JAVA FRAMEWORKS AND COMPONENTS

This book is a practical tool for Java programmers. It provides the necessary information for them to find, evaluate, and select suitable application frameworks. This work explains in plain language the benefits of frameworks and component technologies, specifically in relation to web application development. It is unique in that it does not focus on any specific technology, but uses examples from several different frameworks to explain the underlying principles. It therefore has a broad appeal to developers who are not sure which framework is right for their purpose, and serves also as a practical tool. Application frameworks are large, often complex tools that many developers do not fully understand. Consequently, they cannot take advantage of the substantial benefits such a technology can bring to their development project, as they are often left "reinventing the wheel." As the market for web applications begins its second wave, this book provides the critical information for developers to make the transition into componentized framework-based development, keeping them ahead in an increasingly competitive market. An emphasis on quality and globalization is maintained throughout, as these factors become essential in new projects.

JAVA FRAMEWORKS AND COMPONENTS

ACCELERATE YOUR WEB APPLICATION DEVELOPMENT

MICHAEL NASH
JGlobal Ltd.
Freeport, Bahamas

PUBLISHED BY THE PRESS SYNDICATE OF THE UNIVERSITY OF CAMBRIDGE
The Pitt Building, Trumpington Street, Cambridge, United Kingdom

CAMBRIDGE UNIVERSITY PRESS
The Edinburgh Building, Cambridge CB2 2RU, UK
40 West 20th Street, New York, NY 10011-4211, USA
477 Williamstown Road, Port Melbourne, VIC 3207, Australia
Ruiz de Alarcón 13, 28014 Madrid, Spain
Dock House, The Waterfront, Cape Town 8001, South Africa

http://www.cambridge.org

© Michael Nash 2003

This book is in copyright. Subject to statutory exception
and to the provisions of relevant collective licensing agreements,
no reproduction of any part may take place without
the written permission of Cambridge University Press.

First published 2003

Printed in the United States of America

Typefaces Berkeley Oldstyle 10.75/13.5 pt. and Franklin Gothic   *System* LATEX 2_ε [TB]

A catalog record for this book is available from the British Library.

Library of Congress Cataloging in Publication Data
Nash, Michael, 1964-
　　Java frameworks and components : accelerate your Web application development / Michael Nash.
　　　p.　cm.
　　Includes bibliographical references and index.
　　ISBN 0-521-52059-2 (pb.)
　　1. Java (Computer program language)　2. Application software – Development.　I. Title.
QA76.73.J38N355　2003
005.13′3 – dc21   2002041684

ISBN 0 521 52059 2 paperback

This work is dedicated to my best friend and loving wife, Loretta, without whom none of the work necessary to get it completed would have been possible. Her continual support and encouragement is the foundation of everything I do.

About the Author

Michael Nash attended Acadia University in Canada and then began his own software and consulting service. He has been developing applications for business ever since, from financial software for offshore reinsurance to hotel executive information systems. Mr. Nash has been involved in many open source development projects and was the creator of the Expresso Framework and the team lead for Expresso when it won the 2001 Java Community Award for Outstanding Group Technical Contribution to the Java Community. He is a member of the expert group for JSR 127, the JavaServer Faces specification, and is a core contributor to the Keel meta-framework project. Currently Michael is developing a new line of web applications with JGlobal Limited (www.jglobalonline.com) as well as providing training and consulting services on a number of open source projects.

Contents

Acknowledgments   xv

Chapter 1
Components and Application Frameworks   1

    1.1   Introduction   1
    1.2   What Are They?   2

Chapter 2
Components: The Future of Web-Application Development   35

    2.1   Why Are Components the Future of Web-Application Development?   35
    2.2   A Brief History of Components   40
    2.3   Advantages of Components and Frameworks   42
    2.4   Beyond E-Commerce: Components at Work   52
    2.5   Conclusion: The Future Is Just Beginning   53

Chapter 3
Application Frameworks: What Do They Provide and What Are the Benefits?   54

    3.1   Advantages of Frameworks   55
    3.2   What Is in the Tool Box? (Common Elements in Web-Application Development)   58

Chapter 4
Choosing an Application Framework — 105

- 4.1 Overview — 105
- 4.2 What to Look for — 108
- 4.3 Fit the Tool to the Job — 125
- 4.4 One of the Choices Is NONE – When Frameworks Are Not Appropriate — 125
- 4.5 How to Do the Cost–Benefit Analysis — 126
- 4.6 Conclusion — 130

Chapter 5
A Catalog of Application Frameworks — 131

- 5.1 Complete Application Frameworks — 132
- 5.2 Presentation Frameworks — 165
- 5.3 Other Application-Specific Frameworks — 189
- 5.4 Meta-Frameworks — 210
- 5.5 Summary — 214

Chapter 6
Comparing Frameworks — 215

- 6.1 Comparing Frameworks — 215
- 6.2 Combining Frameworks — 234
- 6.3 A Comparison Matrix — 237
- 6.4 Summary — 243

Chapter 7
Open Source and Components/Frameworks — 244

- 7.1 Overview of Open Source — 244
- 7.2 Frameworks and Open Source — 277
- 7.3 Summary — 295

Chapter 8
Development Methodologies and Design Patterns 296

8.1	Frameworks and Methodologies	296
8.2	Example Methodologies	299
8.3	Select Perspective	305
8.4	Testing and Extreme Programming	305
8.5	UML	310
8.6	MVC Architecture	315
8.7	Design Patterns	317
8.8	Development Phases	329
8.9	Designing with Frameworks	332
8.10	Summary	333

Chapter 9
Integrated Development Environments 334

9.1	General Principles of IDEs in Framework/Component Development	334
9.2	Examples of IDEs and Their Use with Frameworks	340
9.3	Selecting Tools and IDEs	345

Chapter 10
Strategies for Using Frameworks: Best Practices 346

10.1	Initial Adoption	346
10.2	The First Project	348
10.3	Problems and Pitfalls	354
10.4	Future-Proofing	360
10.5	Summary	363

Chapter 11
Conclusions: The Future of Frameworks and Components 364

11.1	Emerging Framework/Component Technologies	364
11.2	Framework Interoperability	375

11.3 Meta-Frameworks 375
11.4 Summary 376

Appendix: Case Studies **377**

Glossary **457**

Index **463**

Acknowledgments

I would like to express my great appreciation to all of the people without whom this book would not have been possible. First, the many developers, contributors, and users of framework and component systems. Their groundbreaking work is helping to shape the nature of software development for decades to come. I am honored to be working with some of them on the next wave of Internet systems development. Secondly, to the great teams at both Cambridge University Press and TechBooks for their efforts in making sure my many typographical and grammatical errors never made it this far, and for their support in making this book happen in the first place. Last, but never least, my deepest thanks to my family for their unfailing support and encouragement.

CHAPTER 1

Components and Application Frameworks

1.1 INTRODUCTION

Welcome, I would like to introduce myself, and discuss the explorations that I would like to take you on in this book. I am a software developer, specifically, an application developer. I build software that people use to get their jobs done – practical, everyday software that is being used.

As part of building applications, in some cases I have also had to build some of the tools I needed including components and an application framework. My programming language of choice for the last several years has been Java. My applications have been targeted for Internet/Intranet uses.

In my exploration, I will examine the nature of software development. It is a complex and demanding process, and developers can use all the tools that are available to them to make it easier and more efficient. We also explore how and why developers resist using those very tools, and how you can make the right decisions in your development projects. It has been a long road, and my hope is to impart some knowledge of its many potholes to you.

I think that I have spent a fair portion of my career in the field resisting the "jargonification" of software development. I am convinced that development can be discussed in plain English, as has been done in this book. It is, however, important to understand the basic terminology used to describe frameworks and components, so we will do this first.

We start by examining what is meant by "web applications," "components," and "application frameworks." In a jargon-ridden industry, it is always important to be sure that a common meaning exists for terms. I will define components and frameworks in terms of what they do, so it will be apparent how each is applied to practical application development in the real world. We also discuss the users of these tools, further defining them and see where the components and application frameworks fit into the environment of the standard Java APIs (application programming interface), JavaBeans, and Enterprise JavaBeans (EJBs).

Then we look at components in more detail, and talk about the advantages of component-based development. We also discuss why these advantages make components such a significant part of the future of Web-application development. We examine exactly what the components and frameworks do, and what you can expect from them.

Then we take a brief look at a number of actual examples of frameworks, comparing their similarities and differences, their strengths and weaknesses, and the design patterns they use. We discuss how open source fits into the framework scenario, and why frameworks are a natural fit for this development model.

Finally, we take a look at the future of components and frameworks, and the new technologies they are incorporating. We conclude with a few actual case studies, putting some frameworks through their paces to create a simple Web application.

1.2 WHAT ARE THEY?

What is a Web application? What is a component? What is an application framework? What are they *not*? These are important questions and deserve carefully considered answers.

To-*may*-to, to-*mah*-to. Like so many things in the software industry, ask nine developers for a definition of components, and you will get eighteen opinions. All of them will have some similarities though – and we find the commonality in them.

1.2.1 Web Applications

This is perhaps the easiest of the three terms we aim to define: almost everyone agrees that a Web application is a piece of interactive software that runs on the

Internet or on a corporate Intranet. A Web application is really a specialized case of a traditional client/server application – in this case, the client is a Web browser or some other Internet-enabled device, the "universal client." So a Web application, simply put, is an application in which the users access business logic via their browser.

The server in a Web application is typically an enhanced Web server: for Java Web applications, this almost always means a server that implements Sun's Java Servlet API, usually in conjunction with the JavaServer Pages (JSP) API. At the top end of the scale, the "server" in fact might be a cluster of systems, each implementing a sophisticated full J2EE (Java 2 Enterprise Edition) application server.

Some examples of Web-application servers are as follows:

- **Tomcat:** an open-source project hosted by the Apache Foundation, Tomcat is the reference implementation for the Servlet API and a popular server for development.
- **Jetty:** another open-source Web server project hosted by Mort Bay Consulting, Jetty is well known for its excellent performance and other features.
- **BEA** WebLogic: a powerful commercial application server, it implements the entire J2EE standard, including EJBs.
- **iPlanet:** a flexible and highly configurable server developed by the Sun/Netscape alliance, iPlanet is available in versions with and without full J2EE capabilities.
- **IBM's** Websphere: also available both with and without EJB capabilities, the Websphere server is an enhanced and commercialized extension of the popular Apache HTTP server.

These are just a few of the more well-known choices. One of the great advantages of Java Web applications is the the fact that a wide range of companies support the standards.

The term "Web application" also has a specific technical meaning within the context of J2EE and its standards: it refers to a means of "packaging" an entire application, complete with code, configuration, HTML (Hyper Text Mark-up Language) and JSP pages into a single archive file – a ".war" file, specifically (Web Application aRchive). This file format is used by almost all current J2EE servers as one of the possible deployment mechanisms for Web applications. The idea is that you can simply place the .war file containing such an application into the appropriate directory, and the server will have everything it needs to fully configure and deploy the application. For the most part, this is true; however, sometimes special circumstances require post-deployment configuration. (And in some cases, "special circumstances" is a term for "mistakes." It is always best to strive to comply with the standards for deployment, making the extra steps at least optional, if not avoiding them altogether.)

Refer to the glossary for detailed definitions of any other terms that are unfamiliar to you.

1.2.2 Components

A "component," according to common usage, is a piece or part. The mind's eye conjures up some kind of mechanical assembly, perhaps consisting of a number of parts, connected and related in some way, but comprising a single complete unit. A software component is similar: it is a collection of parts; in this case these are the methods and objects, which provide some specific functionality. Just like its mechanical counterpart, a component can be simple or complex, and it can work by itself or work only in conjunction with some larger unit.

We can think of components as the software equivalent of Lego (TM), the popular toy with interlocking blocks that can be used to easily assemble many different interesting things. As with Lego, there are different kinds of blocks that have different uses – some are larger, some are smaller, some are more generalized, such as the plain rectangular piece, and some are very specific, such as the block with wheels on it. As with Lego, the most interesting part of these blocks is not so much the individual pieces, but the small interlocking protrusions that let them be easily connected. Components that are designed to work together should have the same kind of generalized way of connecting them – most are perhaps not quite as easy to connect as in Lego, but the principle exists.

To define a component more formally, we can say that it is a "unit of functionality with a contractually specified interface." Note the "interface" part here – the specification of a component always provides a concrete definition of the way we interact with the component. This interface may be divided into two parts: the functional interface, which we use from our application when we want the component to perform its functions, and the configuration interface, which is used to change settings and set properties of the component that modify its behavior in some way.

A component is specifically designed with reuse in mind. Unlike a specific once-off application, the component is intended to be configurable for use in many different completed applications, and should be flexible enough to make this easy, but at the same time it should present a well-defined means to the developer to make the connections to the rest of the application.

1.2.2.1 Separation of Interface and Implementation

One of the key attributes of a component is its separation of *interface* and *implementation*. The internals of the component can change, but the interface of the component with the outside world remains constant. This separation means that the actual implementation of the component is free to be improved, while the improved component remains compatible with the original.

Some components take this a step further, and have a "pluggable" implementation. This is where the actual code that does the work is determined dynamically, perhaps via a configuration setting. An example of this is a user authentication component that can use either an LDAP (Lightweight Directory Access Protocol) data source or a relational database to look up users. The LDAP lookup is one implementation, and the database version is another.

An example of this is explored in detail when we discuss design patterns in Chapter 8.

1.2.2.2 Inversion of Control – Don't call us, We'll call you

A feature of some (but certainly not all) components is that they themselves do not directly access their environment. Instead, they use a design pattern sometimes called "inversion of control," where the container is responsible for "handing" the component everything it needs to perform its tasks. For example, in the case of a component that calculates a customer total and writes to the database, the container would need to pass a database connection to it, as opposed to the component trying to access some external service to "request" a connection. This guarantees the isolation of the component and its independence from the external supporting environment – as long as it is handed the correct inputs, it functions correctly.

This pattern also allows the container or framework to have full control over the sequence of processing, as it always initiates the actions of the component. This lays a strong foundation for work-flow processing, and allows the flow of control to be easily changed without the components themselves requiring modification. Components written to this pattern use a *passive* structure – they act only when requested by the calling object. The calling object must also be carefully constrained: action is *only* initiated by the framework/container, and never by any other objects.

Inversion of control is also a firm foundation for a secure system. It does not guarantee security, but it is a good start. If control can be exercised from only one point, it eliminates the opportunity for component operation to be hijacked at some point in the hierarchy, and makes for only a single point that must be actually secured.

Not all component models adhere to this theory, and some experts argue that it is not necessarily the right idea, but it is a frequently seen pattern for components. Design patterns, as we will see later, are an important topic when discussing both components and frameworks.

Inversion of control is also important when designing a system to achieve scalability by distributing its components among multiple servers – it guarantees that the component does not care *where* it executes, as long as it is handed all the inputs and contexts it requires.

1.2.2.3 Component Execution Environment

Components are designed to operate in a specific environment – for example, EJB (Enterprise Java Beans) components are expected to be deployed in a suitable EJB server. The deployment environment often defines the choice of available components – in other words, if you know you are working in an EJB environment for deployment, then EJB-based components are of course a good choice.

Another term for a component's execution environment is a *container*. Simply put, a container takes components through their life cycles, managing their creation, initialization, operation, and finalization.

It is seldom quite that simple, however, because many components operate in multiple environments. A few frameworks even offer component collections that can scale from a simple JSP/Servlet environment on a single server to a distributed environment.

This is where component standardization comes to a developer's aid: if components are created according to specific standards, then they can be used in more than one environment. It means that the total pool of components available in any given environment gets larger, giving the developer more prebuilt components to choose from.

JavaBeans, for example, are components that operate in many different runtime environments.

1.2.2.4 Components and Objects

Although most components are composed of objects, there are fundamental differences between the two structures. A component can be differentiated from an object in that its "encapsulation" is guaranteed: there are no exposed implementation dependencies. An object might only be used within a single application, but a component has been designed with reuse in mind and cannot assume much about the environment in which it will be used. An object typically defines a much smaller portion of a problem space: an email message, for example. A component operates at a somewhat higher level, for example, for sending and receiving email.

A component typically contains a mechanism for configuring its operation in addition to its basic methods for performing its functions. This provides a means for a component to be adjusted to a range of different preferences, whereas an individual object does not usually provide this range of configurability. Sometimes this mechanism is accessed via a graphical configuration tool – as is often the case with JavaBeans. In this way, the configuration of the component and its current state can be both serialized and restored later for use in the finished application.

A component is often composed of a number of objects, which are designed to work together to provide specific functionality. Some component standards (such as EJB) also provide a recommended means to package their components for deployment (e.g., EJBs in a .jar file, containing the objects themselves and a deployment description file).

OBJECTS COMPARED TO COMPONENTS

OBJECTS	COMPONENTS
MANY INTERDEPENDENCIES	FEW INTERDEPENDENCIES
COMPOSED INTO COMPONENTS	COMPOSED INTO SERVICES
INTERFACE AND IMPLEMENTATION TOGETHER	SEPARATE INTERFACE AND IMPLEMENTATION

1.2.2.5 Component-based Development

Component-based development (sometimes abbreviated "CBD") is a term that describes the process of creating applications from existing components. This is distinct from the process of creating components themselves. Component-based development involves more than just deployment. It begins with the process of analysis and design with components in mind, and continues through an assembly-like development phase, to deployment.

CBD should be differentiated from the process of creating components themselves. This is referred to as component development and is a lower level process than CBD, because it creates the units of functionality, which are later assembled into one application.

One-Off Development versus Component-Based Development

One-Off Development	Component-Based Development
Timeframe hard to predict	Predictable development time
Longer time to completion	Shorter overall time
Infrastructure problems probable	Infrastructure exists, problems less likely
Harder to make flexible	Very flexible
Can't test until created, must test as a unit	Pre-tested building blocks
Integration ability must be created	Built for integration

Examining the process will give us a better understanding of components, and the frameworks within which they operate.

Component-based development begins with analysis and design, just as any other development process. With component-based development, however, the roles of component creator and component consumer are more clearly separated. Often two different companies, or at least two different teams, take on these two roles. When creating a system with component-based development, it is assumed that we are not going to start from scratch – we work with the intent of assembling existing components into an application. Similar in many ways to the roles in J2EE development/deployment, which we will discuss later, there is a distinction between the component creator (or supplier), the component assembler, and often even the component "manager," who administers the operation of the components after assembly and deployment.

Part of the design process involves the determination of the set of components that we have to choose from. Sometimes this is mandated (a company has a specific component library or framework established as a standard), in which case this part of the process is very short indeed. If there is no preordained component library to choose from, however, the same techniques that we discuss later for selecting an application framework can be applied successfully here. Reuse and acquisition, as opposed to development from scratch, are emphasized at this stage.

Once the component library is selected, matching the existing components to the problem at hand is the next step of the design sequence. Traditional software engineering practices do not fit this design process very well, and new approaches and design patterns are appropriate. Later, we discuss in detail design methodologies that are applicable to both component-based and framework-based developments.

The actual "development" phase of a component-based project should primarily be a process of configuration and assembly, with perhaps some coding for the custom business logic of the application at hand. The goal is to maximize reuse and long-term maintainability, and one of the factors that affects this is the amount of custom code that must be created.

Finally, there is the testing and deployment phase, where the finished assembly of components is verified and the component deployment environment is set up. Often, this involves deploying the appropriate support environment for the component library that was chosen: for example, a J2EE server and a related framework. One of the advantages of using the same set of components for subsequent development is that the environment is already in place – only the new components need to be deployed.

So, component-based development primarily consists of the *aggregation* and *interconnection* of components, as well as the configuration of the components themselves. It provides a powerful paradigm for rapid development of reliable, high-quality applications.

1.2.2.5.1 Types of Components
- **Client-side components**: Client-side often describes visual components intended to function on the client – in a Web application, they usually function in the user's browser. Client-side components are often user-interface elements – in other words, components with a visual representation, such as data entry fields, calendar components, folders, and other such elements. In the past these have been relatively low-level components, which are often used for building data entry screens. In the Web-application projects, visual

components can be more complex, often used in conjunction with specific server-side code to form a complete application component, such as an email component, portal components, and so forth.

An Applet is a good example of a client-side component. Not all Applets can be considered components in the strictest sense, because an Applet could comprise an entire application without any ability for reuse in other applications. Often though, Applets are ideal client-side components, operating within the context of a Web application to provide a level of interactivity or visual display that is difficult to achieve with plain HTML.

- **Visual Components**: Visual components can overlap with client-side components: most client-side components are also visual because the best separation of responsibilities is often to have the visual rendering of an application happen on the client system. Many integrated development environments (IDEs), particularly those that support Applet development, provide visual components such as data entry fields, drop-down selection boxes, image frames, and so forth.

  Visual components for a Web application, though, are often generated by means of HTML, XHTML, or JavaScript provided by the server. A text box on an HTML form is a visual component, even though it is created as required by the browser in response to HTML from the server-side application.

  Visual components tend to be fairly "low-level," less complex elements than general client-side components.

- **Server-side components**: Server-side, or nonvisual, components are differentiated from client components usually by the lack of a specific user interface. They may be combined with a user interface (UI) to provide a more complete building block for the application, but this need not be the case.

  Some examples of server-side components are components that provide FTP services, database reporting, XML transformation, and practically any other application service.

1.2.2.6 JavaBeans

The JavaBean specification is an example of a component standard, and has given rise to many component libraries of different types that conform to this standard of access to component functionality. Originally thought of as visual components, JavaBeans can be much more.

First introduced in 1996 during the first JavaOne conference, the Bean API (Application Programming Interface) was initially quite specific: it called for a JavaBean to be a reusable software component that was capable of being manipulated visually in a development/builder tool. JavaBeans have come a long way since then, and have expanded even further in the latest release of the Java development kit (JDK) version 1.4.

A bean is defined as an active component that can be manipulated from within an application builder that possesses certain properties and conforms to certain design patterns. This includes being associated with a BeanInfo object that provides definitions of the bean and its properties, methods, and events. Beans were a departure from other component technologies in that they provided the means for the actual component, not a visual representation, to be manipulated from within a development tool. This is possible for the most part because of the serialization capabilities inherent in beans – they can be "serialized" to and from persistent storage as required, allowing the current state of a bean and its configuration to be stored at any point in time. When a bean is read back from its serialized state, the *core reflection* and *introspection* capabilities of Java allow the bean container to examine the bean to determine its classes, interfaces, methods, and method parameters. The container can then use this information to invoke methods, as required, on the bean itself. This is where method signatures come into play: by following specific patterns when coding the bean, the developer can ensure that its methods conform to the expected signatures and can be invoked at run time by a container that had no previous direct knowledge of the bean.

One of the better known method signatures used in JavaBeans is the set/get pattern for setting and retrieving properties of the bean: a method called "setName" with one parameter is assumed to be the one that is used for setting the property called "name." Correspondingly, the "getName" method is assumed to be the means to retrieve the name later. These patterns are recognized by the core reflection and introspection API, and should be adhered to for best portability of the finished bean.

JavaBeans also utilize a special descriptive class called "BeanInfo." This class can be entirely or partly generated, or can be implemented manually by the bean developer. It describes the bean itself, and is used as the standard "view" of the bean by builder/developer tools so that they can manipulate the bean. This separates the interface and the component implementation, a key element in component design.

An example of a component "container," or execution environment is the simple "bean box" utility provided by Sun as an illustration of JavaBean operation. It provides the necessary services to the JavaBean to configure and run the bean, although not much more, because it is designed as a simple utility and demonstration. Other component containers, such as the Phoenix subproject of the Apache Avalon project, provide much more sophisticated services to their components, such as logging, scheduling, connection pooling, and so forth.

JavaBeans are used extensively within application frameworks. For example, the Struts framework makes use of the bean pattern to allow the developer to associate a bean with every form, and to easily perform validations and data transfers between the bean and the page. Even where JavaBeans are not used directly, the get/set and other patterns that are associated with beans are still accepted as a standard. Coding in accordance with such standards not only ensures that the code is consistently readable, but also helps to enforce proper object-oriented encapsulation. Variables are kept private, and get/set methods are used to access them, hiding the internal operation of the bean from the code that uses it. This allows the internal operation to change without affecting the use of the bean, allowing improvements to be made without any reintegration with the rest of the system.

1.2.3 Application Frameworks

1.2.3.1 What Do They Do?

What are application frameworks? Why are they important to you? What do they provide that can help you get your job done?

A framework's primary purpose is to aid and ease your application development process. It should allow you to develop the application quickly and easily and should result in a superior finished application.

It is important that you see the real benefit to determine whether mounting the learning curve of a framework is worthwhile.

Frameworks, in brief, provide you with a powerful *tool box*. The tools in this box help in many different areas of application development. They provide essential design patterns and structure to your application development project, and also provide the backbone and container for the components you create for your application to operate within. In Chapter 2 we will explore the kinds of services and tools you will commonly find in frameworks.

Frameworks are valuable at all stages of development, from design to deployment and beyond, perhaps more so in ongoing maintenance. They usually apply to almost all stages of the life cycle of an application.

1.2.3.2 Application Framework Characteristics

In the process of creating Web applications, a number of basic tasks are encountered repeatedly. As in most cases of programming, where the code that is needed more than once is broken into methods or procedures, these repeated tasks can be generalized and the code reused across multiple projects. This process of generalization and reuse leads to the creation of most frameworks.

Initially generalization sounds pretty easy when you say it fast: you observe what is being done over and over, and break it into a reusable element. It is not quite that simple. The resulting elements that are broken out must form a cohesive, understandable whole. It is this design process that makes the framework itself so useful later – the basic principles of how everything is supposed to hang together have already been worked out, allowing the developer using the framework to concentrate on the specifics of the application at hand.

In its simplest form, the framework has been in existence for a long while: any body of code, such as a library, that reduces development time on future projects by being reusable, constitutes a framework of sorts. Libraries have previously tended to be specific to one area of the development process, though for example, a graphics library, a floating-point library, and so forth. Web-application development frameworks are more applicable to the entire development process of the finished application, and are often made up of a number of different functional areas, each serving one aspect of the Web-application building process.

Many progressive companies invest in frameworks specifically – either by developing one of their own, or by purchasing or otherwise adopting an existing framework. From their point of view, it is an investment for the future. Such an investment reduces their development time overall, and improves the quality of the finished product. Their developers are able to focus on the unique business requirements of their projects, rather than on infrastructure design and development. Maintainability is also substantially improved, so the money saved in adopting frameworks increases over time.

A framework also provides a well-defined extension mechanism, allowing new capabilities and services to be added without loss of structure due to personal coding styles of individual developers and design decisions. A framework must be inherently extensible, and new services should have the ability to be easily added as required. A well-defined extension mechanism prevents the framework from disintegrating into many different styles.

A framework must be as simple as possible, but no simpler. In other words, unnecessary complexity should not get in the way, and yet there must be enough capability provided that the framework has real and measurable benefit. The framework's API should be consistent across modules within the framework to make it easier to use each module once you have learned the overall style of the API.

A good framework should also have complete documentation – something that unfortunately is fairly rare today. "Complete" documentation means that all functions and parts of the framework are documented. It does not necessarily mean volumes of reference and learning material, as extensive documentation does not necessarily mean better documentation. On the contrary, the *right* documentation is much more essential than having a large tome in which you cannot find what you need. Diagrams and possibly UML serve to provide a good guide to large and complex projects, such as frameworks, and should be used as required.

A framework should be widely applicable – that is, it should have the ability to be used in many different kinds of development scenarios, and its functionality called from many different places, including EJBs, Servlets, regular Java classes, and others. This requires giving careful thought to design, because some techniques (such as thread-safety) must be taken into account. Although a framework hides much complexity from its user, it should still allow all of its functionality to be accessed. This means multiple "levels" of access, so that lower level features (such as database access or file system interaction) as well as higher level functionality (such as UI independence or logic components) can be used directly.

A framework should approach the problem domain from a generic point of view – the more involved a framework is in providing business logic, the less widely applicable it is. Many applications require logging, access to a user interface, configuration, and other common services. Fewer applications require, for example, mortgage rate calculations. If a framework does provide more business-logic level services, they should at least be optional or replaceable, otherwise its applicability might be sharply limited. A framework should also provide its functionality in modular fashion. This avoids the unfortunate fact that the more a framework does often means the less it is reusable. Every project does not need every service – some applications require database access, others do not. Developers will probably resist using a framework that provides substantial database-access features if their application does not need it – even if many other features of the framework would be valuable. If the database-access functionality is optional, however, then there is no need to carry any excess baggage.

There is a trade-off at work when building reusable components. On the positive side, time is saved by reusing the component. This must take into account the number of times it can be reused – for example, in how many projects do you think you will be able to reuse this component? Also, the time to develop the component as a once-off can be subtracted from the total time for each of those projects. On the negative side, the additional time it takes to develop a *reusable* component must be amortized across all of the times it is reused. If, as a crude example, it takes one day to develop the component as a once-off, without taking reuse into account, and it will be used in two projects, then it should not take longer than two days to develop it as a reusable component – or the overall benefit becomes negative. On the other hand, if it takes two days to make it reusable, and it is reused ten times, then the savings are significant. Although this is an oversimplification to some degree, the principle holds in most projects. The difficulty, of course, comes in the fact that it is usually difficult to say how many times a component will be reused. You also have to take into account the improved flexibility of the reusable version of the component, and possibly its lower maintenance cost as a result, and many other factors.

Almost all frameworks evolve, rather than being explicitly developed. A good up-front design will allow the available budget to be used on a basis that is extensible and reusable.

Framework: a supporting or enclosing structure. A basic system or arrangement of ideas.

The name seems to imply something skeletal – an outline of an application, perhaps labeled "some assembly required." Frameworks are often anything but skeletal – most are highly complex and full of functionality, with many different areas providing sophisticated services to the finished application. They are however, an outline: frameworks often help to define the shape and the scope of an application. A framework is frequently composed of a number of components, or it may contain the facilities used to develop components, such as base classes that components can use to extend. A major benefit of many frameworks is that they provide the backbone or software "bus" that allows creation of components that can be easily connected and work together.

A reasonable formal definition of a framework is that a framework is a *reusable problem domain model*. A framework is a reusable design for all or part of a software system. A good framework can reduce the cost of developing an application by an order of magnitude because it allows you to reuse analysis, design, *and* code.

A framework also incorporates a reusable *design*, which usually takes the form of a set of both abstract and concrete classes, and a mechanism for these classes to collaborate. Meaningful reuse of components usually requires a framework: it provides the context for the components to exist within the library, providing the backbone around which they interoperate.

The design of the interfaces and functional components is one of the most difficult aspects of developing software – much more difficult than the actual creation of the code. This is why the benefits of frameworks go beyond the reuse of their components – the reuse of the *design* is almost more important.

Frameworks are a fairly broad topic, and it is fair to say that there are many thousands of frameworks in use today. Narrowing the field to Java reduces the number somewhat, but frameworks are particularly popular in Java, so there are still several of them. We focus on a specific kind of framework, however: frameworks that are intended for use in Web-application development, instead of stand-alone applications or even Applets.

Hierarchy of a Typical Framework-Based Web Application

```
┌─────────────────────────────────────┐
│            APPLICATION              │
└─────────────────────────────────────┘
┌─────────────────────────────────────┐
│            FRAMEWORK                │
└─────────────────────────────────────┘
┌─────────────────────────────────────┐
│    APP SERVER / SERVLET CONTAINER   │
└─────────────────────────────────────┘
┌─────────────────┬───────────────────┐
│       JVM       │       DBMS        │
└─────────────────┴───────────────────┘
┌─────────────────────────────────────┐
│         OPERATING SYSTEM            │
└─────────────────────────────────────┘
```

An application framework, conceptually, fits between the application server or a Servlet container and your own application code. Unlike an IDE or a builder tool, some or all of the code to the framework gets deployed along with your application at the production stage.

1.2.3.3 Who Needs Them

Web applications are developed by a surprisingly diverse group, and with a bewildering array of approaches. There are two broad groups of developers: the traditional developers, that is, people who look at Web application from an "application-oriented" approach. Often, they are developers who had worked on other development technologies, such as client/server or client applications. They look at Web applications as a special category of application, which is of course correct. The other group is page authors, who primarily look at Web applications from a "page-oriented" viewpoint, and see a Web application as a set of Web pages that have a certain degree of dynamic behavior. They are also correct. Sometimes these two functions are embodied in a single person, but for larger projects there may be a number of people involved in each of these two categories. Many frameworks focus specifically on making the interaction between these two categories easier and more effective.

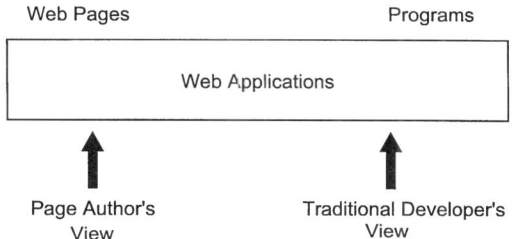

Views of a Web Application

The developer may focus more on the underlying logic, database access, processing, and other traditional software elements of a Web application, but the page author is just as necessary, because the finished application is a collection of Web pages, irrespective of how dynamically they are generated, and the normal Web design constraints apply.

Frameworks have something to offer both these groups, as we will find out. Perhaps more importantly, many frameworks concentrate on the all-important *interface* between these groups, so that the page-oriented nature of the Web can connect properly with the application-oriented code running behind the scenes. Frameworks also offer many benefits to developers who work partly in both these groups: developing application logic, but assisting page designers in accessing scripting and other presentation technologies to enhance their Web pages. By encapsulating scripting support, making presentation flexible and configurable, and providing prebuilt template support for page generation, frameworks make these tasks much easier and maintainable than direct coding.

Any application developer who works with a sufficiently complex project has a need for frameworks. You have to ask: does the use of a framework benefit the project as a whole? A number of factors must be taken into account, including the skill levels of the developers involved. Although a framework can provide a huge productivity boost once the learning curve is mastered, inexperienced developers can find mounting this curve a daunting challenge, and many simpler applications may be better off without a framework. The size of the project is also important – as will be discussed in more detail later, some smaller applications are simply better off being created directly – however, some framework choices are suitable for smaller as well as larger projects. The exact dimensions that make a framework suitable partly depend on the framework, but in general, a project that runs from days to weeks (assuming it is once-off) might be easier to accomplish directly. Any project that involves database persistence, scalability concerns, internationalization, or a project that will run for more than a month can almost certainly benefit from the use of a framework.

Once the learning curve of the framework is behind you, though, nearly every project completed with it will be easier to do and yield better results.

Some industry experts believe that the ultimate goal of a framework is to build applications without writing any code, that is to simply assemble them from existing components. Further, they believe that you do not necessarily have to be a good programmer to write the code, but the framework should make it easy for even nonprogrammers to build applications. I strongly disagree with this view. I am convinced that programmers are much more than code generators, and that they bring the necessary sense of design and balance to an application, at all levels. Although it is true that frameworks are powerful tools, and good frameworks allow you to write less code and achieve more, this does not reduce the need for expertise on the part of the programmer. On the contrary, the more powerful tools require a developer who is familiar with the use of that power, and how the tools work. Just as you would not entrust a powerful construction machine to an inexperienced operator, you must have an experienced and knowledgeable developer to get the most out of the power represented by a good framework.

1.2.3.4 What Are they not?

A framework is *not a Servlet container nor an application server*, although a framework and the applications developed with it are almost always designed to be deployed in an application server or Servlet container. The framework is not the container itself, however, and the best frameworks avoid being tied to any specific application server, thus allowing portability of the finished applications.

A framework is *not an API*. Although there should exist an API that specifies the interface to the various components provided by the framework, the framework is more than an API – the name implies a specific implementation, and a higher level structure than an API. Often a framework provides a number of APIs, but it is more than an API.

A framework is *not a code generator*. It is possible for a framework to perform code generation, but this is only one technique for providing application services. More important than cranking out the physical code is the underlying structure and services provided by the framework.

A framework is *not a finished application*, although it may be provided with one or more example applications. In the same way as an API should not imply or be restricted to one implementation, a framework should not be inextricably linked with a single application. It is frequently the case, however, where a particular framework is intended for use in creating a particular type of application: for example, the IBM SanFransico project and framework is intended for building financial applications. This is a more focused type of framework than, for example, the Apache Struts framework, which can be used for creating a wide variety of applications.

A framework is also *not an IDE nor a development environment*, although most frameworks can be used within integrated development environments and other development tools. Some frameworks are even specific to a single development tool, which is, in my opinion, a disadvantage. Like many developers, I have found that the development tools or IDEs that I use have changed many times over the years, sometimes as a result of a specific project and sometimes as a result of a better tool coming along. Ideally, you do not want to be restricted to one specific development environment when you commit to a particular application framework, and you certainly do not want to be inextricably linked to a single IDE.

A framework is *not a component*. Typically, modern frameworks provide the basis for an execution environment and integration backbone for components. Frameworks are often composed of a set of components – hence the term "component library" is applied to some frameworks. A true framework, however, is more than just a group of components – it should provide mechanisms that support development of new components as well.

A framework is *not a 4GL* (fourth-generation language), although it can provide many of the same benefits in the development process. 4GLs imply vendor lock-in – specific 4GLs are proprietary to commercial vendors and sometimes suffer from a lack of extensibility. It is often difficult to extend their high-level features to perform new tasks, and even when you can, you usually have to change languages (from the 4GL itself to a "lower level" language) to make the extension.

1.2.3.5 Frameworks and J2EE

J2EE set of standards is an important factor in much of Java Web-application development, so we carefully examine it and its relationship with frameworks and components.

J2EE, or Java 2 *Enterprise Edition* is a standard, or more accurately a set of related standards. It is intended for implementing and deploying enterprise applications. J2EE is not a specific implementation – it is more like a blueprint than a building, and many different implementations of all or part of its standards are available, some are better than others, and some are more complete than others. It is important to realize that J2EE does not necessarily imply the use of Enterprise JavaBeans (EJBs).

J2EE applications are intended to consist of more than one *tier*: a client tier, consisting of applications using the services of the other tiers to provide interaction with users; a middle tier, which usually includes an EJB container, a Web container, JNDI (Java Naming and Directory Interface), JMS (Java Messaging Service), and other service providers; and a data or Enterprise Information System tier, which provides access to a persistence mechanism – a database, for example, or perhaps a set of connectors to a legacy system used for data storage.

J2EE is not, on its own, an application framework, at least not in the sense that we will use the term here. Many frameworks, however, depend on some or all of the services and standards that J2EE provides. Such frameworks provide a concrete implementation of many of the J2EE standards, in such a way that a particular class can implement an interface. Most J2EE frameworks concentrate on the middle tier, although some also provide client tier services as well.

J2EE servers typically provide a number of *component containers* – run-time environments for components of various types to run within. The components designed to execute within the J2EE environment can count on certain services to be made available from these containers, so it provides a known background for the development of components.

J2EE provides a number of benefits as a standard for component execution, and frameworks that take advantage of its standards can also offer the same benefits.

- **Division of responsibilities:** By dividing the application development, configuration, and deployment into a number of distinct roles, the J2EE standard provides a means of distributing the effort of creating and deploying an application among a number of people with different skillsets. This fits well the resources available in a larger enterprise.

- **Scalability:** J2EE containers, because of the design of the standard, can be written in such a way as to provide for easy distribution of the various components across a cluster of connected server, and as a result, provide scalability. Most containers are written this way, but definitely not all of them.

- **Ease of Integration:** Almost every enterprise has existing information systems and legacy applications. When they implement new systems using the J2EE standards, they will likely want to integrate with the older systems on some level. Because of the modular nature of J2EE, and the hiding of implementation details at the service layers of the model, it is easy to "plug in" legacy applications by "wrapping" them as a component. From the perspective of other components, they become just one more cog in the mechanism, indistinguishable from the new components of the system.

These are just some of the major advantages to the J2EE environment. At the same time, frameworks that provide these advantages can also be burdened with the following disadvantages:

- **Complexity**: To achieve its scalability, the "full" J2EE environment (e.g., with JNDI, EJBs, etc) takes care of a lot of the "plumbing" necessary to set up a set of clustered servers. This plumbing imposes a certain amount of complexity in and of itself, and this complexity is not necessary for applications that are not deployed in a cluster. The ideal is a framework that lets you develop and deploy in a single server environment – without any complexity you *do not* need, and then scale up easily into a full clusterable environment if and when that becomes necessary. Few frameworks indeed offer this flexibility.

- **Performance Constraints**: Although an oft-cited reason for developing within the J2EE environment is scalability, and the opportunity to gain performance by clustering multiple servers, this argument is two-edged: whereas J2EE servers excel at multiserver environments, and can indeed support many users in such a configuration, they do not scale well in the other direction: *down*. Smaller applications are frequently better off in an environment that does not support all of the overhead of a full-blown J2EE container. Also, depending on the specifics of the application, clustering may not be the best or most direct route to improved scalability – we examine some of the other routes later.

  We discuss performance and the factors that contribute to it in more detail later.

1.2.3.6 Frameworks and Enterprise JavaBeans: To EJB or Not to EJB

We have already mentioned the distinction between the J2EE set of standards and the specific standard within this set called Enterprise JavaBeans. Although most Web-application frameworks rely on portions of the J2EE standard, not all of them rely on the existence of EJB, or its presence in the application development process.

EJB, like any other standard or technology, has its proponents and detractors – any developer should be free to choose the appropriate technology for a particular application, and the existence of EJB simply adds to these choices. It is not the only or necessarily the best means for a given use.

Over-engineering any project is a mistake: if all you know is hammers, everything looks like a nail. Just because EJB technology is available in a particular environment does not make it the right choice. It is important to understand the advantages and disadvantages of a solution, just as it is important to understand the alternatives. Knowledge of the weaknesses of the technology also gives you the best chance of avoiding them, if you do decide that using EJB is the correct approach.

To decide whether EJB is an appropriate part of a project, you need to understand the advantages and weaknesses of the technology. EJB indeed provides many advantages, and we review them first:

The EJB specification lays out a great deal: it specifies types, life cycles, restrictions, roles, and responsibilities. The portability of the EJB standard, if guidelines are followed carefully, allows you to take the finished application and easily deploy it on another vendor's server. The specification also divides the developers who use it into "roles," providing a foundation for coordination between different developers in a team project. This facilitates team development by avoiding the overhead of establishing these separate functions.

Another significant advantage of EJB is the close integration with the underlying J2EE platform, and the rest of the APIs and services that it provides, such as naming, security, transaction handling, life-cycle management, and so on. This supports even the most demanding and complex applications without having to create additional services. EJB has access to the "big guns" to get the largest projects completed.

The primary advantage that many developers choose EJB for is to achieve scalability. The ability to cluster EJB servers, that is, to add multiple inexpensive servers to a group of servers to support higher load, is very attractive. The ability to do this with no application modifications (just configuration changes) adds significantly to EJB's appeal.

Another important advantage is the industry support for EJB technology. With almost every major vendor (with the notable exception of Microsoft) endorsing the standard, the technology is not likely to go away soon – it will probably continue to be very well supported in the foreseeable future, a significant point for a developer who is thinking of long-term maintainability of his finished applications.

All of these are significant advantages of EJB technology. Like every complex technology, however, these advantages come at a price. Now, we consider some of the drawbacks.

The EJB specification is large and complicated, and involves an extensive learning curve. Learning it well enough to use it is significantly different from learning to use it *well*. Many of the advantages of EJB can be partially or even entirely negated when applying the standard incorrectly. For example, over-extensive use of Entity EJBs in particular can result in many objects being created and resultant scalability problems. Many other examples exist. Having a large club is not the same as being able to wield it expertly, and in this sense the complexity of the specification works against it. No other widely accepted technology such as EJB has avoided the same complexity – the .NET platform by Microsoft, for example, is also large and complex, although it is not yet as mature as EJB technology. CORBA (Common Object Request Broker Architecture), as defined by the Object Management Group (OMG), is another example, and some people consider CORBA to be even more complex than EJB, because it addresses an even wider audience of developers and spans multiple programming languages.

Part of the cost of the added complexity of EJB is paid during development – it can take longer to create an EJB solution than one based on the simpler Java APIs. It can also be more difficult to debug – although some of this is again related to the distributed nature of EJBs - it is more difficult to figure out what is going on in multiple Java Virtual machines (VMs) being synchronized across multiple servers than in a single-VM environment.

The "roles" of the developer laid out in the specification can help address this issue, but it is still important to have a certain level of knowledge of the entire specification, even if your own role only interacts with a part of the whole. Appropriate instruction and training of the developer group undertaking the project are essential – EJB is not something you can pick up in a few weekends after reading the manual and expect to be productive.

EJB objects are by their very nature are a bit more involved than normal Java objects: most implementations require three separate objects to be written for every bean (and four for Entity beans). The packaging of the finished bean is specified as part of the specification as well, but a number of implementations include vendor-specific enhancements to make this process easier for their particular server.

EJB (like many other specifications) is somewhat like a moving target: the specification continues to evolve. Currently at version 2.0, having been updated from 1.1 and before that from the 1.0 specification, each major version introduces new capabilities, and in some cases has an impact on existing applications. This is not a disadvantage unique to EJB but it is a factor that must be taken into consideration when undertaking a development project. It is possible to have the specification render part of your work obsolete by coming out with a new release before your application is even completed. This is just one of the hazards of the rapidly evolving standards in today's development world. New things being added to standards makes it a two-edged sword: on one hand, we want the new features, and having them included in the standard makes them "safer" to use than if they were vendor-specific enhancements. On the other hand, it is difficult to comply with the standard if it does not hold still for a while.

EJB container implementations vary in quality. Despite Sun's careful efforts to ensure that a set of sophisticated standard tests are available to ensure compliance with the specification, some EJB servers perform better than others, and some provide a more complete implementation of the specification than others. This means that the level of the specification supported by the target container must be taken into consideration before certain capabilities are used. Another significant pitfall can be found in vendor extensions: it is important for portability not to rely on facilities that are not a part of the EJB specification, although they may be available on a particular platform.

Some of the advantages of the EJB specification may not be required for your solution: if issues such as multithreading, scalability, and transaction management are not key to your project, using EJB may be comparable to killing an ant with an atom bomb – the ant is indeed dead, but there are a number of less desirable side effects that may trouble you for some time to come. Using "straight" Java classes makes more sense in this situation. If time constraints and other factors make adoption of EJB unwise initially, it may make a lot of sense to create your application in an "EJB-friendly" manner. That is, do not utilize EJB, but adopt design and implementation patterns that would make moving into an EJB environment later much easier. This way, when the application becomes more popular and usage increases (which often happens – at least we hope so), you have the option of extending the application to take advantage of the capabilities of EJB without having to rewrite. Several application frameworks that we discuss have facilities specifically intended for this, and it brings the advantage of scalability in *both* upward and downward directions.

Another alternative is to allow your application to scale in a different direction: use of distributed Web services, for example, or JMS as a distributed backbone to create a message-oriented system can be very effective. Also, Java supports the CORBA standard very well, which can lead to better interoperability with distributed components written in different languages, because CORBA is a cross-language standard. JavaSpaces and Jini are also different approaches to scalability that may be worth investigating for your project.

In conclusion, the use of EJB (and some of the "full" J2EE platform) should not be a foregone conclusion for a project. There are compelling reasons to use EJB in some circumstances, and equally compelling reasons in not doing so in others, depending on the projects. The ideal approach is to defer the decision by using a framework that lets you begin without EJB, then ramp up to them later without reinventing anything.

1.2.3.7 Adopting Frameworks

Frameworks bring a number of benefits to the development process. The most obvious benefit is the speed of development – once the learning curve has been overcome, the time required to develop an application by using a framework can be a small fraction of the time required to do the same without using such a framework. There are many more subtle advantages that in the long term might be even more important.

So if these substantial benefits are available, why are not *most* Web applications built with frameworks?

There are a number of reasons:

- **New Technology**: As I am sure you will appreciate, the technologies that you hear being talked about in the trade press and magazines are often *not* what you are actually working with on a day-to-day basis. The real world often lags the "ideal world" talked about in the magazines, and new technology, irrespective of how beneficial it is, can be a hard sell in some organizations. This fact alone can sometimes be the reason for the slow adoption of frameworks. If you ask and the answer is "it's scheduled to be investigated next year," then your organization probably falls into this category.

    In all fairness, Web-application-development frameworks have not been around all that long, so being a relatively new concept, they are kept out of some organizations at least in their current form for Web applications.

- **Learning Curve**: Even organizations that have made an attempt to integrate frameworks into their development process sometimes still do not use them: the learning curve for most frameworks is very steep, and on many occasions the developers assigned do not make it to the top. Instead, they decide that doing things the "old" way is better than going through all this. Sometimes this is a result of selecting the wrong framework, and sometimes it is a result of selecting the wrong developers.

    Actually, to say that the learning curve of frameworks is very steep is not necessarily a negative remark, if you think about it. A "steep" learning curve means that it is possible to learn in a short period of time, but the effort required is fairly large for this short period. It also means that the learning itself is fairly large – for example, a lot of information is gained in a short period of time, and also expertise is built rapidly. It is important to dedicate time to learning a framework – it is not well served by just spending a few minutes, but at the same time the rewards and the increases in effectiveness and productivity follow quickly in response to the proper effort.

- **Open Source:** Many of the best frameworks are open-source products. Open source and frameworks tend to go well together, as the nature of a framework tends to benefit from many different developers in many different situations working on its development. Unfortunately, using open-source software is still a problem for some organizations. We address these concerns in Chapter 7 in more detail.

- **"Not Invented Here" Syndrome:** Sometimes, for good or bad reasons, an organization is unwilling to adopt a technology that it was not created internally. Sometimes this extends to an organization creating its own framework or component library. With what is available today, this is seldom justified. Sometimes these concerns stem from the available solutions being open source, and the unwillingness of the organization to give up what it perceives to be a competitive advantage. Sometimes the concern results from an unwillingness to add dependences – the organization or team wants to be completely independent and rely on their own development and software resources. In practice, this can seldom be achieved completely: using a standard operating system (e.g., Linux, Windows, AIX) introduces a kind of dependency, even if your package is portable across such systems. Being dependent on a particular framework, however, is a bigger leap of faith. If a framework is used for a number of mission-critical applications, the framework itself becomes mission-critical. If future developments in the framework start to negatively influence the existing applications, these future developments will probably be ignored – the organization will not upgrade to the latest and best version of the framework if it means substantial rework of applications already deployed. This can lead to an "orphan" version of the framework being used, which, although manageable in many situations, can negate some of the advantages of using a framework in the first place. Today, much careful design thought goes into helping solve this problem in framework development. Often using a framework in such a critical area of development reminds companies of outsourcing: they effectively outsource some significant portion of not only their software development, but also their software design, and outsourcing has its own set of problems, which most companies that have tried it are aware of. The framework developers do not necessarily have the same standards of quality, design goals, scheduling constraints, and other parameters that the in-house team trying to use the framework does. Some of these concerns are solved by using open-source frameworks, and getting involved in the development of the framework itself. We discuss this in more detail in Chapter 7.

In summary, "not invented here" syndrome can have its roots in genuine and tangible issues, and is not always unjustified. It is not just something you ignore or overcome, it is something that you address the issues for and resolve. Careful consideration must be given to how these issues are addressed when considering an "outside" framework.

1.2.3.8 Good Tools in Bad Times

In times when software development budgets are shrinking, developers must produce more with less. They have less time, fewer people, and limited resources. In this environment, the opportunities presented by frameworks become even more important. The advantages of being able to produce high-quality, highly functional applications in less time with fewer people are even more apparent when times are tough. One of the primary advantages of frameworks is the amount of thought and design that goes into their creation, which is then available to be tapped by the organization or developers using the framework, effectively multiplying their effectiveness without sacrificing quality. As is often said in engineering disciplines, including software, you can have it fast, good, or cheap, pick any two. By leveraging the significant effort that goes into a well-designed framework, you can actually have all three to a greater degree than was possible before.

1.2.3.9 Reinventing the Wheel

No one likes to do work twice. Code reuse is the attempt to do work only once: once you have written a section of code to do a job, theoretically you should never again have to write that section. It seldom works out quite that well – I know I have many times found myself thinking "this feels familiar...," while coding a piece of logic, then starting a hunt through other sections to find a piece of code that was similar, and finally copying the relevant parts.

The job to be done may be very similar to the original job for which the code was written, but not quite the same. This then leads to the problem of deciding whether to reuse an existing piece of code, or whether it is better to create a new functionality. Having a single piece of code, however, means there is only one piece of code to debug – so reuse, whenever possible, has substantial advantages both in time and in the quality of the finished product. Truly, "less is more."

Every developer knows the frustration (not to mention the increased cost) of having to maintain several different "almost identical" copies of a piece of code, rather than a single more flexible and reusable version.

This must, of course, be taken in context: sometimes there is a very good reason to do something again, particularly if it can be done better. This even happens in open-source projects, where theoretically reuse is more heavily practiced. The arguments made above in defense of the "not invented here" syndrome still apply, and when considering reuse it is important not to see it as a silver bullet, or as inarguably a "good thing."

1.2.4 APIs

Application Program Interfaces (APIs) are a different animal from either components or frameworks, although a component as well as a framework may indeed have an API. As before, there are no hard and fast rules, but an API generally presents a fairly low-level interface for other programs to call the method and access the objects of a particular library. An API consists of a list of classes and method calls available in a particular library – it is a description of what is there to be used. An API is like a Java interface, whereas a component is more like a concrete class.

An API, in fact, is just the description of a library – not the implementation. A specific implementation is what we will use for development work, but the API itself is important in its own right, because it defines the standard with which we work, and assures us that we can change implementations as required. Much like using an interface in Java, the API specifies *what*, not necessarily *how*.

The JavaMail API is a good example: a large number of methods are made available, as well as objects that are complex enough to almost be components in their own right. JavaMail, however, does not *do* anything – it provides capabilities for other applications to do things, but it does not stand alone – nor can you develop a complete application using only the services it provides.

An API differs from a component in that it does not have the ability to be "plugged in" as an independent part. APIs are often used to provide services to components, however: for example, an email component can use the JavaMail API to access mail servers.

Frameworks differ again in that they may provide several APIs, and probably make use of a few, but are not designed to provide specific, complete functional units – they do not *do* anything per se, but are used to build components and applications that do. For example, we might use the Struts framework to develop an email application. If we take care to provide a mechanism for integrating this email code into other applications, we may have created a component.

In Web-application development with Java, an important API that we deal with constantly is the *Servlet API*, as defined by Sun Microsystems. This API is well described on Sun's website, and sets the standard for implementations of Servlet containers, or Servlet engines, which are a common element of most Web applications today.

An API, such as the Servlet API, is typically identified by a specific version, so that an implementation of the API can conveniently specify which version it provides. For example, a particular version of Apache Group's Tomcat Servlet engine might implement version 2.3 of the Servlet API – this tells the developer what to expect, and defines in a very specific way what methods and objects are provided by the API.

APIs are often best described by means of JavaDoc documentation, which is the documentation generated by the JavaDoc tool provided by Sun's Java Development Kit. JavaDoc itself is a complete tool, but also involves an API, and is extensible as a result.

1.2.5 Application Servers: The Web-Application Execution Environment

Web-application servers and "Servlet container" applications provide the foundation for almost all Java Web applications. Indeed, some frameworks and components are designed specifically for use with particular application servers such as BEA's Weblogic or IBM's Websphere. Application servers are not frameworks themselves, however.

Application servers provide an execution environment for Web applications and their components – these environments consist of a number of services. Some of the common services are as follows:

- **HTTP services**: HTTP is the protocol that we are all familiar with as the delivery mechanism for Web pages. It is actually much more, and more than Web pages and images can use this familiar protocol to bridge the gap between client and server and also between servers. For example, XML (eXtensible Mark-up Language) data for the SOAP (Simple Access Object Protocol) might use HTTP as its transport mechanism. Servlets and JSP pages also typically interact with the client via HTTP.

- **Servlet Execution:** Servlets are a key technology in many Web applications. They make the connection between Web requests and server-side logic. Conversely, many frameworks implement very few individual Servlets. The Apache Struts framework, for example, implements only one actual Servlet. This one Servlet acts as the dispatcher of requests to other application components. In the MVC (Model, View, Controller) nomenclature, this single Servlet acts as the "controller." MVC is a term and a pattern first discussed in the book *Pattern-Oriented Software Architecture: A System of Patterns*, by Buschmann et al., and widely used to describe a mechanism of separating the functional units of model (application logic), view (user presentation), and controller (user input and interaction) in an application. We will see many examples of this pattern in the frameworks we examine later.

  Why is this a good thing? To maintain good separation of business logic and presentation, it is important that the user interface is not "built-in" to the logic. UIs that are maintained separately from the application logic are easier to change, and this is more readily achieved if the UI is outside the Servlet. One way of doing this is to use JSP pages. Although they compile into Servlets, they are more readily maintained, because they exist on the Web server as regular text files and are compiled automatically. Another example is XSL (eXtensible Style-sheet Language): the style sheets that define the presentation are more readily modified than Java code and do not need to be compiled either.

  A single Servlet also provides a single "control" point, or point of entry, for an application. This makes it easy to ensure that all requests on the application are handled in the same way: just put the control code into the one and only Servlet. Security code is a good example of the advantage of a single point of control. Configuration is also aided by the single-Servlet approach, because the web.xml file of the application need only register that Servlet, and does not need to be modified when new views or business logic are added.

- **JSP Execution:** JavaServer Pages, or JSPs, are simply Servlets in fancy dress; they are created by compiling specially designated Web pages. These pages are automatically compiled when they are first accessed, or when they are updated.

  JSPs, like any of these technologies, can easily be used incorrectly: the flexibility of allowing Java code to be inserted into a JSP page allows logic to creep into what should be entirely a "view" or presentation area. This can lead to all sorts of problems, as it violates the principle of separating logic and presentation. The solution is simple: any Java code embedded in JSP pages should be entirely presentation-oriented. If you need a loop or some logic to display the data correctly, fine. Often, custom tag libraries provide these facilities more easily, allowing a JSP to be built with no code at all.

- **XML transformation services**: We discuss XML and XSL transformations in detail elsewhere. The capability to run such transformations is often provided as a built-in capability of an application server, making it simple to separate content and presentation even for static pages.

- **EJB services**: Usually, when an application server is referred to as a "J2EE server," we assume that the entire J2EE specification is available to us to work with. In actual fact, this is seldom true – some services are not commonly implemented in today's servers (such as JMS (Java Messaging Service)). Common usage does differentiate between a "Servlet server" or "Servlet container," such as Tomcat, and a J2EE server, such as Orion. The Servlet API is itself a part of the J2EE specification, so it is not entirely accurate to make them distinct, but the so-called full J2EE servers usually implement most of the EJB portion of the specification, allowing for the deployment and handling of, at least, Session beans, and more commonly today both Session and Entity beans.

- **Java Naming and Directory Interface (JNDI)**: A key element of any full J2EE server, JNDI services are essential for deployment of EJBs, although they are very useful in other situations (e.g., access to LDAP services).

    A directory service is a mechanism by which distributed components or services locate each other. This is the enabler to allow them to interact, because if they cannot locate each other no collaboration is possible. A directory, as the name implies, is a central repository of names and location information, exactly like a phone directory or a library card catalog. Each distributed component requires only a reference to this directory for locating and communicating with any other component that is listed. JNDI provides a common interface to many existing directory services, allowing previously incompatible directories to be accessed by Java applications.

    A naming service consists of a set of *bindings*. These bindings define the relationship between the *name* of a service or component and its actual "contact information," or its location and means of communication. Some of the more common naming services are COS (Common Object Services), the CORBA naming service, used by several different programming languages including Java, DNS (Domain Name Service), the distributed naming service for the Internet, mapping domain names into Internet protocol (IP) addresses, LDAP, a lightweight derivative of the X.500 standard for network directory services and often used for accessing user authentication and authorization information in Web applications, and NIS (Network Information System), a network naming service developed by Sun. JNDI allows all of these naming services and others to be accessed via a common API.

As JNDI is an interface, not an actual implementation, a specific implementation for each naming service that you need to access must be installed to actually use JNDI with that service. Implementations exist for many different services, and the popular ones are easy to find. Often a framework is available with an implementation for at least LDAP and DNS, for example.

- **Java Message Service (JMS):** A messaging system is a tool used for creating highly scalable and flexible applications by providing a means for distributed components to communicate asynchronously. A messaging system is sometimes used in place of a more traditional peer-to-peer architecture, and has some advantages over such an architecture. Messaging architectures encourage a loose coupling between message producers and message users — the receiver of the message is not necessarily aware of the location or even the identity of the sender, or the time when the message was created.

  As Web applications are built to scale up to ever-increasing demand, we are confronted with issues relating to reliability, security, and synchronization that were not a problem previously. It has been found that a messaging-based system operates more reliably and scales to greater user loads than many other approaches. Individual services and components can be modified without affecting the remainder of the system, as long as the way they deal with messages from and to the remainder of the system remains unchanged. This promotes reuse and component independence, increasing system flexibility substantially. Messaging systems also eliminate the single point of failure found in some client/server and other architectures.

  Java Message Service is an API for sending and receiving "messages" via queuing systems. JMS supports both *point-to-point* and *publish-subscribe* types of messages. Although the definition of the messaging service must be included in a J2EE implementation, an actual implementation of the service is optional. ("Would you like an *engine* with that car, sir?") However, a couple of good open-source implementations as well as connector interfaces to existing commercial messaging systems, such as IBM's MQ product line, are now available.

- **JavaMail and the JavaBeans Activation Framework:** It is actually fairly uncommon to find an application server providing SMTP, or mail server services, although it is straightforward to access email functionality from your Web application via the JavaMail API, which requires the JAF (JavaBeans Activation Framework) jar files to function.

The JavaBeans Activation Framework is a data typing and registry technology, now included in the standard JDK. The JavaBeans specification does not define a complete method for data typing, determining the supported data types of a component, and a means of associating the typed data with the component. In addition to these facilities, JAF allows an application to discover the operations available to an element of data and instantiate the appropriate object to perform those operations.

- **JTA:** JTA (the Java Transaction API) defines the required interfaces between a transaction manager, which handles the coordination of a distributed transaction, and all of the components and elements involved in the transaction itself, both at the application and server side of the transaction.

- **JTS:** The Java Transaction Service (JTS) provides an implementation of the OMG Object Transaction Service specification. It utilizes the normal CORBA IIOP (Internet Inter-ORB Protocol) to facilitate transactions between JTS transaction managers. JTS provides its transaction services to the application server, the resource manager, and the communication resource manager, as well as to a transaction application. The JTS transaction manager implements the JTA API discussed above.

- **CORBA:** CORBA is a multilanguage standard for distributed component interoperability. It is a complex and sophisticated standard, and provides many facilities to manage and permit communication between distributed elements. Frequently seen as the architecture of choice when a project spans multiple languages, CORBA can be used for projects created entirely in Java as well, although other options exist for entirely Java projects, such as Remote Method Invokation (RMI). CORBA involves defining interfaces between components in the Interface Definition Language (IDL), a programming-language-independent specification language designed just for this purpose. Mapping IDL to Java is straightforward, and tools that perform this mapping are included in the standard JDK from Sun.

- **JDBC Pooling:** Although JDBC itself is not a service, most J2EE application servers provide a pooling capability, allowing applications access to a configurable pool for connection to J2EE data sources. Most frameworks provide their own connection pooling, both when their applications are deployed in an environment that does not supply its own such pool, and in circumstances where the framework's own pooling is superior to the implementation provided by the J2EE server vendor.

Many application servers offer extensions and enhancements beyond the basic J2EE services (even if they do not fully implement all of the J2EE standards themselves). This is a two-edged sword, and use of these extensions should be approached with caution. Of the great benefits of Java is its vendor independence. Although Java itself may be controlled by the Sun-led *Java Community Process*, the number of vendors providing Java platforms is large. With these large bases comes the flexibility to change platforms which leads to business pressures that drive competition for vendors to provide better and better platforms. However, in an effort to differentiate themselves from their competitors in what has started to become essentially a commodity market, vendors attempt to "extend" their offering with nonstandard services. Applications that use these services then become dependent on the specific platform, which is one thing, but at the same time become dependent on that particular vendor, which is something else again. This stifles the whole process of freedom from vendor lock-in that is such a large benefit of Java itself. Irrespective of how large or powerful the vendor is, you are essentially handing a certain amount of control – control over *your* business or organization –to a vendor when you use a feature that locks you in to that vendor's platform. Irrespective of how good a feature the extension looks like at the time, this is never a wise decision in the long term.

One way to blunt this two-edged sword, however, is to utilize products that provide their own source code. Sometimes this means open source but not always – there are commercial products that offer the same advantage, although often at a steep price. Having source code, however, helps you pry open the trap of vendor lock-in, as it is always possible for you to maintain your own code for the required platform. Few companies want to get into the business of maintaining their own server platform, irrespective of how difficult it might be – this is possible but not necessarily practical. Again, the solution is to avoid the vendor lock-in in the first place, by sticking to cross-platform standards.

CHAPTER 2

Components: The Future of Web-Application Development

2.1 WHY ARE COMPONENTS THE FUTURE OF WEB-APPLICATION DEVELOPMENT?

In this chapter we discuss the *why* of components and frameworks and the rationale behind their use. We also talk about the current state of Web-application development and where the industry perceives it is going to establish a firm foundation and justification for the use and development of components and frameworks.

We also look briefly at Java's suitability for component-based development and for the development of application frameworks, as well as for the specialized features of the extended Java platform and associated APIs that make them ideal to this task, including JavaBeans, Enterprise JavaBeans, and Reflection.

2.1.1 Where We Are Today

The software industry is, for the most part, still creating much of its product in a "monolithic" fashion. The products may be more modular and configurable than they used to be, but most projects cannot be said to be truly component based. Even some projects being built with component-enabled technologies are not taking full advantage of the component model. It is quite possible to misuse component capabilities and as a result, to forfeit many of their benefits.

Many companies and organizations are becoming aware of the advantages and are getting their developers trained in the new technologies and the proper way to use them. It takes time for an organization to adopt such a significant change in their current practices. Some of the trade magazines would have us believe that the industry is years ahead of where it truly is – those of us in the trenches know that the reaction time is a little longer in the real world. The change to component-based development has begun, however.

2.1.2 The Market

The market for software components was expected to grow to around $4.4 billion by the end of 2002, $1.0 billion from products and $3.4 billion from related services, according to the research done by PriceWaterhouse Coopers.

There is no doubt that people are willing to pay for components. The questions are: why and what do they perceive are the business benefits?

We are living in an era of unprecedented change in the software industry. From the great boom in the late 1990s to the slump in 2001, two factors that have remained constant in the software industry are change and growth. Even as some software companies fall on hard times, others prosper – the difference is usually in the way they perceive the software marketplace. Software is no longer entirely an art form or a process of creating one unique masterpiece at a time. It has evolved into more of an engineering discipline, one driven by the real-world economics of what works and what does not. Simply stated, components and component-based development are one of the things that work.

The signals from the software market are clear: products that exhibit poor quality, inflexibility, and significant schedule overruns are increasingly being rejected in favor of the new breed of component-based systems. As the infrastructure to support components becomes more mature and standardized, and as cross-architecture integration tools such as SOAP (Simple Object Access Protocol) become widely available, the component marketplace will likely grow even more rapidly.

However, industry analysts' reports are sometimes overly optimistic, and the predicted boom in the reusable component marketplace has not (yet) materialized.

Most other technical industries have been using the component-based model of development for years. For example, in electronics, if you want to create a new television set, you do not begin by reinventing the picture tube, the transistor, and the remote control. You design by considering how you can use existing components, such as available picture tubes, transistors, circuit boards, amplifiers, power supplies, and remote controls, and by adjusting their behavior, configuring them in a certain way, and interrelating them, to achieve a better television set.

Likewise in the automotive industry, you seldom hear about a car manufacturer designing a car that doesn't run at all when designing next year's model. You also don't usually need a new road on which to drive that new car. This is because car companies start with something that works (usually last year's model), and they extend, customize, and improve it through the use of existing cost-effective components.

Components represent the "transistor" of the software industry, or perhaps more accurately, the "integrated circuit." They provide a known quantity, a building block of established functionality and quality that can be used to assemble applications in a way more akin to assembly of a television than traditional development of an application. This is not to say that the assembly is necessarily simple, by any means. After all, can *you* put together a television from a collection of parts?

Component-based development, discussed in detail later in this chapter, is still an exacting process, but it is a more rapid, reliable, and predictable process. It is easier to say how long it will take, what will be needed, and how the finished product will work – all very desirable attributes in any engineering discipline, including software engineering.

The history of software engineering has been, by and large, the history of a battle against ever-increasing complexity. Object-oriented design and development was one of the big guns in this battle, and components and frameworks, correctly applied, are the biggest yet. In 1968, a NATO-sponsored conference met to discuss what was called at the time the "Software Crisis." The crisis is not over, but with the new tools available to developers, it is a lot better than it used to be. Components provide one of the most potent tools to overcome this crisis, addressing the underlying concerns of productivity, reuse, reliability, and quality.

2.1.3 Why Projects Fail

The reasons for software project failures are varied, but they often fall into one of a few categories:

- *Schedule:* One of the key reasons for project failure is the inability to achieve scheduled milestones. Companies often simply cannot continue spending time on a project. Sometimes it is a matter of unrealistic goals having been imposed on a development team – this is not a software problem, this is a management problem. No manager should ever set a schedule without consulting in detail with the people who will actually make it happen – the developers themselves – but they do.

    Because component-based development timeframes are much more predictable, the developer can give better defined estimates to management, and management can rely on them with more confidence. Even tasks that are common to component-based and noncomponent-based developments, such as capturing user requirements, analysis, and design, can benefit from prebuilt structures in which such capture and analysis can be made. Usually the largest gains, however, are in the actual construction of the application itself.
- *Specification changes during development:* Another common reason for failure is that a project's goals change so radically while it is under development that the current project can no longer be adapted to serve the newly defined purpose. The greater flexibility of component-based systems can help avoid this in the first place, and the shorter development time gives less opportunity for significant "spec creep" to occur.

    When specification changes occur during a project, despite the faster development, the fact that components are usually, by their nature, more configurable and flexible than custom-created system elements gives a further advantage: they can simply be reorganized and reconfigured in many instances to adapt to the change in specification. If the change is substantial, then new components to provide the additional functionality can be added to the existing set more easily than in traditional development.
- *Project management failure:* Perhaps the most common reason of all is a failure in the project management. It may be that the specification did not change, but that the project team's understanding of it was never complete, and they did not have access to the customer for clarification. Also, it may be that the schedule was being adhered to by the project team, but the customer was under a different impression as to what that schedule was. These are not technical problems; they are again management issues – primarily

communication issues, in fact. A closer connection between the project leadership and management and the development team, of course, is the first step toward avoiding such problems.

The ability of component-based development to shorten project life cycles, to make elements of the project more predictable, and to provide prototypes very early in the process helps avoid the communication gaps that result from management problems. Component-based development cannot do anything to solve bad project management, of course, and component-based projects can fail through bad management just like any other project. However, the component-based process encourages good practices that facilitate management of the project, making component-based projects a little easier to handle than projects that do not use the technique.

Component-based projects also have advantages when keeping the customer of the project informed and satisfied: essential application functionality is available earlier when assembling from components, so progress can be demonstrated easily. The risk of failure is reduced by involving the customer or end user as early as possible. After all, an operational application communicates progress much more capably than a status report. Rapid assembly of components facilitates not only early delivery of essential functionality but also staged delivery of the entire project. This in turn makes more options available throughout the project. If the specification is misunderstood or changed, both the developers and the customer can find out earlier, when there is still time – and budget – to do something about it. Problems with scheduling become apparent to everyone involved early on, as each increment is delivered either on time or late, with the same benefit: time to correct the issue before the end of the project. The staged deliveries also provide an opportunity to consider specification and scope changes at more frequent milestones, accommodating even rapidly changing project goals more easily.

In the software market, fear of failure of a project is very real and well justified. An embarrassingly large percentage of major software projects fail completely or fail to meet their overall goals, schedule, and budget. Information technology (IT) spending is no longer driven by the technology, if it ever was; it is now almost exclusively driven by the need to fulfill business requirements. Companies are seeing component-based technologies as the most cost-effective way to meet these requirements, with the lowest risk of failure. Where the market demand goes, development follows. Projects happening on "Internet time" simply are not allowed the luxury of time to develop entirely new architectures and low-level capabilities from scratch – the schedules (and, to a degree, the budgets) simply demand reuse, and components fill this demand. The unit of purchase used to be the application – an entire solution providing full capability in a particular area of business, say purchasing or customer relationship management (CRM) – but the unit of purchase is shifting to the component or the service, providing a single unit of service that is then combined with others to provide full capability.

Components bring advantages to the entire process of development. During design, finding components with the right kind of interface is an essential part of the process. If components need to be developed, the external interface can be defined, and then development can proceed in parallel. This is the "black box" approach to components. You do not look inside; you simply deal with the component as a unit that performs its contracted function without concern for *how* it does it. By assembling components, you are able to deal with larger programs than in a monolithic one-piece design. Components are insulated from one another, and the development of one component team is independent of the developments of any other, reducing bugs and unexpected interactions. The design process becomes mostly concerned with decomposing the application into components, as opposed to being oriented around either procuring or creating these components.

In the development process of the components themselves, quality is aided by defining the interface and the contract the component will fulfill early in the process. Then the component can be tested during development to ensure correctness by checking whether it fulfills this contract. Indeed, some methodologies advocate creating the unit test that verifies the contract as the first step, before the component itself is procured or created.

Once the components are assembled into the application and you determine that each component and the container and interactions are bug-free, then you can be confident that the overall application is of high quality.

2.2 A Brief History of Components

The history of components parallels the history of software development itself. When software was in its infancy, it was considered sophisticated to be able to reuse code at all, rather than having to flip all those switches again. We have come a long way since then. Even in the early days of assembly language, the concepts of reuse began to emerge with subroutines or segments of code called from more than one point in the overall program. Even the crude technique of copying and pasting code for a particular routine was an early form of reuse.

Function libraries took this a substantial step forward. Here we saw the emergence of subroutines specifically intended to be used in more than one application.

The first pass at generalization when creating frameworks is *parameterization*. This is the process of delaying certain design decisions until run time – that is, when there is more than one way of dealing with a particular algorithm, allowing the user (or at least the deployer) to make those decisions by means of parameters and configuration.

A problem that arises frequently in large development projects is when a particular algorithm or component exists in many *nearly* identical forms. Since they are not *entirely* identical, they must all be separate, and each one consumes development and maintenance resources that would be better used elsewhere. Developers use the dreaded cut-and-paste method of development: they cut out the sections of an existing working application that does nearly what they want or most of what they want, and modify only the parts that need changing. Although this is very effective in the short term (you get the application done quickly), it is very ineffective in the long term, as it will give you much more code to maintain and document. You are also unable to benefit from a bug being fixed in one component, as the change will not automatically propagate to others.

Developers who wanted to work smarter instead of harder quickly sought a solution to this issue (those who did not simply move on to another project or company when such problems arose). Of course, object-oriented techniques in and of themselves are part of the solution: inheritance and polymorphism combat the problem of "cut-and-paste" development if applied correctly. Even before object-oriented development, the creation of software "libraries" was addressing this need – in the object-oriented world, such libraries are even more widely applicable. Indeed, virtually no Java Web application is created without making use of literally dozens of such libraries.

The use of other design patterns quickly extended the reach of libraries into what we now think of as frameworks: particularly delegation and forwarding, combined with the dynamic class loading capabilities of a language, such as Java.

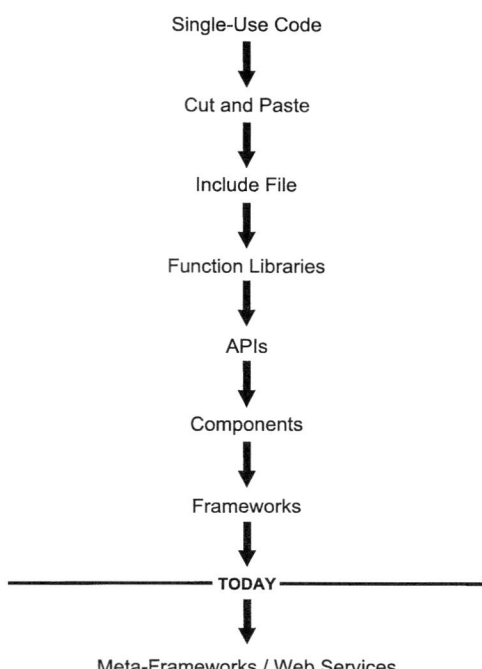

2.3 ADVANTAGES OF COMPONENTS AND FRAMEWORKS

Let us look in more detail at some of the specific advantages of components and the frameworks that support them.

2.3.1 Time to Market

Most of us are in the software business to make money. The industry moves quickly, and often the first to market has opportunities that others do not. Sometimes it is the opportunity to be the first to go belly-up, if applications are built quickly and without regard to quality – but if the job is done right, the first to market can establish themselves as a leader early on, and this advantage often lasts. Components help with this; they let the job of building an application proceed much more quickly, without sacrificing quality.

Building with components goes much faster because the detailed logic to perform each individual service is already complete – it is just a matter of wiring up the pieces. The time saved by not having to design and create sophisticated infrastructure is also very important. Even when custom logic is required, creating it is faster when you start with an existing component architecture.

The time to respond to changes in the market is often shortened by components as well, allowing a company to not only be the first out of the gate, but also faster and more nimble in the twists and turns involved in changing their product to keep up with changes in the market demands and in technology over time.

For example, a component-based word processor might be able to quickly react to an industry trend toward importing and exporting XML by being able to plug in components to read, parse, and export XML. A monolithic word processor would have a more difficult time making the adaptation, as its code for loading and saving is woven into an overall application architecture.

Some surveys indicate that at least double, or perhaps as much as a fivefold decrease in the time to market can be achieved in a component-based development project.

2.3.2 Quality

What do we mean by "quality"? Why is it important? Quality describes the abilities of a product to meet stated or implied needs – in other words, to get the job done. It is more than this bare definition, however; quality affects the entire life cycle of a software product, from design to long-term maintenance.

The old view that some defects are inevitable, and that to maximize profitability a certain percentage of defects must still reach the customer, is being seriously challenged today. Particularly by using components and frameworks, we have the ability to build quality from the outset, rather than correcting defects later in the develop–test–debug cycle.

Why quality? Simply put, quality software makes good business sense. The true cost of creating, selling, and supporting high-quality software is overall far lower than the cost of low-quality software. One of the least expensive ways to improve software development *productivity* is to improve software *quality*. Quality, therefore, is cost effective – it retains customers, and has become a key competitive issue in software development.

As the practice of application development continues to mature, becoming less of an "art" and more of an engineering discipline, the lessons of quality learned in the manufacturing and engineering world can be applied to it more readily.

To increase software quality, the people involved and the processes they work with are even more important than the tools they use. Frameworks and component technology provide more than tools; they provide a philosophy of development that is quality oriented.

One of the advantages of a reusable component is that it has been, well, reused. This means that it has been tried and tested in other applications and is known to perform its particular function correctly. All other things being equal, a known quantity is better than an unknown one when you are building an application. As one pundit put it "if we built houses like we build software, the first woodpecker to come along would destroy all of civilization." Components allow creation of software that is a bit more "woodpecker-proof," and allow us as developers to be part of the solution to the software quality crisis that plagues our industry, rather than part of the problem.

Components themselves demand higher quality: in once-off software development, a particular function of an application may be rarely used, or rarely used in a certain way. A defect in the rarely used area might never be noticed, or might not be perceived as a significant problem even if it is. With components, however, the component developer does not necessarily know how the finished component will be used when it is assembled into an entire application. A function he thought was of little importance might be the cornerstone of an application, and defects in that function would be completely unacceptable. As a result, it is essential that every part of a component be of as high quality as possible. Because of the reuse of components, any defect is likely to be replicated into many applications, creating a bigger problem. On the other hand, the benefits of extra effort (if any – as quality can actually be easier) in developing quality software in the first place are also replicated. This makes the effort all the more worthwhile, the more the component is reused.

Code quality is more than just code that does not break – it goes all the way from design to deployment. A framework that is used widely has a better chance of producing a high-quality application partly because it is used in many different ways, in many different environments. The tools in a framework must be resilient enough to work correctly in all of these different environments – this means they are resilient when presented with an unexpected situation in your application.

Because the components in a framework do not have any knowledge of your specific application, they are more independent of a particular application – this usually makes them more reliable overall. After all, if you are building something to be used once (say, a disposable plastic fork), quality is not as essential as if you are building something to be used again and again (say, a fine

Advantages of Components and Frameworks
45

piece of formal silverware). As software life spans very often far exceed their initial estimates, it is always better to assume a long life than a short one, and build accordingly.

The commitment to quality must come from the top to bottom in any development project – the project leaders must be committed to a specific methodology and all team members must share this commitment. Basing development on a framework gives this process a jump start.

Let us examine some of the key areas of quality in software, and how component- and framework-based development can help in these areas.

- **Quality environment**: The first step in achieving a quality application is the environment in which it is developed. By this we mean all of the factors around the application, including the corporate infrastructure, the physical environment, the corporate culture, and more.

  In a corporate environment where development is thought of as a necessary evil, it will be difficult to achieve quality. If management is only concerned about getting it done, and spending as little time and money as possible, quality is hard to achieve.

  If the corporate culture is such that developers are an afterthought in the IT infrastructure, and are not given the tools to do a job well, chances are that the job will not get done properly. This includes everything from a quiet, isolated workspace ("open plan" offices and software development being entirely incompatible) to proper software tools, and sufficient time to do the job right. Unrealistic schedules do not inspire faster work – quality software development, like quality in any engineering discipline, takes careful planning and sufficient time.

  Proper tools for a job are, of course, essential. This starts from the hardware up all the way to the Integrated Development Environment (IDE) and the documentation tools. Some IT managers have, for example, the absurd notion that developers should have the slowest machines, and are under the impression that this will somehow make sure they develop faster code. The same managers then skimp on a test environment, denying the opportunity to test in a realistic deployment scenario. Such misconceptions do not permit quality development.

  Managers without development experience dictating schedules to the actual developers is a recipe for poor quality.

  Although a framework does not necessarily influence any of these things directly, its use does imply certain attitudes about development. Using a framework represents a commitment to a training cycle. It represents a decision on the part of the organization to produce an application that is better equipped than something that could be developed independently, and this in itself gives an indication of the attitude of the organization toward development – that it should be done right, and with the right tools.

- **Design quality:** As we have said before, a framework is not just a collection of components and abstract classes. It is also a set of design patterns, and defined ways for these patterns to interact. In the process of developing a framework, these abstractions are created, usually from existing applications in the problem domain. A well-designed framework represents the distillation of many different application design principals into a cohesive and usable whole, and therefore provides a substantial jump start on the design process for the application overall.

  Developers are free to concentrate on the functional and business design aspects of their application, leaving the design of the supporting capabilities (such as database access, security, administration, etc.) up to the existing design of the framework. This promotes quality at the design level.

- **Meeting of stated and implied requirements:** By definition, quality includes the ability of the finished application to meet the stated and implied requirements. "Stated" requirements are not too bad – generally there is some consensus between the developer and the user on what these are at least. "Implied" requirements are bit harder. If you are like me, and operate with a somewhat clouded crystal ball, you may discover that the user or customer was under the impression that much more was implied than you were led to believe. You have created the user a fine and strong outhouse, according to the specification, and he was expecting a skyscraper. To address this "grey zone," it is necessary to make the application flexible: to allow it to expand during the development process as the user's needs become better defined (or as they are extracted painfully by means of iterative prototyping, as the case may be).

  A framework assists substantially in this area as well, as it supports the need for the application to change or even expand during the development process by providing prebuilt functionality, even if this functionality was not seen as part of the requirements for the project initially. The user decides that the new application is going to be used by 200 people, not 20 as in the original estimate, for example. This is not a problem – your framework supports multiple database engines, and you simply change to Oracle rather than Access.

- **Prevention of defects – proper planning:** An important part of preventing defects early in the development process is to have a proper project plan for the development. Correct and realistic scheduling, for example, is an essential part of this process. Nothing creates the opportunity for defects better than late specification changes – they cause new functionality to be "shoe-horned" into a design that was not intended for it. A framework-based project has the advantage here as well. Rather than leaving the development process open to "surprises" later on, a framework gives you an almost "paint-by-numbers" level of control over the development. You know what the capabilities of the framework are, and what is provided. You are assembling parts, rather than embarking on journeys of discovery. You will not have a "surprise" half-way through the development when you discover that a feature planned for development takes much longer time than anticipated, or that a driver does not work with the database you have been planning to use. An existing framework with functioning examples takes the mystery out – you know applications in the same problem domain as yours have been developed using this tool-set. You can plan better by working with the known components, and this makes for a better overall project plan, and enhanced quality. You have a map, rather than feeling your way along in the dark.

- **Avoid coding defects:** The best way to avoid coding errors is to write less code. By using a framework, the total number of lines of code that need to be developed for any given application is an order of magnitude less than it would otherwise be, and the preexisting code of the framework is likely far better tested than any single application's code. This leads to much lower incidence of coding errors, and at the same time provides more time for the code that *does* need to be written, increasing its quality as well. Real-world experience has indicated that use (and reuse) of components can reduce the occurrence of defects from five to ten *times* compared to once-off code.

- **Coding standards:** By establishing coding standards and sticking with them, coding defects can be reduced further, and existing problems can be more readily discovered. Coding standards also make it much easier for teams of developers to read and understand each other's code, thereby promoting team development.

    Starting with a framework brings a set of coding standards to a project automatically, and this tends to form good habits in developers as they extend and customize for their own projects, with the classes provided.

- **Detection of defects and testing:** If you have a hundred identical parts lying on the table in front of you, it is easy to scan them all for defects: you look for what stands out, what is different and not in conformance with the rest. It is much harder if you have got a hundred different parts – you cannot scan for patterns, you must examine each one individually.

The same is true of components developed from a framework. For example, if you were using the Expresso framework and created a hundred different subclasses of the Database Object Class (a class providing object/relational mapping and database persistence in Expresso), then it is easy to test those objects to ensure they all function as database objects should – you know what a database object should be able to do, and each of these hundred objects should be able to do those things (in addition, of course, to their custom logic).

This kind of consistency provided by frameworks makes a major difference when it comes to detection of defects, and this again enhances overall quality. After all, you cannot *fix* them if you cannot *find* them.

- **Documentation quality:** The same consistency that makes it easier to locate defects in framework-based code than in custom code also makes it easier to produce quality documentation for your project. You get to concentrate on describing the logic of your application, the parts that actually do the work, rather than writing a lot of documentation to describe your custom method of connecting to a database, for example.

  Documentation quality should not be confused with quantity: many good frameworks (and applications, for that matter) do not require vast volumes of documentation. An elegant and flexible design is always easier and faster to document than a monolithic one.

  The uniformity of design also makes it much easier to document the design of your application. If you were describing a car, for example, you do not need to explain what a car *is*, just how *this* car is different from other cars. The same is true of an application built on a framework – you can describe what makes this application unique, and the "standard" capabilities provided by the framework are always the same between its applications. This again puts more time into the important documentation, enhancing its quality in the finished product.

- **Support quality:** Quality of support and training for an application is also an important factor. The best application is not meeting its stated and implied requirements, after all, if no one can understand how to use it. This is another area where the consistency of development created by the use of a framework comes into play. For example, if I have a support representative who is familiar with applications built on a certain design pattern – for example, financial components produced by a certain company – then they will probably be able to do a good job of assisting a user with a module of these financials even if it is not the one they have specific experience with. If the screens are always organized the same way, and the menus follow a certain structure, then the support representative will have an easier time, because he can expect a certain structure to the application. The same is true with applications built with a framework: they are easier to support because of their consistent design, allowing superior quality support to be delivered to the end user.

- **Maintainability:** To continue providing a quality solution to its users, any application must be maintained over time. New features will be added, integration with other applications will be made, user-interfaces may be enhanced, and so forth. Using components and frameworks makes a significant difference here, because by their very nature, reusable components are intended for many different purposes. Therefore, as the purpose of the application is extended and changes over time, you are more likely to be able to adapt components to these changes than to adapt custom-built code. In addition, the clean encapsulation of components means that individual components can have their implementations replaced easily – without disrupting the remainder of the application. For example, an application may originally be written to use flat files for its data storage. A later upgrade then requires a relational database – the component relating to data storage can be upgraded to one that is database-capable, whereas the remainder of the application remains unchanged. If, instead, custom file access code was used throughout the application, it may not have been viable to upgrade at all.

  Although it is hard to measure the ability to maintain software, most experts agree that component-based systems are much easier to maintain than their monolithic counterparts.

Therefore, as we have seen, component-based development can indeed make a significant difference in the most serious problem with software development in today's industry: quality. Not only can components address this issue, but they can do it while at the same time increasing developer productivity, decreasing the time to market, and with greater adaptability than any other approach.

2.3.3 Cost

Partly as a result of the issues discussed earlier, the overall cost of building with components, despite the extra work of achieving reuse and the other qualities required by a good component, is lower than once-off development. This becomes even more the case when the components can simply be assembled, rather than created. Time is literally money in the software business, so the time saved in development by assembling components contributes to the cost savings.

Even commercial components that have a direct cost associated with their use can still sometimes make the overall project cost lower.

Not only is the cost often lower for components than for single-purpose-built software, but, almost more importantly, it is *predictable*. You know the cost of using a component ahead of time, this means one less variable in the complex equation for forecasting a project's overall budget.

Decisions that make overall architectural changes to a project are often those that incur the maximum cost, and the most risk. Designing a new infrastructure is not easy or quick, and a mistake at this level can be disastrous to a project. Standardizing on a tried and true component model eliminates this risk, further contributing to control of cost.

2.3.4 Adaptability – Change by Reconfiguring, Not Rewriting

Components, by their nature as reusable pieces, tend to be more configurable and adaptable than code that is written as a one-of-a-kind. This flexibility is then available when (not if) the specifications and scope of the original development change. It is usually possible to change the components by simply reconfiguring them, as opposed to having to open the black box and start tinkering inside. This means the adaptability is gained without a loss of quality. This has a direct impact on the maintainability of the overall project.

Like most techniques, however, use of configurable components can have its down-side if applied incorrectly. Some components are not good candidates for being made highly configurable – performance can suffer, and the component complexity can increase substantially. Sometimes separate implementations are a better approach than a component with a huge number of configurable options. Finding a balance in this trade-off is part of the skill of an expert component developer, and when it is done well, it becomes another reason to prefer well-built components over single-use software elements.

As most projects have over 80 percent of the development effort they absorb spent on maintenance, this adaptability is a major benefit in terms of cost.

Sometimes the advantage that adaptability brings to the potential reuse of entire applications is overlooked. If the application is component based and configurable, it may make the difference between being able to use it – perhaps with modifications – and having to begin a completely new project.

2.3.5 Scalability

Components, if built correctly in the first place, can often provide a basis for better scalability than custom code. Because the scope of the component is known ahead of time, its place in the architecture is better understood in advance, giving an opportunity for the component to be made distributed and clusterable, opening the door to enhanced scalability.

The design pattern of having a component called by its container, and never the reverse, can be applied for scalability: if the component is always handed what it needs to operate, it does not care where those things came from. This allows the component to be relocatable in a cluster, allowing the container to make decisions about load-sharing for best performance.

2.3.6 Integration

By design, components are intended to plug into other things – they are not a complete application on their own, so integration is expected. This tends to make components easier to integrate with just about any other code elements, and raises the integration capabilities of the whole application.

This means components and component-based systems are ideal for connection to legacy systems – indeed, components are often created to "wrap" legacy applications, allowing them to be used just like any other component.

The increasing interest in components, due to the advantages they offer, has in turn spawned an urgent interest in the technologies that connect them together and support them. The two major leaders in the race to provide such connections and infrastructure are Java, and in particular the J2EE platform, and Microsoft, who arrived late to the game, but are aiming their .NET platform at the same space. Interestingly, the business requirements becoming the driving force in the market has pushed vendor preferences lower on the importance scale than it used to be: people are less interested in who they are doing business with than the quality of the results to their business. This drives the requirement for multivendor solutions to integrate more frequently, as IT departments become "multivendor" shops. One of the emerging technologies in this area that has great promise is Web services, and in particular the SOAP protocol. We will explore this important trend, and its relationship to the overall component and framework marketplace, in detail later.

2.4 BEYOND E-COMMERCE: COMPONENTS AT WORK

The newer the sector of the IT industry, the more you will find components there. When something works, organizations tend to leave it alone – many legacy systems that predate component technology are still out there, ticking away, performing their functions. New developments, however, have a better chance of being created with component development, and e-commerce is one such development.

Before the Internet, there was no such animal: e-commerce has come about with the rise of the Internet – or more specifically, the World Wide Web. E-commerce is generally thought of as the process of offering products or services for sale via the Web. The condensed time frame of trends on the Internet has prompted companies trying to get on the rapidly moving bandwagon to try out components and other rapid development technologies, such as scripting languages.

The scripting route, using technologies such as Javascript, ASP, CGI, and so forth, was faster, at least initially. Like a Hollywood set though, many such solutions were all scenery, with little substance. They looked good, but did not have the back-end power to connect to essential business systems, as necessary when weaving e-commerce into a cohesive part of an overall company strategy. The solutions built with components tend to fare a little better – although some of these were all flash and no bang.

E-commerce, however, was only the beginning – the first ripple of a much larger wave. The second phase was *e-business*. This is where not just a company's interaction with customers and potential customers is carried out in part over the Web, but where a company also interacts with its peers and business partners via the medium of the Internet. Suppliers, distributors, and wholesalers – the volume and critical nature of the Web interactions was suddenly much higher than when the Web was just one more means of reaching customers.

Now the Web was essential to business, and significant competitive advantages could be gained by leveraging it correctly. Component-based development became the technology of choice for creating these new business-to-business Internet applications. Its standard and easily connected attributes, and its ability to adapt quickly, became essential facilities.

Business-to-Business (B2B) has already become a more important form of e-business than Business-to-Consumer (B2C), and the growth is still rapid. As more organizations begin to take advantage of these new opportunities, they will increasingly find component and framework development an essential tool.

2.5 CONCLUSION: THE FUTURE IS JUST BEGINNING

We have seen why all of the interest in components and the frameworks that support and foster them, has come about. In Chapter 3, we will examine the kinds of capabilities that components and application frameworks provide, and how they deliver these advantages to your projects. We will discuss what to expect as this new wave in the software industry begins to crest.

To entirely mangle a famous saying, however, a rose by any other name is just a red flower with sharp thorns. Calling something a component does not make it so, and definitely does not magically convey the advantages we have discussed on the product so named. Marketing and hype being what they are in the software industry, it is easy to make a product buzzword compliant, but not as easy to actually do the engineering necessary to make it worthy of the name 'component.' Searching the net, it is easy to believe that the whole software world has jumped on the bandwagon of components, and that virtually any product is built of these wonderful, configurable, and reusable pieces. In reality, the battle for components has only just gotten underway, and the big guns have just started firing recently. So beware of any solution that promises to be the end-all and be-all of component development. Ask the questions that can determine just which of the many advantages of components the solution is providing, and how.

The great wave of component-based development is so far just a ripple. It is a great concept, but the groundwork that had to be laid is only just propagating to companies' IT departments. Once the enablers are in place though, dramatic strides forward in quality, productivity, and interoperability will be seen. This is not theory – many companies are there already, and are showing the way to the future.

CHAPTER 3

Application Frameworks: What Do They Provide and What Are the Benefits?

In Chapter 2, we have discussed components and described their benefits. The software architecture that supports the operation of components is called the component "container." It provides the environment in which a particular type of component can be run and manipulated.

Components come in many different forms, from the ubiquitous JavaBean to Web services, and at many different levels of scale. At the small-scale level, components with a visual aspect, such as drop-down boxes, tree lists, and buttons, are assembled into a single form. At the high-scale level, entire services such as order entry, billing, and inventory update are combined into a complete application.

All levels of components, however, have one thing in common: they all operate within some specific component container. Often, this container is one of the services provided by a framework.

A framework is not only a component deployment environment, but also it is used throughout the development of an application and its components. It is a part of both the development and the run-time life of your application.

In this chapter we explore frameworks in more detail. We describe the features you will likely find, and the benefits they provide to your development project.

We also include what application development frameworks provide in broad terms and how they relate to APIs (e.g., JavaMail). We discuss the common elements found in many Web applications, and how appropriate components and frameworks can be used to provide these elements. That is not to say that these services and facilities are all that a framework can provide – indeed, many frameworks go far beyond them.

3.1 ADVANTAGES OF FRAMEWORKS

When managing the complexity of a software development effort, a number of factors must be considered. Let us look at how frameworks and their components help us address these concerns in real-world projects.

First, it is always important to keep development projects as simple as possible – that is not only should they be limited in functionality, but given two different approaches to a problem, the least complex one is most likely to have the least problems in terms of time, cost, and maintenance. Simple is good – as long as the specification is still being met.

Frameworks, despite sometimes being complex if taken as a whole, bring simplicity to development by decomposing the problem space into separate elements, such as authentication, database access, and user interface. Each of these elements if dealt with independently and consistently gives rise to a solution that is, overall, less intricate than one that deals with them collectively, and allows them to have arbitrary interconnections.

It is important to design systems in a modular fashion, and frameworks by their very nature as generic application building tools encourage this approach. An application built using a framework is much more likely to be built using a modular design than a "once-off" application.

The resulting flexibility helps the new application become more resistant to evolving requirements – modules can be replaced or upgraded as specifications change rather than building a whole new structure. The same modularity also promotes reuse.

Errors made in the design and architecture phases of a project tend to magnify later and prove much more expensive to rectify than coding problems. The structure and design patterns provided by a framework ensure that your project is being built on solid ground, and help avoid these issues before they can occur.

Documentation is always an essential part of a project, both for usability and for later maintenance. Starting from a framework gives your project a leg up here as well, because the consistency of using the same base patterns means that these patterns only need to be documented once – probably, they are already documented in the framework itself.

Frameworks provide benefit at many different levels of application development. We examine some of the more important areas in detail.

3.1.1 Structure

Frameworks provide a structure for application development – a backbone to build from, making the development process a little less "freehand" and slightly more "paint by number." They ensure that your project includes all of the key elements such as security, database access, UI, and so forth by providing an outline into which the details of your particular application are filled.

The existence of such a structure allows easy parallel development – more than one developer can work on parts of the project knowing that the pieces will fit together correctly later.

The design stage of the project is also speeded up, and can be more concentrated on the application-specific concerns, rather than on infrastructure.

Even though a framework brings a powerful tool set to an application development effort, it is often the design patterns and structure that it provides that give the biggest boost to development. Particularly with less experienced developers, one can focus on the application at hand, rather than figuring out what works and what does not. In Chapter 8, we will explore some of the powerful design patterns frameworks bring to your projects.

The kind of structure that a framework applies to its own services can be examined to understand how that particular framework approaches application problems. Some frameworks, for example, take a very "service-oriented" approach, where each aspect of your application is considered a service. Typically, a service-oriented framework will also structure its own capabilities as services.

Several of the more popular application frameworks help in the development effort by creating some, or even most, of the code for you. This is known as "code generation," and it is a technology that has been in use for many years, often with great success. Sometimes code generation is performed by a third-party tool, such as the webAppWriter project, which generates Expresso applications. In other cases, code generation is a facility of the framework itself, such as the Torque module of Turbine.

Code generation can be a great time saver, but certain disadvantages apply: if it is not possible to regenerate code without losing modifications you have made, the generation has to be done for any customization. One technique to avoid this is to extend the generated classes, and put your customizations in the extensions; in this way the generated classes can be regenerated without losing any customized code. More advanced code-generation techniques use a synchronization mechanism, whereby changes made by the developer in the generated code can be "synchronized" with the original and preserved in future generated versions.

Code generation can also be capably applied in situations where standard code must be added to or generated from custom functionality: for example, the interfaces required for deployment of an Enterprise JavaBean can often be generated from the underlying bean. Code can also be generated to "wrap" legacy applications and provide a Java interface to their functionality. Like most tools, code generation when correctly applied can be very powerful – but can be a serious hazard when misused.

3.1.2 Services

A framework provides a wide array of services to its applications, for use in both the development and deployment phases. These services very often begin with either a component container, or access to a component container provided by the application server. Frameworks designed for operation in a J2EE EJB-enabled environment often rely on the Session EJB object for their component element. Some frameworks provide their own component model, more or less compatible with EJB standards – this allows the framework to be used both in EJB and in non-EJB environments. Avalon is one example of such a framework.

The component container service is only one of many possible services provided by a framework, however. In fact, some frameworks concentrate on only specific areas of the application, such as presentation. Such frameworks provide the connection to the component model for application logic, but leave the choice of component model to the developer. An example of such a framework is the Apache Struts project.

3.1.3 Completeness

Most application development projects are on a budget – both of time and money. This means, as a developer, you are interested in getting the job done, and usually do not have enough time for much more than the job – no time for extras or items categorized as "nice to have" but not required. If your projects are similar to mine, there is usually enough pressure to get just the specified functionality completed in the alloted time.

Using a framework can expand the horizons slightly: if adding some of the "nice to have" functionality does not cost any additional time, you can end up with a richer, more complete application that is comparatively more polished than it could have been without the framework. For example, say your application could benefit from more sophisticated error handling, but you would not normally have time to build it. If this functionality is already included in your framework, then you are able to build a better and more complete project in the same amount of time.

At the time of maintenance, the extra capabilities become even more appreciated. Remember, you may end up having to maintain the project yourself, so be kind to future developers.

In Section 2 we see the kinds of services and tools that frameworks typically provide, and how they are used in the development process.

3.2 What Is in the Tool Box? (Common Elements in Web-Application Development)

Let us rummage in the tool box of a typical framework and see what it normally provides. Much like the tool box stashed in many people's car trunks, there are a number of things that you almost always find, and a number of things that are less common.

3.2.1 Application Logic

The architecture of the Web is based on a request/response model. A client requests a page, and the server responds. The client fills out a form and submits it, and the application responds.

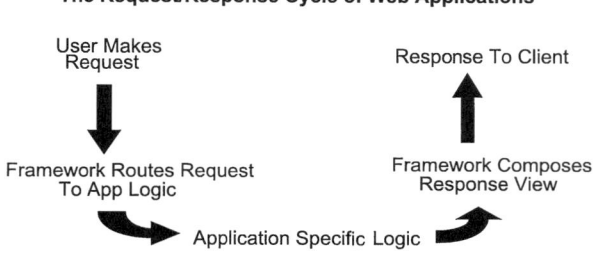

The Request/Response Cycle of Web Applications

Most frameworks for Web applications try to work with this model. Since the days of the 5250 protocol for the so-called dumb terminals, it has been recognized that most of the time spent by any interactive application is waiting for the user. This is, of course, the basis of timesharing theory. Web applications can take advantage of the same technique, albeit somewhat more up-to-date.

Therefore, handling application logic is the process of routing requests – from users or other sources – to the logic of the application.

Most application frameworks, even those that concentrate primarily on the user interface and presentation issues, provide some means to organize and interface with the application logic. The application logic is normally separated from the presentation quite intentionally, and a mechanism must exist to connect the two (providing the "controller" in the model-view-controller pattern). The flow of control between the various logic elements of the application must also be defined, and frameworks must provide this mechanism as well.

In a Web application, the initial request from a user is almost always accessing a URL. This URL then must present a page to the user, which provides access to the next step in the application and so on. This is the beginning of the *flow of control* mechanism of the application and is the first step in connecting the user to the application logic.

Frameworks use a different terminology here to describe the transition of the application from one state to another and the logic that creates the transition. Struts, for example, calls the classes that provide this logic as "actions," whereas Turbine talks about "modules" and "screens." Regardless of its terminology, a basic function of almost all frameworks is to make this connection from requests to logic.

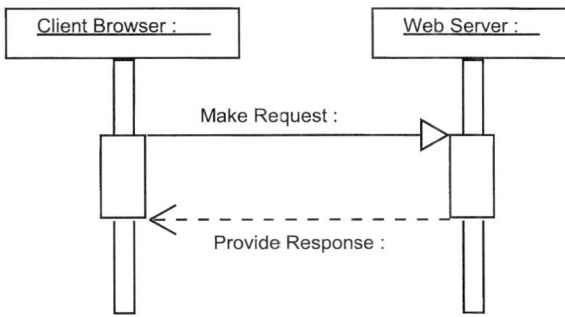

The application logic "unit" in frameworks attempts to satisfy a number of goals:

- **Support easy creation of the application logic:** Any framework should make creation of the logic as easy as possible, without getting in the way. You should not have to jump through hoops to conform to the framework's implementation. Implementation of a simple interface or extension of a base class are two simple methods.

- **Support scalability:** The logic container must be highly scalable, because it is frequently an area of the application that accounts for much of the processing time spent servicing user requests. This may involve making the logic container "thread-safe," that is, allowing no instance variables (only method-scope variables) to allow many separate threads to use the logic without conflict or locking. Struts action objects are one example of this, but it is a common pattern.

- **Support standards:** All things being equal, it is usually better to support a standard than reinvent a new way of doing something. Of course, things are not always equal. Sometimes there are good reasons for deviating from various degrees of standard – to achieve better performance, higher reliability, or some other goals.

    Where possible, however, the logic container for a framework should work with existing standards, for example, using the JavaBeans patterns for getting and setting the attributes. It means interoperability with the EJB standard, for instance.

3.2.2 Database Access

Most sophisticated applications being developed today interact with some kind of database. This is also true of Web applications, and most frameworks provide a mechanism for easier access to databases.

Often this mechanism takes the form of a "mapping" between relational database tables and objects. This allows you to deal with Java objects that correspond to a database record (or a group of records), without having to deal with SQL or JDBC directly. This gives you a number of advantages:

- **Object access:** With an object/relational layer doing the dirty work, you can concentrate on your application logic in a more object-oriented fashion.

OBJECT / RELATIONAL MAPPING LAYER

```
                    APPLICATION
                    MANIPULATES
         OBJECT   OBJECT   OBJECT   OBJECT

         OBJECT / RELATIONAL MAPPING OF FRAMEWORK

RDBMS:    TABLE   TABLE   TABLE   TABLE
```

When you need a customer record, for example, you just instantiate an object and call a method. When you need to store the record, you call another method. You do not have to switch between thinking in SQL and thinking in Java.

There are a number of different techniques for providing object/relational mapping and persistence. Each has its advantages and disadvantages, depending on the application at hand.

The general technique is simple enough: provide a Java object that corresponds to data in the relational database. Allow this object to be populated and manipulated, and then provide a way for the object to synchronize its data with the underlying database.

The object/relational layer is also an optimal region to apply security and control constraints. For example, if all objects accessing the database are extensions of a particular parent object, the parent object can determine whether the current user has access to perform the specific database operation being requested. This allows the individual persistent objects to be written without having to think about security, and still be fully secured. Control constraints, such as audit ability, can also be applied at this layer. If a particular persistent object is set up as "auditable," for instance, it can automatically write all accesses (particular write accesses, such as updates and deletes) to the appropriate audit trail table or file.

In short, an object/relational mapping layer can provide powerful capabilities to your persistence mechanism without any extra coding effort: an ideal example of the application of a framework to a development project.

- **Database independence**: Frameworks frequently provide independence from the underlying choice of database, making it easier to move the finished application from one vendor's database to another. Of course, the JDBC standard makes this much easier, but even when using JDBC it is very easy to end up with code that works only on one type of database.

  Some capabilities of an object/relational mapping layer can extend beyond JDBC's capabilities. For example, creation and modification of the underlying tables, indices, table relationships, and triggers may be supported. Often, these features of databases require some vendor-specific extensions to SQL, so sophisticated configuration mechanisms are used to support multiple database engines from a single code base.

- **Caching**: Frequently, the database connectivity part of a framework will provide a means of caching data, making read operations many times faster than if they had to go directly to the database itself.

  When done correctly, this can be a substantial performance gain – it is, however, important to understand the scalability issues that are related to the caching mechanism. For example, how does caching operate in a clustered multiserver environment? Can you cache things other than database information?

- **Speed**: One of the less apparent benefits of using a framework can be overall application performance. If you are building an application from scratch, it is all too easy to slip in sections of code that become performance bottlenecks – particularly when you are building the "low-level" facilities for your application: its persistence mechanism, for example. When using a framework that has had many eyes and minds behind its development, these issues likely already have been found and addressed. This means that if you use the framework facilities, you get the benefit of the optimization effort put into its components for free. In a large or complex application, this can be a substantial benefit for using the framework in the first place.

  A common example is the ability to reuse a component rather than instantiating several different objects. Not only does this prevent the overhead of creating objects, it also (often) reduces memory and the time spent on interobject communication. In many cases, a framework provides a sophisticated component manager that will pool and reuse component instances as appropriate, providing further savings. A framework also frequently supports the use of caching at various levels of its operation to increase performance. Your project can get this advantage without any additional effort – for example, if the framework applies caching to its object/relational layer, your database access can be several times faster than the same operation made via direct SQL calls to the database.

So what does this tool do for you? It lets you build in the database access portion of your application faster, knowing it will be reliable, portable, and scalable. Data integrity can be automatically guaranteed, and excess coding can be avoided.

When examining the persistence layer of many frameworks, we find it relies on object/relational mapping – why not use an actual object database (OODBMS – Object-Oriented Database Management System) instead? There are number of reasons: OODBMS are good at processing complex data, and they are intrinsically object based, as the name implies. However, a great deal of existing data exists in relational database form. Using an OODBMS in this case would require conversion, which is not always practical if the relational data source is in use by other existing applications. The query and reporting tools for OODBMS also often lag their relational counterparts in features and flexibility – for example, the powerful "join" capability of relational databases is difficult to duplicate in an OODBMS. The concurrency control and transaction handling of OODBMS are also primitive in some products, and performance can be an issue. All of these factors mean that most frameworks assume that you will be using JDBC to talk to a relational database for your persistence needs. A number of major software companies have announced extensions for their products that may be the best of both worlds: Object/Relational Database Systems (ORDBMS), so this distinction may be a slightly blurred in the future in any case.

An important element in many database-based applications is support for "atomic" transactions – that is, a group of operations that must either complete successfully, or be reversed (rolled back). An incomplete operation cannot be permitted. The classic example of this is a bank account transfer – you cannot have a system that deducts the amount from one customer's account balance, but fails when trying to add it to another, leaving the total amount incorrect. Many different approaches to transaction handling exist, as we will see later in more detail when examining a framework's transaction services.

3.2.2.1 Java Data Objects (JDO)

A specification for an extension to the standard Java API called JDO, or Java Data Objects, has been recently finalized and released.

JDO proposes to do two things: provide a means for application developers to deal with Java objects that represent a view of persistent data, both local and enterprise, and allow "pluggable" implementations of the actual persistence mechanism.

Some debate continues about its merits, because JDO takes a somewhat different approach than most other object-relational mapping tools: it aims for complete persistence transparency – in other words, the persistence of an object is largely hidden from the application developer. The developer simply deals with an object that determines at which point it must be synchronized with a persistence mechanism, such as a relational database. Although this approach shows the promise of providing much in the way of simplicity for the application component developer, it is, however, not as simple to be implemented successfully. Some developers argue that it is not even the correct approach to persistence, that is, making persistence transparent is not that much of an advantage, because it obscures concerns such as locking and concurrency over which the developer should have more explicit control.

Most developers agree, however, that independence from the persistence mechanism itself is desirable. JDO also provides this by separating the concept of a persistent object (e.g., one that is saved to a persistent store such as a database) from the persistence implementation. In this way, an application using persistent objects can work immediately in a deployment with a different persistence mechanism. This is a capability beyond mere database portability in that it allows an application, for example, that originally worked with a relational database as its persistence mechanism to be run with a file-system-based storage mechanism.

JDO deals with developers in two different roles: those who create a JDO implementation for a specific data storage mechanism (such as a relational database), and application developers who use a JDO implementation to provide persistence for their own objects.

The specifics of the database-access technique, of course, can vary widely. Some frameworks use Java's reflection API to determine the fields in an object, and then automatically map these fields to database columns, optionally using external configuration files to tailor the mapping (to specify which Java types get mapped to which DBMS types, for example). This is a very Java-like way of working – you work and think in objects, not in tables and records. Other frameworks take an approach that is closer to the database. The objects that correspond to database tables must explicitly declare which fields are to be persisted, and which database columns and types they correspond to. For developers more familiar with relational database access and SQL, this can be a very natural approach.

3.2.3 Database Maintenance

In addition to providing programs with an easy way to access database records, many frameworks also provide an easy way to build database maintenance capabilities. The uncomplimentary acronym "CRUD," for "Create," "Read," "Update," and "Delete" is sometimes used to describe the functions needed. Users frequently need to be able to search through a database table by means of a query, update, or add records, and sometimes delete existing records. Often, these things happen as a result of the operation of your application itself, transparently to the user. Sometimes, however, the easiest way to allow the user to maintain certain sets of information is to provide them with "CRUD" functions directly.

The built-in database maintenance functionality of many frameworks typically allows existing databases to be used. This makes access to legacy information quick and easy, because practically any data source can be accessed via JDBC.

Prototyping is also easier; rather than spending time building data maintenance features, you can concentrate on the unique functional aspects of your application.

This feature also serves as a valuable test and debugging tool, because you can directly set up test data sets, and examine the results in the tables after the test runs.

Database maintenance capabilities let you get on with the important part of your application, freeing you from having to code this repetitive function, and allowing data entry capability early in your application's life cycle. This is particularly useful for prototyping, where direct database maintenance is often the easiest way of setting up test data.

3.2.4 Logging

Logging is sometimes frowned upon as either a necessary evil, to be avoided whenever possible, or a low-tech replacement for proper debugging. Proper logging is neither of these, but is in fact a highly valuable technique that can be applied in many of today's most sophisticated applications. It has also been said that too much logging can make source code illegible and difficult to follow – the reverse is true of correctly applied logging. Modern logging can increase the overall legibility of any code, particularly in distributed applications where traditional debugging tools are difficult to apply. It can act as an ideal guide to application logic and flow for a newcomer, and then can be turned off to minimize its impact where it is not needed. It is also an invaluable aid to debugging: when an error occurs and is able to be related to a detailed log, the bug can often be isolated in a moment, and repaired just as quickly.

Many toolkits have been built that provide logging capabilities, often used to track the operation of an application for debugging purposes. Frameworks often include such toolkits, making it easy to add code that allows your application to log its progress in one way or another. The best such capabilities do their work with a minimum impact on the performance of your finished application, and allow the logging to be tuned easily for various levels of detail without changing code.

Logging is often already built-in to the components of the framework itself, which means that tracking the operation of those components is straightforward. This can be very useful when learning the framework – sometimes it is useful to know what goes on inside the black box.

It is important to understand what the performance penalty is for using logging – and to be able to make a decision on what the proper level of logging is for particular situations.

Most logging toolkits use a method of configuring multiple logging levels. This allows the developer to turn detailed logging on and off as required. Ideally, the performance impact when logging is set to a minimum should be zero – allowing the logging code to be left in place even in production code. This then allows it to be used again in case of a problem, without changing the code.

Built-in logging capability saves you from having to use debugging capabilities, and enables you to track application function at different levels. These advantages can be gained without having to create the infrastructure for good and flexible logging – which reduces the time taken in the overall development effort of your project.

We have already discussed some of the attributes to look for in a logging system: it should be configurable, with multiple levels or channels of logging that can be turned on and off without having to change source code. It should be a low-impact one, for example, it should not impose a large performance or maintenance burden on the application, either at run time or development time. It must also be "fail-safe," that is, a failure to log a message should not bring the whole application down – logging is generally a low-priority function, with the possible exception of error logging. Often, a background thread is used to allow "lazy logging" where the actual log entries are written when CPU time is available, rather than in real time. Logging must be manageable – ideally incorporating the concept of file "roll-over," starting a new file and perhaps renaming the old one when writing to the file system, to prevent any one log from getting too large and unusable. Ideally, the log output relating to a specific client request should be uniquely identified, making resolution of an issue related to one particular request easier.

3.2.5 Event Handling

Most frameworks have one or more means to deal with "events." The term "event" can be used to describe processing at many different levels of an application. There are UI/presentation-related events where, for example, a user clicks a button or selects a control. Events can also be internal to an application, or data related. For example, an event can be generated when a certain record is saved to the database, or a cache has expired. The actual meaning of "event" depends entirely on the framework in question. The AWT and Swing UI APIs, for example, have a specific meaning in mind when they discuss "events." Triggering actions based on an event that has occurred is a common technique for driving the application logic.

Events are also sometimes used as a communication mechanism between distributed components – systems using Java Messaging Service (JMS) often use this technique. This mechanism is frequently given the name "distributed event handling."

A common design pattern applied to events is to have two elements involved: the element that triggers the event itself, and the event "listener." Often, the way other classes become aware of events is by "subscribing" to the event, registering themselves as a listener to a particular event. For example, if a piece of logic must be triggered every time a new customer is added, the class or component implementing that logic "registers" itself as a listener with the object that stores the new customer. When the event occurs, the "new customer" object goes through its list of registered listeners and sends each of them some kind of message: an event notification, telling them that the event they have signed up for has just occurred. Sometimes an intermediary is used here, a kind of event manager, where objects can register the events they emit, and listeners can sign up to register themselves as listeners for particular events.

Ideally, a framework should use a generalized event handling mechanism, so events at all levels of an application can have listeners registered, and have certain actions take place when the event occurs. Some common uses for events in frameworks are as follows:

- **User interface event:** A user clicks a button, submits a URL, or manipulates a control in some way.

- **Database event:** A new write (or sometimes even read) operation has taken place on a particular table.

- **Timed or scheduled event:** A specific date or time has past, and scheduled events are emitted to trigger certain actions at that date or time.

- **Log in/log out:** A common technique is to emit an event whenever users authenticate with the system, or when they log out (or their session expires).

Event-driven logic has traditionally been used mostly in the area of the user interface, but the technique is gaining popularity among developers for use in many other areas of application development.

3.2.6 Caching

Caching, or the holding of calculated or retrieved results temporarily in memory, is a well-known mechanism for improving application performance. Any data that is expensive to create or retrieve can potentially benefit from caching. Common examples are database retrievals and the results of complex computations.

Most frameworks provide a mechanism for caching. Sometimes this mechanism focuses entirely on caching database or other persistent store data, but often the cache is general-purpose, and can store almost any object that can be identified by means of a key.

Caches found in frameworks often also provide memory-management capabilities, so the cache itself does not use too much of the available memory. They incorporate algorithms to use the available cache most efficiently, such as a least frequently used algorithm to select items to remove from cache when it is full.

A Java Specification Request (JSR) has been submitted, JSR 107, to create a standard extension to Java for caching APIs. Currently, the many different caching specifications used by frameworks are not necessarily compatible with each other.

3.2.7 Configuration

In the early days of application development, providing facilities for configuration was easy: a setup file was often used, containing a few settings and options required for an application to know where its data directory was, the name of the database to be used, and other basic information. If a change was necessary, the application was shut down, and the file was edited. On startup, the new settings were read, and the application went about its business.

Multiuser applications began to complicate this straightforward scenario. Often, the solution was to provide each user with a "personal settings" file, and retain a common file for configuration of the entire application. As applications became more flexible, the setup files began to get more complex. Often, an easy-to-use graphical user interface (GUI) replaced the old form of editing the file with a text editor.

With the advent of Web applications the situation became even more complex. Now we have many users, some of them are anonymous, some not. We have a requirement now for applications to continue running for twenty-four hours and seven days a week. The application cannot be restarted arbitrarily, even when configuration changes are required. Configuration files usually cannot be stored on the client's PC, so some registry of user preferences must be maintained on the server.

The added complexity of the applications and the greater options for flexible configuration often lead to configuration data being stored in XML, not flat files any more.

All these changes result in the need for a framework to provide configuration services to its applications and components. Such a service must be able to support multiple applications, each potentially with multiple configuration contexts. Each application may be accessed even while changes to configuration are being made. Usually these configuration services are based on XML files, or possibly on database tables.

3.2.8 Scheduling

Many application frameworks provide scheduling services. Sometimes these services are combined with event management, and sometimes they are independent. Most allow for repetitive tasks, for example, a task run every Thursday at 12 P.M., or every day at 2 A.M.

The task being run could be virtually any sequence or component. Often a framework that provides a logic container will allow this logic to be scheduled. For example, if the logic container is a Session Bean, the scheduler can launch any method of a Session Bean.

3.2.9 Messaging

The ability to communicate, both synchronously and asynchronously, is essential to many applications. Communications must occur between the user and the application. This is the job of the user interface. The user clicks a button, or fills in a field, and the application responds. The user does something else, and the application responds again. This is the synchronous side. The asynchronous side is also important. If the user were to request an operation that takes longer than is reasonable for the user to wait (about two seconds, in an application that is perceived as "responsive"), the application needs an *asynchronous* way to communicate its results. This can take one of many forms: email is a common mechanism. The application simply sends an email to the user to let him know that the request has been completed. Another option is to wait until the user logs in to the regular user interface and then notify him – although this could take longer, but this might be less convenient than the alternative. If the delay is not long (e.g., it is a matter of a minute or even several seconds), the user might still be logged in. In this case, the message might be able to fit in to the normal synchronous communication with the user (e.g., through a pop-up box or other such means).

All of these capabilities are the job of the messaging service of an application framework. Several frameworks provide at least the email option – others go further, and include an interface to a generic messaging system, such as JMS, which we will examine in more detail later.

The second type of messaging service provided by frameworks is the messaging between application elements. These can be components on the same system, or across the network. They might be parts of the same application, or even elements of multiple applications collaborating on a single process, such as a business-to-business order processing transaction. Messaging of this type can still be synchronous or asynchronous, and the same mechanisms are sometimes utilized: a real-time connection can be used for synchronous connections (Web services via SOAP are one example of how this can be achieved), and an email can be used for nonsynchronous messaging – although this is more uncommon.

A framework will probably provide at least some means of user messaging, and the more capable ones will provide a wide range of options for messaging between all of the entities involved, both human and software.

3.2.10 Error Handling

Java, of course, provides a mechanism of exceptions to make it easier to deal with errors – but exceptions do not do the whole job. Once a piece of code has a problem, and throws an exception, what happens? Does it simply throw up its hands and land the problem in the user's lap, leaving them staring at an incomprehensible stack trace? Clearly that is the worst case – most developers make at least some attempts to provide a "polite" delivery of the bad news.

Frameworks typically help out by providing a standardized way of handling and tracking errors. Several goals can be consistently achieved this way:

- **Tracking the problem for correction**: Tracking the problem usually involves some kind of logging, either in a file or into a database. It is important to note that whatever mechanism is used to record *enough* information to accurately locate and correct a problem, it is not *so much* that it is impossible to weed out the problem from the mass of logging data. Logging can also become a burden on the performance of a system, and a good framework will have a way to reduce this burden, especially in a production system, while still allowing for serious problems to be logged as needed.

- **Informing the user, if appropriate**: If the problem is the type that the user can do something about, by all means, tell him. If you are going to tell the user, always make sure to use plain English (or plain French, or plain German, as appropriate). This is not as easy as it sounds, and often frameworks provide the means to "translate" the internal rumblings of the application into something the user can understand and take appropriate action. It might be as simple as "you need to put a number in there," or "no such entry," but if it is wrongly presented, it is not information, it is a "bug" – from the user's perspective. After all, it is the user whose perspective matters in the end. Conversely, if it is not something the user can do anything about, then perhaps the best route is to simply not tell them – but make sure to tell *somebody*. The worst problem is a "silent" error – better that it arrives with bells on than to slink about in the shadows, sabotaging the function of the application with no evidence of a problem.

In the case of a data entry problem, or input validation error, the best course of action is to present the user with the input screen again, this time highlighting the field or fields that had the problem. The page should also include a description of what the problem is, preferably near the field itself. A particularly important feature is to retain any data the user has already entered. Nothing is more annoying to the user than having to rekey data.

- **Informing the system administrator, if appropriate**: If the problem is not a simple mistake on the part of the user (like our example of just keying an incorrect number), then it may indicate a more serious problem. Often, frameworks provide a way to have certain levels of error trigger a notification to a system administrator, or a group of administrators. This frequently takes the form of an email, containing sufficient detail that the administrator can take constructive action to solve the problem. For example, if the system frequently runs out of memory, the administrator can begin configuring caches to compensate.

- **Fixing the problem, or at least working around it**: Even better than carefully tracking the problem and notifying the proper people about it, a framework can take action to try to solve certain issues. Running out of database connections, for example, could trigger the framework to scan the connection pool for idle or broken connections, and reestablish new connections. This "self-correcting" behavior is sometimes provided by the more sophisticated frameworks.

- **Easy implementation**: The error handling in a framework must be easy to incorporate. It should not impose a lot of extra work on the developer – in fact, ideally you should not have to do any extra work at all. A valuable way to make error handling transparent to the developer, one used by many frameworks, is to implement "nested" exceptions: allowing one exception to be nested within another. It is common to see code such as:

```
try {
  ...
} catch(YourException e) {
   throw new MyException();
}
```

The problem with this technique is that although it allows one exception to throw another, it loses information from the original exception, making debugging much more difficult. It is much better if you can build code such as :

```
try {
  ...
} catch(YourException e) {
    throw new MyException(e);
}
```

Typically, a framework provides a number of constructors for these nested exceptions, and also allows the printStackTrace method to print the entire nested stack of exceptions, allowing the true root cause of a problem to be seen in stack outputs and logs.

In the case of JDK 1.4, handling of nested exceptions is built into Java itself, so it makes good sense to become familiar with the technique.

The consistency of always using the same generalized components to handle errors means that these features will always be applied, whether the problem is relatively common, or something that happens rarely. As any quality-assurance person can tell you, the most obscure error will be the first thing the unsuspecting user will run into.

Like logging, advanced error handling tends to go by the wayside as project schedules and resources get tight (which always happens). Using a frameworks' error handling mechanism avoids having to reinvent error handling, and usually provides a much more sophisticated mechanism than would be built for a once-off.

3.2.11 Monitoring and Testing

Every Web application is built on the top of a totem-pole. This totem-pole consists of all of the other layers of technology necessary for its operation, and usually includes at least an operating system, a virtual machine, a Servlet container/application server, databases, communications, and many others. Perched on this pinnacle, there are many factors that can affect the performance of finished applications.

Many frameworks provide tools for measuring and monitoring an application's performance. Entire projects have been built (e.g., the Apache Cactus project) to perform testing and to measure performance of Web applications.

Ideally, this performance should be able to be monitored in the actual deployment configuration – it is not as good to measure in a test environment. At the same time, it is important to be able to measure performance of individual components to determine where bottlenecks are occurring.

Some of the monitoring capabilities provided by frameworks are:

- **Load generation:** Creating pseudorandom test data sets to simulate user data. This allows for as realistic test as can be performed without actual users on the system.

- **Test harness:** The ability to simulate users with multiple threads. This permits "load" or "stress" testing, often at simulated user levels far above what are anticipated, to determine what problems might occur at times of high system load.

- **Production monitoring:** The process of continuing periodic tests on the production system to ensure that it continues to operate properly. This allows a failure or impending failure to be dealt with by sending warning or error notifications to the responsible party, helping avoid extended down-time by notifying the system administrator of a problem right away. In the case of performance monitoring, the administrator can begin reallocating resources or adjusting parameters to assist with a slowdown as soon as it begins, and in the ideal situation might even be able to bring more servers online to eliminate the bottleneck without the system grinding to a halt.

- **Notification:** In addition to the notification from the production monitoring, other events can be tracked and automatic notifications can be sent. For example, log files being rolled over, caches operating above a certain percentage, new user registrations, and other occurrences can trigger notifications, allowing the administrators to be aware of the load and operation of the system.

- **Logging:** All of the monitoring, tests, and notifications should be logged, to provide an over-time record of the system's performance. This allows an analysis that can determine times of higher load, or situations that seem to cause more system errors or problems, and for those situations to be tracked to other occurrences in the same time frame. Perhaps every time more than 100 users are logged in, some particular database exceptions are noted. Perhaps Tuesdays are prone to higher loads than any other days of the week. All of these kinds of trends can be spotted with adequate logging.

3.2.11.1 Performance

"Performance" is not quite as simple as it sounds. Modern hardware is many times more capable than systems only a few years old, yet users become accustomed to greater speed very easily, and so do developers. Applications swell with features, seemingly expanding to fill all available memory and consume all available CPU power. Modern users have certain expectations – they look at a measure called "perceived performance," which is not the same as raw computational speed.

Performance can be measured in a number of ways, and we need to examine how an application framework can benefit each of them. Web applications in particular need to pay special attention to performance due to the environment within which they operate. In a "closed" network, such as a typical client-server system, the maximum number of users is known and the user load, at least to a degree, is predictable. In a Web application, especially on the open Internet, the user load can vary widely, and it is difficult to predict what the load will be at any particular time until the application is deployed. Even then, additional efforts at promotion can result in huge swings in load from one day to the next. Raw computational performance is only one part of the picture, although it is often the focus of many optimization and performance-tuning efforts. Computational performance relates to the amount of overhead incurred by a particular application – this overhead can be an issue with some deployment environments, and a well-crafted framework will seek to carefully minimize it. Each individual algorithm in a framework should be selected for best performance, because the conditions under which it will be used – what kind of application will be created – is not known ahead of time. If the framework provides you with efficient and speedy building blocks, you have a headstart on creating an application that will perform well overall.

The amount of memory available and consumed is often critical to performance, because Java does well with plenty of available RAM. Exceeding the limit available to the VM can result in swapping, however, which is to performance what hitting a brick wall is to a race car – a show-stopper. It is essential that your application be tested in a memory environment similar to its deployment environment to ensure it does not exceed what is available and cause this issue. In a hosting environment, where a single server is shared among more than one customer, or multiple Web applications and sites for a single customer, this issue becomes even more critical. Sometimes one of the easiest and cheapest performance boosts you can achieve is to simply move the application to its own machine – the hardware today is, frankly, cheap, and trying to overuse one particular system is seldom worth it.

Performance also needs to remain constant in relation to load over time – that is, if an application starts up and runs reasonably quickly at first, the same number of users should get the same response from it even four hours later. Slow degradation of performance is often indicative of resource or memory leaks – a pool of objects always getting larger, or a new object getting created and never dereferenced. The design patterns and (hopefully) well-tested code of a good framework can help you avoid this, provided the framework itself is applied correctly. However, the responsibility to manage the number of objects created and watched for open-ended resource allocation still lies with the application developer.

As load increases, performance should decrease in a predictable slow pattern – it is of course perfectly normal for a system to slow down gradually as the overall load increases. If the performance curve shows a sharp increase in time for the operations to be completed, however, you are probably running into some kind of resource limitation at that point. Either the amount of RAM needed to support that many sessions is not available, the number of database connections has exceeded the available maximum, or there are some other hard limitations. It is important to be able to load-test under realistic deployment conditions to determine these limits. As long as they are high enough, and the system deals with the overload relatively gracefully, all is well. There are always *some* performance and load limits to a system, at least in a practical sense. One such limit is the old maxim that the user is seldom willing to wait for a response from any system for more than two seconds. This rule of thumb has been in existence since the days of client/server systems, and in fact users on a website might be accustomed to a bit more lag – but they may not like it. If a system can produce most of its responses within two seconds, the perception of performance by the user will likely be fairly good, and this is indeed a key measure. Some frameworks provide a load-testing harness that can operate the functions of the applications under simulated user load to test this kind of responsiveness and track the results. Obviously, for real-world deployment this is an essential tool, and if your framework does not do this itself you should consider a third-party package that does so. The load testing should take into account network traffic and be as similar as possible to a group of actual users interacting with the system, which can be difficult to achieve.

The ability of a particular system to respond well to larger user loads without hitting a performance threshold is the system's *scalability*. A system is said to be scalable if it can easily support higher user loads with increased capabilities: for example, if you allow five database connections, and the system can support

200 users, can you increase the database connections to ten and support 400, or even 500 users? If there is an artificial limit brought on by the design of the system, it is said to not scale well. Scalable distributed systems take this a step further – they support the ability to add more than one *server* to the single application, thereby bringing to bear on the performance issue resources beyond the reach of any single system. This is of course one of the key benefits promoted for the J2EE/EJB platform. A truly scalable system, one that can have a large number of servers added to its cluster for a single application, is not so easy to achieve. Even a well-designed distributed system using EJBs is not necessarily scalable – for example, it may rely on a single database, and the database becomes a bottleneck over a certain number of simultaneous connections. A good framework will support the appropriate design patterns to avoid such bottlenecks. Not all do – and do not believe that just because a framework supports J2EE/EJB, or distributed applications, a silver bullet will slay all your performance issues.

An essential benefit that frameworks bring to the performance process is the ability to switch environments: most frameworks, for example, allow you to easily switch database engines or persistence mechanisms. If you have originally created your application using the Hypersonic SQL database, for example, and discover that the user load will be much higher than you originally expected, you can switch easily and with no coding to Oracle, or some other high-performance database manager. This flexibility is a key attribute, and one that is not likely to be built into an application designed for a single environment without a framework.

Assuming you have designed a system with your framework that will scale to the limits you require, how can you make best use of the framework to maximize perceived performance? If the application itself processes quickly, what can be done to make the user see that? Part of the answer lies in the user interface. The Web is a request/response model, and making and breaking connections can be expensive. In the Web environment, you also do not necessarily have control over the performance of the client's connection and should not make assumptions that everyone has a high-bandwidth link to your application. The user interface to your application should be responsive, which involves intelligent use of the appropriate markup (often HTML). Just as with static Web pages, large images and busy pages will be perceived as slow irrespective of how fast the back-end processing is. Just because the application cranks out the page in a split second does not mean that the 4 MB GIF can be downloaded over the user's modem any faster. Smart use of HTTP/HTML and page layout is as essential a part of performance as optimizing the back-end processing, and its effects can be felt even at lower user loads, where the network latency and browser overhead are more significant parts of the overall time.

A framework should provide you with a backbone that is designed for performance and scalability. Through repeated use in many different applications, the developers of the framework will have found out many things that work – and many more that do not. Take advantage of their experience and try to use the performance and scalability features of your framework appropriately.

3.2.12 Security

A key element of many Web applications is to provide appropriate levels of security. An application designed for public access on the Internet might not need digital certificates and secure socket layer (SSL), for example. The best frameworks provide selectable levels of security, so you can use the right size of lock.

Security is a matter of applying the right safeguards at each level of the overall implementation of your application. Let us examine each of these levels, and how the security capabilities provided by frameworks apply to each one.

3.2.12.1 System Security

Overall application security begins from the basis of system security. The best application security does not help much if the user can bypass it by going directly to the underlying system. Let us look at the totem-pole of services on which our application must perch:

- **Hardware:** An issue that is often and easily overlooked is physical hardware security. It does not help to have the world's finest security software if someone steals your backup tapes, for example. A server console left logged in as superuser is also easy to avoid.

- **Operating system:** Things get slightly more interesting at the operating system level. There are many more "holes" that must be considered, and frameworks can only do a little to help at this level. The techniques for applying operating system security are well documented elsewhere – it suffices to say that the choice of operating system and security policy are critical foundations for any Web application.

- **Web/application server**: Security becomes more complex at the level of the Web and/or application server: this is the server that provides the application with its infrastructure, and this infrastructure itself must be secure or the application security is not useful. A cracker can bypass application security and get what he wants from the application server directly if there is a weak infrastructure security.

- **Application**: Application-level security is where frameworks can be of greatest use. They can provide an application with a number of mechanisms for authentication of users, ranging from the simple "basic" authentication to smart cards all the way to biometrics, such as voice and retinal recognition. The application then uses this authentication, which identifies the user, to determine a set of authorizations – what the user is allowed to do within the application.

    A specification known as Java Authentication and Authorization Service (JAAS), developed through the Java Community Process, brings some unity to this area of security – we will discuss it in detail later on, and see how it is used with frameworks to provide pluggable and flexible authentication mechanisms.

- **Browser**: Security can even be compromised from the browser level. For maximum convenience, Web applications often let a user store a "cookie" on the browser that will facilitate future logins. It is assumed, often incorrectly, that in this technique only the same user will access the application from the same PC. As a security practice, it is right up there with sticking a post-it with your user name and password to your monitor – in other words, it is not a safe plan! The browser itself is also responsible for its side of the encrypted communication in SSL/HTTPS mode, and can provide a potential security problem if this mode logs its data in a nonsecure manner.

Security is a *process*, not a one-time function. The ability to routinely audit any running Web application and server is required to maintain proper security, and is highly desirable in any framework.

Just like home security, there is no such concept as completely impenetrable security. It is a matter of making it difficult – all right, *very* difficult – for the would-be hacker to break in. If they happen have a couple of supercomputers sitting around, and an endless supply of experts, they probably *will* eventually get your data. The point is to make it as difficult as possible for them. Just as most home burglaries are a result of a careless mistake, such as leaving a window open or a door unlocked, most system break-ins on the Net are due to the cyber equivalent of such mistakes, and are just as easy to avoid.

Specifically with frameworks and Java Web applications, here are a few points to keep in mind:

- **Use the most up-to-date stable version of the framework available**: older versions sometimes have bugs that become known over time that can be exploited as security "holes." (The same is true, incidentally, of your application server and your Java VM – it is always best to stay as up-to-date as possible with them as well.)
- **Install strong encryption if it is available**: Some frameworks provide the option of using "obfuscation" or actual encryption – if you have a choice, always select the "hard stuff." The best possible encryption may be slightly harder to set up, but for security in your finished application it will be worth the extra trouble.
- **Use a Java security policy**: In the case of JDK version 1.2, Java itself provides a detailed security mechanism in the form of Java security policies. These can be used to enhance Web-application security by:
  - Limiting the classes that can access to the file system to only those required. In many frameworks, configuration files and log files are the only two file-system accesses needed for most applications – if you locate the classes responsible for this and allow only these classes, then yet another avenue of problems is avoided.
  - Limiting the classes that can request network connections and limiting what IP addresses connections can be initiated from. This is particularly important when your application is dependent on another server application for its operation – in this situation, you will probably only want inbound connections from one specific server. This prevents the introduction of a class that collects passwords via a network connection.
  - Limit access to system properties to only those classes in the framework that require them – this reduces the chance of malicious code altering system properties.

  See your JDK documentation for more information on creating a policy file.
- **Secure the file system**: Any Web application can be compromised if the intruder gets access to the application server directories, or (worse) the Web-application directory. Valid code can be replaced, and configuration files might be cracked. File-system security is the prevention here. It is very important not to allow directory access or to place configuration or class files in directories that are for static Web pages. The user account under

which the Web server application runs should require read-only and execute permission only – not write permission. This blocks one avenue of attack. If it is necessary to grant write access to the application file, limit it to specific directories only, as any writable file is a potential point of vulnerability.
- **Secure database JDBC drivers**: Ensure that the JDBC drivers you are using are configured to accept only connections you know will be required – typically by default many configurations allow any requests.
- **Use firewalls between the Internet and your database**: Enough has been written elsewhere about firewalls and their implementation, but it suffices to say that this is a necessary step in a truly secure configuration. You want to protect your database by all available means, and a proper firewall is a potent tool for this.
- **Secure the database connection point**: Almost all frameworks have some form of database access. This means that somewhere in its structure the framework connects to the database via JDBC, using a login and a password for your database server. To implement connection pooling, it is common to use a single user name and password for all connections. The easiest way to ensure that the framework and its applications have access to all of the tables they need is to give them the administrative user name and password, which grants full access to the database. There is a danger in this, however – if the configuration file is compromised, the intruder gains high-level access to your database. It is instead better to grant only the level of access required by the framework as a whole. This may vary – during setup and configuration the framework may need CREATE TABLE and DROP TABLE permission, for example, but this is not usually needed during an ongoing operation. Grant only the security required to minimize the risk.

  It is also a good idea to limit the network access to the database – most databases have the ability to allow connections only from a specific IP address or a group of addresses – the server on which your framework application runs should be the only server with such permission. This way, even if the intruders have the password, unless they are logged in to the application server system, it does them no good. Two gates to come through are better than one.
- **Remove all unnecessary services**: Most frameworks, and for that matter, most application servers, come with many different services. The default configuration of the server or the framework may have these services enabled, but they may not be required by your application. If they are not strictly required, turn them off. Any active service presents another opportunity for an intruder to gain access – and often a service that is on by default will have

some kind of default security or password applied to it that leaves an open door.

The same is true for any Servlets configured in your application's web.xml file that are not needed – comment them out or remove them altogether. The fewer Servlets configured, the fewer elements you have to worry about securing.

- **Change all "default" passwords:** Most servers, databases, and other applications come with some kind of default security setup, usually including a default password for the master access account. It is important to locate each and every one of these and either change the default password or remove the account altogether, if it is not needed. Otherwise, all your intruder has to do is install a copy of the same server, or read its documentation to determine the default password, and he is in – with "root" access, no less. This is one of the most overlooked but easiest to implement security measures.

  Look for default passwords and accounts for each of these:
  - Operating System, including telnet, FTP, NFS, Samba, and other network services.
  - Web servers, such as Apache or other HTTP service.
  - Database Server, for example, Oracle, Sybase, MySQL, and so forth.
  - Application server/J2EE server, such as Weblogic, Websphere, Orion, Tomcat, and so forth.
  - Application framework.
  - Any installed commercial applications, in particular those with network access, such as email servers, collaboration products, chat tools, and so forth.

- **Monitor for intrusions:** Despite the best precautions, a determined intruder will probably find a weakness somewhere. Just like physical security, the idea is to make intrusion as difficult as possible, so the prospective attacker would find it worth their while not to break into *your* system.

  As a result, it is best to run some kind of monitoring application, an intrusion detection system. These systems monitor your server for unexpected or nontypical activity and alert you to it. There are also companies that offer intrusion detection as an external service. This gives you the means to determine if your security has been breached and be able to do something about it rapidly.

- **External Security audits:** The best way to truly ensure that you have covered all the bases is to hire an external security firm to perform an audit of your security system and policies. It is often difficult to see your own mistakes, and an external pair of eyes can spot things much more easily. Many companies avoid this route for various reasons, but it is better to have someone paid to find your security holes than to wait until someone who is not paid to find them.

3.2.12.2 Authentication and Authorization

Most business logic that a user wants to access requires some form of identification of the user, a way for the program to tell who is making the request. Just as you log in to your email account with a login name and password, most Web applications use a mechanism of a user name and password to identify who is requesting what.

Authentication refers to the process of determining *who* is making an application request. It is quite distinct from authorization, which is the process of determining, which functions that particular user is allowed to perform. Frameworks typically provide flexible mechanisms for both of these.

Often, the means of securing the login process can be configured: simple HTML form logins can be compromised and displaying the password as "*."s as it is typed is not that much help. Using Secure Sockets Layer to transmit the password and login via an encrypted channel is better, and a more robust method such as Kerberos, where authentication is encoded in time-stamped "tickets," is a step up again. The correct level for a particular application should be chosen, and good frameworks give you the choice.

A pluggable authentication mechanism usually allows a way to access different data stores of user information. These choices usually include access to a Lightweight Directory Access Protocol server (LDAP), operating system user lists, custom database tables created for the purpose, and legacy user databases.

An essential adjunct to authentication is the ability to handle sessions: unlike the situation with a client-server application, where the one instance of the object code remains operating during the entire time the user interacts with it, Web applications work in what is essentially a stateless environment. Users, however, need the ability to maintain the state across individual requests, and almost all frameworks provide a means to do this well. The underlying Servlet API provides the key element – the ability to establish and maintain a "session," some consistent record that says that this request is related to other requests by the same user. Frameworks frequently make use of this session to maintain at least the user identity, allowing the user to remain "logged in" and authenticated for the duration of the session. More advanced frameworks extend this ability across secure and nonsecure pages – allowing a session established via an SSL login page to be used in non-SSL pages as well, for example, or allowing a single authorization to be carried across multiple Web applications or even across multiple servers.

3.2.12.2.1 JAAS

The JAAS standard, first published in 1999, provides some extensions to the normal Java 2 security model that are of particular interest to Web applications.

The previous Java 2 security model does a good job of providing policy-based access control to Java objects, addressing the potential security issues of Java's dynamic class-loading abilities. This provides security based on the origin of code, and optionally on who "signed" the code. What it does not address, however, is who is *running* the code.

Most programming environments take the opposite approach, starting first with user authentication and authorization. Java, with its early use on the Internet as downloadable code, started with code-origin security first.

JAAS adds to these abilities the knowledge of the identity of the user, and the ability to use this identity to specify personalized permissions for the user.

In the case of Java 1.4, JAAS is integrated with the Java base distribution, so its capabilities are automatically available to Web applications deployed on this platform. Independent releases of JAAS are available for JDK 1.3.

JAAS provides a straightforward, configurable authentication mechanism. The exact mechanism for authentication can be exchanged, allowing many different mechanisms to be used as appropriate. Applications that are not security-critical can use the default configuration-file-based mechanism, imposing no unnecessary complexity, while still allowing security as required. For more security sensitive applications, more rigorous authentication is easily added – such as Kerberos, or certificate-based methods. It is even possible to require multiple methods of authentication as required.

JAAS defines a user as an extension of the Java security.Principal class. A collection of Principals makes up a javax.security.auth.Subject.

Principals are expected to provide some kind of proof of identity, which could range from a basic password all the way to advanced biometrics, such as retinal scans. These credentials are divided into private and public categories. It is possible to configure JAAS so that all multiple authentications must be verified before the user is fully validated: for example, a legacy application login and a database login.

Applications can easily make use of JAAS by calling for a Login Context object, which accesses a JAAS configuration file to determine the appropriate Login Module to be used. The Login Context mechanism allows the use of a general purpose call-back handler to support all the information required for different authorization mechanisms.

Once authentication has been established, the access to functionality is controlled via authorization.

Authorizations can be specified in an extended version of the security policy file, by specifying a code-base and a particular permission, as in a pre-JAAS policy file, but in addition specifying a Principal that must be a member of the Subject that requests the secured function.

3.2.12.3 Data Security

I am sure we have all heard the terrible tales of companies' databases getting pilfered for their credit card data. Often, these attacks are caused by a complete lack of the most rudimentary security measures, but sometimes the hackers really have to work for their spoils. The job of data security is to make their job as difficult as possible – without locking out the users and applications that *should* have access at the same time.

There are a number of different approaches to data security. Many rely on the pluggable encryption mechanism made available by the Java Cryptography Extensions (JCE), now a built-in part of Java according to JDK 1.4.

Data security is in fact related to another essential security concern: data *privacy*.

Although most companies doing business online have a privacy policy, and take into consideration the privacy of the data they collect, if they are unable to provide adequate security for the data itself, the policy will not stop a third party who gains access from making use of the private data as it sees fit. The essential backbone to any privacy policy is having the technology in place to make it enforceable.

Several areas of overall security must be considered when thinking about data security:

- **Data acquisition:** When data is first acquired, the means of collecting it must be secure. You must not only ensure that the data is not being copied by a third party, but must have a mechanism of knowing that the party providing it is in fact who they say they are. Frameworks address this by providing access to SSL forms, using the HTTPS protocol, and by providing basic mechanisms to verify identity with return emails. Although not foolproof, these provide at least a basic means to verify that the information collected is valid and not intercepted while being collected.

- **Data communications:** Once the data is collected, security must be considered every time it is transferred from one place to another. This includes the transfer between components of a distributed application. Scalability needs often drive applications to be distributed across multiple physical servers, and when these servers exchange data, the exchange itself can be vulnerable to interception, particularly if it uses geographically remote servers. For example, you may collect the credit card information from a customer via a secure form, and use a means to be assured that it is indeed the customer who is providing the information, but when authenticating the credit card use a nonsecure communications mechanism.

  Frameworks should provide a secure mechanism for inter-server communications, especially if the component model they support encourages distributed applications.

- **Data storage:** This is where most peoples' thoughts turn when considering data security: when the data is present in the database. As we have seen, it is not the only place to consider, but it is essential for several reasons. First, the application likely no longer has control over the data – the database system's own security is now responsible for who has access to a particular record, and as we have seen, there are areas of weakness between the application and the database security layer in some instances. The best way to ensure data security here is via encryption: making sure that even if the data itself is compromised, it is in a form that renders itself useless to anyone else. Many different standards for encryption exist, including complex "one-way" encryption mechanisms that make a particular element of data gibberish to any user other than the originating user. In this method, the data is scrambled and stored – no way exists to unscramble it, but the encryption mechanism can be reapplied, and the same original data will result in the same scrambled data. For example, a password "secret" is encrypted, and a string "*7xhedh" is generated in its place and no algorithm is provided to turn "*7xhedh" back into "secret." When the user logs in, however, the password they key is again run through the same encryption process, then compared to "*7xhedh." If the scrambled strings agree, the user is logged in. In this way, the problem of storing the password itself is side stepped completely.

  However, there are problems with this approach. Only by comparison to the original data can information be retrieved: it is not useful for information that must be deencrypted back to its original form from the encrypted, stored version. It also makes it difficult to use the searching and retrieval capabilities of a database: if you want a customer named "Smith," but the names are all encrypted, you cannot search for "Smith" – you must search for the encrypted form, or go through and decrypt each customer to see if the name was "Smith." This can cause some difficulty in application design that your framework should help you with.

- **Data retrieval**: We have discussed earlier how retrieval of encrypted data can complicate an application's life span. Retrieval of information must be easy for those appropriately authorized, and this relates back to the entire structure of an application's authentication and authorization. Any weak point in this chain can inadvertently allow unauthorized access to confidential data.

- **Data expiration**: If you no longer have the data, you cannot compromise its security. As the old saying goes "dead men tell no tales," the same is applicable for deleted data, assuming the deleting mechanism you use is complete, and overwrites the old data appropriately. Many databases, for example, have the ability to "undelete" a deleted record, which could comprise a serious security risk. The security of your application is only as good as its weakest link. Even file systems can sometimes be reread after being deleted, and in some special circumstances even files that have been intentionally overwritten can be retrieved partially. How to get rid of data is as important a topic as how to acquire it.

    It is also important to remove and purge confidential data as soon as it is no longer required, but not before. Expiration on data should be marked, and a process run periodically to locate records that can be purged appropriately. Users and authentication can also be granted limited lifetimes: this is a useful technique in security generally, because it prevents "old" user names and passwords from being used after they are no longer legitimately active. Several frameworks provide this "expiration" mechanism for user accounts, although few provide sophisticated purge mechanisms for obsolete data – often this is an issue that must be handled by your database of choice.

3.2.12.3.1 Methods of Attack on a Web Application

Examining the different ways that Web applications can be attacked, we can better understand the ways we can defend against such attacks. Like the security consulting services hiring reformed thieves, we can learn much by getting inside the hacker's head.

An attack on a Web application first requires a point of access. The intruder can gain access to a system in many ways, and we have already looked at the importance of reducing the number of ways available by disabling services that are not required, such as FTP, NFS, and other port/socket-based protocols that are not in use.

Once a point of access is found, the security behind that point of access is attacked. The goals vary and can include:

- **Capture of passwords**: The intruder may want to access existing valid passwords – so it is essential that unencrypted passwords are not stored, and that communications between the user and the system when passwords are being exchanged are encrypted. The authentication mechanism in many frameworks addresses this by using SSL security when passwords are entered. More robust mechanisms than passwords can also be used (such as certificates, pass-phrases, biometrics, location-based authentication, etc.).
- **Access to data**: Although easy access to data for authorized users is essential, it is equally essential that unauthorized access be made as difficult as possible. Changing default passwords is an often-overlooked route of access to databases, as is file-based access directly to the database files. Storing data in an encrypted form is one option, although it can have a searching and performance penalty associated with it.
- **Damage**: Creating a problem, disabling your system, or destroying information might be the goal. Preventing write access to data on a production system can deflect this kind of attack in many circumstances, and intrusion detection and logging are essential to become aware of any damage that has occurred. Although prevention is better than cure, applications that can perform rapid self-verification and validation of data can be recovered from this type of attack more easily than others. An off-system backup is essential, which should go without saying.
- **Denial of service**: A common form of attack is to simply make your system so busy fulfilling what appear to be valid requests that it is effectively denied to other legitimate users. Some frameworks can help with this by providing detection of rapidly repeated requests from the same client, and limiting the amount of resources and/or connections that can be allocated to a single client at any given time. Intentional delays in the login progress when invalid entries are made can defer not only denial of service but other attempts to obtain entry.

Of course, this is hardly a complete list, because the innovativeness of intrusions appears to be always growing, but with some simple preventive measures and good commonsense you can prevent most casual attacks, and certainly make life more difficult for even the most determined intruder.

3.2.12.3.2 Auditability

An often-overlooked area of security is auditability – the capability to track critical events, logging them so that a sequence of actions by a particular user can be reproduced after the fact.

To be useful, it is important that the auditing process does not become such a performance burden on the application that it is invariably turned off. It should be separate from the normal logging functions of the application, because they serve two different purposes. Finally, the audit trail should be easily searchable, so that finding activity between specified times or from particular users is quick and easy. Storing the audit trail in a database table is often a good choice – assuming the performance constraints are satisfied.

3.2.13 Presentation and User Interface

Some frameworks concentrate on providing the visual side of applications – the user interface. In the context of Web applications, this can range from basic HTML through XHTML to XML transformations via XSL all the way to full GUI applications using Applets or client-side applications for their presentation.

Handling presentation for an application involves providing a number of services. We explore each of these below. Presentation can also take many forms, as we will see, and the best frameworks leave the technique employed up to the developer.

3.2.13.1 Internationalization

The issues involved in internationalization, although perceived mostly as a presentation issue have an impact on all parts of an application. The best frameworks take this into account, and at the same time do not make internationalization so *intrusive* that it becomes too difficult to write the application.

Here are a few of the areas where a framework should provide support for internationalization:

- **Pages and forms**: Each page must, of course, have the ability to be generated in the appropriate language, as must each form for data entry. A framework should provide the ability to build pages and forms in a language-independent way, with a way to specify keys to an external, translatable language file or resource.

- **Menus**: Menus must also be easily translatable, and this usually means either avoiding the use of "graphical" menus (where the menu choices are images or icons with words on them), or using a technique whereby the appropriate icon can be selected depending on the current locale.

Image maps are also an area that can make internationalization difficult, and even icons must be carefully selected, because they are often culture dependent: an icon whose meaning is reasonably obvious to an English-speaking westerner might not be clear to a native Russian speaker, for example.

- **Error messages**: Even the lowly error message must be able to be internationalized easily – in fact, this is a particularly important area that the framework must provide. Nothing is more annoying than to hit an error and be given a message describing it in a language you cannot understand!

- **Character sets**: Some language translations require alternate character sets. Whereas the English language typically uses ISO-8896-1, many eastern languages use Big5 or other character sets for their presentation, and the framework should support this capability to truly support internationalization.

- **Multibyte support for presentation**: Along with alternate character sets, some languages require more than one byte to express each character or symbol in the language – Java supports this well, but the capability for it must be included in the framework itself.

- **Multibyte support for storage**: In addition to supporting multibyte character sets for presentation of pages and forms, the framework must provide an easy method of storing multibyte character data in its persistence mechanism. Ideally, this should work on a database that is not necessarily set up to store multibyte data, to provide maximum flexibility of a database engine. This can be done via an encoding mechanism, whereby the multibyte data is encoded when stored and decoded when read again: the hidden danger in this technique is the difficulty in searching for encoded data.

- **Different display orders**: The user interface mechanisms of the framework must be flexible enough to allow for different orderings in some languages (e.g., Arabic), and for, sometimes, large differences in the length of certain terms in some languages. It is not uncommon for the same term to vary in length by 30 percent or more between languages. Screen layout must be flexible enough to accommodate this.

- **Numeric formats and currency handling**: Numeric formats also vary from locale to locale – particularly currency values. Although this may be a minor issue in the overall scheme of things, it is an issue well appreciated by international users of the finished application.

- **Date formats**: The same is true of data formats, only more so: date formats can be particularly misleading if presented the wrong way. One way of avoiding this is to use "day-month-year," where the month is represented in letters, for example, "01 Aug 2002." Of course, then you run into the language issue again. This is an issue that a framework should provide help for.

Given the nature of the Web, a truly internationalized Web application must support multiple languages simultaneously – presenting the appropriate language (in the appropriate character set) to each user. This means that the application must dynamically associate each user (each session) with a locale, and apply this locale appropriately when building each page for that user. Of course, Java's own built-in support for the Unicode standard makes this considerably easier, and the internationalization support of the language itself is also an essential building block. It is the job of a framework, however, to make these facilities easily and transparently accessible to the developer.

An application accessed by a Web browser has the ability to determine the user's language preference directly from the browser – most frameworks take advantage of this capability to determine the appropriate locale, and then use this locale to build the proper local-language page for the user as requests are made.

A couple of primary approaches are used by frameworks to support internationalization, each having their advantages and disadvantages:

- **Message files**: Many frameworks take advantage of Java's built-in support for locales and its support for message bundle files. A message bundle file associates a "key" with a particular string in the local language. For example, the English message file might have

    ```
    greeting = Hello!
    ```

Although the French message file has the same key, but a different is string associated:

```
greeting = Bonjour!
```

Frameworks allow the "keys" defined in these message bundle files to be used in many different places within the framework, such as labels and messages within the Presentation components. It is essential that any area where the string may be used in the user interface or messages to the user be able to use these keys, otherwise parts of the user's interaction will still happen in the original language, providing an unfinished feel to the entire application.

- **Multiple templates:** Another technique used by frameworks when providing internationalized user interfaces is to divide the page templates for each page presented to the user into separate languages. For example, with JavaServer Pages (JSP), an English JSP would be created that is identical to the French JSP, at first. Then the French JSP is translated directly. When users connect to the application, their language preference is used to select the template itself. The effort of creating these templates can be considerable, but automated tools are often used to ease this burden (see the Barracuda presentation framework for an example of this).

    This technique allows for completely separate page layouts to be used for each local language, which can be useful for languages that have considerably different word lengths (such as German and English), or where the order of presentation is different (such as French and Chinese). It is also a technique easily applied with frameworks that use XSL Transformation (XSLT) as their presentation technology, because this transformation can select a different style sheet for each language, allowing the specifics of the local-language version to be collected into a single style sheet.

    The multiple-template technique also can easily support languages that utilize a completely different sequence – such as Arabic, which is read from right to left, and not from left to right like many European languages. This is the kind of true internationalization that is difficult to support with just message strings, because the entire page must often be restructured depending on the currently selected language.

- **Multiple data storage:** An application that is used simultaneously by users in different languages has another challenge: the stored data, or data made persistent by the application in any kind of database. If the data was keyed in by a user in one language, but then later read by a user in another, it may not be understandable. In some cases this is not important, such as an application where personalized information is written and read by the same user. In other cases it may present a problem, such as a catalog used by people in two different countries. If the catalog presents the field "ProductName" that was keyed in by users in Germany to users in Japan, misunderstandings are possible. One approach to this, supported by frameworks, is the idea of multiple "versions" of a single field. The data is stored separately for each language, and the records related within the database. If a local-language version of a particular field or record is available, it is used – this prevents a record that does not have a German translation, for example, from appearing completely blank. This is a complex but powerful process, and it is only supported by a limited number of tools. The need must exist in sufficient force to make such a complex technique worth applying, and then testing is complicated considerably.

The technique (or techniques) applied by any given application must depend on the circumstances, but in general the level of internationalization supported by Web applications is currently inadequate. Given the truly international nature of the Web, and with more than half of the users on the Web having a native language other than English, it becomes essential to choose a toolkit that lets you apply practical internationalization to your development projects. There is no single "suitable" technique – most good frameworks provide a combination of the above approaches.

3.2.13.2 Web UI options

Web applications have a number of choices when it comes to their user interface. These choices fall into two categories: those that do not require anything "special" on the client side, and those that do. For example, HTML is generally a choice that most browsers can understand unassisted – it falls into the category of a UI that requires no special client-side software. Applets, on the other hand, require that at least a JVM of the appropriate version exist on the client, and are an example of a UI choice with special requirements. Depending on the nature of the Web application and its intended deployment environment, one of these choices may make more sense than the other – if you deploy a general-audience website on the Internet, for example, you may want to lean toward not requiring anything special on the client side.

3.2.13.2.1 Applets

Although Applets have somewhat fallen out of favor, for both valid and invalid reasons, they are still a viable and useful approach to Web user interfaces.

Applets are able to provide a substantially more flexible GUI experience to the user because the display is not constrained to what is possible with straight HTML, or even HTML and JavaScript.

One of the issues that was a problem for Applets in the past is that different browsers used different versions of the Java platform itself, rendering some Applets incompatible on some browsers. One answer to this that has emerged is the Java "Plug-In" provided by Sun Microsystems – it allows the appropriate version to be automatically downloaded as required to the user's browser, eliminating some of the compatibility concerns. Applets deployed in an Intranet environment, where the clients are under closer control of a central support facility, also avoid this issue to some degree. In the past, Applet performance has been less than acceptable on some platforms – this too has been largely made an obsolete concern, both by better client-side VMs and the improvements in the standard APIs for Applet display.

3.2.13.2.2 JSP

JSP technology provides both Web-application developers and Web designers to rapidly create dynamic Web pages that provide access to business logic and data. The promise of JSP is to separate the user interface from content generation and business logic, while still providing the portability of Java and the ease of use of HTML, allowing Web designers to alter page layout and design without affecting the dynamic content of the page. HTML and other layout instructions in the page are simply "passed through," while special tags are processed as the connection points to program logic.

JSP is actually an extension to the Servlet API – a JSP page is compiled when it is first accessed to create a Servlet, and this Servlet is then automatically run every time the JSP page is accessed. If the page is changed, the compilation automatically takes place again on the next access to the page, making maintenance quick and easy.

As discussed earlier, however, there is an opportunity for misuse of the capabilities of JSP, but the wise developer can see the pitfalls and easily avoid them.

Many frameworks provide support for JSP as their user interface method of choice, most notably the Apache Struts framework. JSP enables the use of Custom Tag libraries, and indeed most frameworks that use JSP extensively provide their own tag libraries. There is an effort underway by Sun to define, via the Java Community Process, a set of standard tags (the Java Standard Tag Library) that can be used by many different frameworks and development tools. The tags that are provided with standard JSP provide many functions but they fall short of the full range of features required to build complex UIs quickly and easily. Custom tag libraries provide additional functionality, without violating the principal of separation between model and view – without embedding custom application logic in the JSP. Custom tags that provide access to the application logic and data (the model) can be created and can be used just like ordinary HTML or JSP tags, as if they were part of the normal markup in the page. They can also be called with parameters, allowing different operations to be called based on user input and selections, and they can return markup back to the page, providing content generated from the application logic where needed. Page authors can use prebuilt tags, integrating the application logic and data into their page design, without ever having to see a line of Java code.

A tag library is built from Java classes, which extend the javax.servlet.jsp.tagext.TagSupport class, implementing the methods they need to perform their operations. Operations within the tag class have access to the output stream of the JSP page, as well as the request and response objects, allowing the tag to have easy access to the session, includes, and other JSP/Servlet functionality. These Java classes are then listed and organized in a "tld" file, or a tag library description file, which uses an XML format to specify how the tag may be used on a JSP page.

```
 1: <tag>
 2:     <name>Login</name>
 3:     <tagclass>com.yourcompany.taglib.Login</tagclass>
 4:     <bodycontent>empty</bodycontent>
 5:     <attribute>
 6:         <name>db</name>
 7:         <required>false</required>
 8:         <rtexprvalue>true</rtexprvalue>
 9:     </attribute>
10:     <attribute>
11:         <name>forward</name>
12:         <required>false</required>
13:         <rtexprvalue>true</rtexprvalue>
14:     </attribute>
15: </tag>
```

The excerpt above shows a tag called "Login" being defined. The logic is contained in the class com.yourcompany.taglib.Login. These tags can then be accessed by referring to the tag library that describes them, similar to the way Java classes are "imported" before they are referenced:

```
<%@ taglib uri="/WEB-INF/tld/mytags.tld" prefix="mytag" %>
```

This statement associates a "prefix" with the tag library, so the Login tag can be referred to in the JSP page with this prefix and its name, as defined in the tld file:

```
<p>SomeMarkup<p>
<mytag:Login db="abc"/>
<p>More Markup...<p>
```

Any output generated by the tag would be seen on the page between the "SomeMarkup" and "More Markup" paragraphs.

This easy way to extend JSP's functionality has led to many thousands of custom tags, for every conceivable purpose. They also provide an ideal way for a framework to provide access to its functionality in a way that fits well into the JSP model.

3.2.13.2.3 XML/XSL

XML is a powerful and flexible data representation standard. In combination with XSL, it can become a powerful mechanism to create extremely flexible UIs. If you think of XML as a stream of data, and XSL as a filter, you have got the general idea; XML content is "transformed" via eXtensible Stylesheet Language (XSL) into its final presentation format. XSL is extremely capable, but not as easy for nonprogrammers to grasp sometimes, so, like many other things, the trade-off between power and ease of use must be taken into account.

We explore XSL transformation again in Chapter 5 when we discuss some of the frameworks that put it to use.

XSL is a language with a specific purpose: to express "style sheets." It consists of three basic elements:

- **XSL Transformations (XSLT)**: a language for transforming XML documents from one format to another.

- **XML Path Language (XPath)**: an expression language used by XSLT to access and refer to portions of an XML document. XPath is also used in linking XML documents.

- **XSL Formatting Objects (XSL-FO)**: an XML vocabulary for specifying formatting semantics. This is the part of XSL that is used when creating Portable Document Format (PDF) files, for example.

An XSL style sheet specifies presentation by forming a description of how one XML document is transformed into another XML document that uses its formatting vocabulary.

One aspect where XML/XSL is particularly good at is transforming data conditionally; that is, doing a different transformation depending on the user (or the device) requesting the output. This makes it a good choice when supporting different Web devices, such as regular HTML browsers and WML mobile devices. You can even use a series of XSL style sheets to convert XML content into Adobe's PDF format, or even into Rich Text Format (RTF).

The separation of content and presentation is very "clean" with XML: there are no "hidden" formatting concepts in XML that make it more difficult to present in multiple formats. Although it is possible (and common) to include formatting "hints" in the XML information itself, these "hints" can be interpreted by different presentation style sheets as required (or ignored completely if necessary).

The original XML content can even be something other than a file; it could even be a combination of two or more XML data streams. This allows XML/XSL to be used in situations where other UI technologies are not capable of handling the complexities involved. It is also easy for an XSL transformation to select only the required "subset" of the original data, allowing only the desired elements to be passed on for final formatting for summary or high-level views of the content.

XML itself is not a fixed set of tags, like HTML or WML. There is no "meaning" implied in XML data that can be used for presentation directly – therefore, something must provide the formatting for presentation. XSL fills this gap. As a transformation technology, XSLT allows the same data to be presented in almost any format – this supports the use of different formats for print, online viewing, different devices, and even different languages.

Although it is currently common for XSLT-based user interfaces to perform the XSL transformation on the server, modern browsers are beginning to offer the ability to do the transformation on the client side, further offloading the server. There are some difficulties, however, with this approach, because the level of XSL support on the different browsers varies considerably, and the developer using this technique runs the risk of limiting his application to one brand of browser, which is never a good idea.

XSL is still somewhat of a moving target as far as a standard is concerned, but sufficient standards have been agreed on to make it a highly practical tool.

A powerful combination can be attained by using JSP pages to generate XML, which can then be further transformed via XSL as required for formatting – the two technologies fit together well.

Several other options are available, including a technique of using XML to express the connection to application logic via custom style sheets, such as Cocoon's XSP, and Barracuda's XML-based approach, both of which are examined later in detail.

3.2.13.2.4 Flash and Other Options

The MacroMedia Flash product is also a viable choice for an application's UI. More than just a media display mechanism, the most recent incarnations of

Flash provide a highly flexible, XML-driven plug-in to modern browsers that can be driven by an appropriate back-end Servlet. The display possibilities with Flash are virtually endless, and are far greater than what can be achieved with HTML alone. The drawback, of course, is that Flash is a commercial product, and appropriate licensing applies, along with the possibility of vendor lock-in to a certain degree. Also, the Flash plug-in is not guaranteed to be present on all your client's systems, particularly if you are creating an application used on the Internet.

Other options for user interface also exist, and have their place as well. The "older" technique of generating HTML directly from a Servlet has its disadvantages, as discussed, but by the use of powerful libraries that generate the HTML from visual component definitions, these disadvantages can be outweighed by the ability to create a user interface in a programmatic way. A UI can be built, for example, using the Element Construction Set (ECS) library (an Apache project), which is entirely generated from the back-end Servlet, with no templates, markup, or HTML required. The Echo framework, which we examine in more detail later, also offers a Swing-like library of components that provide complete control over the windows and display of the browser from the application.

3.2.13.2.5 Supporting Flexible UIs

One of the goals of separating business logic from presentation is to allow easy changes to the user interface, without affecting the underlying logic. Most frameworks support this, but a few take it to the next state entirely, that is, they allow you to choose the user interface *methodology* as required. This allows, for example, part of the UI of an application to be built using JSP, and another part to be built using XML/XSL, or part with WebMacro and part with Barracuda.

As part of the process of supporting flexible user interface options, the framework must allow for an abstraction layer between the application logic and the presentation mechanism. This layer must be sufficiently abstract to allow different presentation mechanisms, yet support a rich enough set of UI elements to allow the developer to build a sufficiently expressive connection to the logic elements.

The UI abstraction layer is in fact bidirectional: UI events are triggered by the user's actions, and form elements representing the user's data entry flow from the user to the controller and on to the application logic.

Frameworks take a number of different approaches to the UI abstraction issue. Some handle the presentation as an application issue, allowing the application to have fairly complete control over the design and layout. Others handle presentation as entirely a page-designer issue – the application has

What Is in the Tool Box?

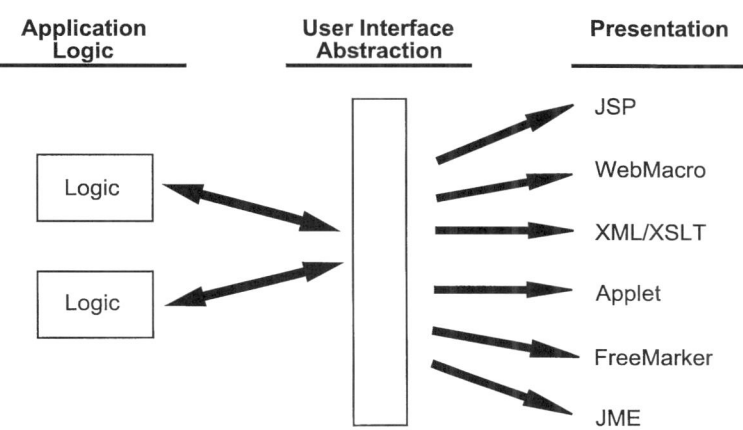

Flexible User Interface Abstraction

comparatively little control over the look of the pages created. The difference in these approaches is the difference between Web pages and a traditional UI toolkit, such as Swing. Swing brings many highly flexible options to the developer: the ability to manipulate multiple windows, handle low-level components, lay out the page in a flexible way by means of panes and grids, and many other advantages. It is not, however, intended for a page designer to use directly: the Swing approach is almost entirely Java code. Although some UI builders make the creation of Swing UIs graphical, and allow nondevelopers to configure beans that make up the interface in a graphical builder application, the bottom line is that the result is Java, not markup.

Some frameworks proceed in this direction – the Echo framework, for example, provides a rich Swing-like UI that provides many of Swing's advantages to the Web-application developer. The ArsDigita BeBop tool does something very similar, but also links in XML and XSL transformations to allow "style" to be applied to the presentation after it is created.

Other frameworks go the other way: they generate their results from logic in a completely UI-agnostic format, a nonvisual representation of results. The UI layer, whether it is XML, JSP, or a template language, is then responsible for the layout of each element, and for separating out the components it wants to use when building the presentation. The developer does not say "make this a check box," he simply produces the output, and the page designer chooses whether to use a check box, a radio group, or a drop-down menu. The developer does not even specify the layout of the results on the page, other than perhaps by their nesting in the nonvisual structure. Expresso's ControllerResponse object takes this nonvisual approach, as one example. We will see many other variations on these themes, as well as discuss a new proposed Java standard (JavaServer Faces) that attempts to provide a common ground for presentation.

Java Micro Edition. Java Micro Edition is Sun's package of Java technologies designed for consumer and wireless devices. It differs from WML in that JME is intended to actually run the Java technology within the consumer device, be it a cell phone, PDA, smart card, and so forth, whereas WML is markup designed to allow small display devices to access Web services.

Java Micro Edition effectively represents another "user interface" to Web applications, because these smart devices frequently connect to Web capabilities to perform their functions. The level of user-interface independence in a given framework should be sufficient to allow even such a completely non-HTML-like user interface to access business logic online.

3.2.13.3 Portal

Some frameworks, as we will see, go beyond GUI capability and provide portal services to their applications and components. Portal capability is more than just a user interface function.

Portals provide a unified point of access for multiple resources. Access to these resources is part of the job of a framework's services, and a number of standards exist for such access. When we examine a couple of portal frameworks, we explore these standards in more detail.

Portals are a lot more than just a specialized way of presenting a user interface. In fact, presentation is one of the least important aspects of a portal: its underlying structure, and the abilities it has to access content, applications, and other data are the best measures of its abilities. We explore two portal frameworks in Chapter 5.

3.2.13.4 Web Services

The term "Web services" has recently been popularized to mean the interaction of applications via XML-based messages, using the standard HTTP protocols of the Web as a transport. Web services promise to provide a valuable mechanism for widespread integration between components, even components created on different platforms (as Web services are language independent).

Few frameworks (yet) provide direct support for Web services, but we explore how this is changing rapidly, and also explore the tools being used to make this happen.

We discuss Web services in more detail, including their impact on the future of components and frameworks, in Chapter 11.

3.2.14 Legacy Application Integration

Although the facilities we have seen so far provide many services that are useful when integrating with existing applications, many frameworks provide facilities specifically designed for this. These facilities can provide access to both the data from a legacy application and its functionality. The former is more common: for example, many legacy data sources can be accessed via JDBC, so the object/relational mapping tool of a framework can be used for this purpose, particularly if the tool provides reverse-engineering of existing data sources. The latter is a bit more sophisticated: allowing for a means to actually call the functionality of the legacy applications. This is sometimes found in application-specific frameworks, such as IBM's Java Toolkit for the AS/400. More generically, it can take the form of tools and services to make CORBA connections to legacy objects, or Web service access, perhaps via a SOAP protocol.

Often, frameworks provide the means to create "wrappers" around legacy applications, or portions of them. This allows a legacy application to "appear" as a component, and be accessed by new applications without regard to its origins.

Legacy Applications "Wrapped" as Components

```
Web Application  | Component | Component | Component | Component | Component |
    Server       |           |           |           |           |           |
-----------------|-----------|-----------|-----------|-----------|-----------|
    Legacy                               |  Legacy   |
    Server                               | Application |
                                    CORBA, JDBC, SOAP
                                    or other Multi-Platform
                                    protocol provides interface
```

A final means of access to legacy applications is primitive by comparison, but no less useful: a framework should provide a means to make calls to operating system command scripts, and to retrieve the output from them. This is particularly valuable on Unix systems, because the rich shell commands allow for other applications to be called and their output manipulated before returning them to the new application. Sometimes hitting it with a rock is as high-tech as you need to get!

3.2.15 Utilities

Almost all frameworks have some capabilities that do not really fit into the other categories of services they provide. For example, many have the ability to generate the database tables required by the application being installed. This kind of capability comes under the heading "utility."

The utilities provided by frameworks are often stand-alone programs, or even complete GUI applications, designed to be run independently from the rest of the framework. Often they generate code, or perform specific setup functions.

Some of the utilities provided by various frameworks are as follows:

- **Database generation:** Many frameworks, particularly those that have an object/relational mapping service, provide the mechanism to create the database tables, fields, and indices required by both the framework and the finished application. This frequently takes the form of a separate utility because it is usually only performed once. Sometimes this is done directly via JDBC, or it may be done by generating the appropriate SQL statements into a file, which can then be executed by the database front-end directly.

- **Code generation:** Some frameworks ease the burden of creating your objects by automatically generating Java code, usually based on some key information you provide about the application to be generated. This gives you a "headstart" on coding the actual application. Code generation must allow for the specification to change once the generation is complete, however, either regenerating only portions of the generated code, or allowing customized changes to the generated code to be isolated.

- **Template generation:** Frameworks can also provide the ability to generate presentation templates, often from the database definition. This makes the job of creating a basic user interface for database maintenance much easier.

- **Internationalization:** Internationalizing an application can be a tedious job – frameworks provide various utilities that can assist. Barracuda, for example, provides a mechanism for generating localized templates, combining a master template with local-language files. Expresso provides a utility for cross-checking localized MessageBundle files, verifying that all strings are accounted for in every language.

- **Monitoring:** Some frameworks provide a special "status" utility for monitoring not only the operation of the framework's basic services, but also the ongoing operation of your own application. Sometimes this is combined with a performance testing and/or unit testing mechanism.

- **Testing:** Almost all frameworks today (the good ones, at any rate) provide for their own unit tests. Frequently, a standard unit test framework, such as JUnit, is used. Ideally, this utility should be usable by your own applications, allowing them to be tested easily and frequently during the development process.
- **Bundling and installation:** Frameworks sometimes provide utilities to aid in the creation of an installation bundle of your finished application. This often takes the form of a ".war," or Web Application aRchive file, the standard format for Web applications to be deployed in an application server.

3.2.16 Others

Frameworks provide many other services than that are explored here. Application-specific frameworks particularly tend to have more specialized capabilities and services, a few of which will be discussed briefly below:

- **Agents:** A category of software for which Java is particularly well suited is the development of *agents*. An agent is an autonomous application that handles events, recognizes conditions, and performs appropriate actions based on its programmed goals. Frequently, such agents use intelligent behavior, employing rule-based and heuristic algorithms to determine what action to take on the user's behalf. Agents are useful for information searching, content filtering, and many other applications.

    Agents may work alone, processing toward a specific goal, or they may collaborate with other agents to achieve their purposes. They can reside on a specific server, or may even be *mobile*, moving around a network as required to complete their functions – again, Java is ideal due to its portability and built-in networking capabilities.

    All of these factors make agents a good candidate for development with frameworks, and indeed a number of frameworks and related tools already exist for this purpose, including JADE, IBM's Aglet Workbench, ObjectSpace Inc's Voyager, General Magic's Odyssey, JATLite, and others.
- **Scripting support:** Some frameworks provide explicit support for integration with scripting languages, such as Perl, JavaScript, ASP, PHP, and so forth.

These services make it easy to integrate the rapid and flexible development of scripting with the more structured capabilities of Java. They also allow existing applications written with these scripting languages to easily connect with Java server applications, providing a cross-language solution.

- **Platform-specific services**: Frameworks such as the Java Micro Edition, the Roaming Media Framework, and others designed for specific platform environments (such as mobile devices, for example) frequently bring services to the application process that are appropriate only in these environments.

3.2.17 Summary

In this chapter, we have discussed some of the capabilities frameworks provide. As you can see, it is a broad pallet. In general, some capabilities are found more often than others, and each framework has its particular advantages: some frameworks do better in the database connectivity/persistence area, others are strong in work flow, and still others bring powerful design patterns to the table, and are suited to large and complex Web-application-development projects.

In later chapters we examine specific examples of frameworks and their components, and see how well they provide all of the advantages we have discussed here. We discuss how to make the best choice between frameworks, and how to fit them to your projects, because not every project needs all, or even most, of the capabilities that may be provided.

It is difficult to deny, however, that practically any serious Web-application-development project can benefit from the use of the appropriate framework. Now that you know more about what to expect, you will be better able to make the transition and start reaping the benefits.

CHAPTER 4

Choosing an Application Framework

In this chapter, we look at the differentiating factors of frameworks, and give you a set of techniques for choosing frameworks. We also look at how you can determine whether a particular framework fits your needs. We concentrate on the practical job of choosing the right pieces to get the job done, and give you the information you need to choose the right tool.

4.1 OVERVIEW

Let us say that you are convinced that the benefits of frameworks are real, and that it would make good business sense for you and your organization to adopt an appropriate framework. Now what? Where do you go to find frameworks, and how do you go about evaluating them? When you first start evaluating frameworks, there are some high-level observations you can make right away. Let us examine them first and then get into more details.

4.1.1 Identification

There is sometimes a fine line between a component library and an application framework. Some products are oriented more toward providing a set of application elements, rather than providing the backbone to build an entire application. Often, component libraries are more focused, concentrating on a particular area of the application, such as file access, visual presentation, or middleware elements. In general, a component library is defined as a collection of fully-developed components, and may include capabilities for generating your own components. A framework may include a component library, or they may be separate – the framework providing the backbone and infrastructure, and the component library providing specific services built using this infrastructure.

Sometimes it takes a certain level of investigation to really understand what the product being investigated consists of. An API is sometimes confused with, called, a framework; and the name "component" is hung on everything but the sides of trucks it seems sometimes. The definitions in Chapters 1 and 2 should be helpful here, but the bottom line is still whether or not the product provides the benefits, and not what it is called.

4.1.2 License

The license under which a framework is distributed is critical. It is the key element that tells you what you can and what you cannot do, and for the things you can do, what the limitations and costs are.

Basically, there are two general categories of frameworks when it comes to their license: open source and proprietary. As explained in Chapter 7, there are many variations on the theme of "open source." It is important to examine the *specific* license, and make no assumptions. Sometimes a small variation in wording from one license to another can make a large difference in its applicability to your project.

For proprietary frameworks, you have the added factor of price, and the way price and licensing correspond. Frameworks are an odd beast compared to other software products – they are not just installed and put into use, they are used to *create* other applications. Does the commercial license involve any royalties on the applications you create? Are there any limitations on how you can license what you create? How many developers are permitted to use the framework for each license? These are all valid and important questions when considering a commercial framework. You must also take into account the usual considerations when contemplating an important software purchase: support, viability of the company, references from other users, and so forth. As with any software project, it is important to understand who holds the copyright to each portion of code used to build the finished application, starting from the operating system.

If a system is developed under contract to a client, what are the implications for ownership? Are all of the licensing considerations taken into account? These are important questions, and often are not given sufficient consideration in any project, whether it uses open source or proprietary/commercial software.

One consideration that might be particularly important with commercial (nonopen-source) frameworks is a licensing stipulation that guarantees access to the source code of the framework if the company that supplies it is no longer able to provide support. This is a well-established practice in large-enterprise software purchases, and has been in existence for many years. Often referred to as "escrow service," or "source escrow," the general idea is that if you do not ordinarily have access to the full source code of the product, that the source code be placed with a third party. The third party is under instructions that in the event of some agreed-upon circumstance (the supplier goes out of business, or some other trigger), they will release the source code they are holding into your (the clients') hands. Frequently, this service will include provision for periodic updates, so the source that is held is still relatively current.

4.1.3 Complexity

A framework must be simple enough to be learned fairly readily, but at the same time provide enough features so that it can be used effectively. A framework always embodies a theory of the problem domain, developed either explicitly or informally. It has a specific way of tackling application development. Understanding this model goes a long way toward demystifying the framework itself. It is important to dedicate enough time to understand a framework before jumping in to evaluate its specific features. It may have many useful facilities, but if the high-level design patterns are flawed, or the structure is unable to scale, the deficiencies might not be detected until a very unfortunate stage of the project lifecycle.

Modularization is a key to handling complexity. Just like the framework itself, such modularization seeks to decompose the framework itself into units that deal with one specific problem domain at a time. Persistence, presentation, configuration, and security are good candidates for framework modules. Ideally, this modularization should allow you to choose only the elements of the framework you need, making it easier to deal with the complexity of the entire framework by breaking it into bite-sized pieces. These pieces can then be documented and diagramed (e.g., using Unified Modelling Language (UML) diagrams), making the whole understandable.

4.2 What to Look for

When studying frameworks, it is important to narrow the field to those that provide components and services that are appropriate for your selected deployment environment. For example, if you are planning on deployment in a non-EJB environment, then a component library based on EJBs cannot be considered. If, on the other hand, your deployment environment is a hosted server where EJB and distributed processing are not options, you want to make sure that the framework does not have requirements that you will not be able to fulfill.

4.2.1 Design Patterns

A good framework is not just a set of abstract classes that you can inherit from, but it is a design: a set of patterns that defines *how* those instances should collaborate to build a working application. You should look for these patterns in a framework and the cohesion that they can bring to your application development. It is essential that you understand the underlying design patterns behind a particular framework, and how they interrelate. This is more important than just knowing how the framework operates or how to use it to create an application. In many cases, the diagrams showing the structure and patterns used are an essential part of understanding the toolkit and its design. UML is often used to good effect in this instance, as we will see later.

It is more essential to understand the design patterns used in a complete application framework than in frameworks that only provide a part of the application functionality. The patterns you buy into now will be an essential part of all future developments you perform within this framework; therefore, choose them carefully.

In Chapter 8, we will examine some of the design patterns commonly used in frameworks.

4.2.2 Examples

A complete application framework should supply a number of examples, both simple "hello, world" level examples, to help you learn how the framework is applied, and more complex examples: at least one complete, real-world application. This application gives you an idea of the product in actual use – often you can deconstruct the example, or parts of it, to create your first application with the framework.

4.2.3 Documentation

Documentation, of course, is an essential part of any usable framework. Do not rely on JavaDoc-based documentation (unless it is augmented with special extensions, such as DocBookLet, which allows entire sets of XML/SGML documentation to be embedded into the source, to be extracted later and processed into different documentation formats).

Some noteworthy documentation associated with a framework are as follows:

- **Catalog/feature list**: A high-level list of the features that the framework provides, perhaps with a short description of how it is provided. Often this catalog is augmented with use-case and other UML diagrams to provide visual backup to the textual descriptions.

- **Cook book**: A step-by-step guide that describes the steps involved in creating a new application, and how to make use of each of the framework's facilities. This cookbook should provide examples of usage – preferably several different examples, including complete applications.

- **Design documentation**: A document that describes the key design patterns used by the framework, and the rationale behind their use. Describing the overall philosophy behind the framework's design is very helpful as well. What kinds of applications is it designed to support? Which areas of the development process does it apply? Is it intended to be lightweight, to be used with other APIs or frameworks, or is it meant to provide every facility of the finished application from its own set of services?

- **Status documentation**: Frameworks grow and evolve in response to use, and from the feedback of those that apply them. A status document gives you an idea as to what stage of its life the framework is in. Are all of its features implemented? Are some frameworks more mature than others? Are some frameworks just experimental or deprecated, slated for removal? Look for a date on a status document – the Internet overflows with obsolete information.

- **Road-map/direction document**: Knowledge of the intended development direction of the framework is very important to you. If you are going to make the often considerable effort to learn and adopt a framework, knowing its intended future direction is only prudent. No one can predict the future with certainty, but knowledge of the agenda of the key developers and contributors can help you make a decision on whether to adopt a particular framework or not.

- **Source code**: A final source of documentation on a framework is the source code. Indeed, it is the final word on how the framework actually functions, and how to use it. Almost all frameworks have some or all of their source code, and it should be evident from browsing the source that the code has been created according to consistent coding standards.

  It does not matter much if the coding standards are the same as your team's – as long as they are applied consistently. A carefully applied coding standard also tells you about the framework team – are they coordinated in their approach to coding? If you can see an easily recognizable style between modules developed by different contributors, it is an indication of the care and consistency that is likely carried over into other parts of the project, which speaks well for the framework as a whole.

4.2.4 Support

An essential criterion when evaluating any framework is its support. Some of the factors involved in evaluating support are as follows:

- **Who provides it?**: What options do you have in terms of who provides support? Sometimes with an open-source project, your only option is the community of developers and contributors of the project itself. Often, however, this community will consist of one or more developers who are willing to provide commercial, paid support. Sometimes there are even specific companies that provide support for open-source projects; these might be the same companies that sponsor the project or a third party. It is important to understand early on what the options are.

- **What is the procedure?**: What is the support procedure? How do you ask questions? These are often poorly defined areas of support in open-source projects, and sometimes they are not very clear even with commercial support. A specific help-desk or bug tracker program is a good indicator, which indicates that the project leadership has put specific support mechanisms in place.

- **What is the cost?**: Commercial support is easy enough to evaluate in terms of cost, but it is important to understand exactly what you get for your money. I would recommend a written support contract, because misunderstandings by either party can lead to serious problems later, just when you do not need them in your project's development.

Community or "free" support is a different story. All anecdotes about no such thing as free lunches aside, there is indeed often a kind of "price" for even community support for an open-source product. No one on the mailing list of the product will appreciate a user who always asks and takes, and never gives back. After all, open-source developers are often volunteers, and if there is no feedback, and no contribution to the effort, community support can dry up quickly. The "price" for community support, then, is an attempt on your part to give something back to the community that provides the support. In Chapter 7, we examine details of exactly how you can do this.

- **What is the level of expertise?**: Probably the single most important statistic about the support, however it is supplied, is the level of expertise of the person or group providing that support. The software industry as a whole has an abysmal reputation in this area, but often you will find that the situation for framework support is better than the average. Companies or groups providing support for frameworks understand that their primary user is himself a developer. The "high-school-student reading the manual" approach will not cut it with this audience! Determining whether the available support staff indeed possesses the required level of expertise can be an issue – one approach is to speak with (or email) the support staff during the evaluation of a framework.

- **What is the response time?**: Generally, community support for an open-source framework does not have any kind of guaranteed response time. You can somewhat gauge the average response time by reading the list and considering the kind of reactions other users have received to their questions, but, of course, this is not a reliable indicator. Commercial support, however, will often provide some kind of indication of the expected response time for support issues. Of course, a "response" does not necessarily mean your problem is solved, and guaranteed response time is not really all that valuable an attribute.

- **Self-support**: We have discussed the importance of documentation of all forms of a framework, and what should one look for in good documentation. Documentation is the vanguard of any self-support effort. Ideally, the documentation should be sufficiently complete and comprehensive that no other support is required. Anyone reading this who has worked with almost any software will undoubtedly stifle a chuckle – although the situation is much better in many areas than it used to be, it is a constant in the software industry that documentation lags behind the product in most cases. Again, properly constructed UML and other structure diagrams can help provide the necessary tools for self-support.

Self-support goes beyond documentation, however. Often it includes internally generated documentation, specific to how the product is used within your own organization. You may also find that it is helpful to have an in-house "expert group," whose experience with framework makes a resource for other novice users to refer to.

4.2.5 Standards Compliance

It is important to understand the level of compliance with standards that exist in a particular framework. Of course, the disadvantage of standards is that there are so many to choose from. Determination of *which* standard to follow, however, is often simple in Java world. The Java Community Process, the means by which Sun adopts new standards for the Java platform itself, provides part of the answer. If a particular standard has been adopted through the JCP process, it becomes a somewhat safer bet for the future.

It is also particularly important to understand the difference between the accepted standard and the so-called extensions to the standard. Although in some cases extensions may be permitted by the specification, the developer must always be aware that any vendor-specific extensions, irrespective of their usefulness, are by definition *not* part of the standard itself, and therefore their use can cost the application its portability. Sometimes this seems a reasonable price to pay compared to the advantages the extensions bring, but this is seldom true in the long run.

4.2.5.1 Why Standards?

Why do you care if your framework supports standards? It is a matter of long-term viability and basic business sense. If a standard emerges, and is adopted by the industry, a large number of developers can be trained in that standard. This means that as implementations of the standard become more prevalent, they provide options for the user of the standard in the event of nonviability of a supplier. J2EE is a good example of this process, along with many of the standards it contains. A popular, well-accepted standard means that there will be multiple commercial sources, and possibly even open sources for the implementations of the standard. Take Java Messaging Service (JMS), for example. There are a number of excellent commercial implementations, and at least three open-source versions. There are connectors from the standard to other messaging products, more documentation, tutorials, and a large community of developers who know how to use it. All of these are advantages of standards.

Standards bring to the software market the same kind of advantages as design patterns bring to development; they codify a specific way of doing something, and allow it to be reliably reproduced in many different circumstances. They are like interfaces in Java; they separate the definition from the implementation. A correctly designed standard will enable interoperability without stifling innovation.

4.2.5.2 Which Standards?

In the Java frameworks world, the standards that are worth complying with are reasonably obvious. The standard APIs such as the Servlet API, JNDI, JDBC, JMS, JMX, and so forth, are all good candidates. As a general rule, there must be a good reason to deviate from a standard, if one has been well established.

For frameworks, compliance with the set of standards and APIs that make up J2EE are a fair bet.

4.2.5.3 Choice and Innovation

Of course, just because there is a standard does not guarantee that it is worth the silicon on which it runs. Better ways of doing things are constantly being invented, and standards should not be simply a speed bump on the road to innovation. A well-designed standard allows for substantial innovation before the noose tightens: implementations can take advantage of new capabilities and development, but still remain compatible with the standard.

Sometimes a so-called defacto standard is just another way of describing the lemming response: just because everyone flings themselves off a particular cliff does not necessarily mean that it is a good idea. Frameworks often challenge standards by providing alternatives – this lets the people in the trenches decide what actually works best for them, and often establishes a new standard as a result. The eXtensible Server Pages (XSP) technology in the Cocoon framework is a good example: it is a different way of doing things than the de facto standard of JSP, but it has its advantages in the right situation. There are many examples of this.

Sometimes the standard itself is poor, and frameworks frequently provide alternatives in these situations. Just because the alternatives are not "standard" does not mean they cannot be used effectively. It is a matter of weighing the advantages and disadvantages when choosing to take the well-trodden road of the standard or the potential shortcut.

4.2.6 Component Support

One of the key elements provided by most frameworks is a component support environment: the backbone around which components can be deployed, and the tools that make creation of the components easy. The mechanism by which a framework does this is an essential factor when choosing a tool.

Some frameworks use an EJB approach to components: their central component is often the Session Bean. In Chapter 1 we have discussed the pros and cons of EJBs in general, and how they cannot be assumed to be the right answer in every single situation. Many more frameworks take an EJB-agnostic approach; you *can* use EJB, but you do not *have* to do so. Often, this provides the best of both worlds, providing this flexibility does not come at a cost of much greater effort, or that the mechanism that provides the interface to EJB does not gum up the works so much that performance and scalability suffer.

It is important to examine a framework and find out what its approach to component support is: ideally, you will see high-level design patterns that implement all of the essential component design patterns. You will see things like inversion of control, loose coupling, pluggability of key implementations, and so forth.

Now that we have explored some of the attributes to watch for when examining a prospective framework, let us look at the major categories of frameworks and discuss some key attributes that are unique to these categories.

Application frameworks fall into three broad categories. Frameworks that provide services for most, if not all, of the application development effort are called "complete" application frameworks. Frameworks that concentrate more or less exclusively on the presentation or user interface issues are called "presentation," and thirdly, frameworks that are suitable only for a relatively small number of problem domains are called "application specific."

There are also a few frameworks that concentrate on an area of application development other than presentation, but are still general enough to be used in almost any kind of application. An example is a framework that concentrates exclusively on an object/relational mapping capability. We look at an example of one such framework in Chapter 5.

4.2.7 Complete Application Frameworks

Some application frameworks provide components and services that help in almost every aspect of a Web application's development, and they are applicable when building almost any type of Web application. We refer to these as "complete application frameworks," and look at a number of examples.

Complete application frameworks are intended to provide service and tools in many, if not all, of the functional areas discussed earlier. They always provide a mechanism for at least presentation, persistence, and logic handling. Often they provide almost all of the services an application requires, including logging, security, database connectivity and maintenance, email connectivity, Web services, and more. An all-encompassing framework can be a large and complex system, with a significant learning curve.

4.2.8 Application-Specific Frameworks

Unlike frameworks designed to be used in the development of any kind of finished application, application-specific frameworks are used to develop finished applications in a more specific category. For example, a framework designed for developing portals may be a skeletal portal application in and of itself – where the user of the framework basically "fleshes out" the functionality to their specific needs.

4.2.8.1 Vertical Market Frameworks

Frameworks that focus on a single industry such as legal documents, accounting, or construction are sometimes called vertical market frameworks. A vertical market framework will not work well in other industries, and contains functionality very specific to its targeted market.

Examples include frameworks designed for specific deployment environments, such as mobile wireless devices, and frameworks focused on creating applications of one specific type, such as agent development frameworks. An application-specific framework may also focus on a particular problem domain, such as publishing or portal building.

An application-specific framework may be an ideal choice for a project within its domain – a portal-building project will likely proceed much faster with a dedicated portal framework than with a generic Web-application framework. At the same time, a domain-specific framework may bring a certain set of assumptions about the design of the application that are not desirable in a particular project. A publishing framework may be oriented around XML content handling, for example, when the project calls for content in a relational database instead.

When choosing an application-specific framework, the factors influencing the decision are even more narrowly defined: if the framework focuses, for example, on accounting, does it approach the problems of accounting in the way you want for your project? The appeal of a vertical framework is likely to be less broad, it will likely have a smaller user base, and possibly lower levels of support. A framework that is more horizontal, but applies to a specific area of the development process (e.g., a persistence framework or presentation framework) is a different story. It will likely have broader appeal and support, but, of course, it does not necessarily provide any specific functionality for your accounting program.

4.2.8.2 Presentation Frameworks

If your primary need for application is assistance with the presentation, then you may be looking at a framework that only provides this need. Some projects where a decision is made to use EJB for the persistence and application logic level, for example, might only need a presentation tool as a framework.

Presentation frameworks should provide all of the key attributes of a complete application framework, but with special attention to a few areas in addition. We discuss these areas in the next section.

4.2.8.2.1 Templates or Transformations?

Two of the major techniques used by presentation frameworks are templates and transformations. Understanding which technique is being employed in a specific framework will help you evaluate it more easily.

Templates: The template technique drives the user interface from the markup level. The presentation begins with a template, and this template usually includes tags or tokens to denote where the dynamic content will be placed when the application runs. The Velocity project is a popular example of a template-based presentation framework.

The template technique was the first step toward having application logic generate HTML directly (or via a library such as Element Construction Set (ECS)). In most dynamic Web pages, a large portion of the markup on the page does not change, and remains constant from one invocation of the page to the next. At a minimum, the layout is constant: the format that defines where the dynamic content will be placed, and how it is decorated on the page does not change. Keeping the constant markup in a reusable file also provides the separation called for in the model–view–controller architecture, not to mention being easier to maintain than a bunch of strings within your application logic.

But how can we associate the dynamic content with the static markup? When we have, for example, the results of an SQL query to fit into an HTML table, we must have a way of intermingling the dynamic results with our static content, and putting the dynamic portions at precisely defined places on the page. Template engines solve this by embedding special markers, or *tags* in the markup. These tags are associated at run time with the proper pieces of the dynamic content, and the resulting combined page is presented to the user. This has the advantage that nonprogrammers can easily manipulate static content, and even the tags to denote the location of the dynamic content, if they are straightforward enough. If the tags are defined in the proper way, graphical HTML editors, such as Dreamweaver and FrontPage, can still be used to create attractive templates easily and quickly.

The most popular form of tag is rather HTML-like: this is the approach that JSP (especially with the use of custom-tag libraries) takes. Tags might take the form of <html:form action="test">, which is in fact well-formed XML. This usually works well with the graphical HTML editors, because they often allow "custom" HTML tags to be used, and simply treat them as valid HTML on the page. To take this to the next step, some template engines use well-formed XML as their tags. Provided that the HTML markup is also well-formed XML (e.g., XHTML), this provides the advantage that the whole page is XML. This allows parsers, for example, to read and manipulate the page, and for it to be compared against a DTD to provide a validity check. This is somewhat similar to a "compile-time" check with Java: it allows you to see whether your page is at least structurally correct before actually trying it at run time.

Other tags are more "textlike" – they appear as ordinary text in most graphical HTML editors. Velocity and WebMacro are examples of template engines that use textlike tags: they look almost like the old "mail-merge" tags used in word processors, and are easy to read and understand, for example, "$foreach customer" or "$client-name." Often they are less verbose than their XML counterparts. Unfortunately, other than the template engines themselves, no standards exist for validating such tags.

Some template engines and techniques allow you to go beyond the tags embedded in the markup: they allow any arbitrary code to be included, allowing a certain amount of logic within the template. Ideally, this logic should be restricted to the kinds of looping and branching constructs required for presentation: the actual business logic should not be tangled with the presentation in this way. Velocity, for example, only allows an intentionally limited set of logic operations in its own macro language to be embedded. JSP, on the other hand, allows practically any valid Java to be included.

The downside of too many macros or programming within the page is that it limits the ability of the a nonprogrammer to work with the page: page designers are soon lost in the complexities of actual programming, irrespective of how much of a subset of a "full" programming language is used. Fortunately, most markup does not require complex logic, and page designers can be taught simple iteration, and even some, branching fairly easily. Embedded code can also rapidly become a maintenance burden: the different formatting rules of the markup and the logic mean that often no proper coding standards are applied, and the embedded code becomes a mass of unformatted logic that even its originator cannot properly maintain.

The ability to extend the tags available with custom tags, however, shifts this burden back to the programmer. JSP, for example, allows any new tag to be created, which the page designer can simply place on the page. Irrespective of how complex the logic "wrapped" in the tag is, it is still a single tag, and the separation between model and view is maintained. Other template languages allow "macros" to be written in external files, or helper classes to be created that provide higher level tags to be used.

For many presentation needs, templates and their associated tags provide a good solution. It is only when the presentation logic becomes very complex that some problems start to arise. If many sections of the page are conditional – for example, they are only displayed when a specific situation occurs – it becomes very difficult to test and debug the page. Sometimes, unusual conditions from the application logic can result in invalid markup because of conditional sections, causing an actual failure of the application, at least from the user's point of view. Ideally, even simple conditions should be the domain of the application developer, not the page designer, and should be handled in the code. For example, if any prices below ten dollars should be highlighted, it is better to say

```
<myStore:specialPrice>
    <b>The price is only $<myStore:price>
today!</b>
<myStore:specialPrice>
<myStore:normalPrice>
    The price is $<myStore:price>
</myStore:normalPrice>
```

than

```
<myStore:IfPrice < 10>
    <b>The price is only $<myStore:price>
today!</b>
</myStore:IfPrice>
<myStore:IfPrice> 10>
    The price is $<myStore:price>
</myStore:IfPrice>
```

Not only does the first approach take the hard-coded price of ten dollars out of the markup, and put it in the domain of the application (where it could be more easily read from a database or configuration), it also highlights another problem: the page designer is probably not a programmer, and might not detect the bug in the second example that the programmer would – if the price is exactly ten dollars, no price is displayed at all.

Template systems must also take performance into account: compiling the template and creating the appropriate internal representation that can then be combined with the dynamic content can often be done once, and the results cached. This is the technique used by JSP by default – it automatically regenerates a Servlet class and compiles it whenever the original JSP page is used. Of course, the cost of any kind of dynamic page generation, whether it is template based or transformation based is that the processing time contributes to the overall time the user must wait to see the finished page. Because this time is already far too long on many sites, intelligent caching and carefully controlled use of dynamic content must be practiced to prevent the site from being unused.

Transformations: The transformation technique drives the user interface by applying a series of changes, or transformations, to the output produced by the application. Often this utilizes XML/XSL transformation, which we discuss in detail in Chapter 5, but other methods have been used successfully as well.

In the transformation technique, when the user requests a dynamic page, the application logic runs as before and produces the dynamic content. It generates this content in a special format that can then be "transformed" by a special filtering program (often an XSLT processor). This transformation wraps the dynamic content by matching it with sections of a style sheet, and sends the combination of the two to the user. Sometimes more than one style sheet is applied, with the final result of the pipeline being the finished HTML markup.

Some designers have a difficult time envisioning the finished page in the transformation technique, but at the same time, the opportunity to use the same transformations consistently allows for uniform formatting on a site with many pages.

The most popular way to write transformation presentation layers is to use XML/XSL. XSL is based on a pattern-matching mechanism, where each part of the result data from the application is "matched up" with a section of the style sheet, indicating how it is to be processed. This implies "built-in" iteration, usually eliminating the need for the page designer (in this case, the style sheet designer) to have to think about iterating over a collection of elements. The page designer simply says "apply this format to customers," and the format is applied to *all* customers, automatically. XML/XSL transformation requires the application logic results to be either XML or something that can be rendered readily as XML – this is not usually a problem, and many good tools exist for serializing data to XML format.

The choice between transformation and template is not necessarily cut-and-dried. There are some frameworks for presentation that use both, even allowing a combination of the two to be used for a single page. There is nothing that stops most template engines from generating XML, instead of HTML, and in turn processing this XML via an XSL transformation, providing, potentially, the best of both worlds. The choice is often made on the basis of the presence of appropriate tools, however, and the expertise of the team using them: if the team is skilled in XML and XSL and has appropriate tools, the advantages of using the transformation technique are considerable. If the page authors are mostly skilled in straight HTML, however, and have access to HTML-authoring products, the template technique may be a better approach. The best frameworks allow both, as needed.

Transformation offers the ability to restrict the amount of logic in the style sheet, but good programming disciplines can solve this issue even with the template technique, so one does not necessarily have an advantage over the other on this count. Just because a developer *can* use a tool incorrectly is no indication that he will do so.

4.2.8.2.2 To JSP or not to JSP?

When Servlets were first introduced, their benefits were quickly realized. Portability was achieved, and performance was good. All of the other capabilities of Java including database access were accessible. This facilitated rapid development of early Web applications. It quickly became evident that the inclusion of HTML input in Servlets was a tedious, error-, and maintenance-prone process. There was also no distinction between the tasks of a Java developer and those of a Web-page designer: any changes in logic had to be made by the developer.

The JSP specification was then introduced, providing a way for Servlets to be created automatically, from markup HTML pages containing small pieces of Java code. The HTML markup was automatically included in the generated Servlet. Page developers were able to edit the markup, simply leaving the "scriplets" that provided the logic.

Incorporating the logic into the markup still had many of the same problems as the reverse situation, however. The JavaBean specification provided a means to interface with logic that was better than scriplets: it allowed for access to methods and properties of JavaBean objects from within the markup of the JSP. This promoted the separation of the logic into other nonvisual objects, and the presentation into JavaBeans that were in turn accessed by the JSP.

This separation led to what has been called "Model 1," where the JSP acted as the view and the controller, and other Java objects acted as the model, containing the application logic.

JSPs are not the ideal controller technology; however, they are better suited to the "view" role, so further refinement made it possible to separate the controller into a dedicated Servlet, and the view into one or more JSP pages. This is referred to as "Model 2," and is used by several frameworks, including Struts. In this model, the client request is handled by a controller Servlet, which invokes the appropriate logic, and then passes control to the appropriate JSP page, which builds and delivers the response.

We review Models 1 and 2 MVC in more detail when we examine design patterns in Chapter 8.

This is the current state of the art in JSP and when combined with the more recent improved custom-tag libraries, they make a powerful UI combination. With custom tags, scriplets can be avoided in the markup entirely – a development, in some developers' eyes, that makes JSP another template engine.

4.2.8.2.3 Template Engines

One can ask the question, "why not use a template engine directly"? Of course, template engines have existed even longer than JSP. Some of the more popular engines are WebMacro, Tea, Freemarker, and Velocity. A template engine accepts a template, in the form of markup with some special tokens embedded, and replaces the tokens with data from the logic portion of the application. This is a slightly simple view: the tokens used by most template engines form a basic scripting language, and usually permit at least looping and conditionals.

Template engines address some of the potential concerns of using JSP. They do not allow arbitrary Java code in the markup, so the temptation to mix markup and logic is avoided entirely. The scripting capabilities of template engines are also able to perform the logic operations required for presentation, which is why sometimes scriplets creep into JSP. Many template engines, despite their capabilities, have a syntax that is easier to learn than that of JSP.

From a deployment point of view, template engines avoid the necessity of a Java compiler to which JSP pages must have access when they automatically regenerate their corresponding Servlet. The direct access of template engines to their template files also provides better error reporting – JSP pages are notorious for their cryptic error messages. Template engines often also provide a smaller memory and disk footprint.

There is, however, no universally agreed standard for templates, nor for the syntax of their scripting language. JSP, for all its faults, has substantial industry support. With the advent of readily available and powerful custom tag libraries,

JSP is further narrowing the gap to template systems. Given its wide support and a stable standard, JSP provides a good choice in many situations.

4.2.8.2.4 XSP

Another alternative to JSP, which can have benefits in some areas is a technology called XSP, or eXtensible Server Pages. We will discuss this when we look at the Cocoon framework in Chapter 5.

XSP provides a technology similar to that found in JSP, with some important differences. XSP is XML based, and an XSP page is valid XML. JSP pages can also use XML, but are more often marked up directly with HTML. JSP and its custom tags allow markup to access logic as required, providing the connection point between the view and the model. XSP pages are not, in themselves, the view. Instead, they make a more complete separation of the logic: the logic is accessed, or even entirely contained within the XSP page itself. The presentation, which is defined in one or more XSL style sheets, is then applied to the XML resulting from the XSP page.

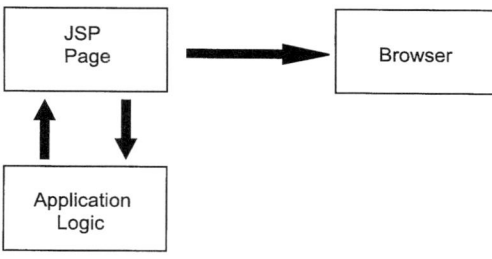

JSP compared to XSP

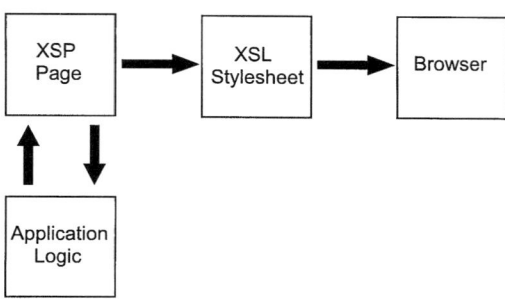

TRANSFORMATION

Using an example of what is nearly the simplest possible XSP and JSP pages illustrates this well.

First, let us look at an extremely simple JSP page:

```
<html>
<head>
<title>Hello World</title>
</head>
<body>
<p align="center">Hello, World</p>
</body>
</html>
```

Looks like HTML, right? In fact it is. In this example, we are not accessing any application logic: if we did, we would either be embedding code, or using a custom tag library to link through the application itself. This simple file, if stored as a .jsp, is simply translated into a Servlet that produces the same HTML code directly. It is a single-step process.

Now let us look at something similar to XSP:

```
<?xml version="1.0" encoding="ISO-8859-1"?>

<xsp:page language="java"
        xmlns:xsp="http://apache.org/xsp">

  <page>
    <title>Hello World</title>
    <content>
     <para>Hello, World</para>
    </content>
  </page>

</xsp:page>
```

Now, the XSP does not look much like HTML, and it is not. Actually it uses special XSP tags, such as "page," "content," and "para" to specify the general layout of a page, but not the actual markup. Unlike its JSP counterpart, the XSP requires one more step to actually generate the markup to be sent to the browser. An XSL style sheet is used to transform the markup from the above XSP page into valid HTML. Is this not more work? In a very simple example like this, yes, it is. However, the key point here is that the XSP page does *not* specify the end presentation format. It effectively uses presentation *placeholders* such as "para," which are then processed through the appropriate XSL. The XSL is in fact where the true presentation is specified, separating it from the XSP and the logic entirely. With JSP, both are in the same file. What is the point? We could easily, in our example, replace the default XSL style sheet, which generates HTML, with one that generates wireless markup language (WML), or SVG (a graphics format for vector drawings). With the JSP page, we would have to actually change the original JSP page, whereas these changes would require no change to our XSP page. This is a more complete separation of logic and presentation, and can have its advantages in situations where multiple presentation options are required.

A fine example might be a report, where the output is designed to be either viewed on the screen or printed. HTML, although a good markup for viewing online, is not always ideal for printing on paper. We would like to have our printed version use Portable Document Format (PDF, an relative of PostScript) instead. With JSP, we need to have two separate JSP pages, one that produces the output in HTML, with the embedded markup, and a second one, which outputs the format suitable for translation to PDF. (This is actually quite difficult with JSP – we might even end up coding a JSP page that outputs XML, and then use XSL to translate this to PDF.)

With XSP, these machinations are not required: we simply prepare one XSP page that gets the data and organizes it for presentation, and then write two style sheets, one for HTML, just like the original JSP format, and another for PDF, probably going through two stages, first to XML-FO (formatting objects) and then finally to PDF. A separate link is used to access the same XSP but indicating which of these style sheets have been applied.

Let us look at the advantages of this; say, for example, we want to add a new field, to our report. With the JSP version, we must alter both JSP pages. We must ensure that the changes are equivalent, for example that the new field appears in the same column in both new versions. For XSP, we simply alter the one XSP page, adding the new column. The formatting for both PDF and HTML remains the same, because it is done via a transformation, and knows nothing about how many fields it must process. There is no opportunity for the two formats to become different, because they both read from the same place: the XSP.

This is, of course, a very trivial example, but serves to highlight how, in some situations, alternative technologies, such as XSP, can have an advantage.

In this section, we have explored some of the major approaches to presentation that you find in frameworks. Often, complete application frameworks provide a choice among several of these alternatives, or even the ability to combine several techniques at once. Because the interface between presentation and logic consumes a great deal of the development time in a typical project, knowing what you're getting into in this area is essential before selecting a framework.

4.2.8.3 Database Access Frameworks

Another category of application-specific framework that is often encountered is what we call "database access" frameworks. These are frameworks that concentrate on providing services for connecting to a database, and often include an object/relational mapping layer.

The approaches of these frameworks vary considerably: with the advent of the new Java Data Objects (JDO) standard, the range has increased further. Some work best with only one type of database. Others provide database independence, and still others work with not any kind of database, but with different types of persistence mechanisms, such as OODBMS, LDAP, and so forth. In Chapter 2, we explored what you can expect from the database access portion of a framework, and these services are what you find in frameworks of this category.

4.3 FIT THE TOOL TO THE JOB

It is very important to select the appropriate framework for the job – although a number of application frameworks are widely applicable to a number of different kinds of applications, there is always one tool that is the best for the job at hand.

To determine this, it is necessary to understand the nature and specifications of the application to be written, and the nature and capabilities provided by the various frameworks. A third factor that also influences the decision – and in fact is more significant sometimes than the other two – is the knowledge of a particular framework that the developers involved in the project have.

Knowledge of a particular framework, having overcome its learning curve, can sometimes make it a better choice than another framework that is unknown.

4.4 ONE OF THE CHOICES IS NONE – WHEN FRAMEWORKS ARE NOT APPROPRIATE

There are some situations where an application framework is not appropriate, for example, applications that do not use the common services provided by frameworks, or applications where there are very specific performance constraints. To be honest, most applications do not fall into this category – and most *can* benefit greatly from the right choice of framework.

Frameworks are only applicable when a number of applications are required to be developed within a specific problem domain, allowing the opportunity to recoup the time invested to build the framework. This is why widely shared frameworks make sense, while in-house-developed frameworks are less practical.

Another valid reason for selecting not to use a framework is when the application already exists – and requires maintenance. In this case, sometimes retrofitting a framework can be less advantageous than the resultant benefit – but sometimes it is still worthwhile in the long run.

4.5 How to Do the Cost–Benefit Analysis

An essential part of the high-level planning process in any business, when considering a new project, is working out the expected benefits, and comparing these benefits to the anticipated cost. This is not just a matter of dollars and cents, unfortunately, because it would be easy if it were. What you must determine is whether or not the benefits – both short-term and long-term – outweigh the cost in both time and money that must be expended to gain these benefits. The costs might also include migration of existing applications, which is more difficult to estimate sometimes than the cost of creating new applications.

Choosing an application framework can be thought of in the same way: it is a major investment, probably requiring more time and attention than money, but major nonetheless. Any organization thinking of such an expenditure should reasonably expect to get substantial benefits in return. Often an evolutionary approach is best: use the new framework on some small new projects at first, and slowly adopt it into larger and more critical projects when the benefits are proven.

So how do you figure out whether a particular project can benefit from applying a particular framework? In Chapter 6, we present a simple method for comparing frameworks and their suitability to a particular project. Even having selected a framework that appears suitable, however, does not necessarily mean that applying it is automatically profitable in terms of time and/or money.

For this we need to do a cost–benefit analysis. Let us explore some of the factors involved:

- **Match specification to services:** Even if the project does not have a specification that is nailed down 100 percent yet, you should be able to compare the general capabilities you want in your finished application with the kinds of services the framework provides. For example, if you know your finished application will make extensive use of a relational database, and the framework provides a powerful mechanism for doing object/relational mapping and many database access and manipulation services, this is probably a good match on the particular specification area. Even if there are a number of areas where there is no match, the importance of each service that *does* must be examined. If, for example, the application makes substantial use of XML/XSL capabilities, and also uses an applet for its UI, a framework that provides exactly what you need as far as the XML/XSL tools may be a better choice than one that is excellent at building Applets.

- **Compare costs:** The costs of developing the application without the framework can be calculated fairly easily, although the estimating process for software development is sometimes an inexact science and deserves a book all to itself. Assuming this is known, however, we then need to try to calculate the cost of completing the project *with* the framework.

- **Cost of acquisition:** Does it cost anything to acquire and use the framework? Keep in mind that even with open-source frameworks, management may require that some kind of support be purchased, so take this into account.

- **Learning curve:** This is often the big item. What will it take to master the framework, at least sufficiently for the project at hand? This is difficult to estimate, because it depends on the skill level of the developers doing the work, the support community, and documentation of the framework, the time constraints of the project and other factors. Keep in mind, however, that this learning curve only has to be climbed once, and then this experience can be applied to multiple projects, making the effort more effective. Of course, if you are considering hiring consulting assistance to shorten the learning time, this is a hard cost that must be taken into account as well – often the cost of consulting is more than made up for by efficiencies realized by the faster, more effective adoption of the tool.

- **Cost of ownership:** What is the ongoing cost of using this framework within the organization? For some open-source projects, for example, it is important to estimate the time duration of keeping the latest version of the framework on the company's server, and for updating any older applications to work with the latest (or a more recent) version. When considering updates, companies often look upon the latest version of any technology with a jaundiced eye. They think of "pioneers" as people up in front lying face down with the arrows in their back, and their pioneering spirit is channeled more into making sure systems stay up. Such companies must consider both the cost of remaining up-to-date *and* the cost of not doing so. The cost of updating is clear: time spent, effort expended, possibly upheaval to existing applications if any backward-compatibility issues arise. The cost of *not* upgrading is slightly more subtle, but no less real. By not upgrading to at least the most recent "stable" version of a framework, companies lose the advantages of the latest bug fixes. If time is spent in dealing with a bug that has subsequently been fixed, it is clearly a loss due to the decision not to upgrade. The loss due to an inability to utilize the latest and greatest features is not as easy to see, but if you consider any developer's time spent within the company to achieve functionality that has already been incorporated into the framework it becomes more clear.

The final, and probably the most serious in the long term, cost of not upgrading is the danger of creating an "orphan." If the version of a framework being used by a company deviates significantly from the "core" version of the framework provided by its supplier, the fixes and enhancements made to the core version become unusable, or usable only with greater and greater difficulty. This is in itself a cost, but it gets worse: rather than being able to rely on the supplier of the framework to maintain the framework over time, the maintenance burden shifts more and more to the company using it. They find themselves less able over time to rely on the maintenance and support of the external supplier(s) of the framework, and the cost goes up.

So, when considering the cost of ownership, budget time to stay up-to-date, or budget time to "adopt" the project entirely, because one or the other will happen.

Of course, for a commercial framework, the ongoing costs of licensing (if any) and any required support or updates may be significant.

The nature of the framework or toolkit itself also plays a role in determining ongoing maintenance costs. Web applications, by their nature, tend to be relatively lower in their maintenance costs due to their server-oriented nature – for example, you do not need to update three thousand client systems out in the field, but just one (or a few) server(s) to install a new version. Not all frameworks have this advantage, however: if you require any kind of custom client-side software (including even a specific version of a browser), then upgrade costs to clients are indeed a factor to consider.

Now, it is a matter of comparing the costs to the benefits and seeing if it is worthwhile to utilize a particular framework in this situation. The two values must be computed into some common unit. If you are budgeting the benefit in terms of time saved, you must convert the cost to time as well.

There is an essential caveat in this process, however. A simple comparison can be misleading: for example, will you create a far better finished application with the framework than without it? Will it be much easier to do the next project, which may have to integrate with the first project? All these factors must also play a role in the decision-making process. The most important factor in computing the benefit is the number of projects that will be undertaken with the new framework. Every new project reaps benefit, while increasing the cost of adopting the tool either very little or not at all. Because many companies that adopt frameworks are in the business of software development, this has a powerful effect on the decision-making process. Even a fairly large IT department in a company that has nothing to do with software development can have the same argument weight in favor of adoption: even a few projects spread the cost of adoption significantly, and show geometrically increasing benefit.

Sometimes it is also necessary to make all or part of the decision to adopt a framework for strategic reasons – in the case, for example, where there will be a large number of projects, but their actual specifications are poorly defined. It can be reasoned that the repeated use of a framework in such a situation is bound to reap benefits over the creation of each project without such a framework, based solely on the fact that there are many projects to be done.

4.5.1 Build or Buy?

Closely related to the decision to adopt a framework is the decision to either buy (or otherwise acquire, in the case of open source) a framework, or build it entirely or partly. There are again a number of factors to consider in this situation. If, for example, there are essential trade-secret issues that need to be incorporated, then the decision to "build" may be the only choice. Although it is difficult to comprehend that the "cost" of even an open-source framework can be substantial, it is a factor to consider: as most professionals know already, total cost of ownership involves much more than just purchase price.

Of course, if what you need in a framework is simply not available, then the decision to build may also of necessity be the only choice. Sometimes an opportunity arises to partner with another group or company to spread the development cost, because creating even a simple framework can be a sizable investment.

4.6 Conclusion

Ultimately, the choice of an application framework will have a massive impact on the development of an application for you and your organization. It is worth spending the time to consider and weigh all of the factors we have discussed. In Chapter 5, we will review some actual frameworks and get an idea of what is currently on the market. You can then apply the techniques and criteria we have discussed here to see how the various options stand up to your needs

CHAPTER 5

A Catalog of Application Frameworks

In this chapter, we will take a brief look at a number of more popular and extensive Web application frameworks. It is not our intention to reproduce the frameworks' own documentation here: you may refer to the appropriate website for each framework for technical and user documentation. What we want to do is observe the frameworks as examples of Web application building frameworks in general, and to outline their major capabilities. Each framework has its strengths and weaknesses, which we will explore in detail later when we compare frameworks in Chapter 6.

Many of these frameworks would take an entire book to fully explore, so what we discuss here is just an outline of what they have to offer. A large number of frameworks are open-source projects, and are actively under development – so it is important to see what has changed and what is new when you review the framework yourself.

You will not find here an evaluation of the framework. It is not possible to judge the suitability of a framework for your particular task without the knowledge of a great many factors, some of which we will explore in Chapter 6, where we will show how to match up the problem with the potential solutions and choose a suitable framework for your task. There are no absolute measures by which we can say this framework is "better" than some other one – you must decide that based on your requirements.

5.1 Complete Application Frameworks

Complete application frameworks provide services for all portions of a typical application's development. Typically, this includes at least presentation, persistence, configuration, application logic, and logging. Often it includes much more. It is often difficult to draw the line between a complete application framework and one that concentrates on a specific area of the application, as it depends to a large degree on the application. If an application has very little or no need for persistence or database access, for example, then a framework such as Struts, which concentrates fairly heavily on the presentation side of the application development process, might well be considered a complete application framework in that context.

We will start our review of complete application frameworks with one that takes a particularly design-pattern intensive view of application development:

5.1.1 Avalon

Name	Avalon
Website	http://jakarta.apache.org/avalon/index.html
Supplier	Apache Software Foundation
License	Apache License
Focus	Server Components
Feature Summary	Strong and Flexible Design patterns

The Apache Avalon project, formerly known as the Java Apache Server Framework, was one of the first open-source Java application frameworks created. It evolved from the production of the Apache JServ project, which added support for the Servlet API to the ubiquitous Apache HTTP server. Avalon is a highly sophisticated framework that spends a lot of time providing powerful design patterns and structure to a finished application. Although not as well known as many other framework projects, it may well be the most capable and the most advanced in design.

Avalon comprises five primary subprojects: Framework, Excalibur, LogKit, Phoenix, and Cornerstone. This breaks the framework into more manageable chunks and facilitates learning. Most of its design patterns are embodied in the Framework portion. We discuss below how all of the subprojects fit together and what they provide.

Although Avalon is specifically targeted at server-side application construction, much of its functionality is applicable in stand-alone or desktop applications as well.

5.1.1.1 Framework

The Framework subproject contains the backbone of Avalon: the interfaces and default implementations for much of its functionality are here. It is the most mature of the subprojects, and, in many applications, is the most heavily used.

Every component defined within Avalon's framework implements (or extends, if it is also an interface) the Component marker interface. (We discuss the *marker interface* design pattern in detail in Chapter 8). This indicates that the Component can be managed by a ComponentManager (a default implementation that is supplied). A Composable object (which implements the Composable interface) is a user of components. It uses a ComponentManager to get access by components, and it requests this access by means of a component's "role." Several components can have the same role, and therefore, are interchangeable – effectively different implementations of the same functionality. Logging, for example: the single role of logging can be fulfilled by one of several different logging components supplied with Avalon. By using components via their role, instead of directly, Composable objects can utilize any implementation of that role, making the entire application completely configurable.

In more recent versions of Avalon, some of its containers support accessing components that do not implement Component as an interface. This makes it even more flexible.

The Framework portion of Avalon goes on to define other interfaces that refine the definition of each component, describing its capabilities and its requirements from its container. These include:

- *Disposable:* A component that requires its "dispose" method called to release and clean up resources prior to its termination. This can be used, for example, to close database connections, files, and so forth.
- *Executable:* A component that performs some specific task in response to its "execute" method being called. This is one option for encapsulating your application logic elements in Avalon.
- *Initializable:* A component that requires an initialization step, possibly to allocate or acquire resources it uses. A connection pool, for example, could establish its connections to the database at this point. A logging component could open or initialize its log file, and so forth.

- *Startable:* A component that can be started and stopped, and remains running once started until stopped, such as a service. An FTP component or event listener might be Startable.
- *Suspendable:* A component whose operation can be suspended, or temporarily stopped and later started again. This is distinct from a service that is shut down completely in that it may be start up again later if it is Suspendable.
- *Configurable:* A component that requires a Configuration object to be supplied before it is used. Configuration objects contain generic configuration information that a component can use to customize its operation based on settings. Any component that needs configuration information implements Configurable. If its configuration information can be updated after it is initially set, it implements Reconfigurable as well.
- *Contextualizable:* Components that require a "Context," (e.g., application, component, session or request context information) to be passed from the container implement this interface.
- *LogEnabled:* The component must be supplied with a "logger," an object capable of writing to the selected logging mechanism. The "logger" object is then used as necessary to send messages to the appropriate logging mechanism.
- *Parameterizable:* Components that need to be supplied with run-time parameters (but not necessarily with full Configuration) implement this interface. This is a "lightweight" alternative to Configurable.

There are a number of other interfaces, for components that require a certain treatment of information from the container, but the general principle of inversion of control is maintained throughout: the container *always* calls the component, never the other way around. In more recent versions of containers, these life-cycle interfaces are *extensible*, that is, additional lifecycle interfaces can easily be added.

5.1.1.2 Excalibur

The Excalibur subproject of Avalon provides a number of basic server-side component implementations. Excalibur is still actively in development, so the API of some of these subprojects are not yet finalized, and more subprojects will likely be added in the near future. Some of the components provided by Excalibur are as follows:

- **AltRMI:** An alternative implementation of Remote Method Invocation, with some important differences. AltRMI has a different approach to exception handling than the "normal" RMI capabilities of Java; methods do not have to throw RemoteException, as the AltRMI equivalent is a subclass of RuntimeException (which need not be declared). There are other important differences, and AltRMI is still under development – be sure to check the site for the latest status.

- **BZip2**: As the name implies, components that are able to compress and decompress using the BZip2 format, a popular archive format on Unix and Linux systems.
- **Baxter**: Component providing JMX-Managed bean capabilities. JMX (Java Management eXtensions) provides a series of interfaces to allow Java services and components to be "managed" by an external management application.
- **CLI**: Component providing parsing and management of command-line parameters.
- **Cache**: Configurable caching capability, with pluggable replacement algorithms and storage mechanisms.
- **Collections:** Advanced collection and set capabilities, extending what is normally available in the standard java.util package.
- **Command:** Asynchronous command event processing (related closely to the Event component).
- **Component:** Provides the essential default component manager, which allows components to be selected by "role," allowing different implementations to be easily exchanged.
- **Concurrent:** Components providing advanced thread-handling capabilities.
- **DataSource**: Allows access to pooled data connections, either directly or via a J2EE server's connection pool.
- **Event**: Generalized event handling, dispatching, and fixed- and variable-sized queuing of events.
- **Extension**: Utilities for determining available or required optional packages.
- **I/O**: Excalibur's Input/Output utilities.
- **Internationalization:** Support components for internationalization, including access to message bundle files in different formats, such as XML.
- **Logger**: Excalibur's components for using the LogKit logging system, providing logging capabilities.

- **Monitor:** Resource management capabilities, allowing objects to be "monitored" and notifications sent when the monitored object changes.

- **Naming:** Generalized name space and naming capabilities. We discussed naming in Chapter 1 in some detail.

- **Pool:** Generalized pooling components, allowing any other resource to be pooled. Used by the DataSource component.

- **Source resolver:** A component that can provide a data stream for any given URI, for multiple protocols.

- **Tar:** Capabilities to read and manipulate "tar" archives.

- **Testcase:** Utility components for creating test cases.

- **Thread:** Thread pool management components. Creating threads, or separate runtime contexts, is a fairly "expensive" operation in terms of performance, so that maintaining threads in a pool allows the same thread to be reused, avoiding this overhead.

- **Util:** Utility components, including the PropertyUtil component for reading property collections.

- **XMLBundle:** XML Resource bundles for use by the internationalization components.

- **Zip:** Capabilities for managing and creating "zip" archives.

5.1.1.3 LogKit

The LogKit subproject is a logging toolkit used by the other subprojects to provide logging capabilities. It is similar in implementation to the JDK 1.4 logging facilities, but does not require JDK 1.4 to be used. Components can implement the Loggable interface in Avalon and have access to any of a number of different logging APIs, such as Log4j, the Apache LogKit project, or the logging capabilities of JDK 1.4 itself.

5.1.1.4 Phoenix

The Phoenix subproject provides for the deployment and execution of "Blocks," or server components. It is effectively the "kernel" of the server applications built with Avalon, and provides a stand-alone runtime environment for Avalon applications.

Complete Application Frameworks

Phoenix defines the interfaces for services provided by the server application, where the entire application is made up of such services.

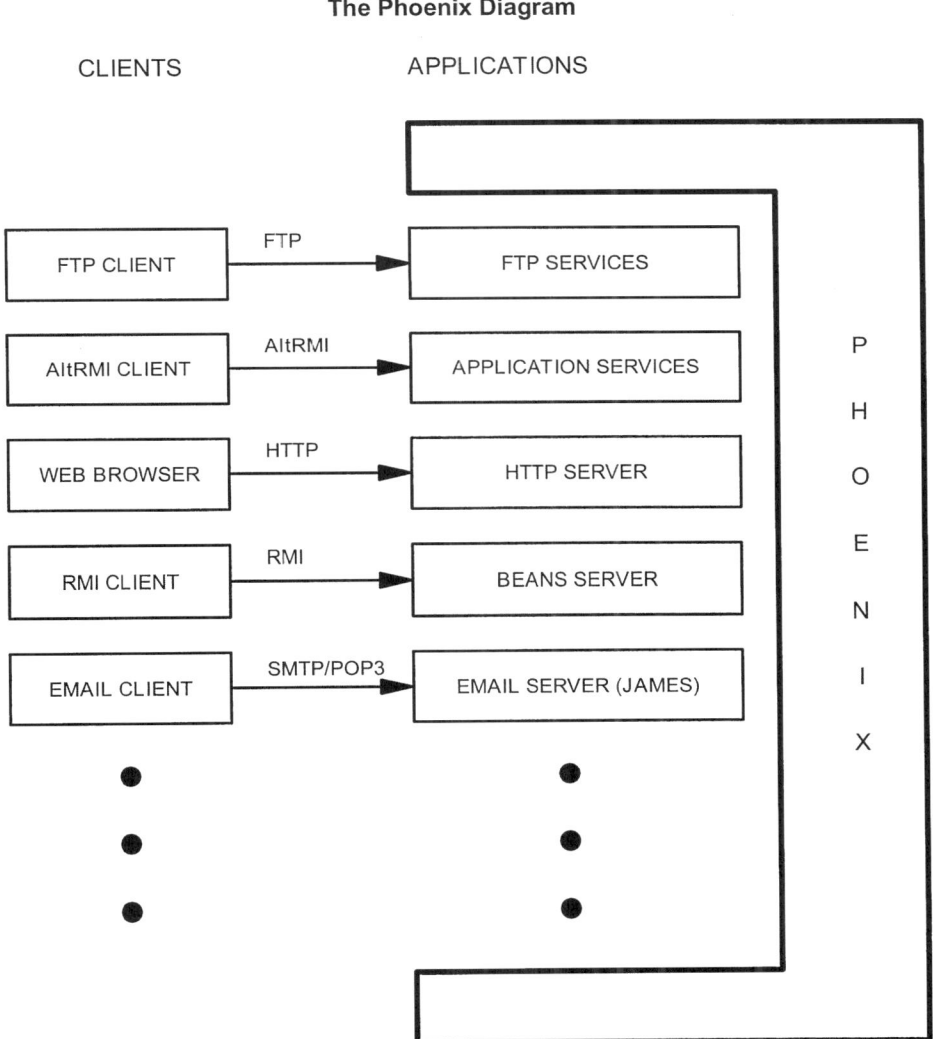

5.1.1.5 Cornerstone
The Cornerstone subproject provides a collection of Blocks that can be deployed in Phoenix, including socket management, job scheduling, principal/role management, and more.

5.1.1.6 Applications

The applications subproject is a directory and repository of server applications that use the Phoenix subproject as their runtime environment. This includes applications developed specifically for Phoenix, and interfaces to third-party applications that were originally developed for other environments. These third-party applications rely on a small piece of connector code that allows them to be launched and managed in a Phoenix server. These applications consist of blocks that can be easily reconfigured and used in your own Avalon applications.

These applications include:

- The obligatory "Hello, World" demo.
- SimpleServer, a demonstration of Phoenix server capabilities.
- HTTP Proxy, providing basic proxy services for HTTP and Web browsing.
- FTP Server, which provides standard FTP services from within Phoenix.
- AvalonDB, a JDBC-compliant DBMS, still under development.
- A wrapper for the popular HypersonicSQL JDBC-compliant database.
- Overlord, a game server, still under development.
- XCommander, a server that responds to XML commands.

5.1.1.7 The Sandbox

Effectively another "subproject" in Avalon is the Sandbox – an area where new capabilities, services, and applications are developed until they are ready for inclusion in one of the other subprojects. As the name implies, it provides a "safe" place to experiment with these new capabilities while they are under development.

Avalon deals with components that are *externally managed*, meaning that the components are provided at run time with the contexts, connections, and logging capabilities they require by the framework. This is a very flexible method of implementing component interaction. It is also an example of the "inversion of control" pattern for components, where the components never call the container, always the reverse.

Avalon also separates the different aspects of component functionality, such as security, manageability, configurability, into independent interfaces. An Avalon component then implements each of these interfaces to provide these functions, keeping them independent. Avalon focuses on providing tools for component-based development, allowing components to be easily assembled into applications and at the same time allowing individual components to be replaced at runtime for complete flexibility. In Avalon, every component has what is called a "role," a signature by which the component can be retrieved.

Avalon components are marked by implementing the Component interface. They then optionally implement other interfaces to specify their areas of concern to their containers, such as LogEnabled, Configurable, Parameterizable, Composable, and so forth. This makes the framework extremely flexible and does not tie it to any one deployment environment.

Avalon can be used in a number of different ways to support Web application development. At the most basic, the framework portion of Avalon can be used to provide structure and important design patterns. Many Web applications, however, can benefit from at least some of the components in the Excalibur subproject: at least logging, default component management, and connection handling. Applications that also utilize the Phoenix kernel take their use a step further – Phoenix can be used in one of several ways in Web applications:

- As a 'stand-alone' application, Phoenix is started up independently from the Servlet engine, in a separate VM (virtual machine). Some means of communication (possibly AltRMI or JMS) is then used to route application requests from the Servlet front-end to the Phoenix server.
- Wrapped in a Servlet, Phoenix can be started in the same VM as the Servlet engine, making for a less complex startup, but providing a somewhat less flexible deployment environment.

Avalon is a very active project, with several busy mailing lists and a number of active developers.

Some of the projects created with Avalon include:

- Cocoon, which we review later in this chapter.
- Apache James, an open-source email server.
- Jesktop, a desktop and application environment.
- Jo!, a lightweight and efficient Web server that can be deployed as a Phoenix block.
- Enterprise Object Broker (EOB), an alternative to EJB.
- JabaServer, a Jabber (a multiprotocol chat client) implementation.

The second framework we will examine is also very popular, although it takes a different approach from Avalon, despite using Avalon in its own construction.

5.1.2 Cocoon

Name	Cocoon
Website	http://xml.apache.org/cocoon/index.html
Supplier	Apache Software Foundation
License	Apache License
Focus	Website publishing and dynamic applications
Feature Summary	Powerful XML and XSL handling, conversion of content to virtually any format, flexible and extensible pipeline processing.

Cocoon is another framework that concentrates primarily on presentation – although it provides a number of very valuable features for use in the entire application development process. Cocoon takes an XML-based approach to many of its functions; XML and XSL transformations are an essential part of its operation. Cocoon is part of the Apache XML project, found at http://xml.apache.org.

Cocoon is actually a framework built on another framework that we discuss: it utilizes the Avalon framework for logging, configuration, threading, and context management. It addresses the issue of the separation of presentation and content for an XML-based website. The "content" in this case, consists of both static and dynamic resources.

Cocoon includes a number of basic mechanisms for processing XML documents. It uses a mechanism called "Transformers" to allow flexible processing of XML generated by "Generators." This can be as simple as XML documents being transformed into HTML via an appropriate XSL transformer, or more complicated, with application logic participating in the Transform process.

5.1.2.1 Matchers

Cocoon ties the request by the user to the appropriate response by means of "Matchers." These matchers control the dispatch in a Cocoon application. Once a generator creates the XML, it can pass through one or more Transformers and/or Aggregators – aggregators being used to combine XML from multiple sources into a single output stream of XML.

A matcher usually defines a URL regular expression, allowing the same matcher to be used for an entire group of URLs, such as:

```
<map:match pattern="xsp/*">
```

This matcher will apply to all URLs beginning with "xsp/," such as "xsp/test," "xsp/abc," but not "xsp/test/one." The "**" wildcard is used to include "subdirectories" in the URL, and thus "xsp/**" would also match "xsp/test/one."

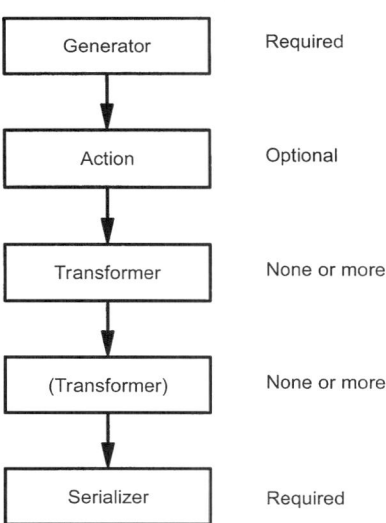

Cocoon: Generator-Transformer-Serializer Diagram

5.1.2.2 Generators

Generators can access and create XML from files, application logic, a relational database, LDAP server, XML-enabled databases, or other data sources.

The "file" generator is the default if no other generator is specified, and simply generates XML from a file or a URL. Other available generators include:

- *request:* A generator that produces XML based on the contents of the servlet request, including header information.
- *status:* A generator that produces status and runtime information in an XML stream, including current memory usage and other statistics.
- *directory:* Produces a listing of the contents of a specified directory in an XML format.
- *imagedirectory:* This is similar to *directory*, but including size information about any image files found in the directory.
- *fragmentextractor:* A generator that can "extract" a portion of an XML stream, passing on only the desired portion to the pipeline.
- *jsp:* Allows JSP pages to be used to initiate the XML stream. The selected JSP page must output valid XML.
- *stream:* Reads XML from a request InputStream and generates SAX Events.
- *html:* Produces valid XML from an HTML input stream – ideal for reading existing HTML content.

- *velocity*: Allows a Velocity template to be used as the initiator of a pipeline – the template must generate valid XML.

The available Generators can easily be extended to include your own custom Generator. As long as it can produce XML output, any component can be used as a Generator.

5.1.2.3 Actions

Action classes can be used as an interface to arbitrary application logic – what we have described as the "application logic container" – for Cocoon. Any parameters or context information already in the pipeline can be passed to the Action, and the Action can respond with additional information used later in the pipeline. Action objects allow a complete separation between logic and presentation, even more so than XSP pages.

Actions are one option when considering where to encapsulate your application logic when building a Cocoon application.

5.1.2.4 Transformers

Transformers take the XML stream produced by a generator and perform a specified manipulation on it, then pass it on to the next step in the pipeline: either another transformer or a serializer. XSLT is only the most obvious example of a transformer; several others are supplied. Transformers that allow other XML streams to be included into the pipeline, allow SQL statements to be run and the results included, extract fragments of the XML stream, and perform internationalization, are supplied, among others.

Multiple transformers can be connected together to produce the output desired.

5.1.2.5 Serializers

Cocoon uses a mechanism called Serializers to render the transformed and aggregated XML into the appropriate markup for the client's browser: HTML, for example. As the XML transformation always changes XML into another form of XML, the resulting markup is always valid and complete (provided that no errors exist in the transformation process). A serializer is the last step in a pipeline, and writes the finished output to the proper location – whether this be the user's browser, a file, a log, or a database.

Serializers exist to produce output for HTML, WML, PDF (Portable Document Format), SVG (Scalable Vector Graphics), RTF (Rich Text Format), and a number of other formats.

Complete Application Frameworks

Cocoon includes a substantial number of examples, ranging from simple examples of basic capabilities all the way to more sophisticated Web applications, including logins, authentication, and database access.

```
 1: <html>
 2: <head>
 3: <title>Hello</title>
 4: </head>

 5: <body vlink="blue"link="blue"alink="red"
 6: bgcolor="white">
 7: <h2 style="color: navy; text-align: center">Hello,
 8: World</h2>

 9: <content>
10: <p align="center">Hello, World!
11: </p>
12: </content>

13: </body>
14: </html>
```

Although this example may look suspiciously like HTML, it is not. It is actually XML, as you can see by the unusual "content" tags (among other differences). Unlike HTML, this content can be transformed – it is a matter of setting up a few configurations to have this simple markup rendered as HTML, XHTML, WML, PDF, SVG, JPEG, VRML, XLS (the file format used by Microsoft Excel) or even PostScript and VoxML (Voice output)! How is that for flexible output formats? Even this trivial example shows some of the power of handling content in XML.

Taking this further, both the source of the XML *and* the transformations it undergoes can be dynamically generated. For example, the capabilities of the browser can be analyzed to determine if HTML or WML transformations should be used. The source XML can also be generated dynamically through the use of XSP (eXtensible Stylesheet Pages). XSP is described in more detail in Chapter 4.

Cocoon requires a different way of thinking about Web applications, but once the paradigm is grasped it is an extremely powerful and efficient way to build them. Cocoon is undergoing active development, and a busy mailing list is available both for users and developers.

Given Cocoon's emphasis on XML and transformation technologies, it can easily be used as a powerful presentation framework in combination with other frameworks, such as object/relational mapping frameworks, or frameworks such as Turbine or Avalon, which provide substantial sets of capabilities for the whole application. At the same time, there is nothing preventing an entire application from being created with Cocoon itself, particularly if the application is heavily oriented toward publishing of content and multiple presentation formats.

The Cocoon project is undergoing steady development, and new versions are released regularly. Because of the unique pipelined approach to content manipulation, it can be a difficult framework for some developers to grasp, but its potential is tremendous for Web application creation.

For an example of Cocoon in use, see the Cocoon case study in the Appendix.

An extensive list of live sites powered by Cocoon is supplied on Cocoon's Web pages.

The next framework takes a more database-centric view of application development, and has been around for nearly as long as Avalon, and before many of the other frameworks we will examine.

5.1.3 Expresso

Name	Expresso
Website	http://www.jcorporate.com
Supplier	Jcorporate Ltd.
License	Apache-Style License
Focus	Database-oriented Web applications
Feature Summary	Rich feature set, flexible UI choices, emphasis on object/relational mapping layer

The Expresso Framework, hosted and sponsored by Jcorporate Ltd. is a complete application framework strongly oriented around database access. At the core of Expresso is a powerful object/relational mapping and persistence mechanism called DBObjects. These DBObjects form the basis of all database access within Expresso, and most of its other services require such database access.

An Expresso application begins with a Schema object, which lists all of the other key objects to be used by this application. The existence of a Schema object allows the application to be configured by Expresso's own facilities, including security and navigation. The Schema object lists the DBObjects, Controller objects, and Job objects used by the application.

Expresso applications have access to two different sources of configuration information: first in an XML file, expresso-config.xml, which specifies one or more "contexts." Each context is normally associated with a separate database, and a single Expresso application can span multiple databases as required. The XML configuration file can also contain application-specific configuration, allowing it to be used for custom preferences. The XML configuration is read at initialization automatically.

The second source of configuration information is a dedicated "set-up value" table that is automatically created in the database for each context. The values stored there can take effect immediately, allowing changes while an application is running.

The major functional elements of an Expresso application are contained within its DBObjects, Controller objects, and Job objects. We will examine each of these individually:

5.1.3.1 DBObject

Classes that inherit from DBObject, or (more likely) SecuredDBObject can be instantiated to represent one or a group of records in a database. DBObjects can handle obtaining their own connection to the database (via the database connection pool service of Expresso), or may be explicitly handed a database connection (to facilitate database transactions).

Subclasses of DBObject need to implement only one or more constructors and the "setupFields" method is ready to use. The setupFields method specifies the database table the object will be associated with, and the fields in those tables that it can access. A special instance of DBObject, called "AutoDBObject" can be used against an arbitrary database table, and can determine the fields available in that table automatically at run time.

Database objects also automatically have caching applied, making their performance highly tunable. The size of the cache is adjustable for each DBObject class individually, and mechanisms for collecting cache statistics are available. These objects also have built-in security (when subclassed from the Secured-DBObject class), allowing access rights to be granted for individual user groups as required.

By means of method calls within the setupFields method, database objects can define:

- auto-incrementing fields, where the next number is supplied by a specialized class that handles sequential number generation.

- valid values for specified fields, including regular expression masks.
- indices to be created on the database for enhanced retrieval performance.
- virtual fields – fields whose value is computed on the fly from other fields.
- referential integrity constraints, including relationships with other database objects, in a database-independent way.
- "details" of objects associated with the specified database object – this allows cascading deletes to be applied, where the related detail records are deleted in the same operation as the parent record when required.

The rich selection of methods available in a DBObject make virtually any database operation a matter of a single method call.

5.1.3.2 Controllers

The "Controller" class (and its subclasses) are the basic unit of business logic in Expresso. They provide the "C" in the MVC pattern, routing requests for logic to "states," or methods that provide that logic. These "states" can be either methods internal to the Controller object itself, or actual "State" objects external to the controller. So, effectively, a Controller is a collection of states, like a finite-state machine.

The Controller object transitions from state to state normally by means of user actions: for example, clicking a link, pushing a button on a form, or some other UI action. Controllers are by nature completely UI-independent: they make no assumptions about the nature of the UI that interacts with the user. Instead, they deal with the outside world by emitting "ControllerElement" objects when they transition into each new state. These "ControllerElement" objects take one of four types of objects:

- *Outputs:* An output object is just what it says – the result of some processing on the part of the State that emits it. This could be as simple as a total, or as complex as any Java object. Outputs are the way Controllers express their results.
- *Inputs:* An input is a request for information, normally rendered as a field that the user fills in on a form of some kind. It may take the form of a list of valid values, from which the user may choose, and a default value might be supplied by the controller – which may or may not be used by the UI. A label is also supplied as part of the input object.
- *Transitions:* A transition is simply a navigation tool – it provides the user with a way to move to another state, either in the same Controller or another. They are normally rendered as links, icons, or buttons on a form. Clicking one of

Complete Application Frameworks

these icons takes the user to a new state, which then in turn emits its inputs, outputs, and controllers. This describes the flow of control in all Expresso applications.
- *Blocks:* A block is simply a container for other ControllerElements. It allows the UI to be better organized, by providing a means for a controller to group related ControllerElements together. All elements relating to a customer, for example, can be gathered together into a Block called "Customer." It is strictly an organizational tool, and implies no constraints on the presentation layer.

A controller object is stateless – it knows only what it is handed as arguments as it transitions from state to state. (Each "state" of a controller should not be confused with the "state" of a session). This allows controllers to be fully reentrant and thread-safe, and a single instance is normally used for all requests to a particular controller, making them very efficient containers for application logic. If a state is required by a controller, it should be passed in as one of its parameters from the preceding state. The framework contains many examples of this.

In many Expresso applications, Controllers are accessed via the Struts framework, which is incorporated into and included with Expresso. Special URLs (by default ending in "do") are mapped to Controller objects, which are themselves extensions of Struts "Action" objects. The Controller is then invoked, transitions into its appropriate state, and produces its inputs, outputs, transitions, and blocks. These are then rendered back to the user's browser by one of the supported UI technologies in Expresso. The different UI options are called "View Handlers," and several are included with Expresso (and more can be added):

- **Default view**: If no view is specified for a particular state, a simple HTML view will be automatically generated. This is useful for utility controllers, whose functions might only be used infrequently, as no specific UI need be written for them. It is also handy when prototyping a new application, as you are able to concentrate on functionality and logic and leave the UI for later.
- **XML/XSL view:** This UI option allows a state's output to be produced in XML format. This XML can optionally be transformed by a specified XSL stylesheet, allowing it to generate HTML, XHTML, WML, PDF, or whatever other format is required for that instance. The stylesheet that is selected can be adjusted according to the user's browser, allowing multiple devices (e.g., HTML and WML) to be served from the same controller automatically. It is also possible to skip the XSL transformation step and generate XML directly, providing a valuable tool for debugging.

- **JSP view:** A common option for the view is to create a JSP page. Expresso is fully integrated with the Struts framework (discussed in detail in its own section), so the highly flexible tag libraries included with Struts can be used to build JSP pages quickly and easily. Special extensions to Struts' normal tags make it easy to access ControllerElements, thereby translating the UI-independent response from a controller into a usable JSP page UI is simplified.

5.1.3.3 Jobs

A Job object is designed to be used for processing that is not interactive. Typically, processing that takes any longer than a few seconds is not a good candidate for interactive use. A user is typically annoyed if a task takes any longer than perhaps two seconds. For longer tasks, Job objects are used. A Job object is similar to a controller in that is has no UI dependence, but unlike a controller it is not designed to be interactive. Jobs are "queued" by creating entries describing the job object to be executed in a special database table, and a background thread called the Job Handler "picks up" these queued entries and executes the associated job object. The job object can call other jobs, call controllers, use database objects, and generally perform any required processing. It is common (but not required) for a job object to indicate its successful completion via an email sent back to the user that requested it be queued originally.

Job objects can also be *scheduled*, that is, set up for execution at a specific date and time. This scheduling can also be repetitive, ideal for jobs that are run once a day or once a week, for example.

In addition to Controllers, DBObjects, and Jobs, Expresso provides a number of other services. These services can be used by any of the core objects discussed previously and are used to build the functionality of the application as required. These services can be broken down into the following groups:

- **Database maintenance:** Expresso contains a controller called DBMaint that can be immediately used with any Database Object to provide database maintenance. This controller comes supplied with a default (but customizable) JSP-based view that allows records to be added, updated, deleted, and searched. This provides the ability for an application's database to be quickly populated when testing and prototyping, and removes the necessity of coding database maintenance logic for any of the application's tables.

    DBMaint also handles database objects that participate in a master/detail relationship, automatically generating a "tabbed" user interface to allow the master record and associated details to be edited on a single form.
- **Security:** Security is applied at multiple levels of an Expresso application. Initial authentication is normally achieved by logging in, providing a user

name and password. The authentication process uses a "pluggable" object to determine where it will get its authentication information, allowing LDAP, database, and Operating System security to be used as appropriate to provide the list of authenticated users. Once authentication is achieved, the user is associated with one or more groups, and authorization is provided to the groups. Database objects have authorization associated with them for each of the database operations (add, update, delete, search). Controllers have authorization to each of their states, allowing the application's logic to be secured at any level required. And finally, Job objects have authorization to the job itself, and to any special "functions" within the job (if required).

In this way, an Expresso application can be secured at any level required without the need to write any authorization or authentication code. The framework uses either "weak" security (basic encryption), or ties into the Java encryption packages to optionally provide highly sophisticated encryption, for both passwords, and security data and database data, as required.

Security is also taken into account in a number of other areas of Expresso, such as the filtering mechanism applied to data entered on forms – to prevent malicious script from being introduced as data.

- **Caching**: Expresso automatically uses its own Caching mechanism to a provide middle-tier caching for set-up and other configuration data. Caching can also be applied to any database object, multiplying database performance considerably. The cache uses a least frequently used algorithm to maintain a minimum level of free memory, preventing conflict between the memory needs of the cache and the remainder of the application. The cache can be finely tuned, with the amount of caching applied to individual database objects adjusted based on data collected from actual operation of the finished application.

  Caching can also be applied to any object that implements to a cacheable interface, allowing easy access to cache functionality for the finished application.

- **Configuration and initialization**: Another service provided by the framework is Configuration and Initialization. When the Servlet engine starts, a special start-up Servlet runs to load initial configuration information, initialize connection pools, and start logging services and job handlers. The initial configuration information loaded can be customized as required for a particular application, and each application's configuration can be maintained in a separate XML file, simplifying administration of multiple applications in the same Web application context.

- **Logging**: Expresso uses the Apache Log4j project to provide its logging capabilities. Logging is set up for each application independently, and multiple

logging "categories" can be adjusted for different logging levels independently. This allows specific areas of finished applications to log more detail, for instance, making debugging much easier.
- **URL mapping:** Through its integration with the Apache Struts framework, Expresso provides "URL mapping," that is, the ability for specialized URLs (by default ending with the ".do" extension) to be mapped to the appropriate Controller object, and to invoke the proper state on that object (based on URL parameters). This provides access to the application logic through a series of logically organized URLs. The mappings are controlled via extended versions of the normal XML configuration files used for Struts, with the addition that each application again has its own file, making administration more straightforward.
- **Testing and performance monitoring:** Expresso also provides a service to test and monitor the performance of both the framework itself and the applications you build with it. In addition to unit tests (built using the JUnit framework, also incorporated into Expresso), the framework provides a database of tests, where each test consists of a series of URLs. This series of URLs is executed in sequence, and allows sessions to be created (so the action of logging in, for example, can be tested). Because each URL is executed, the response is compared to a specified "expect string" to see if it is correct, and the result of the comparison noted. The time for the response to be completed is also recorded, and is compared to a series of expected timings – this allows a particular run of the test to be graded as to its speed. When many tests are run at once, this allows the performance of the system under load to be tested at a very fine granularity, as particular URLs running slower than normal will indicate the source of performance issues.

  Other performance-monitoring mechanisms are built in at other areas of the framework: Controller objects, for example, can be timed, allowing the actual execution of the application logic to be analyzed. Database object accesses can be counted and timed as well, allowing the database configuration to be optimized easily.
- **Utilities:** Like most frameworks, a number of utility functions are provided with Expresso. These include things such as utilities to generate the database structure (by reading the definitions of each database object), run unit and performance tests, and run Controller objects from the command line (for easy debugging and prototyping).
- **Internationalization:** Internationalization has been given careful treatment in Expresso. Through its integration with Struts, tags are available to allow text on any JSP page to be read from a message bundle file, where the message bundle file to be used is determined per user (and per application). This

allows multiple users to each see the application in their own native language. In addition, separate character sets are available for each language option.

Normally, the authentication (e.g., login) process determines the preferred language by reading the options set for the user's browser, but these can also be specified as user preferences in the database.

Commercial support for Expresso is sold by its host company, and a number of other projects have been created that use Expresso's services to build other projects, both open-source and commercial.

Expresso is an active framework, with ongoing development taking place on a daily basis. There is a moderately active mailing list, and a number of online forums dedicated to discussing both the framework and various projects built with it.

For an example of Expresso in use, see the Expresso case study in the Appendix.

A number of projects, both commercial and open-source, have been created using Expresso. A list is included on the Expresso Website, and includes:

- *eForum:* An open-source discussion forum application
- *WebAppWriter:* An online application for creating new Expresso applications automatically from templates.
- *eContent:* A commercial content-management application.
- *ePoll:* An open-source polling and voting application.

This next framework is similar in many ways to Avalon, because it concentrates mostly on the component structure and design patterns of the nonvisual portions of application development, unlike Expresso, which encompasses the view layer as well.

5.1.4 Arch4J

Name	Arch4J
Website	http://arch4j.sourceforge.net/
Supplier	Sycamore Group, LLC
License	SpiderLogic Open-sources Software License
Focus	Complete application framework; concentrates on the model portion of the MVC architecture, business services.
Feature Summary	Applies design patterns to achieve implementation/interface independence for many essential application and business services.

The Arch4J framework provides a well-designed infrastructure for building Web applications. Unlike most other frameworks, it makes no attempt to deal with the "view" portion of the MVC architecture directly: it concentrates instead on the "Model" part of the architecture. Arch4J provides the concept of a business service: a state change in the business being modeled by the application. Business service calls represent the only way for the model to move from one state to another, ensuring all changes to the model go through a single process.

Arch4J specifies a structure for business services, but leaves the actual implementation of the services to the developer to specify. This ensures that the actual service is easily replaceable with another, whereas the application written to use those services can remain unchanged.

The business services architecture is broken down into a number of individual service areas:

- **Base:** Includes logging and property management components.
- **Base Services:** Access to the system services supplied by a particular application server.
- **Business data:** Defines the container object for business data.
- **Client controller:** Provides the abstract ActionHandler interface, and classes concerned with accepting client requests and routing them to the appropriate handler in the business logic.
- **Data access:** This component provides a layer of abstraction above the normal JDBC level, automatically handling connections and allowing a specific method to be called for each row in a resulting set. It does not provide an object/relational persistence layer itself, but can be used as the interface to other persistence mechanisms.
- **Data domain:** A data domain allows a specific range of valid data values to be defined, allowing implicit validation.
- **EJB:** This component acts as an interface to EJB Session Beans.
- **Java class generator:** Provides a mechanism for programmatically generating Java source code.
- **Messaging:** Provides an interface to messaging systems, such as JMS, for both point-to-point and publish/subscribe functionality, without any provider dependences.

- **Data parser:** A generalized mechanism for reading records in either fixed or delimited formats.

- **Persistence:** Provides an abstract mechanism for accessing persistence mechanisms, with an implementation for the Castor persistence framework.

- **Property tree:** A component to build hierarchies of properties from files, including XML files.

- **XML wrapper:** A component used to abstract the connection to a specific XML parser, with an implementation included for the Apache Xerces parser.

Arch4J is a relatively recent addition to the framework world, and will no doubt be further developed over time. It provides a well thought out architectural layer for integration with other tools, keeping the application logic abstracted from dependences, even on the "model" side.

In Arch4J we see the same kind of "pluggability" that is an important part of Avalon and Turbine: the ability to assign a specific implementation by changing the configuration. This flexibility is a common feature of a number of frameworks, but the level to which it is applied varies considerably.

The next framework we examine also has a long history, and is used in many diverse applications currently running on the Internet. It is, similar to Expresso, a company-sponsored open-source project, and also has commercial applications built from its foundation. It includes a unique and powerful presentation layer that can be used independently of the framework as a whole.

5.1.5 ArsDigita ACSJ

Name	ACSJ
Website	http://developer.arsdigita.com/acs-java/
Supplier	Red Hat Software
License	ArsDigita Public License
Focus	Complete application development
Feature summary	Flexible Swing-like UI components, object/relational mapping layer, Integrated with Content Management

The ArsDigita Community System framework is a complete application framework, released in open source under a modification to the Mozilla open-sources license (which we discuss in Chapter 7). ACS consists of both a Core module, for general application support, and a more specialized Content

Management module, specifically aimed at providing services for creation, management, and publication of Web content.

The ArsDigita Core system provides user and group management, authorizations, and various other services such as versioning, email, and categorization. The Core consists of an infrastructure layer, handling issues such as startup, database connections, logging, among others, the Kernel layer, handling authentication, authorization, request dispatching and related functions, and the services layer, providing a higher level of functionality such as email handling, categorization, and page generation.

5.1.5.1 BeBop
The presentation layer of ACSJ makes use of BeBop, a toolkit for server-side Web user interfaces. BeBop provides a UI capability similar to the Swing UI for client-side Java applications, but specifically created for and optimized for performance in the Web environment. BeBop automatically preserves the state of the UI from one request to another, allowing the developer to build rich interactive UIs from reusable components without having to explicitly handle state for each component. BeBop produces XML, which is then transformed via an appropriate XSL stylesheet to produce the markup for the specific browser. BeBop's basic building block is a "Page" class, which contains a hierarchical structure of BeBop components. The Page object is instantiated and mapped to a specific URL when the system is initialized. Each request to that URL is then served by the same Page object, with listeners being used to tie the components to specific application logic as required.

5.1.5.2 Application Objects
ACSJ represents logic via Application Objects. These objects belong to one of two categories: Domain Objects, or elements from the problem domain, such as a product, account, customer, etc., and Process Objects, which contain logic for using domain objects to perform a task, such as "bill the customer," "credit the account," and so forth. Domain objects have a specific state and identity at any point in time, while process objects are generally stateless. Requests by the user are routed via a Dispatcher object to the appropriate application logic.

5.1.5.3 Data Objects
The persistence mechanism in ACSJ is provided by Data Objects, which allow the data of a domain object to be stored and retrieved. Basic add, update, and delete functionality are provided for by data objects. Each domain object is

defined in a Persistence Definition Language (PDL), which specifies the mapping between the database tables and domain objects, providing it in an XML format usable by the persistence layer. Data can also be accessed via other persistence stores, such as LDAP servers.

ACSJ has been around for a while, and has experienced a great deal of development. It is currently undergoing some refactoring toward a new release, and supports an active mailing list.

Next we will examine one of the most feature-rich frameworks available, also hosted by the Apache Foundation, and the basis of one of the other projects we examine later. Turbine also interfaces well with several of the presentation frameworks we will examine.

5.1.6 Turbine

Name	Turbine
Website	http://jakarta.apache.org/turbine/index.html
Supplier	Apache Software Foundation
License	Apache License
Focus	Complete Application Framework
Feature Summary	Modular design, oriented to the Web developer, flexible persistence layer, configurable UI system

One of the most comprehensive application frameworks available today, Turbine has a large and active developer community. It provides services to the entire application development life cycle, allowing database-oriented Web applications to be created quickly and easily.

Turbine is a full-featured application framework provided by the Apache foundation. It consists of over 200 classes separated into five basic modules, and provides services for virtually any type of Web application.

Turbine's intended audience is Web engineers, not necessarily Web designers. It provides tools for integrating with presentation technologies (such as JSP, Velocity, Freemarker, and Cocoon's XSP), but Turbine itself concentrates on providing application services.

Turbine has recently been segmented into a number of subprojects that combine to form the whole framework. This allows components of Turbine to be used outside the framework itself, so developers can choose the portions of Turbine that they need for a particular project, and even use Turbine components in other frameworks if required.

5.1.6.1 Torque

Torque is the persistence layer for Turbine, and is responsible for generating both the code and the required SQL statements needed to access a database. Torque works from an XML database design file, generating code to use Turbine's Peer mechanism as an object-relational mapping for the specified database. It is also able to create HTML documentation describing the database for easy reference. Torque provides tasks that can be accessed via the Ant build utility to create databases, generate DTDs, import and export data, generate XML schema information, create Velocity templates, generate SQL, and generate documentation. Torque also provides the runtime environment in which the generated code can operate, including connection pooling to the appropriate database. It supports a wide variety of popular database engines, and others can be readily added as required. Torque uses the Peer mechanism, which evolved from and uses an older project called Village. A Peer is a class with a one-to-one mapping to a database table. An adaptor mechanism connects the Peer to the selected database, allowing the same object to be used across multiple database engines. A Data Object is then used to access each row within the specified database table. The Peer system and its related objects provide the ability to select, update, and add data, and allow complex multitable queries to be quickly created without having to utilize the underlying SQL directly.

5.1.6.2 Fulcrum

Fulcrum is the services framework portion of Turbine – it provides a backbone for services to integrate with, and can be used independently of the entire Turbine framework. Fulcrum allows "pluggable" implementations to be used for all of its services, enabling complete customization of each service for a particular use. (Work is currently underway to use Avalon for this instead.)

Some of the services connected to Fulcrum are caching, Intake (a service for receiving input from forms and providing appropriate validations as specified in an XML definitions file), localization, pooling, scheduling, file upload, and XSL transformation among many others.

5.1.6.3 Stratum

Stratum is more of a collection of subprojects that are still under development and not really a subproject. Some of these components will likely be relocated into other subprojects, and include general-purpose configuration capabilities (including support for XML-based configuration), exception handling (with chained/multitiered exceptions), generic Factory handling code, a global caching system, and pooling and lifecycle components.

5.1.6.4 Maven
The Maven project is an effort to unify management for software development projects. Based on a project "model," Maven brings together project information, documentation, metrics, and cross-references. It is a tool to assist developers, particularly developers on large and complex interrelated projects. Although still evolving, Maven is already bringing significant benefits to the Turbine development effort, and is slated for use in a number of other popular open-sources projects.

Turbine has a few key classes that encapsulate logic and control application flow. They fall into the following groups:

5.1.6.5 Actions
User requests are first routed by the Turbine Servlet to a "Page" module, which contains the remainder of the elements required to prepare the response. A Page class uses a Screen class to access the layout of the page it will generate. This Screen class calls a reusable Layout object to specify the overall orientation of the response page; that is, the sections of the page such as the header, footer, and body, which can be populated with navigation and content. The specific Screen used can be determined by the Action module, discussed below, and a default layout is provided. A Screen class provides the means for the markup to be generated that forms the body of the completed Web page.

An Action class is the primary logic wrapper for Turbine. This is where the application logic goes, and an action is called in response to user requests. When a user request is made, the Turbine Servlet (the controller Servlet in the MVC model) executes the appropriate Page. The Page in turn is responsible for running the Screen, providing layout and navigation, and linking through to the Action class for application results. This division allows an individual Action object to be reused in different areas of the application.

5.1.6.6 Navigation
Part of a page's response is to provide navigation for the application. The Layout object used to prepare a page response to the client executes a Navigation class to determine what form this navigation information will take. Because it is normal for the same navigation to be provided to many different pages, the Navigation (and Layout) object can be reused as necessary, in combination with different Action classes, to built the complete application.

Turbine is a very active framework, with extensive development and frequent releases. It is among the more mature frameworks available today, and supports a busy mailing list and a large developer community. It is the foundation for a number of other Apache projects, such as the portal framework Jetspeed, which we will examine in more detail later in this chapter.

For an example of Turbine at work, see the Turbine case study in the Appendix.

Next we examine a commercial offering, a framework well suited to large J2EE application development.

5.1.7 Wakesoft Architecture Server

Name	Wakesoft Architecture Server
Website	http://www.wakesoft.com
Supplier	Wakesoft
License	Commercial
Focus	J2EE Application Development
Feature Summary	J2EE design pattern implementations, tool integration.

The Wakesoft Architecture Server, a commercially available framework, provides frameworks and facilities for all areas of application development, including application logic, persistence, and presentation. It is designed for easy customization and extension.

Wakesoft provides an implementation of the core J2EE design patterns as recommended by Sun Microsystems, as well as extensive services to Web applications, including:

- *Application logic:* Provides a service-oriented mechanism for containing your application logic and connecting it to requests and views.
- *Persistence:* Provides a configurable persistence framework for data storage and retrieval.
- *XML integration:* Allows XML data to be easily integrated into your application from multiple sources.

The product provides integration with the TogetherJ and Rational Rose UML/design tools, and is compatible with a number of different application servers.

Like many other frameworks, Wakesoft allows the Struts framework to be integrated for presentation support.

Wakesoft's product is built around nine distinct sub-frameworks, each providing specific services to your application:

- **Server-side presentation**: Provides services for creating presentation logic, focusing on providing reusable components for JSP pages.
- **Navigation Framework**: Provides the Controller in the MVC pattern, and provides the mechanism by which requests are routed to the appropriate application logic.
- **XML Information Exchange Framework**: Provides services for reading and writing XML data streams.
- **Business Object Framework**: Provides an architecture for containing business data and relationships independent of your choice of persistence mechanism.
- **Application State Management Framework**: Provides configurable and flexible data caching mechanisms.
- **Application Logic Framework**: Encapsulates application logic components and provides for their collection into specific processes.
- **Persistence Framework**: Provides object persistence independent of the exact storage mechanism (e.g., Entity Beans or Data Access Objects).
- **Object Key Framework**: Provides a unique key (sequence) generator service.
- **Logging Framework**: Configurable logging mechanisms for use by all application components.

Our next framework takes the opposite extreme from Wakesoft and Turbine: it is a lightweight, minimalist framework providing primarily presentation support (with multiple options as to the actual presentation layer used) and a flexible database persistence mechanism.

5.1.8 Niggle

Name	Niggle
Website	http://www.niggle.org
Supplier	Jonathan Revusky
License	BSD-Style License
Focus	Persistence and User Interface
Feature Summary	Simple and powerful persistence layer, pluggable user interface layer.

Niggle is a complete application framework that focuses on a flexible UI implementation and on a powerful data persistence capability. It allows Servlet-based applications to be created rapidly and with far fewer lines of code than would normally be required by providing a high-level library for the application to build on.

Created in 1999, Niggle originated from a development project to allow UI flexibility for an existing application. By providing a higher level API, Niggle allowed multiple templating engines to work with a single application. Niggle partitions the application development process into distinct areas, providing a backbone for component reuse and speeding application development considerably.

5.1.8.1 Persistence

Niggle provides a persistence mechanism independent of any specific data source, isolating the application from the exact mechanism used to store and manipulate data. Relational databases, XML databases, or plain ASCII data files are all options for the storage mechanism. Niggle uses a data API called Oreo to provide this independence, and provides three implementations of the Oreo interfaces with the package: text file persistence, Relational Database Persistence (RDP), and XML file persistence. Custom implementations are straightforward to add.

External XML files specify the data source information and the "record metadata," or definitions of specific record types. Records are defined and associated with a particular class, which must implement Oreo's "Record" interface, or the DefaultRecord implementation will be used automatically if no class is specified. The individual fields of each record are then defined, each field being associated with a type and a name. The type of each field is again defined as a specific class, and various default types are included. A regular expression for field validation can also be defined in the XML file.

Once this external definition has been created, Niggle applications can access the appropriate record object, create "mutable" (changeable) copies of any existing record, and update the changes back to the data source. The application is not concerned with the nature of the persistence mechanism, allowing an application to begin by using simple text (or XML) files for persistence and later be converted to use a relational database by changing nothing by the external configuration file.

5.1.8.2 Presentation

Niggle provides a generic presentation API, where the implementation can be any of several choices, by default Freemarker, but allowing WebMacro and Velocity as supported options.

All requests are responded to with a "Page" object, created by an appropriate PageFactory, where this page is rendered back to the client in response, after the appropriate application logic has been applied. The selected template engine then processes the page as required to intermix the application data and markup.

The Niggle project has a low-traffic mailing list and substantial documentation on its website.

Now we examine a commercial offering again, this time a framework focused on Web services – we examine Web services in Chapter 11 in detail.

5.1.9 Systinet WASP

Name	WASP
Website	http://www.systinet.com
Supplier	Systinet
License	Custom Evaluation and Commercial License
Focus	Web Services
Feature Summary	Strong integration with various IDEs, easy creation of Web Services

One of several software products available from the Systinet company, WASP is a development framework oriented around Web services. It is a commercial product, but is available at no charge for noncommercial or development use. WASP is oriented for use within the Sun Forte integrated development environment.

WASP allows the creation of a Web service from three basic elements: its interface, embodied by the WSDL file for the service, the actual implementation of the service (e.g., the application logic), and the deployment information, specifying the deployment portion of the WSDL description of the service.

A group of Web services that make up a complete "Deployment Package" comprise the finished application.

Systinet provides a series of products that make up the WASP series, including:

- **WASP developer:** Tools to integrate with your IDE (Integrated Development Environment) to enable the creation of Web Services quickly and easily. Includes specific versions for Forte, Jbuilder, and Eclipse.
- **WASP server:** A server environment for deploying Web services, with support for SOAP and WSDL. A "lite" version is available free for commercial use.
- **WASP UDDI:** An implementation of the Universal Discovery and Directory Interface (UDDI) allows clients to locate and get information about available Web services. We discuss UDDI in detail in Chapter 11.
- **WASP security:** An implementation of a Web service to provide single sign-on for a domain of authenticated users.

Web services are a new and vital part of the Web application development community, and their importance is likely to grow in the future. We discuss the impact of Web services in detail in Chapter 11.

Our next framework is also a commercial product. Like Wakesoft's offering, it focuses on J2EE application development including EJBs.

5.1.10 realMethods

Name	realMethods Framework
Website	http://www.realmethods.com/framework.html
Supplier	realMethods
License	Commercial license, per developer seat or unlimited
Focus	Complete application framework for full J2EE environments
Feature Summary	Extensive support for the whole J2EE environment with concrete implementations of best practice design patterns

The realMethods framework, a commercial product, takes a very thorough pattern-based approach to framework design. Applications built with this framework are designed specifically for deployment in a full J2EE environment, utilizing EJB and providing a concrete implementation of the Sun J2EE blueprints for application developers to build from.

The framework provides design pattern implementations on each of the three J2EE "tiers." The framework uses a single entry-point Servlet, and has been successfully integrated with the Apache Struts framework for enhanced JSP functionality.

The view of a realMethods framework can utilize JSP, Servlet, and other presentation technologies. The framework handles the routing to appropriate views, as well as the connection of request to the appropriate business logic. "Worker Beans" provide the connection between the presentation tier and the application logic, with every action being associated with a worker bean as required.

Using the proxy pattern, requests for logic are delivered to EJBs, typically Session beans, for processing. This provides for a separation of the MVC layers so essential to application maintainability. Session beans access the data access objects, which in turn provide the connection to the Entity beans with their persistent data in the application.

Data Access objects provide connection handling, as well as forming the access mechanism to application data. Pluggable implementations allow different persistence mechanisms to be used, and a default implementation is provided by the framework.

The application logic is accessed via a JMS Queue, implementing a version of the "command" design pattern (which we explore in detail in Chapter 8). This isolates the logic from the request and presentation portions, allowing individual logic elements to easily be reused. realMethods provides a base class for creating message-driven beans, via the JMS Command/Task Architecture. A single message-driven bean is used as an interface to Task and Command Java classes, eliminating the need to create individual JMS-enabled objects individually.

realMethods allows many different options for the presentation layer, including the popular Struts framework, which we discuss later in this chapter in more detail.

The next framework, another open-source project, again takes a unique approach to application "assembly."

5.1.11 Brazil

Name   Brazil
Website   http://research.sun.com/brazil/
Supplier   Sun Microsystems
License   Sun Public License
Focus   Server-building framework
Feature Summary Content aggregation and portal services

The Brazil framework takes the concept of a "server" beyond a simple mechanism for providing content stored in files: it allows the creation of URL-based interfaces to many different applications that were not originally Web-enabled. Brazil provides a toolkit of reusable components, enabling applications to be constructed by assembling their parts via these components.

Brazil introduces the concept of a "meta-server," that is, a server comprising the aggregation of a number of other servers. The meta-server provides portal and intermediary services, collecting the content (both dynamic and static) from multiple locations and providing a single access point. It allows content from other servers (or sites) to be automatically transformed into a cohesive format.

The basic component of Brazil that facilitates application assembly is the Handler. Handlers are provided for accessing URLs, parsing XML/HTML, template handling, and many other services. New Handlers can be implemented to extend and customize the framework's functionality. Handlers can be created to access any source of content, even legacy applications, allowing that content to be consolidated into a single site seamlessly.

Brazil is a research project of Sun Microsystems, and incorporates access to a number of other standard Java technologies, such as JMS (Java Messaging Service), Jini, and JRMS (Java Reliable Multicast Services).

5.1.12 OpenSymphony

Name	OpenSymphony
Website	http://www.opensymphony.com
Supplier	The OpenSymphony Group
License	Apache-Style License
Focus	Flexible J2EE Framework
Feature Summary	Set of J2EE components for easy integration into existing environment, many subprojects and modules. Meta-framework like integration capabilities.

OpenSymphony is an open-source complete application framework that provides a rich set of J2EE-compliant components for assembling Web applications. It is divided into a core set and a number of optional subprojects.

- *OSCore:* A set of core components and utilities common to all applications and submodules built using OpenSymphony.
- *PropertySet:* A component to manage typed mappings of property names and values, backed by a pluggable persistence mechanism that can use one of a number of actual peristence implementations: e.g., XML, EJB, Castor, etc.
- *SiteMesh:* A set of components designed to allow a website to produce content with a consistent look and feel and navigation system quickly and easily, using a combination of JSP and XML.
- *WebWork:* A set of components providing a "pull HMVC (Hierarchical Model/View/Controller)" presentation mechanism for Web applications. Multiple mechanisms for generating the resulting HTML are supported, including JSP, Velocity, and XML/XSL.
- *OSWorkFlow:* A low-level workflow component implementation, proving a basis for applications to utilize workflow capabilities.
- *OSCache:* A flexible, stable, and fast-caching mechanism that can be used for many different types of cacheable content.
- *OSAccess:* Components providing securable access to site data, based on user identification – providing the ability for users to only see their own data, for example. This is distinct from the OSUser subproject, which provides high-level user management and authorization.

A number of other components are under development for integration with OpenSymphony, and the project has a large and active developer community.

Some of OpenSymphony's components depend on a full J2EE (in other words, are EJB-enabled) container, whereas others are suitable for use in a servlet-only container (such as Tomcat).

5.2 PRESENTATION FRAMEWORKS

What is a "presentation framework"? In the most basic definition, a presentation framework is any library or framework that provides tools making it easier for a developer to build the user interface, or "presentation" side of a Web application. In your development, you probably already have encountered the problem: the easiest way to solve the problems of presentation often turns out to be the worst way, in the long run. When Java Servlets first came along, it was simple enough to embed a "print" statemente that wrote back to the HTTP response output with HTML (or WML) directly. Setting aside the problem of violating the principles of MVC, this solution also quickly becomes unmanageable due to the close coupling between the code and the markup – even the slightest change to the resulting page means recompiling the Java Servlet, and redeploying it.

JSP, by itself, as we have discussed earlier, makes the problem a bit easier, but it is not the whole answer. Often "basic" JSP does not have the advanced presentation power required, and developers resort to "scriptlets," which brings back the whole problem of markup embedded in code (or, in this case, code embedded in markup).

Some frameworks concentrate primarily on the presentation side of Web application development. They provide a way to separate the concerns of application developers from UI designers/creators, emphasizing the separation of logic and presentation, and at the same time facilitating the connection between those two concerns.

Presentation is an issue in Web application development for a number of reasons:

- The presentation mechanisms on the Web vary widely in both their markup and their capabilities. There is, of course, HTML (at various levels of standards), XHTML, JavaScript embedded in HTML, XML, Java Applets, Flash and all of its variations, WML for mobile devices, CSS in combination with HTML or other presentations, and so on. To make matters worse, a single application is often required to support more than one of these standards at the same time. This is somewhat similar to the problems of early "green screen" applications when they were faced with the multiple "clients" of

different terminal types – you wanted one application to appear correctly on many different manufacturer's terminals. In the old "terminal" days, however, you could count on at least some basic standards: a terminal normally had 80 columns, 23 or more lines. With the Web, however, a WML display area might be a matter of 2 square inches, whereas the same application also needs to work correctly for the user with a 23-inch flat-screen monitor.
- The Web is a request/response-based technology, by and large. HTTP is called a "connectionless" protocol, and is designed to have resources "requested" and then at the end of a request to send a "response," which the user then reads, possibly fills in some information, and then submits as a new "request," then the cycle repeats. This is quite different from client/server computing, in which the connection to the client side of the application is maintained continuously. It is a bit similar to some of the older "terminal" protocols, however, such as IBM's 5250, which had a similar "request/response" mechanism. This paradigm means that user interfaces should ideally be focused around a "page-at-a-time" interface, making ports of older applications to an Internet UI sometimes difficult.
- As one observer put it "the great thing about standards is that there's so many to choose from." Even amongst a single UI technology, such as good old HTML, there are variations in the supported level of the standard from one browser to another. Writing your interface to the lowest common denominator can lead to some bland, overly simplistic interfaces. Depending on features that may not be supported by your client's browser, however, can lead to complete failure of the application. Walking the line between these two can be greatly assisted by a flexible UI technology, where your application can "read" the capabilities of the client browser and adjust its responses accordingly, using as much as they have available and no more.

In an attempt to satisfy all of these requirements, presentation frameworks have sprung up that address these needs with varying degrees of success.

5.2.1 JavaServer Faces (JSF)

A specification has recently been developed (and was released in 2002) via the Java Community Process (JCP) to "define an architecture and APIs that simplify the creation and maintenance of Java Server application GUIs." This specification would provide, when completed, a standardized set of JSP tags and classes to provide a higher level tool kit for assembling GUIs for Web applications.

Development tools can then be built to take advantage of these standards to provide more advanced facilities for building GUIs than exist currently. Like many existing presentation tools, one of the goals of JSF is to allow the application developer to focus on the application logic, allowing the presentation to be created independently.

The JSF standard itself defines the API for device-independent user interface components. These components are then processed via a "rendering kit" to produce the visual representation to the user. As the user interacts with the UI, appropriate events are propagated back from the components to the application logic. This separation of layers ensures that any of these levels can be customized or replaced, allowing for compatibility with many different existing display technologies. For example, UI components can be rendered via an Applet where appropriate, or into HTML via JSP tags – the underlying application is not affected. This level of flexibility also allows JSF to interoperate with many existing presentation frameworks, augmenting their abilities. Although JSF is designed to allow easy access by page designers via visual tools, it also exposes the API to allow developers direct access where required – providing the best of both approaches in the proper circumstances.

JSF's components can maintain "state" information between requests, allowing multipage forms and a "wizard-like" series of pages to be easily constructed. Components can handle input data other than strings, making complex parsing and associated error checking unnecessary. Sophisticated validation layers allow UI-level validation to be handled independently of application logic, and an advanced and configurable error-handling mechanism also relieves the developer of the burden of creating a usable UI exception-handling mechanism.

Much like component-based development itself, JSF targets a number of different roles. The page designer, responsible for creating the user interface to the website or application, can assemble pages from a combination of markup and prebuild UI components. When used in conjunction with JSP, these will take the form of configurable custom tags. It is expected that visual design tools will make this process even easier over time. The component developer role in JSF is entirely separate: this is the job of creating the UI components themselves – often this will not even be a necessary role for many application development efforts, as existing component kits will be adequate for the majority of uses. The role of the application developer is separated from either of these – he or she needs only to be concerned with creating the application logic, along with any persistence mechanism (such as DBMS access), and provide application-level event handlers that respond to the events generated by the user's interaction with the visual components. These event handlers then pass on the information that the application itself needs to do its job, no matter what mechanism is being used to actually interact with the user.

Although it is not an established standard yet, JSF will soon have a significant impact on the presentation framework landscape. Although it is certainly not going to displace all other methods, JSF will establish a standard with which, no doubt, other presentation frameworks will become compatible with over time. The establishment of a standard will enable tool developers (such as IDEs and presentation-building visual tools) to work with a single established standard across all compliant frameworks. This will result in the release of visual tools rivalling the ease of use of Microsoft's Visual Basic (and, more recently .NET Studio), while at the same time preserving the greater flexibility and portability of Java Web applications.

None of the presentation tools available today make it as easy as a tool like VisualBasic to create flexible Web-based user interfaces, and the corporate developer is faced with a no-win choice. JSF and the subsequent adoption of it as a standard will change all of that, and the corporate developer will have a superior choice without sacrificing ease of use.

The creation of the JSF standard will no doubt have an impact on almost all of the presentation frameworks we discuss here over time – but its flexibility ensures that the unique advantages of existing presentation frameworks can be maintained while still providing a standard approach to interaction with a user interface.

There are a number of different approaches to content generation that are seen in presentation frameworks:

- **Servlets**: Simply writing Servlets with presentation markup embedded is the simplest approach, and is the one taken by many basic Web applications, or in situations where the client is known (such as with an intranet implementation). The disadvantages are, of course, what we have discussed above, and very few modern presentation frameworks use this approach any more.
- **Markup "construction kits"**: The next step up from embedded markup is the so-called "construction" libraries, where Java code is used to construct markup elements as objects, and a rendering step is made at the end of the process to convert the objects into the appropriate markup. An Apache project called Element Construction Set (ECS) was one of the best of these libraries, and is still in widespread use. It was powerful enough to allow many different options at time of rendering, and was suitable for more than

just HTML markup. It is still a somewhat dated technique in light of more recent developments.
- **Template engines:** The next generation of presentation tool was the template engine. A "template" containing "meta-markup" in the form of special tokens embedded in HTML (or WML, etc.) is created by the user-interface designer. Then this template is "populated" at the appropriate point before being presented to the user with the actual data from the application. The "tokens" or "templating language" used by the template was usually limited in the amount of logic it could perform – quite intentionally, as the forced separation of concerns of Model, View, and Controller is the desired result.

    Unfortunately, no standard exists for such a templating language (other than, perhaps, the de facto standard of JSP, which many consider to be a templating language), and each of the template engine approaches had incompatible scripting languages.

    Examples of this approach are Velocity, WebMacro, FreeMarker, and Tea, among others.
- **JSP:** JSP has become the de facto standard when it comes to HTML scripting in Java Web applications. Despite vocal criticism, and despite being compared to Active Scripting by Microsoft, JSP has developed and matured to the point where it is a highly functional approach to separating presentation and templating – if used correctly. As we discuss elsewhere, it is sometimes all too common for it to be used incorrectly, and to suffer the same problems as are encountered when embedding markup into Java Servlets directly.
- **XML transformation:** Having an application generate its user-interface objects and rendering those objects as XML has a number of advantages, as we discuss in detail elsewhere. The XML can be transformed, via the XSL stylesheet language(s) into any kind of markup – in this way a single set of UI objects can be rendered as HTML, WML, DHTML, etc. as appropriate, depending on the interaction with the client at the time. This is an approach used by a number of presentation frameworks, including especially the presentation portion of the Cocoon framework. It is also an option for several others, such as Struts, Expresso, and Turbine.
- **DOM manipulation:** A final approach is used by at least one presentation framework: Barracuda uses the technique of accessing the markup via the XML Document Object Model (DOM) – viewing markup as a "tree" of objects representing the XML form of that markup, then allowing the application to manipulate the XML before it is regenerated as markup for presentation to the client.

This provides good separation of the content from the code, and allows the logic to remain entirely in the Java code, while using programmatic "hooks" in the markup to make it easier for the developer to manipulate nodes in the DOM hierarchy.

There are a number of frameworks that concentrate on a specific area of the application development process. A number concentrate on the "presentation" or User Interface area, making it easier to write applications in a way that makes them as independent as possible of their user interface techniques. We will look at a number of the more popular techniques, and see what their similarities and differences are.

5.2.2 Struts

Name	Struts
Website	http://jakarta.apache.org/struts/index.html
Supplier	Apache Software Foundation
License	Apache License
Focus	JSP presentation, flexible connection to application logic
Feature Summary	Strong and Flexible Design patterns powerful tag library

The open-source Struts framework, which is one of the most successful and popular Web-application frameworks available, provides key capabilities to the developer for building virtually any Web application – especially those that make use of JSP pages as their user interface technology. Struts can, however, interact with many other presentation technologies that include XML/XSLT and Velocity.

Struts is more than a presentation framework, even though its focus is on the view and controller side of application building. It also provides services for configuration, internationalization, and application logic.

Struts uses a special Servlet to provide the "C" in MVC – the Controller. In Struts, the controller is a powerful routing system, passing requests made by the user on to the correct application logic and then directing the results to the appropriate "view." This provides a clean separation between the Controller and the View, as well as the more common separation of the Model from the other two.

Struts provides for encapsulation of the logic for an application in objects called "Actions." These actions are triggered by requests from the user. Typically, for every JSP page in the finished application there will be one or more Action classes, and possibly an ActionForm class as well. Pages are associated with Actions via a central configuration file, and the resulting "view" from each action is specified in this file as well, allowing the application to be configured easily and quickly.

A major capability of Struts is the included JSP custom tag library. Custom tags allow the standard capabilities of JSP to be extended with tags that are particular to an application. Struts provides several categories of custom tags, which can be used to rapidly build sophisticated views for the application, while at the same time avoiding the pitfall of embedded logic in presentation pages.

The tags are collected into tag libraries, where each library provides a specific group of functionality:

- **HTML tags:** This tag library provides custom tags for building HTML-based user interfaces, especially forms for user input. Tags include custom internationalization tags, which read the appropriate language- and locale-specific string from an external messages file, conditional display of context-specific error messages, and tags for building links to other pages with the correct URL encoding.
- **Template tags:** The template tag library provides tags used for consolidating several files into a single page – it allows for easy reuse of standard headers, footers, and other common page elements. The template library has a number of proposed extensions that provide even more sophisticated templating and portal-building capabilities. These extensions will probably become a part of the standard Struts distribution over the next few versions of the framework.
- **Logic tags:** The logic library provides tags that allow looping and branching. This eliminates the need to write "scriptlets" into JSP pages (a practice that is not recommended for any use of JSP), whereas still allowing collections of objects to be used and decisions on presentation issues to be made at the time the page is rendered.
- **Bean tags:** This library provides the ability to manipulate objects provided by the logic of the application as JavaBeans. This provides the means to display application data, and to access special "ActionForm" beans that act as the middleman between the JSP and the underlying Action objects that hold the application logic. JSP provides special tags to access the properties in JavaBean objects, and the Struts Bean tag library builds on this, providing means to create new bean objects and access properties quickly and easily.

Struts has complete documentation, especially for its tag library. It includes sample applications – an essential for any framework.

Struts is also well known for its stability – its straightforward design facilitates use in large projects without introducing errors.

Struts relies on a single-key Servlet, the ActionServlet, that routes all requests to the appropriate Action object, and then on to the view.

The configuration of the Action Servlet in the web.xml file, also includes key configuration information for the framework, including the location of the single configuration file, struts-config.xml. All Struts actions are mapped to a specific extension, such as ".do" or ".action." All requests are then prefixed by an action prefix, followed by this special suffix.

Struts also allows a single action to be associated with multiple views, allowing the same logic to present different user interfaces. For example, a default view might be the normal UI, then an alternate UI specified as an "error" UI, to notify the user of a problem. The mapping from an Action to its potential "views" is done in a single XML file, allowing the view to be changed without any impact on application logic. This central configuration file contains all of Struts' startup information, including:

- **Data source configuration:** Struts provides access to JDBC data sources, any number of which can be defined.
- **Form bean definitions:** Struts allows a JavaBean class to be associated with any form to facilitate the transfer and validation of data to and from the form.
- **Global forwards:** This is the ability to define a logical name and associate it with either an Action or a specific view – for example, "error" can be defined as a global forward to "/something/displayerror.jsp." This global forward can then be used instead of specific URLs later in the configuration, allowing all references to be changed at once if required.
- **Action mappings:** The bulk of the configuration file is usually used for defining the associations between a specific Action class and a path associated with that class: e.g., "/Login" can be associated with "com.yourcompany.actions.LoginAction." Each action/path combination is then associated with a number of "forwards," which specify the valid views from that action. There may be more than one view specified, and the Action logic can forward to the selected view by means of a logical name, allowing pathnames to be kept out of the actual application logic. For example, the Action might call the view named "approved," which might map to a JSP page in "/something/views/approval.jsp." If the jsp ever changed, only the configuration file would need to be updated.

Presentation Frameworks   **173**

Many third-party additions and extensions to Struts have been created, and a number of these are being actively considered as candidates for inclusion in the "base" Struts project. They provide capabilities such as XML/XSL-based views, SSL security, and portal-type UI extensions to Struts.

In addition, a number of Struts components are sufficiently capable of being used on their own that they have been "separated" from Struts to enable them to be used in other ways – these include many of the JSP custom tags (which have been included in the Apache Taglib project, separate from Struts itself), and the Digester – the utility in Struts that reads its XML-based configuration information.

A Struts page is very familiar to anyone experienced with JSP, but a well-written Struts JSP avoids any scriptlets at all, using, instead, the rich tag library available with the framework. For example:

```
1: <%@ page language="java" %>
2: <%@ taglib uri="/WEB-INF/tld/struts-html.tld"
3: prefix="html" %>
4: <%@ taglib uri="/WEB-INF/tld/struts-bean.tld"
5: prefix="bean" %>

6: <html:html locale="true">
7: <head>
8: <title>
9: <bean:message key="hello.title"/>
10: </title>
11: <html:base/>
12: </head>
13: <body bgcolor="white">

14: <html:errors/>

15: <html:form action="/helloworld" focus="yourname">
16: <table border="1">
17: <tr>
18: <th align="left">
19: <bean:message key="hello.name"/>
20: </th>
21: <td align="left">
```

```
22: <html:text property="yourname" size="20"
23: maxlength="30"/>
24: </td>
25: </tr>
26: </table>

27: <p align="center">
28: <html:submit property="submit" value="Say Hello"/>
29: </p>

30: </table>

31: </html:form>

32: </body>
33: </html:html>
```

In the above example, the Struts-specific usage begins with line 2, where we "import" the two tag libraries used on this page. Then we use the tags to prepare an internationalized dynamic page:

- On line 14 we use a high-level error-handling tag: if the user's input is not valid (they enter their name in the wrong format, presumably), this form will be redisplayed, but with the "html:errors" tag expanded to describe what the validation error was, so the user can try again.
- On line 9 we use the "bean:message" tag to access an externally supplied message bundle file. The string associated with the key "hello.title" will be substituted, presumably saying the immortal call "Hello, World" in the appropriate local language.
- On line 15 we see the use of the "html:form" tag, associating this form with an action, in this case, the URL "/helloworld."
  We would have mapped this URL in our struts-config.xml file to be identified with an appropriate Action class. Nothing about this form dictates what that action does, or what the next view might be.

This is an extremely simple example of the most basic capabilities of the tag library, but already the capabilities of Struts are providing enhanced application functionality and ease of development.

Struts is one of the most popular and widely used application frameworks in existence today, and supports a busy mailing list and an active developer community. A number of books are available specifically about Struts and its use in Web application development. Many other frameworks also either incorporate Struts directly (such as Expresso), or allow it as one of the options to be used as a presentation layer (such as realMethods, Wakesoft, and several others).

For an example of a Struts application, see the Struts case study in the Appendix.

5.2.3 Maverick

Name	Maverick
Website	http://mav.sourceforge.net
Supplier	Infohazard.org
License	MIT X-Consortium license
Focus	Presentation
Feature Summary	Lightweight MVC Web-publishing framework

Maverick is a lightweight MVC-based framework for Web application development. It provides a pluggable mechanism for selecting a view mechanism; any of several different templating engines can be used as required.

Maverick provides support for internationalization, and allows transformation via both XSL and other technologies (such as DVSL, a Velocity-templating language).

The Maverick framework is supplied with substantial documentation and a good set of example applications showing its use with a number of different template engines.

5.2.3.1 Domify

Maverick includes and utilizes another project, called Domify. Domify is essentially the opposite of an XML parser – it is an XML generator, where the XML Document Object Model is generated from any arbitrary structure of objects. This permits existing object hierarchies and structures to be emitted as XML, making it simpler to "XML-enable" your application.

Our next presentation framework takes an approach that differs considerably from the template engine way of handling presentation. It allows Web UIs to be built in a manner more closely resembling the way desktop applications with Swing are constructed.

5.2.4 Scope

Name	Scope
Website	http://scope.sourceforge.net
Supplier	Steve Meyfroidt
License	BSD-type license
Focus	HMVC Presentation
Feature Summary	Provides sophisticated swing-compatible user interface for Web applications

The Scope framework provides a different approach to presentation for Web applications. Generally, the HMVC (Hierarchical Model View Controller) model is considered less than suitable for Web application development, because it implies fairly "heavyweight" architecture for user interfaces. Scope overcomes that problem, however, and provides a very rich UI mechanism that can allow an application to be used with either the standard Swing user interface directly, or a Swing-like front end suitable for Web deployment.

Scope provides field validation and event handling, coupled with a model that makes it easy to get data to and from the appropriate user interface pages. When a user makes a request, a Control object begins a sequence of events that result in the appropriate model (or application logic) element being notified. When the application state changes as a result of logic, the reverse sequence allows the model to notify the view, via a hierarchy of components back to the user's page. This two-way synchronization allows a Web application to provide a kind of interactive experience normally only seen with Applets or desktop applications. Any JavaBean model object can be used as the application logic connector, and Scope is designed to allow new kinds of beans to easily be "plugged in" to this layer.

Scope also provides localization support, and a set of unit tests to verify the function of the framework itself.

Scope's approach to user interface construction more closely resembles that of a desktop application, and is very useful for applications that need to be highly interactive.

Good documentation is available for the project, along with a number of simple example applications.

The next presentation framework we examine is one of the more popular template engine solutions – it is incorporated as the presentation mechanism to many applications in daily use.

5.2.5 WebMacro

Name	WebMacro
Website	http://www.Webmacro.org
Supplier	Semiotek Inc.
License	Apache-style License
Focus	Template Processing
Feature Summary	Template Language

WebMacro is a popular and well-established presentation-oriented framework: it concentrates on providing an alternative to JSP and other UI technologies. It is released under an open-source license, and closely follows the Model–View–Controller pattern.

WebMacro provides a highly focused template-scripting language, and a powerful class analyzer to connect elements referred to in the script to application classes. It allows you, as the developer, to avoid HTML in code, and at the same time keeps the code out of the HTML. This prevents page designers from having to be dependent on Java programmers, and vice versa, providing independence to these two tasks and allowing page design and development to proceed in parallel.

WebMacro requires a Servlet engine, but not necessarily a full J2EE-compliant server, allowing it to scale from small single-server deployments into larger clustered deployments. The framework is configured via a single properties file and is easy to install even in conjunction with other frameworks.

The template-scripting language in WebMacro is specifically designed for presentation: it is, quite intentionally, not a general-purpose programming language. Arbitrary logic is not allowed – only logic appropriate to presenting data in a page is permitted. WebMacro's scripting language can access fields directly in Java objects, or can use JavaBean "accessor" (get/set) method. For example, if an object has a getTotal() method (following the JavaBeans design pattern), then

```
$theClass.Total
```

can be used in the WebMacro template to refer to the current value of the Total field, as retrieved by the getTotal method. You can also refer to non-JavaBean style methods, such as "total()" (as opposed to getTotal()):

```
$theClass.total()
```

Java developers find this an entirely natural notation, and page designers adapt to it easily. Methods can also be called with arguments from the template:

```
$theClass.calculateTotal("param," $otherParam);
```

This shows an example of a scripting variable used as one of the parameters. This method of calling methods, however, requires the page designer to have a direct understanding of what methods are available and the appropriate meaning of parameters, blurring the line between page design and development somewhat more than is recommended.

WebMacro builds on the JavaBeans specification for its class analysis, the mechanism that allows the templates to be "hooked up" to the business logic of the application. By analyzing your business logic classes and looking for specific method signatures, WebMacro can access field names, accessor (get/set) methods, and hashtable accessor methods. The results of this class analysis determine the variables and methods that are available to the template-scripting language.

For efficiency, WebMacro caches the results of its class analysis, so this processor-intensive step is not repeated for every request. The actual invocation of the accessor methods (via Java's reflection API) is the only repeated process at run time.

WebMacro supports high concurrency by making each template thread-safe: multiple threads can be accessing the same template at the same time.

In Chapter 7, we discuss the concept of an open-sources project being available under two separate licenses – WebMacro is an example of this technique in use.

Our next framework is a new approach to the same template issues as addressed by WebMacro. This one, however, is developed from a different codebase, by a different group.

5.2.6 Velocity

Name	Velocity
Website	http://jakarta.apache.org/velocity/index.html
Supplier	Apache Software Foundation
License	Apache License
Focus	Template Engine
Feature Summary	Template capabilities with Macros, extensive tool support

Velocity is much like WebMacro: quite intentionally. As a result of a licensing conflict, performance concerns, and other circumstances, the Velocity project attempted to recreate the bulk of the functionality of the WebMacro framework, but starting without the benefit of the WebMacro code base.

Velocity is used as a service in many other frameworks, and is designed to be used either stand-alone, or "plugged in" as a general-purpose templating capability into virtually any project. It provides a simple yet capable macro language, and can be used to generate either Web-browser-compatible markup, such as HTML or WML, or even SQL, XML, and Java code.

A Velocity page looks a lot like a WebMacro page, understandably. Here is a simple example of a Velocity template:

```
 1: <html>
 2: <head>
 3: <title>Hello Someone!</title></head>
 4: <body>
 5: <p align="center">
 6: Hello, $request.getParameter("name")
 7: </p>
 8: </body>
 9: </html>
10: </programlisting>
```

As you can see, this template consists almost entirely of standard HTML, with only one line (line 6) using anything specific to Velocity – in this case, displaying the value of the request parameter "name." Accessing model data is equally straightforward:

```
...
<td>Product: $product.descrip</td>
<td>Price: $product.price</td>
...
```

This clean and simple syntax is quick and easy for page designers to learn, and it does not disrupt the flow of the markup like JSP scriptlets can. Most page design tools will allow Velocity tags to be embedded without errors, allowing the page designer to use their existing tools for page creation. Add-ons for many popular development tools are available that make using Velocity templates easier, including IntelliJ IDEA, UltraEdit, JEdit, TextPad, Emacs, and others.

Velocity also uses an efficient one-time compilation, creating a compiled version of templates for efficiency once and updating it as needed if templates change. No Java compiler is required at run time, as templates are not translated into Java Servlets. Templates can even be stored in repositories other than the file system – for example, in a database, allowing great flexibility.

Error handling is also more manageable in Velocity, as the templates cannot contain any Java code, eliminating the possibility of Java errors in templates at run time, and providing more specific and straightforward errors when a template is incorrect.

A number of other projects utilize Velocity to provide specific template-based services, such as:

- *Texen:* A general-purpose text-generating utility, integrated with the Ant build tool, able to produce virtually any text output such as SQL, Java Code, etc.
- *Anakia:* A Velocity-based XML transformation tool, frequently used to generate documentation from XML source documents.
- *Declarative Velocity Style Language (DVSL):* A tool similar to XSLT, providing XML transformations using Velocity templates, but with easy access to arbitrary Java objects.
- *Veltag:* Access to Velocity template language directives via a custom JSP tag library.

A popular and stable project, Velocity still undergoes frequent new releases for new features, performance enhancements, and other updates. A moderately busy mailing list for both users and developers is available.

Other more complex examples can be seen in the code listings for the Turbine case study, in the Appendix.

Tapestry takes another approach to presentation. It allows complex user interfaces to be built easily from components and yet allows for page designers to create the markup itself.

5.2.7 Tapestry

Name	Tapestry
Website	http://tapestry.sourceforge.net
Supplier	Howard Lewis Ship
License	LGPL (Library GNU Public License)
Focus	User interface
Feature Summary	Allows creation and interaction with highly dynamic pages and forms

Presentation Frameworks   **181**

The Tapestry framework is another approach to the user interface issue in Web applications. It is an alternative to JSP and other similar approaches, and relies on a sophisticated object model instead of a pure templating approach.

In keeping with our habit of show more, tell less, we will examine a quick snippet of an HTML file used by Tapestry:

```
<p>Hello, <span jwcid="insertName">Mr. User</span></p>
```

As you can see, Tapestry uses a special attribute of the span tag to identify a portion of the markup as a component (jwcid stands for Java Web Component Identifier). This element is then available to be populated by the application logic as a component in the user interface. The default value, "Mr. User," is automatically replaced at run time with the correct dynamic value.

Each component is then further defined in a component specification file, a special XML-based configuration file with a .jwc extension. The jwc file specifies the bindings of a particular UI component to the associated property of an object, and the binding of the component's parameters. This forms the association between the component as specified in the markup and the actual runtime objects in the finished application. An entire Page is a specialized type of component with no parameters – it contains all the other components that make up the finished page.

Unlike many other UI technologies, Tapestry allows the UI specifications to be largely made external to the application code, keeping the actual amount of code that must be created to an absolute minimum.

Tapestry pages may have a "state," comprising the set of values for all of the components of the page. The lifespan of each component can be either persistent, where the state is recorded and the values persist between request cycles (specific to each user), transient, where the state is reset at the end of the current request, or dynamic, where the property can change even while the page is displayed, and again reset at the end of a request.

5.2.7.1 *Spindle*

The Spindle project deserves special mention in connection with Tapestry. In Chapter 8, we examine the relationships between IDEs (Integrated Development Environments) and frameworks. Spindle is a project that connects the Tapestry framework to the Eclipse IDE, providing wizards and editors that run within Eclipse. These wizards allow Tapestry user interfaces to be easily created from within the IDE.

Now we examine a hybrid approach, combining some of the best capabilities of XML and XSLT with component-based user interfaces.

5.2.8 Barracuda

Name	Barracuda
Website	http://barracuda.enhydra.org
Supplier	Lutris Technologies/Enhydra.org
License	Enhydra Public License
Focus	Server Components
Feature Summary	Unique and flexible XMLC-based approach to template handling and content generation.

The Barracuda project is a presentation framework specifically designed for Web applications. It provides an extremely clean separation between application logic and presentation by means of event-driven processing. Event-driven processing of course, is nothing new, but has been used successfully in client/server applications for a long time. Barracuda is aimed at the Java Developer, not the page author necessarily.

Barracuda is a very modular presentation framework, consisting of a number of components that can be used or replaced as required, providing substantial flexibility to the developer. The template engine in Barracuda is a component itself, and can be combined with other UI approaches, rather than forcing the developer to pick one particular approach to the exclusion of others. Barracuda's component-oriented approach also makes it highly extensible, which we will discuss further on.

Instead of providing a way to incorporate logic into the presentation, Barracuda takes the opposite approach: the presentation templates are compiled into Java classes. These classes are then instantiated and manipulated using standard W3C DOM (Document Object Model) interfaces, and the resulting combination produces the final presentation to the client. The idea here is a familiar one to many frameworks: allow the developers to concentrate on coding, and allow Web designers to concentrate on markup and presentation.

A drawback to this approach is the complexity of the normal DOM interfaces — Barracuda addresses this by providing a set of components that provide elements for building the user interface, much like the Swing framework. The developer simply implements a Model interface to provide the connection to the application logic, and the components provide the actual rendering required.

Presentation Frameworks

Barracuda provides specific tools for dealing with HTML forms, providing a mechanism for developers to "map" form fields and elements to Java objects. These objects can then be handled by the application logic directly. Special validators are also provided to allow creation of sophisticated data-entry validations by assembling preexisting components.

Barracuda builds on the presentation technology called XMLC, which provides your application with the ability to read and parse an HTML (or other markup) file and manipulate it as a DOM object tree. This provides the application with complete access to the markup to insert dynamic content as required. The markup is enhanced with id and class attributes to allow the application logic to locate the appropriate portion of the DOM tree at run time. Once the application has manipulated the DOM tree to include the appropriate dynamic portion, it is then rendered back to the client as the response page, possibly including processing via XSLT if required.

For example, if we look at the following segment of valid HTML 4.0 markup:

```
1: <HTML>
2: <HEAD>
3: <TITLE id="title">My Title</TITLE>
4: </HEAD>
5: <BODY BGCOLOR="white">
6: <SPAN id="text1">First bit of Text Goes
7: Here</SPAN>
8: <P>Some Static text</P>
9: </HTML>
```

We see the use of the "id" attribute for the TITLE tag on line 3, and the SPAN tag with the id attribute to enclose text on line 6. These become the elements visible from our application logic later on. The following code fragment might be used to manipulate the DOM tree generated from this markup:

```
1: HelloWorldExample ex = new HelloWorldExample();
2: HTMLTitleElement title = ex.getElementTitle();
3: title.setText("Hello, World!");
4: ex.setTextText1("Hello Again, World!");
```

Here we see the title element accessed, and the contained text set to "Hello, World!," instead of the "My Title" originally seen in our HTML. The same is done with the text labeled "text1" (between our SPAN tags) – it is replaced with "Hello Again, World!" by our application at run time.

Barracuda provides a unique and powerful presentation technology, which is being extensively used in many new applications. The supplying organization, Enhydra.org, provides a number of other related tools and technologies, and supports an active Website and development community.

Now we will examine a commercial offering that provides a UI methodology compatible with the JSF (JavaServer Faces) API, still undergoing the final specification building via the Java Community Process.

5.2.9 HyperQbs

Name	HyperQBS
Website	http://www.qbizm.cz/hyperqbs.html
Supplier	Qbizm Technologies
License	Commercial License
Focus	Flexible UI creation
Feature Summary	Building reusable and highly flexible server-side UI components.

HyperQbs is a commercially licensed product, designed as a framework for rapid development of J2EE applications. It supports the MVC architecture, and complies with the design goals of the JavaServer Faces JSR (JSR-127) (discussed in detail earlier in this chapter).

HyperQbs provides a set of reusable plug-in components for the presentation layer of Web applications. Its Configurable Application Flow rule engine allows custom component assembly without coding. HyperQbs's abilities make it possible to create your application independent of any user interface protocol. It supports fast prototyping, personalization and localization, multiple devices (HTML, WAP, voice, multimedia and others) and is both scalable and extensible.

Prebuilt components for user interface assembly make prototyping of applications fast and easy using HyperQbs, and yet custom components can easily be added, then reused on other projects. The finished user interface is device-neutral, can be used with HTML, WML, and virtually any other markup language, and supports full internationalization and localization. Each presentation component (or "Qb" (Cube)) can be packaged independently and deployed as required in any application.

As an early adopter of the JavaServer Faces API, HyperQbs brings many of its proposed benefits to Web developers today, and is an important presentation tool.

Next we will examine a framework that provides template capabilities in a lightweight, portable form, and encourages complete isolation between application logic and the view.

5.2.10 Tea

Name	Tea
Website	http://opensource.go.com/
Supplier	Walt Disney Internet Group
License	Tea Software License (similar to Apache)
Focus	Presentation and Template engine
Feature Summary	Lightweight Servlet template engine

Tea is another example of the concept of a templating engine. It is a framework for generating dynamic Web pages via a Servlet (the TeaServlet), enforcing the separation between logic and presentation. At the same time, Tea provides the essential basic programming capabilities needed for flexible and attractive user interfaces with its templating language.

The templating language is easy to learn and use, making it approachable by page designers with no specific programming experience. Tea isolates the application and presentation completely, preventing direct access to data sources from the template and preventing the template from initiating logic. This prevents incorrect or intentionally harmful templates from causing application problems. Tea templates are compiled into byte code, just like a Servlet, and executed like ordinary Java classes at run time.

Tea templates consist of text regions and code regions. Text regions are ordinary markup – such as HTML, WML, etc., and are sent verbatim to the client. Code regions, delimited by <% and>, contain the logic statements.

5.2.10.1 Kettle

Kettle is an IDE designed specifically for editing Tea templates. It provides special features that make it easier to create and manipulate Tea templates with Kettle compared to a general-purpose text editor, including grouping of multiple templates into projects, viewing of template source code and HTML output, compilation and error checking of Tea templates, and syntax highlighting.

5.2.10.2 Trove

Trove, a separate subproject, is a library of collected classes used by Tea and the TeaServlet runtime. It includes APIs for creating Java class files, logging to both files and databases, and utilities such as caching, property file management, and thread pooling.

Trove can be used independently of the other Tea components in your own applications.

Another lightweight and performance-conscious framework, Freemarker is one of the original open-sources template engines.

5.2.11 Freemarker

Name	FreeMarker
Website	http://freemarker.sourceforge.net/
Supplier	Benjamin Geer, Johnathan Revusky
License	BSD License
Focus	Template engine for presentation
Feature Summary	Lightweight, high-performance template solution

Another template engine approach, Freemarker provides a high-performance, easy-to-use template language for application presentation.

Freemarker provides a Template object that your application instantiates in order to retrieve a reference to a particular compiled template. Application data is then supplied to the template as a "tree" structure, making it available to tags in the template for display. Although templates are frequently used for Web presentation, Freemarker can be used for any templating requirement, including Java code generation, email personalization, text and XML transformation, and more.

Let us consider a simple Freemarker template:

```
1: <html>
2: <head>
3: <title>Hello, World</title>
4: </head> <body bgcolor="#FFFFFF">
5: <p>${message}</p>
6: </body>
7: </html>
```

As you can see, this is for the most part just HTML – with a single special token for the "message" to be provided at run time. Now, we can access the template from a Servlet such as:

```
1: private Template myTemplate;
   ...
2: String templatePath =
3: getServletContext().getRealPath("/hello-world.html");
4: try {
5: template = new Template(templatePath);
6: } catch (IOException e) {
7: throw ...
8: }
```

Now that we have a reference to the appropriate template (which in a production application would be read by some type of configuration, as opposed to being hard-coded as in our example, of course),we can use it as follows:

```
1: SimpleHash modelRoot = new SimpleHash();
2: modelRoot.put("message,"
3: new SimpleScalar("Hello, world!")); // Process the
   template.
4: template.process(modelRcot, res.getWriter());
```

Freemarker is a very straightforward extension to the basic Servlet model, and is readily understood by most Servlet programmers without a large learning curve. It is high performance and lightweight, making it well suited for combination with other frameworks that provide application services, or with existing applications that currently embed HTML in Servlets.

Freemarker includes an Ant task, allowing transformations to be made from within an Ant build process.

Our next framework utilizes the client-side capabilities and power of JavaScript to provide a rich and flexible UI driven entirely by the application.

5.2.12 Echo

Name	Echo
Website	http://www.nextapp.com/products/echo/
Supplier	NextApp
License	LGPL (Library GNU Public License)
Focus	Sophisticated user interfaces for Web Application
Feature Summary	Event-driven multiwindow user interfaces for Web application development

The Echo framework takes a different focus on supporting Web application development. Concentrating on providing an alternative to other methods of handling presentation, Echo allows the developer to concentrate on application logic. It provides an event-driven framework that parses HTTP requests, and passes on user actions as events to the application logic.

Echo provides an extensive library of visual components that are combined into finished user interfaces. No HTML need be created, and the interface can easily utilize multiple windows, as the UI can extend beyond the standard page-oriented style common to Web applications. This is more like the style used in traditional desktop applications than the approach taken by most current Web applications.

By integrating Javascript, Echo's UI can support multiple layouts, scrollable panes, and other features usually only associated with desktop GUI applications.

Custom GUI components can be created and reused. They can combine any of the base components into a high level form or element of the finished application.

Echo is ideal for a developer-oriented project, where page design is not imperative, as no HTML or Javascript experience is required.

Consider the following code fragment:

```
Window window = new Window();
ContentPane content = new ContentPane();
window.setContent(content);
Label label = new Label("Hello, World!");
content.add(label);
```

In the above, we see a new "window" (literally, a window in the browser when deploying on the Web) being defined. A ContentPane (which contains all content) is associated with this window, then a simple label with the inevitable "Hello, World!" is added to this pane. When the finished window is displayed, the text is displayed with the appropriate markup in the user's browser. No templates, no markup, just straight application-driven user interface functionality.

As Web applications become more widespread, functions traditionally provided by desktop programs will be taken on more and more by new Web applications. These applications will require the level of user interface responsiveness and flexibility that desktop users are accustomed to, as opposed to the more "content-oriented" design of many of today's Web applications. Echo is an ideal tool for just this purpose.

5.3 OTHER APPLICATION-SPECIFIC FRAMEWORKS

We will now look at a few of the more popular application-specific frameworks – frameworks designed to handle either a particular type of problem domain (such as accounting), or to deal with a specific part of the development process, such as presentation, database persistence, or XML handling. Some of these frameworks border on APIs, in that they provide a pallet of services that requires other framework elements before they can be assembled into a complete application – the line between a library and a framework blurs a bit with application-specific projects.

A category of application-specific frameworks are frameworks that are intended for use on any kind of application, but only provide *part* of the services needed to complete an entire application. The most common type of framework in this category is the presentation framework – they are of different types and are treated in a separate section above. Other examples abound, however, and often these frameworks are incorporated into complete application frameworks to provide part of their overall services. A fine example of this is the Xerces XML parser framework, which is extensively used by other frameworks that need to deal with XML, such as Struts, Expresso, Cocoon, and many others.

Such "horizontal" application-specific frameworks are differentiated from "vertical" frameworks. Vertical frameworks are usually intended for use within a specific business problem domain, such as accounting or insurance. Vertical frameworks provide services that are specific to their domain – like calculating exchange rates, making actuarial forecasts, and so forth. The more vertical they are – that is, the more specific, and the more services they provide to the particular area – the less reusable they are in other application areas. There are few examples of vertical frameworks for Web applications, as the advantages of a framework diminish when the problem domain becomes too focused. Reuse becomes more difficult, as the domain-specific features of an application are often its key differentiator, so the advantages of offering those features for reuse are offset by the advantage of keeping them proprietary.

What differentiates a framework providing application-specific functionality and an API? Sometimes the line is thin, but in general, the most distinguishing feature is that the frameworks tend to have pluggable implementations, and provide a complete set of capabilities in a specific area of functionality. APIs tend to provide only one service, whereas most frameworks provide several related services. As we have mentioned in Chapter 1, an API is essentially an interface, so any framework can be said to possess an API as part of its capabilities – the interface by which applications make use of their services.

We will start this review with one of the most widely used frameworks in this category, the Apache Xerces XML project.

5.3.1 Xerces

Name	Xerces
Website	http://xml.apache.org/xerces2-j/index.html
Supplier	Apache Software Foundation
License	Apache License
Focus	XML Parsing and Processing
Feature Summary	Supports a rich set of parsing and processing options for both SAX and DOM standards for handling XML documents.

Xerces is a framework dedicated to a specific part of application functionality: for example, XML. Used extensively in both open-source and commercial application frameworks, for both the Web and desktop, Xerces provides a highly flexible XML parser and related tools.

Xerces supports the XML 1.0 standard, with the second edition recommendations, DOM (Document Object Model) level 2, including numerous recommendations of this standard, the SAX (Simple API for XML) 2.0 specification, and implements the Java API for XML Processing (JAXP) version 1.1.

Xerces is also a "fully conforming" processor of XML schemas (version 1.0, with additional recommendations), meaning that it complies with the most extensive standard for XML schema processing defined by the XML schema specification.

Xerces provides the means for many applications to interact with XML documents or data streams. The DOM standard allows an XML document to be treated as a "tree" of objects, and traversed and manipulated as required. It is highly flexible, but sometimes for very large documents it can be very memory intensive. SAX, on the other hand, is more "stream" oriented. It processes an XML document or stream by "walking" the structure, and triggering events as necessary as each node and element is encountered. This makes it ideal for very large data sources or XML documents, and for situations where only a part of the source needs be dealt with.

5.3.1.1 XNI

Xerces contains a specification called the Xerces Native Interface, or XNI. This is a framework and set of interfaces used for implementing parsing components and for transmitted streaming document information. The Xerces2 parser is one instance of an implementation of the XNI interfaces, but others can be plugged in as necessary.

XNI is not a specification that the user of XML services from Xerces needs to deal with: the developer can utilize the normal JAXP, SAX, and DOM protocols without ever having to see XNI. It is only when a different parser behavior or implementation is required that this flexible underlying mechanism is used to integrate the new implementation.

Now let us look at a common companion to Xerces, used in many different frameworks to provide XML transformation capabilities.

5.3.2 Xalan

Name	Xalan
Website	http://xml.apache.org/xalan-j/index.html
Supplier	Apache Software Foundation
License	Apache License
Focus	XSL Transformation
Feature Summary	Flexible and powerful XML transformation services, allowing XML to be changed into any other XML-compliant format, such as HTML, WML, etc.

The Xalan XML transformation framework is frequently used in conjunction with the Xerces parser. It allows the parsed XML to be *transformed* into any other XML-based format, according to a set of rules and specifications supplied by the XNI.

In its latest incarnation (version 2), Xalan is an implementation of the TRaX interfaces (Transformation API for XML), a part of the JAXP specification. TRaX uses configuration properties to determine which XML parser and XML transformation capability to apply at runtime, allowing an application complete flexibility in implementation.

Xalan provides a complete implementation of the XSL Transformations standard, version 1.0, and the XPath (XML Path Language) specification, also version 1.0.

5.3.2.1 *XSLT*

XSL, or the eXtensible Stylesheet Language, consists of two transformation specifications. The first is XSLT, or XSL transformations. This refers to the process of converting, or "transforming" one XML document of a particular class (or DTD) into another. The second specification is XSL-FO, or XSL Formatting

Objects. XML-FO is an XML language for specifying formatting in a highly detailed and fairly low-level format – it is in fact used in some instances for preparing printed pages, or the pages of PDF documents.

XML Transformation Process

```
                                    XML with any valid format
    ┌─────────────┐
    │ Source XML  │
    └──────┬──────┘
           │         XSL Stylesheet(s)
           │                │
           │                ▼
           │        ┌───────────────┐
           └───────▶│ XSL Processor │
                    └───────┬───────┘
                            │
                            ▼
                    ┌───────────────┐      HTML
                    │  Output XML   │      PDF
                    └───────────────┘      FOP
                                           SVG
                                           WML
                                           etc.
```

The stylesheet containing the XSL is specified as a declarative set of transformations. Pattern matching is used to select the subtrees and elements from the source XML, then to map these subtrees and elements to specific outputs in the resulting XML. XSL is an expressive language – computations, iterations, and other logic functions can be performed as part of the transformation process, allowing for enormous flexibility in the transformations themselves.

XSL is used for more than formatting transformations, however; it is also a powerful data format conversion tool. For example, if we have an application that stores name and address information, like a Rolodex, it may be able to output its data in an XML stream that looks somewhat similar to this:

```
1: <contact>
2: <name>Fred Burns</name>
3: <title>President</title>
4: <company>XYZ Software</company>
5: <email>fred@xyzsoft.com</email>
6: <phone>(242) 352-1414</phone>
7: </contact>
```

Other Application-Specific Frameworks

Our email program can import XML, but requires rather the following format:

```
1: <address>
2: <person>Fred Burns</person>
3: <email>fred@xyzsoft.com</email>
4: </address>
```

We can use XSL to transform the input into the output. As you can see, we need to select only a subset of the available information, as well as change the names of one of the elements, mapping "name" to "person," for example. This is a *very* simple example, and vastly more complex transformations are commonplace. The following XSL will do the job for us:

```
 1: <xsl:stylesheet
 2: xmlns:xsl="http://www.w3.org/1999/XSL/Transform"
 3: version="1.0"
 4: xmlns="http://www.w3.org/1999/xhtml">
 5: <xsl:template match="contact">
 6: <address>
 7: <person><xsl:value-of
 8: select="name/text()"/></person>
 9: <email><xsl:value-of
10: select="email/text()"/></email>
11: </address>
12: </xsl:template>
13: </xsl:stylesheet>
```

This XSL can just as easily contain HTML fragments, WML markup, or any other template information to transform the same input stream into multiple formats on output, each output format being specified by a particular stylesheet.

In summary, XSLT and stylesheets are a powerful facility that can be utilized in many different areas of your Web application. Xalan is a popular tool for providing this functionality, both for data conversion and user interface generation.

One of the most popular latest technologies currently in the Web application world is Web services, and an essential element of Web services and their interoperability is Apache's SOAP project.

5.3.3 Apache SOAP and Axis

Name   Apache SOAP
Website   http://xml.apache.org/axis/index.html
Supplier   Apache Software Foundation
License   Apache License
Focus   Java access to Web Services and the SOAP protocol
Feature Summary   Ability to publish and subscribe to Web services, plus utilities for generating necessary WSDL and Java classes.

The Apache SOAP (Simple Object Access Protocol) project provides an implementation of the SOAP version 1.1 protocol in an open-source project. It is frequently used with other complete application frameworks to provide SOAP-based access to their services and components. The project provides both client and server capability, and support SOAP messages with attachments.

SOAP, the protocol used by applications to access and provide XML-based Web Services, is an essential part of many new business-to-business Web applications on the Internet today. We examine Web Services and SOAP in more detail in the Web Services section of Chapter 11.

As a client library, Apache SOAP can be used to access and use services provided by other applications via HTTP or SMTP. These services do not need to be Java applications, allowing it to provide a cross-language link. The project provides an API for both sending and receiving SOAP messages from any Java client application.

As a server, Apache SOAP provides the necessary APIs to create message-accessible services from any Servlet container. It is used in conjunction with a Servlet container providing the HTTP support, such as Apache Tomcat. SOAP can be used to publish services from other applications without modifying the existing code, making it an ideal mechanism for opening up access to legacy data and services.

Apache SOAP requires some configuration in the form of XML parser libraries, secure socket extensions (if SSL is to be used), and of course the Servlet engine (or SMTP and POP3 protocol support if using SOAP over those protocols).

5.3.3.1 Axis

The Apache SOAP project is in the process of evolving into a new project for its version 3.0 release, the Apache Axis project. Axis is a rework and redesign of Apache SOAP to use an internal SAX-based model, rather than the DOM model

Other Application-Specific Frameworks

of the existing SOAP project, so as to increase performance and flexibility. It is intended to eventually supersede the SOAP project when it is finally released.

Our next framework focuses on content management, and on providing services appropriate for building applications that need this facility specifically. It is a good example of a framework that addresses a specific need while still remaining extensible and configurable enough to provide a true toolkit approach.

5.3.4 Slide

Name	Slide
Website	http://jakarta.apache.org/slide/index.html
Supplier	Apache Software Foundation
License	Apache License
Focus	Content Management
Feature Summary	Extensible WebDAV capabilities for Content Management

The Apache Slide project provides a framework for the construction of content management, as well as many out-of-the-box content management facilities. It provides an API for access to content management functions, as well as a complete implementation of the WebDAV (Web-based Distributed Authoring and Versioning) protocol, both for the client and server side of the protocol.

Slide includes a client for WebDAV, for both the command line and the Swing UI. This is a supplement to the built-in WebDAV capability that some desktop and authoring tools are now providing, including Adobe Acrobat 5 and GoLive, DreamWeaver, Microsoft Internet Explorer, and Office 2000, and other popular applications. Slide can provide WebDAV interfacing to many different types of repository, such as databases, file servers, XML content stores, and others. Each repository type involves coding a small abstraction layer to allow the slide to interact with it. The slide's WebDAV server module is implemented as a Servlet and can operate in virtually any Servlet container, including Apache's Tomcat, for example.

5.3.4.1 WebDAV

WebDAV, or the Web-based Distributed Authoring and Versioning protocol, defines a standard for collaborative applications. It provides a layer on top of the HTTP protocol for *writing* information, not just reading it. It specifies how to upload, edit, create, and delete "subdirectories" (which may or may not represent physical directories on the file system of the server) and to manage files via HTTP.

WebDAV support provides a number of powerful advantages: users can now access appropriate Internet repositories directly from their desktop applications that are WebDAV-enabled, allowing them to manage their own content and information directly. This allows geographically separated teams to collaborate on documents and content easily, and to manage versions and locking of the shared resource. These facilities can be applied to any type of document, not just HTML or XML, making WebDAV-enabled sites appear like network file systems, an approach many users are already familiar with.

Slide combines with a preconfigured version of the Tomcat Servlet engine/server for quick and easy deployment.

Now we examine a specialized commercial framework, one designed to provide services for a specific kind of client: portable devices.

5.3.5 Roaming Wireless Framework

Name	Roaming Wireless Framework
Website	http://www.objectventure.com/products/rwf.html
Supplier	Object Venture Inc.
License	Commercial (Customer Open-sources)
Focus	Access to wireless devices
Feature Summary	Framework for creation of applications requiring access to mobile and wireless devices of different types.

Roaming Wireless Framework is a commercial offering from ObjectVenture. It provides device-independent services for applications intended for wireless clients.

Incorporating open standards such as JSP with custom tag libraries, XML, and EJB, Roaming Wireless Framework operates in conjunction with ObjectVenture's ObjectAssembler product, a J2EE application development environment. The product allows an application to send the appropriate markup for a specific device type, determining the device type dynamically as required. The framework provides a JSP tag library that takes advantage of this: high-level tags are used that render device-dependent content automatically, and browser-specific libraries allow the special features of a particular device type to be accessed when available. Other custom tags allow access to EJBs for application logic, SQL for database access and XML content. Each tag is backed by an extensible object hierarchy, making customization easy.

Special support for Java 2 Micro Edition (J2ME) is provided – this is a special subset of the usual Java platform designed expressly for mobile devices.

Other Application-Specific Frameworks

Other services available to applications using the framework include security and session management for the mobile client, messaging and notifications including support for Short Message Service (SMS), and data-publishing capabilities for accessing data as XML (with optional XSL transformation).

Roaming Wireless Framework is released under a commercial source code license, providing source code advantages in a proprietary product.

For even more specialized types of applications, our next framework provides unique services. It is designed for creating agent-based applications, where the application logic is portable across servers.

5.3.6 JADE

Name	Jade
Website	http://sharon.cselt.it/projects/jade/
Supplier	Telecom Lab Italia
License	LGPL (Library GNU Public License)
Focus	Agent Development
Feature Summary	FIPA-compliant agent development framework

JADE, which stands for Java Agent DEvelopment framework, is specifically aimed at development of agents and multiagent systems. It provides a middleware layer that complies with the FIPA (Foundation for Intelligent Physical Agents) specifications as well as a set of tools for both development and deployment of agents. A configuration GUI that can manage applications on multiple systems is included.

FIPA works toward standards for agent communication and key agent definitions required for the management of an agent-based system.

The agents developed can be deployed across multiple systems and multiple platforms, and configurations can be altered even on a running system. Agents, by their nature, can move from one system to another as necessary.

Not many actual agent-based systems have been deployed, overall. Part of the reason for their slow adoption has been a lack of widespread acceptance of the standards to support them. Several other agent frameworks support the use of the well-known agent communication language, KQML. The FIPA 97 specification provides for an agent communication language similar to but functionally richer and more completely specified than KQML. JADE provides a FIPA-compliant platform for agent operation, and implements the Agent Management System, Directory Facilitator, and Agent Communication portions of the specification. The platform can be distributed across multiple servers.

JADE is distributed under the LGPL license.

Translation and transformation of data is not just a concern for presentation frameworks; however, many applications have a requirement to move data from one data source to another, usually with some kind of conversion, at least in format. Our next framework specializes in providing exactly that type of service.

5.3.7 Openadaptor

Name	Openadaptor (tm)
Website	http://www.openadaptor.org
Supplier	The Software Conservancy
License	BSD-type Open-sources License
Focus	Data integration and transfer
Feature Summary	Provides a flexible structure for transfer, integration, and transformation of data.

Openadaptor is an open-source project providing quick and simple business system integration, minimizing or eliminating custom integration development. It utilizes XML as a key data exchange format, and allows easy extension to support virtually any source and destination of data. Openadaptor makes B2B (business-to-business) integration much easier, reducing the cost of integration and making it more profitable.

Openadaptor provides the concept of "Sinks," or destinations or consumers of data, "Sources," or providers of data, and "Pipes," or transfer conduits and transformation mechanisms for data. Each of these components is fully extensible, allowing new data extractions, output formats, and conversions to be added easily, while maintaining the overall structure. Pipes are optional, so the simplest data exchange is directly from a source to a sink, with no conversion or transformation occurring at all.

Some of the immediately supported sources and sinks are databases, files, TCP/IP sockets, RMI, and several messaging protocols.

Data exchange can also be more complex than just point-to-point: mechanisms can be set up where a single source is sent to multiple sinks, optionally though one or more pipes. Pipes can be connected in sequence, allowing complex transformation and filtering to be accomplished.

Openadaptor provides a controller mechanism to provide startup and configuration of transfers, handle transaction management, and coordinating

Other Application-Specific Frameworks

communication between the sources, sinks and pipes as required. A powerful GUI configuration mechanism is provided for setting up transfers.

Default configurations allow for basic transfer to be accomplished with little configuration, providing "out-of-the-box" capabilities. For example, the provided "FileSource" can be connected to the "JdbcSink" to load data into a database directly. Default pipes provide basic transformation capabilities, including renaming and repositioning of source data, adding time stamps, and encryption/decryption of data.

Some of the more advanced features include "benchmarking" sources, allowing pseudo-random data to be generated at specific intervals for testing, and "remote control" capabilities allowing Openadaptor's operation to be monitored via a Web browser and various other management interfaces, including JMX.

Testing and verification is an essential process for any application, and several frameworks concentrate on exactly that. We will examine two different approaches to testing with our next frameworks.

5.3.8 JUnit

Name	JUnit
Website	http://www.junit.org
Supplier	JUnit Group
License	Common Public License
Focus	Unit testing
Feature Summary	Lightweight framework for defining Unit Tests, Test Suites, and Fixtures

JUnit is one of the group of projects collectively known as the XUnit testing frameworks, with the "X" being specific to each language: JUnit, of course, being the Java implementation.

We discuss the importance of unit testing, and its relationship to the Extreme Programming methodology in Chapter 8. JUnit provides a simple, easily implemented framework for unit tests. Each test is easy to create, collect into test suites, and to run.

5.3.8.1 Unit Tests

When a specific unit of code needs to be tested (or, preferably, when a test needs to be created *before* a unit of code is written), all that is necessary is to subclass the TestCase abstract class, and implement the constructor and one required method: runTest(). In the runTest method the actual code to perform the test is created – the assertTrue method can be used to determine if a test condition has been successfully met.

5.3.8.2 Fixtures

When a particular test case needs to be reused on other similar objects, a test fixture can be created. This is simply an extended test case with more than one testing method. A single setup() and tearDown() method for the fixture handles initialization and clean-up, then each of the tests can be run against the configuration. Often the set-up for a test is more complex than the test itself, particularly if it involves getting the application into a specific state, or populating a database with a particular assortment of test data before tests are run.

5.3.8.3 Test Suites

A collection of different unit tests can be gathered together into a test suite. A test suite can be automatically created from all available unit tests, and then the resulting suite can be run as a single operation. This allows a complex series of tests to be executed all together, and the results reviewed, and eliminates the need to test each unit individually.

5.3.8.4 Running Tests

Once test suites have been identified, JUnit provides a mechanism for executing those suites: test runners. Both a command-line test runner and a test runner with a Swing-based GUI are included with the framework. A number of extensions have also added Servlet and JSP-based test runners, making Web application testing more straightforward.

The test runners automatically run an entire suite of tests, and record both the failures and errors – a failure is an anticipated condition where a particular test is false, and an error is an unexpected condition such as an exception being thrown. The test runner shows the particulars of the test that failed, along with appropriate stack traces and statistics on the overall suite of tests.

JUnit is commonly incorporated into other frameworks, and is used extensively throughout the Java development community. Many extensions and customizations have been made to JUnit, and a large number of other more specialized testing products are available that are compatible with the framework, including products specific to testing XML, databases, and other application areas. Functional testing extensions have also been created that allow testing of an integrated application complete in its runtime environment, a topic that goes beyond unit testing.

5.3.9 Anteater

Name	Anteater
Website	http://aft.sourceforge.net
Supplier	Ovidiu Predescu, Jeff Turner
License	Apache-style License
Focus	Functional Testing
Feature Summary	Integration with Ant for functional testing Web applications and SOAP services

The Anteater framework is designed for the creation and execution of *functional* tests. It extends the popular "Ant" utility (an Apache project) with custom tasks. Ant is a highly configurable replacement for the venerable "make" utility. It improves on "make" in a great many areas, however, one of them being the ability to easily extend Ant with custom tasks. Ant itself is written in Java as well, and is therefore highly portable.

Anteater is an example of a framework that is generally used in the development and test phases of your project – it is not necessarily included with the run time version of your finished application, unlike most frameworks we have examined.

Anteater extends Ant with three custom task types:

- Action tasks
  An action task is used to emit or receive an HTTP request. When receiving, an Action task is defined to contain multiple matches, which are evaluated when the appropriate request is received. When sending, an action task begins the sequence of a functional test.
- Matcher tasks
  Action tasks can contain one or many matcher tasks, which define the response you expect to receive. If all tests associated with a matcher task succeed, the matcher task itself is successful. Each matcher task associated with an action task is checked in turn until one succeeds. Once a matcher for an action succeeds, the action itself is successful. An action with no matchers is immediately successful.
- Test tasks
  Test tasks are contained within matcher tasks. A test task is used to examine some attribute of a response and compare it to a specified value. If the test is successful, the next test is evaluated (if any) until the entire matcher task is either successful or fails.

Given this structure, Anteater tasks can be written so that they can send a request to a specific server (using either GET or POST-type requests), receive the response, and check the response headers and body for particular properties.

The reverse is also possible: Anteater can listen for incoming requests at an specific URL, test that request, and return an appropriate response.

Anteater tests can even be configured to operate through firewalls (with an appropriate proxy server), and contain special functionality for use with SOAP services.

Given the importance of testing in Web applications, a test tool is valuable, but Anteater fills an especially interesting role. Unlike projects such as JUnit, which concentrate on unit testing, Anteater allows you to test an application in its actual deployment environment. Web applications are complex combinations of a number of different layers, and short of using actual users, the kind of URL-based testing that Anteater provides gives you the best chance of catching problems that might not be obvious when testing individual layers. This is the power of a *functional* testing framework, as opposed to lower level unit testing.

Now, we examine a group of frameworks that bring a specialized capability to not only Web applications, but *groups* of Web applications. Portal frameworks are intended to collect multiple sources of content into a single easy-to-use point of access for users. They often consolidate many different Web applications – possibly from different servers or companies – into one place.

At first glance, it might seem that portal frameworks belong in the section on presentation – their visible aspect being the most obvious, the way they allow a user's screen to be shared by multiple applications, usually providing configuration options to customize the display. However, this is only the visible aspect of portal frameworks – some of their more important features are behind the scenes, as we will see later.

5.3.10 Jetspeed

Name	Jetspeed
Website	http://jakarta.apache.org/jetspeed/site/index.html
Supplier	Apache Software Foundation
License	Apache License
Focus	Portal construction
Feature Summary	Portal building, XML content handling, access to syndicated content

The Jetspeed project is a framework for the construction of Web portals. Portals are gaining popularity in both the Internet and in internal intranet applications, and some de facto standards of portal creation are beginning to emerge.

Making powerful use of XML and XML-oriented content handling, Jetspeed brings many of these standards together, providing a powerful and extensible portal implementation.

Portals provide a common point of access for diverse online resources, such as applications, documents, databases, enterprise information systems, and more. They provide access to these resources for users of multiple device types, such as a Web browser or a portable device (PDAs, Web-enabled cellular phones, and so forth). A portal provides a single junction point where the available resources can be organized according to a user's preferences and authorization, and easily accessed when required.

Unlike many application-specific framework projects, Jetspeed can be set up and used almost immediately, without necessarily writing any code at all. At the same time, it can also be easily extended into a custom portal solution, or to aggregate content types that are specific to a particular deployment.

Jetspeed presents content via a flexible system of templates, and supports use of multiple content publication frameworks, including Cocoon, Velocity, WebMacro, and JSP pages.

The Jetspeed project began its development before the Turbine project, in fact Turbine was started partly in response to the need for a more generic application framework. Jetspeed became more focused on the portal-building capabilities, and now utilizes Turbine as its underlying application framework, providing even easier extensibility for related custom applications.

One of the significant developments in the Jetspeed project has been the creation of a "Portlet" API. Analogous to a Servlet, which runs within a Web server environment, a Portlet is a subapplication that runs within a portal environment. By defining a specific API for Portlets, creation of new custom Portlets is greatly simplified. A Portlet must implement the org.apache.jetspeed.portal.Portlet interface, either directly or through inheritance. Jetspeed provides abstract Portlet classes that implement default behaviors for the Portlet API, making creation of new Portlets simpler. This makes writing a Portlet as easy as implementing a single class to return the Portlet's "content" (the getContent method), although many Portlets are more complex and require more of the Portlet API methods to be implemented for their functionality.

Jetspeed also provides an implementation of an OCS (Open Content Syndication) engine with support for the Rich Site Summary (RSS) standard for site definition and change notification. This allows Jetspeed access to multiple channels of content made available from other sites that provide content in these standards. RSS is an XML format designed to allow changes to a site for easier "broadcast" to all sites using the syndicated content, and OCS provides an XML-based service permitting sites to share their public content with other sites.

Jetspeed also provides a sophisticated content cache to maintain performance, and a powerful security layer with personalization and role-based permissions. Users can customize both their layout and presentation, defining which Portlets will appear on their home portal page, as well as the colors and display attributes of the overall "skin" of their portal.

5.3.11 OpenPortal

Name	OpenPortal
Website	http://openportal.sourceforge.net/
Supplier	Nordija
License	GPL (GNU Public License)
Focus	Portals
Feature Summary	EJB-based portal-building framework

OpenPortal is a framework for creating personalized pages out of multiple "portlets." A portlet can be a Web page, JSP page, Servlet, or several other options.

This project relies on Enterprise JavaBeans, JSP, and Servlets, and must be deployed on an EJB-enabled J2EE server. OpenPortal is in the fairly early stages of development, and documentation is currently a bit sparse.[1]

5.3.12 uPortal

Name	uPortal
Website	http://mis105.mis.udel.edu/ja-sig/uportal/index.html
Supplier	Java in Administration Special Interest Group (JA-SIG)
License	BSD-Type license
Focus	Portal construction
Feature Summary	Flexible and configurable portal services, with an emphasis on features needed by educational institutions

[1] Note: A number of other projects using the name "OpenPortal" exist, so if you are looking for this project, make sure you have the right one.

Other Application-Specific Frameworks

uPortal is another approach to providing portal capabilities in an extensible framework. Created by a group of educational institutions, uPortal provides some specialized capabilities for this group.

uPortal provides services for collecting content from a variety of different sources, then selecting specific "channels" of content for presentation to a particular user, based on their customized layout. This content is then put through a process termed "structure" transformation – that is, where the overall organization of the layout is organized from a user's layout specification. This stage of transformation is not specific to any one markup language. The content is then handled by "theme transformation," where the actual markup is generated and the content from each channel incorporated into the overall presentation to the user.

uPortal makes extensive use of XSL transformation, both for structure transformation and theme transformation. It concentrates on the access and conversion of channel information, and does not itself contain or generate content.

uPortal's channels are defined by a channel-publishing document, which describes the channel, the Java class used to access it, and other configuration information specific to the channel. New channels can be defined by configuring existing channel interfaces, or by implementing the iChannel interface to create news ones. A channel is then registered with the portal, making it available for publication. The channel must then be "published," assigning its configuration and making it ready for users to subscribe.

uPortal can interface with existing authentication and authorization mechanisms, by default using a database store for user login information. Permission is granted as required for specific activities for each channel.

The uPortal project is mature and usable at its current level, and enhancements and additions are made on a regular basis. A great deal of development, deployment, and user documentation are available to allow developers to get started with the framework. uPortal is already powering portal sites for over fifteen universities and schools, with more slated for deployment soon.

Some frameworks specialize in providing the database access services an application needs. These range from simple enhancements of basic JDBC capabilities all the way to full object/relational mapping layers that are independent of the storage mechanism entirely.

When looking at persistence mechanisms, do not forget about the complete application frameworks that have powerful persistence capabilities built in: Turbine, for example, has a persistence layer that can be used with other frameworks, as do several others.

Let us explore a few of the more interesting offerings in this area:

5.3.13 Simper

Name   Simper
Website   http://simper.sourceforge.net
Supplier   Bryan Field-Elliot
License   Apache-style License
Focus   Persistence
Feature Summary Lightweight, simple persistence framework

Simper provides much of the functional capabilities of container-managed persistence with Enterprise JavaBeans, but provides them to applications without the overhead of a full J2EE deployment.

In a small, simple package, Simper provides automatic maintenance of data objects, saving them to the underlying data store as necessary. Persistent objects are JavaBeans, and rely on the method signatures of JavaBeans for getting and setting properties of the object. By the use of "dynabeans," a term coined to indicate JavaBeans that do not have property-specific getter and setter objects, Simper provides the ability to access tables without generating any code for the persistent object.

Simper allows queries to be defined, which can be accessed by means of a convenient mnemonic name for repeated use. Rows can easily be created by a single method call and primary keys are automatically retrieved where appropriate (for sequential identifiers).

For applications that require a framework to wrap raw SQL without a lot of overhead and learning, Simper provides a good choice. Although it does not provide all of the sophisticated features of some of the other choices in this area, not all applications need those choices.

5.3.14 Object/Relational Bridge

Name   Object/Relational Bridge
Website   http://jakarta.apache.org/ojb
Supplier   Thomas Mahler
License   Apache License
Focus   Object/relational mapping and database access
Feature Summary Transparent persistence, full ODMG 3.0 compliant API, JDO compliance (under development)

The Object/Relational Bridge project provides sophisticated object/relational mapping, as the name would imply, and much more. It uses an XML-based mapping between objects and their relational counterparts. The mapping can be dynamically updated, changing the persistence layer's behavior at run time. Bean-managed persistence for Enterprise JavaBeans is supported, allowing Object/Relational Bridge to be used in EJB applications for distributed deployment.

The project provides a PersistenceBroker to allow applications to store and retrieve arbitrary Java objects in any JDBC data source, and to retrieve records as objects from the same data source. It automatically handles references between hierarchies of objects, allowing all related objects to be retrieved from the original object, support one-to-one, one-to-many, and many-to-many relationships. Caching is used to reduce overhead of object retrieval.

Object/Relational bridge handles generation of unique sequential IDs, and provides its own connection pooling and prepared statement pooling.

This framework can be deployed in one of two modes: as a service in the same virtual machine as the application, or as a "server," running independently and providing PersistenceBrokerService to more than one virtual machine – possibly on different servers altogether.

Object/Relational framework is undergoing active development and supports a busy mailing list. JUnit test cases are abundant, and the documentation, although still growing, is already quite substantial and usable. A JDO-compliant interface to Object/Relational is undergoing active development, and should be available soon to the user.

5.3.15 Castor

Name	Castor
Website	http://castor.exolab.org
Supplier	Exolab Group
License	BSD-like
Focus	Persistence and Data Binding
Feature Summary	Data binding with multiple data stores, including XML, SQL tables, and LDAP directories.

Castor is a powerful open-source framework for "data binding," where persistent objects can be bound to one of a number of possible data sources.

Castor's features include access from a Java object hierarchy to and from XML, object persistence to and from virtually any relational database, object access to LDAP directories, exchange of data from LDAP via XML, high-performance caching and "lazy-write" on commit, full support for two-phase commit including rollback, and deadlock detection.

To facilitate queries, Castor provides OQL (Object Query Language) mapping to standard SQL.

Castor's persistence capabilities all start with the PersistenceEngine interface. When an application requires persistence services, it requests an implementation of a PersistenceEngine from the PersistenceEngineFactory. All persistent operations are transactional, meaning they support the idea of an atomic operation that can either be committed or rolled back as a unit, so that all such operations happen within the context of a TransactionContext instance. Every persistent object is identified with a unique object identifier, or OID, and with an object lock. Both read and write locks are supported, with deadlock detection to prevent conflicts. Caching is used for all persistent operations, using an instance of a CacheEngine class.

Castor supports queries by using the PersistenceQuery interface, allowing multiple objects to be returned in response to a query and allowing queries to be reused as required.

Castor provides a sophisticated and well-designed persistence layer for applications, and is used in many Web applications in production.

5.3.16 jRelational Framework

Name	jRelational
Website	http://jrf.sourceforge.net
Supplier	is.com
License	Mozilla Public License
Focus	Database access
Feature Summary	Lightweight object/relational mapping layer

The jRelational framework is designed as a lightweight object/relational mapping layer for applications.

It provides object/relational mapping with support for assigning primary keys. It allows basic operations (add, update, delete, search) as well as permitting custom SQL queries where required. It utilizes an optimistic locking scheme (where the data is assumed not to have changed, and an exception thrown if it turns out that it has when an update is attempted). Persistent objects can access columns from joined tables, permitting cross-table queries.

The basic persistent class in jRelational, the PersistentObject, can be generated from an existing database. Connection pooling is provided, with the provision to use an external pool. The most popular database engines are supported directly, and new databases can be supported by implementing a simple interface (DatabasePolicy).

jRelational is an implementation of the Data Access Object pattern, a design pattern discussed in the Sun recommendations relating to EJB standards, and can easily be used in an EJB environment, although such an environment is not required.

Good documentation, a tutorial, and examples are supplied with the project.

Our next framework goes outside the usual capabilities of Web applications to provide services that enable flexible graphic output, an area often neglected in current Web applications.

5.3.17 Batik

Name	Batik
Website	http://xml.apache.org/batik/
Supplier	Apache Software Foundation
License	Apache License
Focus	Vector Graphics
Feature Summary	Provides ability to generate, manipulate and convert Scalable Vector Graphics

Batik is an open-source framework for manipulating, generating, viewing, and converting Scalable Vector Graphics files (we discuss SVG in detail below).

Batik provides developers with a set of modules that can be used within custom applications as required. These include SVG parsers, generators, and an SVG-DOM implementation, making it easy for applications to access the XML tree of an SVG image directly.

As SVG is a form of XML, custom tags can be used to extend its functionality, making it an ideal format for application-generated images.

Batik includes an SVG browser that allows the created images to be previewed with a Swing user interface. Although the browser is a client application, SVG is a highly suitable format for Web application graphics, due to its vector nature and extremely small image size. The ability for SVG to be generated from existing data sources by accessing them as XML adds to its usefulness in Web application development.

5.3.17.1 SVG

Scalable Vector Graphics is a W3C recommendation for a standard XML-based format for vector graphic drawings. Vector graphics are images that are made up of shapes – lines, polygons, squares, curves – as opposed to bit-mapped graphics comprising pixels. This has a number of advantages for many applications: vector graphics can be rendered at any resolution – they do not lose definition when you zoom in or zoom out (hence the "scalable" part). They are compact – instead of sending a great many pixels over the connection to the client, vector graphics are sent by transmitting a small number of "instructions" to the client. The client then uses these instructions to reproduce the graphic itself. Although bit-mapped images are compressible, SVG is lossless (e.g., the received graphic is the exact same graphic, even in resolution, as the original), and usually so compact as to not require compression at all.

Vector graphics are ideal for application-generated graphics, such as business graphs and diagrams. SVG can even be generated from other XML-compliant formats, allowing the same data, for example, to be rendered as a table of information and a graph.

5.4 META-FRAMEWORKS

One final category of frameworks that is just emerging is what can be termed a "meta-framework." We are using this term to describe a toolkit designed to span, bridge, and connect together *multiple* application frameworks and toolkits, allow multiple component models to interact efficiently, and allow the features and benefits of one framework and toolkit to be used in another. Additionally, meta-frameworks often aim to allow J2EE/EJB to be used transparently when appropriate, allowing developers to choose the best component for the job, no matter what framework or architecture it is from. The term "meta-framework" has also, in some contexts, been used to describe code generators designed to generate source code for customized frameworks for specific purposes – eCommerce, for example. This is not the definition we are working with here, code generators are another kind of tool altogether.

Many frameworks take advantage of other tools: for example, several of the complete application frameworks we examined in the first part of this chapter use the XML parsing capabilities of Xerces. Other frameworks incorporate entirely separate frameworks into their structure – for example, Turbine and Velocity or Expresso and Struts.

The OpenSymphony framework also takes a very integration-friendly approach to its architecture, and is very nearly a meta-framework in its own right.

The Arch4J framework, while oriented particularly toward J2EE/EJB development, also incorporates pluggable interfaces to other frameworks (e.g., Castor) in its structure.

In this sense, these frameworks begin to bridge the gap from a framework to a meta-framework. A true meta-framework, however, is isolated from dependencies on any one supporting framework. It is not a framework in itself, but instead provides an extremely flexible structure to bridge between multiple frameworks.

Although there are a number of commercial offerings that provide meta-framework capabilities, there are only a few fairly new open-sources projects that were intended originally to be meta-frameworks. Many frameworks, however, are extending their reach in this direction, and encouraging interoperability with other frameworks. Avalon, for example, is ideal for this kind of structure, Turbine's flexible architecture is another.

5.4.1 Keel

Let us take a look at one meta-framework project that is open source and was intended as a meta-framework originally.

Name	Keel Meta-Framework
Website	http://www.keelframework.org
Supplier	Keel Group
License	BSD-style License
Focus	Meta-framework: integration of multiple frameworks
Feature Summary	Highly flexible structure designed to allow developers to take advantage of multiple frameworks in a single application, with scalability to J2EE/EJB as required.

The Keel Meta-Framework consists of one core module, Keel-server, and a number of optional modules allowing it to interface with many other frameworks. The core module makes extensive use of the Apache Avalon framework, reviewed earlier in this chapter, and takes its modularity to a new level. Avalon provides multiple container options, and relatively low-level component functionality. Keel builds on this by preserving the same separation of concerns, inversion of control, and other best component practices, while adding higher level component interfaces and specific features for multiframework interoperability. Keel's separation of concerns is maintained throughout its structure, bordering on the domain of aspect-oriented programming in its ability to keep individual components from mixing concerns from multiple areas.

Most frameworks include implementations of the patterns they design – sometimes only a single implementation, sometimes (but much more rarely) more than one. Keel follows this lead in that it provides implementations – usually more than one – for each of the interfaces that it defines. Much like

Avalon itself, however, it does not *constrain* the developer to the specific implementation – it is easy (not just possible) to replace the default implementation with another one, or to switch between the provided implementations simply by changing configuration.

Keel adds to the Avalon base by providing a preconfigured backbone from which to assemble business Web applications. It includes definitions for persistence services (such as database persistence via JDBC, LDAP persistence, simple file persistence, and others), application logic, scheduling, user interface connectivity (with implementations for several of the more popular presentation frameworks), security and encryption, and many others. For each of these implementations at least one default implementation is provided, allowing Keel to be usable "out of the box." Every implementation can be extensively customized through configuration, or easily replaced with an alternative or custom version if desirable. A number of example applications provide not only examples of how to put Keel to work, but also provide immediately usable modules for your own application development, including common functions such as logging in, registration, data maintenance, and polling (voting).

Keel's design encourages extensibility and reusability by isolating what is called the "describing interface" from the functional implementation of that interface. The describing interface tells *what* a component does – not *how* it does it. The "how" is reserved for the implementation.

Keel can be deployed in any of several configurations, depending on the target platform. The simplest is the "single-VM" configuration, where Keel and all of its services and components reside in the same virtual machine as the servlet engine. This would be the choice for a simple nonclustered Web application with modest need for scalability. For more sophisticated deployments, Keel employs JMS (Java Messaging Service) to communicate between the Keel services and components and the front-end being used. For example, a Web application using Struts as its presentation framework can communicate via JMS to Keel, and make use of Keel's services and components. Use of JMS as the middle tier provides substantial scalability, as multiple Keel "servers" can monitor a single queue – for that matter, multiple "client" Web applications can access the same group of servers, eliminating any single point of failure. In still more complex environments requiring even greater scalability, the various Keel services (including application logic and persistence) can be deployed as Enterprise JavaBeans. The core communication mechanism is still JMS, but in an EJB environment the Keel "server" is deployed as a Message-Driven Enterprise bean, and can access other EJBs (both session and entity, optionally and as configured) as needed. In keeping with Keel's "complete pluggability," even the implementation of JMS can be easily changed. Examples are provided using both OpenJMS and the JBoss project's JBossMQ JMS server.

This allows applications developed using the Keel meta-framework to be deployed in a large variety of different configurations, from the simplest server to the most sophisticated cluster of servers. Keel currently includes examples that integrate over eight other existing frameworks, including Struts, Cocoon, Velocity, Turbine, and a number of other frameworks.

Keel takes the reusability of components to a new level, allowing components to not only be independent of each other, and of the container in which they run, but also independent of the framework they are built with. This provides an opportunity to avoid "framework lock-in," a concern that many development shops have about creating applications with a single framework and not being able to later change their mind and use another. Coding to the "meta-framework" allows this choice to not only be deferred, but to be reversible: for example, if the existing developers are already familiar with Struts, it can be used as the presentation mechanism for an application. Later, say, support for mobile devices is required, and an XSL-based presentation layer is required. The same application logic and components can be immediately used with Cocoon, which has the ability to determine browser type and render WML when appropriate. In fact, both UI frameworks can be used at once, accessing the same code running as the back end. Another example might be persistence: let us say that an application is initially coded using a simple JDBC-based persistence mechanism to a local database. Later, it might be desirable for a much larger deployment to use a different persistence mechanism – let us say JDO, or an Object database. Simply writing a "connector" layer from the existing persistence interface to the new implementation is all that is required (plus a change to one line of a configuration file) – no changes to application code are necessary.

Keel also provides JUnit unit tests for all of its functions, where the unit test is designed to ensure that an implementation of a particular service fulfills the contract implied by its interface. Compatibility is guaranteed by the same unit test being used on *all* implementations. Higher level functional tests are also supplied and can be used to verify the operation of an entire finished Web application.

Keel builds on the foundations laid by all of the excellent frameworks already available by not reinventing the wheel – it instead invents the axle, so to speak, providing a point of commonality across multiple application frameworks and component models, allowing the developer to pick the best available elements for their projects, no matter where they come from.

5.5 Summary

You have seen in this chapter a variety of frameworks from different organizations, under many different licenses, providing a wide range of services to application development. This is by no means a complete list – there are literally thousands of frameworks out there, but these are some representative samples of the kinds of frameworks that can be found today.

We, of course, cannot present complete information about any given framework here: we encourage you to review the website for the frameworks you are interested in, because their documentation will be a much more definitive guide than the taste we are able to provide here. Many frameworks are fast-moving targets, and in some cases have even daily updates. It is essential to review the recent postings to a framework's mailing list to understand what the current development focus is.

As you can see, every framework takes a slightly different approach, and addresses a different kind of application need. By seeing concrete examples of what is available, you can understand better the kinds of things you can expect from a framework. In the next chapter, we will discuss how to select the right framework for your project.

CHAPTER 6

Comparing Frameworks

6.1 COMPARING FRAMEWORKS

Now that we have seen a number of different frameworks, we can make some comparisons of what we have seen and draw a few conclusions. It is important to realize that there is no "better" framework in absolute terms.

6.1.1 Comparisons

It is important to realize, as we look at different frameworks and their methods of solving the problems of Web-application development, that no one specific approach is "right" or "wrong." They all have their advantages and disadvantages. Also, do not think that if we have not covered a particular framework in detail that it is not potentially a good choice for your project. We have just looked at a few of the more well-known examples, and there are many others. New frameworks are created frequently, particularly application-specific ones.

We saw in Chapter 4 the wide variety of services provided by frameworks. Now that we have seen different examples of frameworks, we can contrast their approaches, and compare the advantages and disadvantages of those approaches. We will examine each of the most common services provided by frameworks, and see what kinds of approaches the frameworks we have examined use to handle these services, and what are the pros and cons of that approach for different kinds of projects. As we proceed, you will see a number of "themes" that come up repeatedly – some of these are the design patterns that are common to frameworks, which we will examine in Chapter 8 in detail. We will pay special attention to differentiating the approaches – it is a mistake to assume that the way in which any one framework does something is the "right" way, or most especially the "only" way. One thing I can say for sure, having researched all of these different frameworks, is that there is *always* an alternative approach. At first, the alternative might seem strange and unwieldy, but if you give it a bit of time, you will find that understanding several different approaches gives you a broader perspective. Even if you decide that your original approach was the right one, at least you will be making this decision with an understanding of the alternatives.

6.1.1.1 Application Logic
Most of the frameworks we have reviewed provide a means to encapsulate the application logic, tying it to the user interface as appropriate. Many take the approach of mapping, more or less formally, a request URL to a specific piece of application logic. This mapping can be explicit (as with Struts), or could be implied, based on the mappings of URLs to Servlets in the web.xml configuration file.

Barracuda maps all client requests to "event" objects, then dispatches these events to all registered listeners. The framework then guarantees that an HTTP response is generated for every request. The event model is very flexible, as many "listeners" can be registered to receive specific events without necessarily knowing about each other – this allows the application to be easily extended without any impact on existing code.

Struts (and Expresso, which uses Struts) maps requests to a particular "Action" object. This Action object is then responsible for handling the logic of the application (invoking other objects, accessing the database, etc.), after which the response is routed to the appropriate "view" (typically a JSP page) for rendering to the client.

Expresso refines this a bit further by using a Controller object (which is an extension of Strut's Action object). A Controller is basically a finite-state machine, where each request is routed to a specific state, and then, similar to Struts, the reply is routed to an appropriate view. In Expresso's case, there is built-in support for the view to be handled as a JSP page, an XML (with XSL transformation) stream, or automatically generated HTML. Security is automatically applied to Controller objects as appropriate, and mechanisms such as error handling and redirection to other states on error or exceptional conditions are built in, again saving the developer some effort when coding the application logic.

The Controller approach is essentially a form of the "command" pattern, which we will explore in more detail in Chapter 8.

Avalon takes a very design-pattern-oriented approach to application logic. It allows each element of logic to be assigned certain capabilities by implementing specific interfaces. Interfaces such as Configurable, Loggable, and Startable are used to denote actions to be taken by the component manager when handling the component. A Configurable component is handed configuration data, a Loggable component is given a logging manager and so forth. This supports a strict inversion of control.

Understanding where the application logic goes, and how it interfaces with the rest of the framework is an important step in understanding how to correctly and effectively put the framework to use.

Almost all frameworks provide a logic container that can be extended to use EJB as its logic element. By use of the delegate pattern, we can EJB-enable even a framework that was not built necessarily with EJB in mind. There are some exceptions, however: if the framework's design depends on a specific deployment environment for its application logic, you may have to do extra work to achieve the distributed advantages of EJB. For example, let us say our framework uses events to notify the application logic about UI requests, and uses a singleton event manager object for this purpose (a singleton is an object with exactly one instance; we examine this pattern in more detail in Chapter 8). If the singleton event manager expects all of its listeners to be in the same Virtual Machine (VM), you will have to add an extra layer of functionality to distribute these events to multiple servers (or multiple VMs on the same server). If the event manager is pluggable (using the delegation or proxy pattern), then it will be easier to create this new layer.

What do we gain, however? It depends on our project's deployment scenario – if we are dealing with a single server, or a deployment where only the database engine is on a separate server, it may not help much. In fact, the extra overhead may actually slow down our application.

So let us consider the distributed deployment situation: we discussed in Chapter 1 the advantages and disadvantages of EJB – we do get the benefits of a standardized component model, but what about scalability? EJB components can reside on separate servers, so our framework could run on the same server as our Web/application server, and route requests for processing to another server that is hosting the session beans we are using as our application logic container. Assuming that the hardware infrastructure is set up correctly, we are now bringing three or four servers to bear on the problem.

There is still a single point of access for users: the server that runs the Web or application server, but it does not have any of the burden of the application logic. It may not even require a connection to the database, for example. Of course, volumes have been written about how to properly implement distributed components for best scalability, but even our simple example shows how this can be done.

6.1.1.2 Database Access

The presentation frameworks, by and large, do not address database access. Instead, they leave the database access portion of the process up to the developer. Struts goes a step further by providing a database connection definition mechanism, but stops there. The "complete" frameworks, however, almost always provide both a connection pooling mechanism and, at least, one database-to-object connection capability. Turbine, for example, with its flexible service-oriented structure, provides one major object/relational (O/R) mapping layer, Torque. It also provides the ability to use any other mechanism in its place, however. Expresso takes a similar approach, although the flexibility is more constrained in that, the Database Object mechanism, while allowing multiple implementations, provides a much more detailed interface that must be implemented when creating a new persistence mechanism.

Some frameworks provide their own connection pooling mechanism. Connection pooling is very important for overall performance of a Web application, and is used in almost all production Web applications that make heavy use of a database. Expresso, for example, provides a sophisticated and powerful connection pool, as does Turbine. Struts relies on the developer to create a connection pool externally, as does Barracuda. The realMethods framework assumes you will be accessing the connection pool provided by a J2EE/EJB server, and this is often a valid assumption for many frameworks that do not include their own pooling. Sometimes it is valuable to have the option to use externally supplied pooling, however, and some frameworks, including Turbine and Avalon, for example, allow the pool to be "pluggable," and different implementations to be used as and when required.

Several frameworks go beyond simple connection pooling to offer a complete and sophisticated object/relational mapping mechanism. We discussed earlier what this mechanism can do for you. Turbine does a particularly good job here, allowing the object/relational mapping implementation to be "pluggable" as well. Avalon allows for this too, although it does not include its own implementation of such a mechanism – several such mechanisms are included by Turbine. Expresso provides a powerful object/relational mapping mechanism in its DBObject class, and although the implementation is not pluggable, it is very capable and integrated with a performance-enhancing cache layer automatically. Some frameworks provide nothing but object-relational mapping: the Exolab Castor project, for example, Simper, or the Object/Relational Bridge. It is one of the most powerful features of the full application frameworks and that can substantially reduce the amount of code required to create an application. It should be a major focus of your comparison if your application is to be database-dependent.

Avalon provides a sophisticated and configurable pooling mechanism for database connections, but leaves it to the developer (or a third-party library such as Castor) to provide the object-relational mapping.

Niggle provides a simple and elegant O/R layer that is primarily defined in external XML files, making it easier to modify the data model than frameworks, such as Expresso, which embed database field and table names in Java objects.

Cocoon provides connection pooling and easy access to SQL from XSP pages, but stops short of providing O/R mapping.

6.1.1.2.1 Insulation from SQL

Of course, several frameworks, such as jRelational, Castor, and Simper provide nothing but database access services. Using one of these toolkits in conjunction with a framework such as Struts (which concentrates on presentation) can often provide an ideal combination. We discuss later, however, the difficulties encountered when combining frameworks.

When looking at the various database access layers, one of the differences we see is the amount of "insulation" they provide from SQL (assuming they use SQL at all – virtually all do, or at least can). At one end of the spectrum there is a simple database connection. This allows direct execution of SQL itself, as follows:

```
ResultSet rs = stmt.executeQuery("select name, rank,
   serial_number from personnel"
   + "where rank >= " + Ranks.CAPTAIN);
while(rs.next()){
   System.out.println(rs.getString(1) + ", "
   + rs.getString(2) + ", " + rs.getString(3));
}
```

There is effectively no isolation from SQL in this case at all: we can send any SQL that is recognized by our database of choice via our connection. This has the advantage of flexibility – we can do joins, create tables, add indices, select data, and even run stored procedures; in short, we can do anything that we could do with the underlying database itself. SQL is, after all, a very powerful and well-established database query and manipulation language.

Some frameworks leave the situation right here: if database portability is not a strong concern, this can be a perfectly viable approach. Other frameworks take the approach that any SQL is pariah, and must be exorcized completely from the code. To eliminate SQL just for the sake of doing so is not necessarily prudent. Although it is true that having SQL embedded in the code does give the developer two entirely different languages to worry about (Java and SQL), many developers today are expert in SQL; in fact, probably a larger number of developers are experienced in SQL than in Java, as it has been around much longer. The standard JDBC API is sometimes all that is needed for an application, and a balanced approach must be taken to the advantages and disadvantages of SQL in all cases.

The downside of including SQL in the code, however, is, first and foremost, the loss of portability. Unless we are extremely careful, our SQL will have database-specific syntax creep in at some point. Then, although the Java portion of our Web application may be highly portable, we have restricted ourselves to a particular database engine – or, possibly even worse, a particular version of a particular database engine.

SQL is a well-established standard, but not every database implements this standard in exactly the same way. SQL in fact consists of two languages, the query language and the data manipulation/definition language. The query language is usually more standardized across database engines – less so the data definition language (creating tables and so forth).

There are many different approaches seen in the frameworks we have examined to addressing this issue, and most of them involve taking the SQL out of the actual Java code. The simplest approach is simply to define the query itself externally, for example:

```
ResultSet rs = stmt.executeQuery(getQuery
  ("nameRankSerialNumber", Ranks.CAPTAIN);
while(rs.next()){
  System.out.println(rs.getString(1) + ", " +
    rs.getString(2) + ", " + rs.getString(3));
}
```

In this situation, the "getQuery" method is defined to return the actual body of our query. The query might be stored in an external properties file,

```
nameRankSerialNumber=select name, rank, serial_number
from personnel where rank >= $1
```

Now we have the ability to replace just the SQL if we change database engines. This is a simple approach considered by early versions of some frameworks: most of the frameworks have been developed beyond this to store the SQL more flexibly, sometimes in XML format files.

If this is still not enough database independence for you, other frameworks go still further. The next level of isolation is to generate the SQL itself dynamically, based on mappings from relational tables to objects. This is the basic purpose of "object/relational" mapping mechanisms. The application deals directly with some kind of persistent object, such as:

```
PersonnelGroup pg = new PersonnelGroup();
pg.setQuery("rank", "ge", Ranks.CAPTAIN);
pg.runQuery();
while (pg.hasMore()) {
  onePerson = pg.nextElement();
}
```

Although many of the details vary, this is the general approach observed by many of the frameworks we have examined. It has the advantage of containing no direct SQL at all – the query is created on the fly as needed (although it may be cached and prepared statements used for performance reasons). When adding and updating records, such frameworks use a similar approach:

```
Person onePerson = new Person();
onePerson.set("name", newName);
onePerson.set("rank", newRank);
onePerson.set("serial_number", newSerialNumber);
onePerson.add();
```

At this level of insulation from the database, the only elements common to the code and the database are the field names (e.g., name, rank, and serial number). Of course, there is no reason that the field names being used in the code cannot be "symbolic" names, mapped to the actual field names in the database tables at run time by some kind of external configuration.

If we dispense with even the symbolic names, it becomes possible to treat the persistent object as a regular JavaBean, and to use the JavaBean standard method signatures of getters and setters to interact with the persistent object's properties:

```
Person onePerson = new Person();
onePerson.setName(newName);
onePerson.setRank(newRank);
onePerson.setSerialNumber(newSerialNumber);
onePerson.add();
```

Now our isolation from the database is almost complete. What have we gained? Well, we do not have any database-dependent SQL in our code, but we could get it with just simple external property files. We also do not have any tie-in to a particular query or any particular field names – this can be important if the database changes rapidly, but most production systems do not have this problem. Selecting the correct level of insulation from underlying SQL is not as simple as saying that SQL is automatically "bad" and should be eliminated. There are advantages and disadvantages to all of the approaches we see in the various frameworks.

In the above examples, we have shown a simple query and a simple database add. What about more complex database actions: Multitable joins, inner and outer joins, groupings, selecting counts, minimums, maximums, averages, and so forth? These are extremely easy operations with SQL – it was designed for these kinds of operations, and usually does them quite efficiently, considering the inherent limitations of a relational database. Objects have a slightly more difficult time, because there is less agreement on the correct mechanism for creating complex queries of objects. The Object Management Group (OMG) has defined a set of standards for data definition, manipulation, and query for object databases. This object query language, however, is less widely adopted than SQL, just as pure object databases themselves are less widely used. Whether for good or bad reasons, relational databases are here for a while to come yet, and SQL is their standard access mechanism.

One of the advantages of complete isolation from the underlying data query and manipulation, however, is the ability to make even the *type* of data store "pluggable," and not just the brand of database engine. An object/relational mapping layer that provides complete isolation of code and storage can actually use an object database instead of a relational database, or even access objects in an LDAP store, or a native XML database, by simply changing configuration.

The code for the application that accesses the mapping layer remains unchanged. This is a technique sometimes used when allowing authentication/authorization information to be read either from a relational database or from an LDAP store, for example: the configuration changes, but the actual code reading the data does not. In practice, this situation does not arise all that often. An application written explicitly to use an object database seldom ports easily to use a relational database, and vice versa – the paradigms are quite different, and the data organization is quite unique to each application.

In all of the examples we have seen so far, the actual database operation is performed explicitly. We say when to execute the query, and when to add or update the record to the underlying database. Some database access layers (or persistence layers, to use the more generic term for those that can access multiple storage mechanisms) relieve the developer from even this requirement. The JDO standard, for example, handles storing records that have changed automatically when the current transaction is committed. Other persistence layers do the same for queries: we access objects from an apparently limitless cache – the underlying persistence engine handles retrieving the objects we need to access and storing the records we change at the right time. Although this is certainly a powerful approach, and can indeed result in applications with less code and less dependence on the underlying data storage mechanism, many developers are uncomfortable with it in practical terms. The persistence layer cannot always correctly determine the times to read or write to the data store, and locking and concurrency issues must be handled. Such persistence layers tend to be more complex and memory intensive than those where storage and retrieval are explicit, and performance is difficult to manage in large applications.

All of these approaches are seen in various frameworks, and understanding the pros and cons of each is essential when making comparisons.

6.1.1.3 Database Maintenance
Some frameworks go beyond even the object-relational layer to provide built-in database maintenance. They provide facilities to immediately access add, update, delete, and query functions on any persistent object that is defined. This fulfills a common requirement of many Web applications: the need to be able to quickly and easily update and add records to appropriate database tables. Expresso provides the most flexible database maintenance logic in the frameworks we have reviewed – it can be extensively customized by setting various options and altering the user interface. Often, however, an application will require customization beyond the user interface and options available in a standard database-maintenance module.

Turbine, by contrast, also provides a basic database maintenance system, which can be customized by readily altering either the Velocity templates or the code in the associated logic: there is no single component for database maintenance, so custom derivatives are easier to create. Which of these approaches is preferable really depends on what your finished application needs: if you have to have highly customized versions of each maintenance screen, it might be easier to have custom application logic code. If database maintenance is a rarely used mechanism in your application, and it is reasonable to have one generic way of doing it, the approach of a single component might be better. As always, there is no "best" way – it is a matter of fitting with your application development needs.

This capability is usually not a major factor in choosing a framework, although it can be a significant convenience, particularly at an early stage of the development process before your application has its own database maintenance capabilities completed.

Almost all Web applications require some kind of database-maintenance ability, but frameworks often have a hard time providing a service of this nature that is sufficiently flexible. Often, special constraints have to be placed on the maintenance capability, or certain fields must be suppressed, or supplied with a fixed value. Sometimes it is easier to create the database-maintenance logic with these constraints in mind than customize a provided capability.

6.1.1.4 Logging

Logging in a Web application can be very simplistic, or quite sophisticated. The larger your application, the more you will find a need for more capable logging mechanisms. The ability to turn on and off logging in selected modules of the application is essential to find the appropriate messages after a run – if you can only log everything, the log may get very large, very quickly.

Many frameworks make use of existing logging projects to supply their logging capability – a popular example is log4j, but it is not the only choice.

Turbine again provides a completely configurable approach, allowing several different logging mechanisms to be plugged in and used. Avalon also does the same – basing its logging on an interface and allowing even the new built-in logging in JDK 1.4 to provide the implementation. Expresso incorporates the Log4J project, a logging toolkit originally developed by IBM, and now an Apache project.

Logging is a particularly important capability, and should be considered carefully when making your choice.

A framework should provide logging beyond the logging built in to the Servlet API – although Servlet logging might be one choice of output method, the framework should go further to allow the flexibility to log from non-Servlet components. Servlets are only one part of a Web application, and a framework's choice of logging should reflect this.

6.1.1.5 Event Handling

Each framework deals with events a bit differently. In Barracuda, for example, events are primarily an interaction mechanism between the UI layer and the application logic. UI actions by the user trigger events, which are then propagated to the appropriate listeners, in a way somewhat similar to the Swing graphical UI API. Request events are first processed, then the application logic is handled, and response events are triggered. Events are hierarchical and securable, and very lightweight. Events in Barracuda are implementations of an interface, as is the event-dispatching controller, allowing different implementations to be used as required.

In Expresso, by contrast, UI event handling is managed in the same way as Struts — user activities invoke an Action object, and potentially an associated ActionForm, and these objects interact with the model of the application (the business logic), and trigger the associated view when they are complete. Expresso adds the additional concept of "system" events – items like errors, notifications, registrations of new users, and so forth. This type of event can be configured to send a notification email to a specified group of users, and is used as a system-monitoring mechanism, as well as an "early warning" capability of system errors. New events of this type can be created and used anywhere in the system.

Events can, of course, be used as much more than the interface between presentation and application logic: ideally, your framework should allow events to be used within the application logic – for example, to trigger custom functionality when a particular account is updated. This kind of flexibility is seen in event modules such as the one in Avalon's Excalibur project.

6.1.1.6 Caching

An essential ingredient to performance is the intelligent use of caching. Several of the frameworks we reviewed include generic caching mechanisms, allowing them to be used not only for the framework's internal processes, but by your own application as well. Avalon has a sophisticated caching mechanism under development as part of its Excalibur project. Turbine and Expresso provide flexible caching services, as does realMethods. It is important to consider the ability of the cache to scale: is there a mechanism to provide distributed notification of cache updates? If database information is cached, can you perform updates on one server and have the change propagate to others?

Cocoon's caching is highly configurable, and integrated with its XML handling and content-publishing capabilities. It is also available, however, for use by your own applications directly, and because of its foundation in Avalon, allows "pluggable" implementations to be substituted for the default one.

Application-specific frameworks tend to have custom caching mechanisms for their own purposes: Jetspeed, for example, has both in-memory and disk-based cache system for caching content retrieved from other systems, or content that requires time to create or generate – it is highly flexible, but designed for this one purpose. General-purpose caching is seen in more generic frameworks, such as Turbine.

Because caching is a difficult and important subject, particularly as applications scale, it is an area that must also be carefully considered when evaluating frameworks. Simplistic caching can be more of a performance burden than a benefit – a flexible algorithm for deciding when items are to be dropped from the cache, and facilities to monitor the size of a cache are essential.

6.1.1.7 Error Handling

Each framework takes a somewhat different approach to error handling. This is an area where the design pattern and overall concept are important to understand: how does this framework approach error handling? Is it tied to the validation process, where a user's input on a form is checked? Does it handle system errors (e.g., "out of memory" or "database unavailable")? How are the exceptions or errors logged? Is there a notification mechanism? An important part of an overall software engineering project, consistent error handling can be greatly simplified by a framework.

Struts provides powerful mechanisms for validation, allowing errors at this level to be routed back to the original input view for the user to correct. It provides the essential tool of allowing previous input to be preserved – so the user seldom has to rekey an entire form to correct a problem. It does not address overall application error handling, however. Turbine also provides validation error handling, but is somewhat more prone to allowing application problems and sometimes even user exceptions to "fall through" to the underlying Servlet engine. Although this is one approach to error handling, a finished application exposed to real-world users – particularly on the wilds of the Internet – usually calls for something more. Almost all of the frameworks provide easy mechanisms to trap and handle exceptions in custom ways. Expresso provides a mechanism that can automatically email a notification of system and user errors to a group of administrators. This provides a way for even "silent" system errors to be trapped, for example, when a resource becomes unavailable, or the application runs out of database connections. This borders on monitoring, the next subject we will discuss.

Error handling is a perfect example of a repetitive code that needs consistent handling, and is, therefore, a good area to use the abilities of a framework. Many of the existing frameworks have fairly rudimentary error handling, however, and it appears to be an area that is given fairly short shrift overall in Web applications.

6.1.1.8 Monitoring and Testing

Beyond error handling, some frameworks provide built-in testing and monitoring capabilities. Testing can range from basic unit tests, which most of the frameworks provide, all the way to performance-monitoring and tracking subsystems, such as the one found in Expresso. Some frameworks also provide specific hooks for external monitoring and testing applications, such as Cactus or JUnit, to be used.

Built-in unit and self-tests, seen frequently in Avalon and Expresso, are sometimes an indicator of the development methodology used in the framework itself. Extreme Programming (which we will discuss in Chapter 8 in more detail) advocates the development of a test before the development of the code itself. Frameworks built in this way tend to be extremely robust and reliable, and these are the attributes to look for. At a minimum, unit and self-tests are key to ensure that the framework is running properly.

The ability to monitor both the operation of the framework and the finished application is also important: it is essential to determine whether application performance is consistent over time (e.g., the application does not slowly degrade in performance, perhaps due to a memory leak or by holding onto resources that should be released). Frameworks that include this ability can be particularly valuable to a large project.

Of course, some frameworks concentrate entirely on testing, such as JUnit and Anteater. They can be used on their own to add testing to any kind of application, irrespective of the framework it was built with.

6.1.1.9 Security

Security is a vast and complex topic, as we have seen before. Frameworks that provide flexible, pluggable layers for security at multiple levels of your application are the most valuable. Any area of the framework that does not provide security automatically is an area where you will have to provide for it on your own, so keep this in mind when estimating how much development effort and time the framework will save you.

Many frameworks, such as Struts, provide access to basic security in many of their areas, but do not provide the detailed implementations at all levels, such as login pages and encryption capabilities, because they concentrate on a specific area of the application development process. Frameworks that depend on the entire J2EE environment, such as realMethods, tie closely to the J2EE security model. Most frameworks allow at least some flexibility as far as authentication is concerned, such as Turbine's pluggable mechanism for specifying how a user is authenticated. You need to look for the ability to authenticate against, at least, a default mechanism (such as a properties file or database) and the ability to access an LDAP shared authentication store, because this is a requirement of many deployments.

The JAAS standard has brought a thread of consistency to this area of frameworks, and most frameworks are either in the process of implementing it, or have already done so. When such standards exist, it usually makes more sense to adhere to them than not to do so, and JAAS is sufficiently flexible that it is usually a wise choice.

You should look for security at all levels of the framework, including the business logic level, the database, and at the configuration or administrator capability level. Pluggable authentication is highly desirable, and quite popular, and JAAS is a good way for this to be provided. Encryption of key data is also a desirable option, and ideally should be trivial to configure. Not many frameworks address this, due to the restrictions on security capabilities that have only recently been relaxed. Expresso, for example, provides built-in access to encrypting both data and security information (such as passwords), and Turbine's pluggable authentication mechanism allows this to be added easily, even though it is not there by default.

Security, and in particular encryption support, is an area where only a few frameworks place an emphasis, but this will probably change as frameworks continue their development.

6.1.1.10 Presentation UI

A few frameworks, particularly Niggle, Turbine, Expresso, and to a somewhat lesser degree Struts, include the ability to select multiple user interface choices, and to apply a different UI to each different request, if needed.

Barracuda, Turbine, Expresso, Cocoon, Jetspeed, and several other frameworks provide special mechanisms for identifying the client capabilities available (by reading the browser-type code sent from the client), and modifying their UI operation accordingly. This can allow the developer to select not only the appropriate output markup (e.g., HTML, WML, and XML), but also the sub-capabilities within that markup: for example, does the browser support JavaScript – if so, an enhanced version of the form being displayed could utilize JavaScript, otherwise a more portable version is used.

Barracuda compiles the HTML (WML or XML) document used as the UI template into DOM template object, which can then be manipulated programmatically. This is a somewhat different approach than the other frameworks, which tend to follow a templating approach where the template accesses data from some kind of response object. For example, in Struts, a JavaBean object associated with a particular view can be accessed via custom JSP tags to populate the view.

Most of the frameworks provide support for localization: Barracuda, for example, automatically creates a localized version of the DOM template for each appropriate locale, and can detect the client locale. Struts uses an external message file approach, as do Turbine, Struts, and Expresso. Efficient localization requires a careful balancing act between flexibility and performance – looking up every string required to build a page can be very time consuming, so it is important to consider the method used by each framework, and the impact it will have on your performance. Using statically translated templates or pages is one method of improving performance, at the cost of additional disk storage. Barracuda allows this approach inherently: an "Ant"-based build system can be used to generate localized versions of templates at build time. The appropriate template can then be selected based on the locale of the user at run time.

Most of the frameworks also provide a means to partially localize: if a specified string is not available in the appropriate local language, some kind of default language (perhaps English) is used instead. This allows critical areas of the finished application to be localized first, whereas less-important areas can be localized later, without disabling the entire application.

Another important area of UI interaction is the mapping of forms to and from the HTML (or WML, etc.) page, and retrieval of the associated request data into a more accessible structure. This then leads to validation, or verification of the request data (particularly from POST), as appropriate in its context. Struts uses the ActionForm object for this, an extended JavaBean with getter and setter methods that allow each field value to be validated independently. The validation can be any required code, so lookups to database and other such operations are available. The mapping of values from the request to the various bean "getter" and "setter" methods is automatic.

Barracuda takes a slightly different approach: as opposed to a JavaBean, values from the request are mapped into a structure of regular Java objects, whereas Struts uses String values for the "setter" methods of the associated ActionBean. In Barracuda, a Validator can be attached to any collection of values, or to a single field. This facilitates reuse of Validators, because the same Validator (or even a group of validators) can be used on multiple fields or forms.

Expresso takes a different approach again: because the business logic is encapsulated in a Controller object (which is a collection of states), the request data is passed in via parameter values, collected into a "ControllerRequest." This request is not specific to the Servlet API – the mapping from Servlet form values into generic Java variables is done automatically. The Controller's state can then perform any required validation – indeed, some validation is built-in, because certain parameters can be declared as required or optional, and regular expression masks can be applied to their values as basic validation. More complex validation is then performed by the states themselves, and appropriate exceptions are thrown as required to indicate error conditions. Special capabilities for validating parameters against the valid values for fields in Database Objects (DBObjects) are provided, making validation against a field in the database fast and easy.

Regarding user interface, it is also important to consider the best "audience" for a particular UI technology in a framework. Struts, for example, and its primary use of JSP pages, lends itself well to be used by page authors – that is, users familiar with HTML authoring tools and page design in HTML. Many such tools support the creation of JSP pages with custom tags, so, by learning a few custom JSP tags, page authors who are not otherwise developers can create Struts UI "views" easily. This is one of the advantages of JSP technology that ensures its popularity and support by page editors. The same is true of other frameworks that include or link easily with Struts, such as realMethods and Expresso. Turbine's default UI technology, Velocity, is also very easy for page authors to learn – some may argue that it is even easier than JSP and custom tags. Some page editing tools allow Velocity templates to be built easily within their editors, but, because Velocity templates are not JSP, nor are they strictly HTML compliant, some tools object to their use. Barracuda allows regular markup to be created, but it does require the intervention of a developer to make the "hookup" between the finished template and the logic of the application. Because the template itself is "straight" HTML (or XML, WML, etc.), page authors can certainly participate in creating the layout.

The emerging JSF (JavaServer Faces) standard will, hopefully, increase the availability of tools that support UI editing for any compliant framework, expanding the group that is able to create interfaces for such frameworks. Right now, the HyperQBS framework is the closest to a JSF-standard-compliant UI framework. The specification itself is still not finalized.

6.1.1.11 Scheduling

Several frameworks, mostly the complete application frameworks, provide a task-scheduling feature. This brings a capability similar to the Unix "cron" command into the application: tasks can be scheduled for a set time, and executed repeatedly every "x" hours or days. Of course, many of the deployment platforms for a framework, such as Unix, Linux, and Windows 2000/NT, have some form of operating system scheduler. If the framework allows it, this scheduler can be used to initiate tasks in the finished application as well. This is a feature to look for: the ability to trigger a task in the framework from a "command line" or "batch file" – because this is what most schedulers are able to invoke. Turbine, Avalon, and Expresso have this capability "out of the box," but it is not difficult to add to most other frameworks we have reviewed.

As far as built-in schedulers are concerned, the importance of this feature depends heavily on whether or not this is an important capability in your application(s). If you need it, it is extremely beneficial if your framework provides it, because this is a difficult and tedious feature to code. If you do not need it, it should not get in the way. Turbine and Expresso provide scheduler capabilities, with Expresso's scheduler having perhaps a superior user interface, but with Turbine's scheduler being more robust and flexible.

6.1.1.12 Web Services

Web Services, the popular new methodology for providing application logic and data via the HTTP protocol, is a new area to frameworks. The Apache SOAP project, which provides a basis for Web services, can be integrated into the logic capability of almost any framework. No frameworks yet (as of this writing) provide built-in support for Web Services directly, however. This will probably change very soon. Any of the frameworks that provide a specific "container" object for business logic will likely allow those objects to be accessed via SOAP. Frameworks that specifically provide server-oriented services, such as Avalon, are ideal candidates for providing their logic via Web Services as well. The availability of integration with Web Services will likely be an important criterion when selecting your framework.

Web services will also provide a key element in interplatform operation of finished applications including integration with .NET applications. If this integration is important to your finished application, examining frameworks with Web Services capabilities is even more important for you.

We explore Web services in much more detail in Chapter 11.

6.1.1.13 Legacy Application Integration

Integrating with existing logic and data from legacy applications is an essential part of many Web applications. The object/relational mapping layer is one service of frameworks that can be used for this. Given the flexibility of data sources for JDBC, it is often possible to directly access the legacy application's data with object/relational tools, such as Turbine's Peer mechanism, or Expresso's DBObjects. This is sometimes not ideal, however, because the application logic is then bypassed – if certain validations are applied by the legacy application, or if the legacy applications need to invoke specific logic whenever a new record is added, for example, these capabilities will be lost with direct data access. A better solution in these cases is to "wrap" the legacy application with a logic container/object from the framework. For example, you might create a Session bean implementation with realMethods, or a Controller object with Expresso, that acts as the proxy to the legacy application. Then the remainder of your application accesses this object as if it were a "new" object, created directly with the framework, and has access to as many of its operations as you are able to map.

The proxy/worker object capabilities in realMethods are an ideal way to do this, as one example, but it is possible in almost any of the frameworks. Few general-purpose frameworks provide specific functionality for wrapping particular types of legacy applications, however, so it is important to see what kind of access you have to your legacy logic. Can it be called via CORBA, for instance? If it is on the IBM AS/400 system, there is a toolbox API available from IBM to access programs there, as another example. Once this access method is established, the connection between the framework's logic handling capability and this access method is examined.

This is another feature whose importance depends on your needs. If you are creating a new application and not connecting to any legacy data sources, it may be safely ignored. If, alternatively, the focus of the new application is on accessing legacy logic and data, it is, of course, a high priority. Do not expect to find a specific legacy access method in your framework choices; instead, look for the means the framework provides to encapsulate logic, and then examine how this would be connected to the access method available for your legacy applications, possibly through a third-party adaptor object or API.

6.1.1.14 Utilities

All frameworks that we have examined have at least some utility objects built into them, even if only for their own internal use. Some make use of external utility packages: the Struts framework, for example, uses parts of a project called

Jakarta Commons, a set of utility and reusable capabilities used by several frameworks. Turbine collects its utility functions into a specific package, as do many of the other frameworks. Utility functions include enhanced string handling, file and I/O management, and sometimes features such as database creation. A rich set of utility objects and methods can be very valuable in overall application development, so it is worth investigating what is available as you evaluate frameworks. Usually, such utility objects are relatively "stand-alone," that is, they do not necessarily depend on the remainder of the framework for their operations – so they are good candidates for extraction to include them in other projects, possibly projects based on entirely different frameworks.

6.1.1.15 Other

Obviously, these are not the only areas of functionality included in frameworks. Frameworks provide many areas of functionality that we have not included, and some of these may be essential to your particular project. A project-wide view must be considered when evaluating their suitability; in fact, more than that. It is usually impossible to predict what kinds of projects you may develop in the future, but choosing a framework and building expertise in it is an important decision, so ideally you will want to reuse that investment on more than one project. You will therefore be looking for a framework that will not only fit your immediate needs, but also has a good chance of meeting your future needs, as best as you can determine them.

We can draw some conclusions from the frameworks we have examined in Chapter 5. Some generalities emerge that are common themes to all presentation-oriented frameworks for Web applications:

- **MVC separation**: All presentation frameworks agree on one aspect: it is best to provide a separation between the business logic and the presentation or user interface. How far each framework takes this varies widely: Struts, for example, by using JSP pages, provides for a complete separation, but does not necessarily *enforce* this separation. In other words, it is still possible to include code in the UI portion (by writing scriptlets in the JSP page). In fact, this is true of any JSP solution and has sparked a lively debate about the relative merits of allowing this (a summary of this debate is given later in this chapter). Other frameworks, such as Barracuda, enforce a complete separation of the logic and the user interface, ensuring that the two remain independent.
- **"Push" versus "pull" presentation**: For lack of a better term, most presentation frameworks use a "pull" mechanism to get the content and the

markup integrated for transmission to the user. This is the method used by all "template"-type presentation mechanisms: the markup makes references to special tokens or tags, as discussed in previous chapters, and "pulls" the dynamic values in at run time. The combined content and template make up the pages sent to the user's browser.

The other technique can be called "push," in that the markup is either generated dynamically by the presentation layer or read from a specification or template ahead of time, then the entire page is sent directly from the application to the user, with no template involved. This is the technique used by the Barracuda presentation framework, for example, although it also allows transformation of the resulting markup, making it effectively a hybrid between push and pull techniques.

- **XML and JSP:** We discussed in Chapter 4 the technique of combining the features of XML and JSP. Both of these technologies have their advantages, and we discussed these in detail. Most frameworks make a choice between these two technologies as their primary template or markup mechanism, but more often we see frameworks that allow either, or even both, to be used. JSP pages, for example, are entirely capable of generating XML, rather than HTML (or WML or other markup). This allows the standardization of JSP to be put to good use while still retaining the power and flexibility of XML and XSL transformations. Cocoon, for example, supports this combination, allowing a JSP page to be used as the Generator when setting up one of its pipelines.
- **Templating:** The technique of "templating," that is, the creation of a presentation page that has "place-holders" for the application data to be filled in at run time is generally recognized as a good thing by all the presentation frameworks we looked at. At the same time, large differences are evident in *how* this templating is to be achieved. Some frameworks take an entirely different approach, which, as we will also see, has its advantages.

6.2 Combining Frameworks

As we have seen, not all frameworks provide services for the entire development process. Some concentrate on presentation, or on database access, or on some other set of related services, such as XML parsing. To get the best set of capabilities available to your application, you will often find a necessity to combine frameworks. In this section we discuss what is involved there, and some of the advantages and problems with this approach.

In some cases, merging two frameworks that are not designed for such a merging can be akin to merging two freight trains going in opposite directions on the same track. They come together just fine, but it is not pretty, and often it is hard to figure out afterward just where all the pieces go, or to get anything to work again. Early frameworks, particularly complete application frameworks, tend to have this problem. They assumed that they were the "top-level" design mechanism for the completed application, and that they encompassed all of its areas of functionality. Combining them with another framework was fraught with conflicts; if a framework is designed so that its method of accessing configuration values, for example, is tightly integrated with the other services of the framework, it will be difficult to pry it loose without potentially breaking something. At the very least, we will create an orphan of one, if not both, of the frameworks we are bringing together.

More recently, frameworks have adopted a more modular approach, in keeping with the concepts of good component design. If the interface and the implementation are separate for each of the services of the framework, it is much easier to "plug in" new or customized implementations of these services. This allows us to *selectively* apply customizations while not spawning a unique version of the framework itself. If, for example, user presentation is pluggable, it should be easy to switch from using whatever the default mechanism is, say JSPs, to another presentation framework, for example WebMacro. In practice, this is still a bit more difficult than it sounds, but much less painful than it was with earlier generation frameworks.

Taking this concept even further, there is now at least one open-source effort underway to create a tool specifically intended for combining multiple frameworks, providing a structure for different component models to interact. We examined this in Section 4.1 in Chapter 5. If you find that the capabilities of more than one framework are useful in your projects, this is an approach worth examining.

6.2.1 Presentation

Part of the problem of making the presentation layer "pluggable" in a framework is coming up with a suitable abstraction, where the output of the application logic is handled "generically" until the presentation layer comes into play. This is easy enough for template engines: for example, switching between Velocity, WebMacro, FreeMarker, and Tea is relatively easy. They use a common paradigm, with the differences being mostly in the details and the macro capabilities of the various technologies. Barracuda, on the other hand, is an entirely different animal, if you will excuse the pun. It uses a "push"-type mechanism that generates the UI by reading the markup into a DOM structure that is then manipulated by the application logic. Switching from one of these techniques to the other is not impossible, but it is not very common in today's frameworks.

It is important to realize that the concept of the separation of logic and presentation does not necessarily mean a separation between what runs on the client and what runs on the server. Although the client "runs" HTML (or WML, XML, etc.), it is sometimes useful to have at least limited logic functionality when this HTML is prepared: for example, conditionals that say that if a particular condition is true emit this piece of HTML, and if it is not, emit a different piece. This is indeed logic, in the strictest sense, it is generally accepted that the type of logic that is necessary *for* the presentation itself is part of the "view," and not part of the "model." Some frameworks take a hard view, insisting that it is not *possible* to perform logic at the presentation layer, at least not arbitrary logic (they restrict the number of operations possible to a small set of tags, for example), but this does the experienced developer a disservice. An experienced developer should know what it means to perform proper separation of business logic and presentation logic, and should not be constrained artificially to write code to do this. Of course, having said that, there are a great many inexperienced developers, so tools that do provide such constraints indeed have an audience for them. It is important, however, not to reject out of hand any technology that *allows* logic in the presentation layer.

6.2.2 Database Access

The paradigm chosen for the abstract interface is also key when allowing pluggability of persistence layers, or object/relational mapping mechanisms. Some (JDO, for example) handle persistence very transparently – it is not necessary to explicitly "save" or "add" records, the database is updated as needed. Others, such as Expresso's DBObjects, are closer to the relational model: you say "save" when you want a record saved, "update" when you want it updated, and so forth. To have a single interface able to use either of these as the implementation is a complex task, and again one that is not tackled very often. Both approaches, as we have seen before, have their advantages, and proponents of each method have no desire to have their persistence layer reduced to the lowest common denominator.

6.2.3 Modular Frameworks

Most frameworks today take a modular approach: they define a means to add and replace services to the basic framework, such as Turbine's Fulcrum services framework, or Avalon's component and service interfaces. This serves two purposes for the framework: it provides a common backbone for the services themselves, and facilitates new development of services. It also provides a place for services to be replaced by custom or extended implementations.

6.2.4 Meta-Frameworks

One final approach, which we will examine in more detail in Chapter 11, and looked at an example of Chapter 5, is the meta-framework. This is essentially a framework of frameworks – a design and a series of interfaces that find common ground between the different ways that different frameworks provide certain services. For example, a meta-framework might provide a high-level interface and definition for a scheduler service. This service might have a concrete implementation in the form of the scheduler from Turbine in one case, and the scheduler component from Avalon's Excalibur project in another. Normally, these two scheduler services would be incompatible, because the "backbone" for Turbine's scheduler is Fulcrum, the services framework used by Turbine, and the basis for Excalibur's scheduler component is the Component model supplied by Avalon. A meta-framework would provide an "adapter" between these two, allowing a single common interface to access either service on demand.

Consolidation of frameworks along this line can be seen in Turbine even now, as it begins to use Avalon as its component model and basis, and of course, with purpose-built meta-frameworks, such as Keel.

As we have seen, the concept of combining frameworks, or parts of frameworks, can result in a very powerful set of services available to your application development. The difficulties are partially overcome by better framework modularity and separation of concerns, and will probably be addressed even further in the future through the use of specific adapters and meta-frameworks.

6.3 A COMPARISON MATRIX

There are, as you can see, many things to be considered when evaluating a framework. Every factor must be taken into consideration, but the relative importance of various factors changes in any given situation. With the large number of variables, it is sometimes difficult to perform an objective evaluation.

A simple matrix can be used to help you take all of these factors into account, as well as their relative importance for your particular project or projects.

Here we present a basic template for such a matrix, and run through a couple of examples with it. You can then extend this method as required and use it for your decision making.

The matrix is designed to help you do two things: first, to objectively compare two, three, or more frameworks in terms of their specific capabilities and features and second, to compare the importance of each of these features for *your* particular project. Once this is done, you can use the results to evaluate a particular framework while at the same time taking your project into account, and arrive at a final "score" for each framework based on these criteria.

This is how to proceed:

- **List the candidates:** First, make a list of the frameworks you are going to compare. Ideally, they should all be relatively comparable, for example, it is much more difficult to realistically compare a presentation framework with a complete application framework. Two (or more) presentation frameworks, on the other hand, can reasonably be compared with each other.
- **List the features:** Now make a list of all of the features of the frameworks you are going to compare. You need to make this a complete list: if one framework has a feature that others do not have, you still include it. The "ranking" for the frameworks that do not have the feature are zero. We organize this list into a table, such as:

Features	Framework A	Framework B	Framework C	Weight
Database Connection Pooling				
Logging				
Caching				
Security				

- **Weight the features:** Now we must evaluate the *features* in light of our specific project. This is a process to determine how important, on a scale, each of the possible features is. At this stage, we are not considering the frameworks, we are only thinking about how essential each possible feature is in our own

A Comparison Matrix

given context. Often it is easier to select a simple scale, such as 1 through 10 (or if you like zero-indexing, 0 through 9). Two features are given the *same* score if they are *equally* important. For example, if a fairly important feature for your application is security, you might give it 9. If logging is considerably less important, you might give it 4. If scheduling is also a "nice-to-have" but not an essential feature, give it 4 as well. You might need to go back at this point and break down the feature list into a "finer grain." If you have listed, for example, a high-level feature such as "relational/object mapping," you might want to break down further into "relational/object mapping database independence," "relational/object mapping caching," and so forth. It depends on the specifics of the feature set you will need, and on how much detailed information you have about the framework. There is no point in breaking down the features into a fine-grained set if you do not have the ability to evaluate the framework at this level of detail.

Fill in these weights in the rightmost column of your matrix under the "Weight" heading:

Features	*Framework A*	*Framework B*	*Framework C*	*Weight*
Database Connection Pooling				8
Logging				2
Caching				7
Security				9

- **Rank the frameworks on each feature**: Here is the detailed part: rating *each* framework on *each* feature. At this stage, you are examining the framework in light of the feature itself, and comparing it with other frameworks in your matrix. For example, if frameworks A and B use the Log4j package for logging, it might be reasonable to use the same score. Perhaps one framework provides much more sophisticated user interface features – you would rank this framework higher on this feature than one that only provides basic UI ability. This ranking is not an easy process, but it does lead you to a better understanding of each of your chosen frameworks.

    When performing this ranking, it is usually better to use a simple scale again. Some people use a percentage (i.e., 0 to 100 percent), or a simple 1 to 10 scale. The important thing to realize is that the ranking must be a *relative* measure, as much as possible. In other words, if one framework provides mediocre logging capability, you might choose to rank it as 5 (on a 1 to 10 scale). If another framework has a much better capability, ranking it as 10 means that it is *twice as good* as the first one. Sometimes a percentage scale gives you more room to maneuver, but it can be difficult to be subjective. Some people find it helpful to assign simple ranking terms, such as:

- 1: Feature poor or absent
- 2: Feature supported, but not very well
- 3: Feature supported adequately
- 4: Feature supported well
- 5: Feature supported very well – best in class

This is a perfectly adequate scale. It is important to realize that it is not the numbers themselves that count, but how they are applied relative to other frameworks being analyzed: a rank of 3 is always better than a 2, irrespective of what the actual meaning of "3" is compared to "2." On the other hand, if it is a scale of 1 to 100, a rank of 3 is not *much* better than a 2!

Features	Framework A	Framework B	Framework C	Weight
Database Connection Pooling	5	7	7	8
Logging	3	9	5	2
Caching	0	6	5	7
Security	4	6	7	9

- **Compute the weighted score and compare:** Now you have all of the essential information, and it is time to analyze the results. At this point, take each framework's ranking on each feature, and multiply it by the weight for that column. Note the result and repeat the procedure for the next feature. Add this result to the first result. Keep doing this all the way to the last feature, and note the grand total against each framework. This is the framework's *total score* for this particular project. It is *not* that frameworks score in any kind of absolute terms, it is always relative to the given application.

  Now you simply compare the final scores of each framework. It is often helpful to rank them in descending order: theoretically, if you have done the analysis of each framework correctly, and if the weights were accurately assigned, the framework with the highest total score is the best choice for this project. We discuss below the appropriate amount of salt that these results should be taken with.

Features	Framework A	Framework B	Framework C	Weight
Database Connection Pooling	$5 \times 8 = 40$	$7 \times 8 = 56$	$7 \times 8 = 56$	8
Logging	$3 \times 2 = 6$	$9 \times 2 = 18$	$5 \times 2 = 10$	2
Caching	$0 \times 7 = 0$	$6 \times 7 = 42$	$5 \times 7 = 35$	7
Security	$4 \times 9 = 36$	$6 \times 9 = 54$	$7 \times 9 = 63$	9
Total Score	$40 + 6 + 0 + 36 = 82$	$56 + 18 + 42 + 54 = 170$	$56 + 10 + 35 + 63 = 164$	

In our above example, we have compared frameworks A, B, and C. We have shown only a comparison on four features, which is very likely totally inadequate in the real world – hundreds of features would not be unreasonable, and at least dozens are appropriate for any substantial framework. We will assume that A, B, and C are complete application frameworks, each purporting to provide services for a Web application to be developed in its entirety. For the purposes of this example, we have used a 0 to 9 scale for both weights and rankings.

We weighted the features according to our hypothetical project: database connection pooling was apparently quite important, it got 8. Logging was considerably less essential, weighted at 2. Caching was more important, and Security was the most important of the features, weighted at 9.

We then examined our frameworks individually. Frameworks B and C had almost the same level of support for Database Connection Pooling, each ranked at 7 whereas framework A was not as good. Logging was well supported by B apparently, with A ranking below C.

Caching was apparently not supported by A at all, hence the score of zero. B performed slightly better than C in the Caching feature, represented by only a slightly higher score.

Security was provided best by C, with B a close second, and A was a more distant third.

Now we compute: multiplying the rating by the weight, and adding each column gives us a total score of 82 for framework A, 170 for framework B, and 164 for framework C. So, theoretically, framework B would actually be slightly superior to framework C for our project, and framework A would be a fairly distant third.

6.3.1 Serve with Salt

Of course, the final "score" a framework gets is not the only indicator you need to use. One of the things this method does is to get you to think about the importance of each feature, objectively. To assign each feature's weight you must consider its importance, and this is in itself a helpful process. The same is true for a framework's feature set. As you complete the rating for each feature for a particular framework, you must investigate that feature and compare it to how that feature is scored for other frameworks. It narrows your thinking from a somewhat subjective overall impression of the framework to a more objective detailed view of that single feature. When the weights are applied and the score is tallied, it puts back together all of the individual results again in an objective way, through math. The method, of course, has its flaws, but the very process of going through it helps with the analysis.

Often, you will get the results from an analysis like this and disagree with them: your intuitive feeling was that framework "C" was better, but the analysis says framework "B" is. This can be useful in one of two ways. Perhaps you are right (yes, this happens sometimes) and framework "C" is really better. The analysis then, is not taking into consideration *why* it is better. You have either not included an essential feature (perhaps quality, or some other factor that is generally not considered), or you have weighted or ranked features incorrectly. Perhaps you do not have a broad enough scale for either the weight or the ranking – you might need to use a scale of 1 to 100, and not 1 to 10, if the difference between features is that broad, or if there are several features.

On the other hand, if you recheck all of these factors and still come up with the answer saying framework "B" is better, perhaps your intuitive feeling is incorrect, and is based on something that cannot be substantiated and measured. Going through the process, especially with the double-check discussed above, means that you must objectively consider the situation, and normally something that is giving you the impression that framework "C" is indeed better will come up in this process. As with any statistical method or numeric analysis, though, it is easy to skew the results to come up with the answer you want. If that is all your achieving, then do not bother to run the analysis in the first place.

It is also important to understand that the results from using a matrix like this are *only* valid for a specific project. It means nothing to say "framework x scored higher than framework y," you must say "framework x scored higher than framework y *for project z*. Anything else is an unfair judgment of a product against inappropriate criteria.

Given the appropriate skepticism and care, however, a simple analysis like this can be very revealing, and is a useful tool in your comparison of frameworks.

6.4 SUMMARY

We have looked at several different factors that should influence your decision when choosing a framework. As we have seen, there is no "right" answer all the time, and the specifics of your project must be brought to bear. We have also examined a simple method that can be used to help ensure you are objectively evaluating the features and benefits of a number of frameworks.

The different approaches of frameworks have some common elements, typical design patterns, which we will discuss in Chapter 8. The bottom line is that a framework is almost certainly going to bring significant benefits to your development project.

In the following chapters, we will examine in more detail some of the other major factors that you will want to take into account in your choice of frameworks. These factors can then be applied to the method discussed here to help you make a fully informed choice about which framework is suitable for your needs.

CHAPTER 7

Open Source and Components/Frameworks

In this chapter, we discuss the relationship of open source to components and frameworks. We also explore how open source can be of benefit in framework development, and how and why to draw the line between the open-source world and the commercial software world in the right place for your particular project. Although Chapter 8 concentrates on understanding, selection, and *use* of components and frameworks, this chapter deals with their development and ongoing evolution, specifically in relation to the open-source community.

7.1 OVERVIEW OF OPEN SOURCE

First, let us examine what open source is all about. We examine what the term means, how the concept translates into reality, and its impact on the software industry.

7.1.1 What is Open Source?

Open source is a term that is widely used in today's software industry, but it is not always clear what it exactly means. Many people have a specific idea in mind when they hear the term, but misconceptions abound.

Open source seems to imply free of cost, and often this is the case (although not necessarily). Many believe it means complete freedom to do what they wish to do with the software: to copy it, redistribute it, and so forth. This is *not* necessarily true at all.

Many people also have a negative reaction to open-source software, believing that some aspects of it will be harmful to their business or organization. Interestingly enough, they are sometimes right – though more often wrong.

In this chapter we explore the actual definition of open source, and its various forms. We look at what it means for a business to use an open-source project, and how open source affects the development of frameworks and components. Open source is a phenomenon that affects all parts of the software industry, especially Web-application development; so an objective understanding of the topic is essential for any developer today.

7.1.2 Free Software

A special category of open-source software is *free* software. The freedom referred to does not necessarily mean zero cost (although it often does); it refers to the freedom to exercise certain rights granted by the license of the "free" software. We will show some examples to demonstrate the difference between open-source and free software.

7.1.3 Licensing

The copyright holder of a piece of software is generally the author of the software. Copyright laws vary somewhat between countries, but unless specific steps are taken to do otherwise, it is usually the case that a single individual who creates a piece of software owns the copyright, and therefore owns the right to license its use to others. Copyright can be held jointly between more than one person, and it can also be held by a legal entity such as a corporation or a foundation, if it is explicitly transferred to them by the author.

Software is rarely "sold," in actual fact, or even given away. Selling a piece of software implies transferring the copyright of that software to another party in exchange for something. By and large, software is licensed. A license is literally a permission to use, and does not imply a transfer of ownership. It is more akin to a lease than a sale, although most software licenses do not have a specific time limit.

One special case of "licensing" that should be mentioned is public domain. An open-source license does *not* imply or mean that the product being licensed is in the public domain. Public domain specifically refers to a work that is not secured by copyright – it is publicly available and no license is required to use it. Generally, the creator of a piece of software must explicitly place it in the public domain.

A make-or-break criterion when choosing an Open-Source-Software (OSS) framework, or any other framework for that matter, is the license under which it is made available. This can range anything from no license at all, which is a problem in itself in some ways, to a "regular" commercial license, with all of the various terms and conditions that apply. I am no lawyer, but I have dealt with my share of different license agreements over the years and have come to the conclusion that the key to all of them is understanding exactly what is granted and what is not. If it is unclear what you are allowed to do, seek the necessary clarification – ideally, from the copyright holder of the original software, if possible. The copyright holder, after all, has the ability to re release the software under a different license. I have seen this happen a number of times – and there is nothing that prevents a single piece of software from being available under more than one license. In today's environment with so many different patent and license issues, it is almost always a good idea to seek qualified legal advice to ensure everything is in order before undertaking a major project.

What you want to include in a framework license depends, of course, on what you want to do with your finished application. In general, you want as few restrictions as possible on the use of a framework and the applications you build with it. If it is your intention to release the finished application under an open-source license, then the conditions in the license of the framework that require you to do so would not necessarily be a problem. The so-called viral licensing schemes usually require that you release your finished application under either the same or some close variant of the original license, making it doubly important that you understand what is allowed and what is not. Do not take "common usage" as your guide either – just because someone has done a certain thing with an application does not mean that it is necessarily allowed – sometimes it only means that the original copyright holder has not found out about it yet.

For more business-oriented applications, you may want to look for a license that does not place restrictions on whether or how you charge for the finished product. A good example of this kind of license is the BSD license or the Apache license. These licenses mostly exist to ensure that appropriate credit is passed on to the original copyright holder, and to disclaim any implication of warranty. They place almost no other restrictions on how the framework is used – making them good choices where a framework is introduced to a company that is not familiar with open source in general.

7.1.4 Open-Source Licenses

Although saying right up front that I am not a lawyer, and that if you have doubts about a license you must, of course, get proper legal advice, let us have a look at a few common open-source licenses and their advantages and disadvantages. This is not so much to pick out the right kind of license for a particular application, but to get familiar with the various aspects of open-source licenses in general. It is also important to keep in mind that there are often several different versions of a license, released at different times – so it is important to read the "specific" license that comes with the software you are looking at, and not to base any decisions on generalities.

Licenses range from the extremely simple to the mind-numbingly complex. Fortunately, most open-source licenses are fairly straightforward, but the actual terms require different actions and responsibilities to be undertaken by the user of the product so licensed. Before you commit to a framework, ensure that you understand what your responsibilities are: open source does not mean "carte blanche" and universal freedom to do what you wish!

Let us examine some licenses and how they relate to framework products.

7.1.4.1 BSD License

One of the most "open" and simplest open-source license, the BSD license used to have an additional clause compared to the MIT license – the two are now functionally the same. In fact, the BSD license is sufficiently simple that we reproduce an example of the license here:

```
          Copyright (c) (year) (copyright holders)
Permission is hereby granted, free of charge, to any
person obtaining a copy of this software and associated
documentation files (the "Software"), to deal in the
Software without restriction, including without limi-
tation the rights to use, copy, modify, merge, publish,
```

```
distribute, sub-license, and/or sell copies of the Soft-
ware, and to permit persons to whom the Software is
furnished to do so, subject to the following conditions:
The above copyright notice and this permission notice
shall be included in all copies or substantial portions
of the Software.

THE SOFTWARE IS PROVIDED "AS IS", WITHOUT WARRANTY
OF ANY KIND, EXPRESS OR IMPLIED, INCLUDING BUT NOT
LIMITED TO THE WARRANTIES OF MERCHANTABILITY, FITNESS
FOR A PARTICULAR PURPOSE AND NONINFRINGEMENT. IN NO
EVENT SHALL THE AUTHORS OR COPYRIGHT HOLDERS BE LIABLE
FOR ANY CLAIM, DAMAGES OR OTHER LIABILITY, WHETHER IN
AN ACTION OF CONTRACT, TORT OR OTHERWISE, ARISING FROM,
OUT OF OR IN CONNECTION WITH THE SOFTWARE OR THE USE OR
OTHER DEALINGS IN THE SOFTWARE.
```

As you can see, the BSD or MIT license is fundamentally a disclaimer, ensuring that the developer who licenses the software to others is not held liable by any implied warranty, and simply stating that they may "deal in the software" without any restrictions at all. Older versions of this license used to include a clause that restricted the use of the originating organization in any promotions, but this has been removed in more recent versions. Fundamentally, the main requirement of the license is that the copyright notice and permission notice be included with subsequent copies and versions of the software. The license does, however, start with a statement of the copyright, ensuring that the ownership of the software is clear. It also explicitly grants the permission to "deal in the Software without restriction," making it one of the most flexible licenses we examine. It then goes on to list what some of these rights are, without necessarily limiting any that are not mentioned.

This license is notable for what it *does not* include: it says nothing about requiring other products or projects to be released under the same or a similar license. BSD-licensed projects can be included in commercial projects, other open-source projects, and all variations in between without restrictions other than the requirement to include the copyright and license notices.

7.1.4.2 Apache License

The Apache license is one of the simpler and more direct open-source licenses. The primary point of the license is a disclaimer of liability – stating in strong terms that just because you use the software, the copyright holder does not assume any liability for its function. The license permits redistribution without restriction on modifications (unlike some licenses, as we will see). It does, however, impose a few conditions, mostly designed to maintain the copyright notice in any redistributed copies, and to ensure that an appropriate acknowledgment is included in the documentation of any copies, stating the origin of the software.

Other than a few terms restricting the use of the name of the Apache Foundation in promotions, that is about it, this license makes no statement about the use of the software in commercial or noncommercial applications. This makes it a good choice when the finished product is intended to be sold, and not given away. The Apache license is generally regarded as a "business-friendly" license.

The specimen license below is used in the Turbine project – all other Apache projects carry a similar license, with appropriate changes to the project name.

```
Copyright (c) 1997-1999 The Java Apache Project. All
rights reserved.
Redistribution and use in source and binary forms, with
or without modification, are permitted provided that the
following conditions are met:

1. Redistributions of source code must retain the above
   copyright notice, this list of conditions and the
   following disclaimer.
2. Redistributions in binary form must reproduce the
   above copyright notice, this list of conditions and
   the following disclaimer in the documentation and/or
   other materials provided with the distribution.
3. All advertising materials mentioning features or use
   of this software must display the following acknowl-
   edgment:
     "This product includes software developed by the
     Java Apache Project for use in the Apache JServ
     servlet engine project <http://java.apache.org/>."
4. The names "Apache JServ", "Apache JServ Servlet
   Engine", "Turbine", "Apache Turbine", "Turbine
   Project", "Apache Turbine Project" and "Java Apache
   Project" must not be used to endorse or promote
```

> products derived from this software without prior
> written permission.
> Products derived from this software may not be called
> "Apache JServ" nor may "Apache" nor "Apache JServ"
> appear in their names without prior written permis-
> sion of the Java Apache Project.

The above paragraphs protect the integrity and use of the name "Apache" and associated names of both the group and the particular project. This is one of the key differences between this license and the BSD-type license. It has few other constraints, however.

> 5. Redistributions of any form whatsoever must retain
>   the following acknowledgment:
>   "This product includes software developed by the
>   Java Apache Project for use in the Apache JServ
>   servlet engine project <http://java.apache.org/>."

> THIS SOFTWARE IS PROVIDED BY THE JAVA APACHE PROJECT "AS IS" AND ANY EXPRESSED OR IMPLIED WARRANTIES, IN-CLUDING, BUT NOT LIMITED TO, THE IMPLIED WARRANTIES OF MERCHANTABILITY AND FITNESS FOR A PARTICULAR PURPOSE ARE DISCLAIMED. IN NO EVENT SHALL THE JAVA APACHE PROJECT OR ITS CONTRIBUTORS BE LIABLE FOR ANY DIRECT, INDIRECT, INCIDENTAL, SPECIAL, EXEMPLARY, OR CONSEQUENTIAL DAMAGES (INCLUDING, BUT NOT LIMITED TO, PROCUREMENT OF SUBSTI-TUTE GOODS OR SERVICES; LOSS OF USE, DATA, OR PROFITS; OR BUSINESS INTERRUPTION) HOWEVER CAUSED AND ON ANY THE-ORY OF LIABILITY, WHETHER IN CONTRACT, STRICT LIABILITY, OR TORT (INCLUDING NEGLIGENCE OR OTHERWISE) ARISING IN ANY WAY OUT OF THE USE OF THIS SOFTWARE, EVEN IF ADVISED OF THE POSSIBILITY OF SUCH DAMAGE.
> This software consists of voluntary contributions made by many individuals on behalf of the Java Apache Group. For more information on the Java Apache Project and the Apache JServ Servlet Engine project, please see <http://java.apache.org/>.

7.1.4.3 GNU License

There are actually two types of the GNU license that we should examine: the GNU General Public License (GPL) is the first, and is a popular license applied to a number of frameworks.

We comment on some sections of the GPL that are relevant to framework and component development.

```
                GNU GENERAL PUBLIC LICENSE
                   Version 2, June 1991

 Copyright (C) 1989, 1991 Free Software Foundation, Inc.
 59 Temple Place, Suite 330, Boston, MA 02111-1307 USA.
 Everyone is permitted to copy and distribute verbatim
 copies of this license document, but changing it is not
 allowed.

                        Preamble
```

The GPL begins with what is effectively a narrative description, explaining the intent of the license and its many terms.

```
   The licenses for most software are designed to take
 away your freedom to share and change it. By contrast,
 the GNU General Public License is intended to guarantee
 your freedom to share and change free software--to make
 sure the software is free for all its users. This Gen-
 eral Public License applies to most of the Free Software
 Foundation's software and to any other program whose
 authors commit to using it. (Some other Free Software
 Foundation software is covered by the GNU Library Gen-
 eral Public License instead.) You can apply it to your
 programs, too.

   When we speak of free software, we are referring to
 freedom, not price. Our General Public Licenses are
 designed to make sure that you have the freedom to dis-
 tribute copies of free software (and charge for this
 service if you wish), that you receive source code
 or can get it if you want it, that you can change the
```

software or use pieces of it in new free programs; and that you know you can do these things.

To protect your rights, we need to make restrictions that forbid anyone to deny you these rights or to ask you to surrender the rights. These restrictions translate to certain responsibilities for you if you distribute copies of the software, or if you modify it.

For example, if you distribute copies of such a program, whether gratis or for a fee, you must give the recipients all the rights that you have. You must make sure that they, too, receive or can get the source code. And you must show them these terms so they know their rights.

We protect your rights with two steps: (1) copyright the software, and (2) offer you this license which gives you legal permission to copy, distribute and/or modify the software.

Also, for each author's protection and ours, we want to make certain that everyone understands that there is no warranty for this free software. If the software is modified by someone else and passed on, we want its recipients to know that what they have is not the original, so that any problems introduced by others will not reflect on the original authors' reputations.

Finally, any free program is threatened constantly by software patents. We wish to avoid the danger that redistributors of a free program will individually obtain patent licenses, in effect making the program proprietary. To prevent this, we have made it clear that any patent must be licensed for everyone's free use or not licensed at all.

The precise terms and conditions for copying, distribution and modification follow.

After the preamble and description, the main body of the license lays out the legal terms.

```
                GNU GENERAL PUBLIC LICENSE
      TERMS AND CONDITIONS FOR COPYING, DISTRIBUTION
                       AND MODIFICATION

  0. This License applies to any program or other work
which contains a notice placed by the copyright holder
saying it may be distributed under the terms of this
General Public License. The "Program", below, refers
to any such program or work, and a "work based on the
Program" means either the Program or any derivative work
under copyright law: that is to say, a work containing
the Program or a portion of it, either verbatim or with
modifications and/or translated into another language.
(Hereinafter, translation is included without limitation
in the term "modification".) Each licensee is addressed
as "you".
```

The above paragraph is of particular interest to frameworks licensed under the GPL. It discusses the term "derivative work," and this generally applies to applications built using a framework. It goes on to say that a derivative work includes a program that contains a portion of the licensed program. In most cases, a finished application does indeed contain all or a portion of the framework it was created with, as frameworks, unlike code generators, include services used by the application at run time. This then means that applications built with a framework licensed under the GPL will likely also need to be licensed under the GPL.

```
  Activities other than copying, distribution and mod-
  ification are not covered by this License; they are
  outside its scope. The act of running the Program is
  not restricted, and the output from the Program is cov-
  ered only if its contents constitute a work based on
  the Program (independent of having been made by running
  the Program). Whether that is true depends on what the
  Program does.
```

1. You may copy and distribute verbatim copies of the Program's source code as you receive it, in any medium, provided that you conspicuously and appropriately publish on each copy an appropriate copyright notice and disclaimer of warranty; keep intact all the notices that refer to this License and to the absence of any warranty; and give any other recipients of the Program a copy of this License along with the Program.

   You may charge a fee for the physical act of transferring a copy, and you may at your option offer warranty protection in exchange for a fee.

The above paragraph explicitly permits charging for certain services relating to the product, which can be extended when dealing with a framework to charge a client for the transfer of the copy and the related application.

2. You may modify your copy or copies of the Program or any portion of it, thus forming a work based on the Program, and copy and distribute such modifications or work under the terms of Section 1 above, provided that you also meet all of these conditions:
   a) You must cause the modified files to carry prominent notices stating that you changed the files and the date of any change.
   b) You must cause any work that you distribute or publish, that in whole or in part contains or is derived from the Program or any part thereof, to be licensed as a whole at no charge to all third parties under the terms of this License.

The above paragraphs indicate that additions to the framework must be noted as such, and that such additions must also be licensed under the terms of the GPL.

   c) If the modified program normally reads commands interactively when run, you must cause it, when started running for such interactive use in the

> most ordinary way, to print or display an announcement including an appropriate copyright notice and a notice that there is no warranty (or else, saying that you provide a warranty) and that users may redistribute the program under these conditions, and telling the user how to view a copy of this License. (Exception: if the Program itself is interactive but does not normally print such an announcement, your work based on the Program is not required to print an announcement.)

These requirements apply to the modified work as a whole. If identifiable sections of that work are not derived from the Program, and can be reasonably considered independent and separate works in themselves, then this License, and its terms, do not apply to those sections when you distribute them as separate works. But when you distribute the same sections as part of a whole which is a work based on the Program, the distribution of the whole must be on the terms of this License, whose permissions for other licensees extend to the entire whole, and thus to each and every part regardless of who wrote it.

The above paragraph is of particular importance when considering component development. When a component is considered a "separate work," for example, it is distributed independently from the framework that supports it, and the above paragraph indicates the status of this component.

> Thus, it is not the intent of this section to claim rights or contest your rights to work written entirely by you; rather, the intent is to exercise the right to control the distribution of derivative or collective works based on the Program.
>
> In addition, mere aggregation of another work not based on the Program with the Program (or with a work based on the Program) on a volume of a storage or distribution medium does not bring the other work under the scope of this License.

The above paragraph includes the case of using a library of application-specific framework that provides some functionality in conjunction with a library licensed under the GPL. For example, if you have a GPL-licensed framework and also want to use the Xerces XML parser, which is licensed under the Apache license, there is no conflict according to this paragraph – Xerces is not considered to be licensed under the GPL by association.

```
3. You may copy and distribute the Program (or a work
   based on it,under Section 2) in object code or ex-
   ecutable form under the terms of Sections 1 and 2
   above provided that you also do one of the following:
   a) Accompany it with the complete corresponding
      machine-readable source code, which must be dis-
      tributed under the terms of Sections 1 and 2 above
      on a medium customarily used for software inter-
      change; or,
   b) Accompany it with a written offer, valid for at
      least three years, to give any third party, for a
      charge no more than your cost of physically per-
      forming source distribution, a complete machine-
      readable copy of the corresponding source code, to
      be distributed under the terms of Sections 1 and
      2 above on a medium customarily used for software
      interchange; or,
```

The above paragraphs imply specific duties on the distributor of a GPL-licensed program, and ordinarily an application that is built with a framework will indeed require the framework itself to be redistributed with it. The following terms would then apply:

```
   c) Accompany it with the information you received as
      to the offer to distribute corresponding source
      code. (This alternative is allowed only for non-
      commercial distribution and only if you received
      the program in object code or executable form with
      such an offer, in accord with Subsection b above.)

The source code for a work means the preferred form
of the work for making modifications to it. For an
```

executable work, complete source code means all the
source code for all modules it contains, plus any
associated interface definition files, plus the scripts
used to control compilation and installation of the
executable. However, as a special exception, the source
code distributed need not include anything that is
normally distributed (in either source or binary form)
with the major components (compiler, kernel, and so on)
of the operating system on which the executable runs,
unless that component itself accompanies the executable.
If distribution of executable or object code is made by
offering access to copy from a designated place, then
offering equivalent access to copy the source code from
the same place counts as distribution of the source
code, even though third parties are not compelled to
copy the source along with the object code.

4. You may not copy, modify, sub-license, or distribute
   the Program except as expressly provided under this
   License. Any attempt otherwise to copy, modify,
   sublicense or distribute the Program is void, and
   will automatically terminate your rights under this
   License. However, parties who have received copies,
   or rights, from you under this License will not have
   their licenses terminated so long as such parties
   remain in full compliance.

5. You are not required to accept this License, since
   you have not signed it. However, nothing else
   grants you permission to modify or distribute the
   Program or its derivative works. These actions are
   prohibited by law if you do not accept this License.
   Therefore, by modifying or distributing the Program
   (or any work based on the Program), you indicate
   your acceptance of this License to do so, and all
   its terms and conditions for copying, distributing or
   modifying the Program or works based on it.

The above paragraph indicates that using a GPL-licensed framework to create your application *and distributing it with your application* would indeed be considered as an indication of your acceptance of the license for that framework.

6. Each time you redistribute the Program (or any work based on the Program), the recipient automatically receives a license from the original licensor to copy, distribute or modify the Program subject to these terms and conditions. You may not impose any further restrictions on the recipients' exercise of the rights granted herein. You are not responsible for enforcing compliance by third parties to this License.

7. If, as a consequence of a court judgment or allegation of patent infringement or for any other reason (not limited to patent issues), conditions are imposed on you (whether by court order, agreement or otherwise) that contradict the conditions of this License, they do not excuse you from the conditions of this License. If you cannot distribute so as to satisfy simultaneously your obligations under this License and any other pertinent obligations, then as a consequence you may not distribute the Program at all. For example, if a patent license would not permit royalty-free redistribution of the Program by all those who receive copies directly or indirectly through you, then the only way you could satisfy both it and this License would be to refrain entirely from distribution of the Program.

If any portion of this section is held invalid or unenforceable under any particular circumstance, the balance of the section is intended to apply and the section as a whole is intended to apply in other circumstances.

It is not the purpose of this section to induce you to infringe any patents or other property right claims or to contest validity of any such claims; this section has the sole purpose of protecting the integrity of the free software distribution system, which is implemented by public license practices. Many people have made generous contributions to the wide range of software distributed through that system in reliance on consistent application of that system; it is up to the author/donor to decide if he or she is willing to distribute software through any other system and a licensee cannot impose that choice.

This section is intended to make thoroughly clear what is believed to be a consequence of the rest of this License.

8. If the distribution and/or use of the Program is restricted in certain countries either by patents or by copyrighted interfaces, the original copyright holder who places the Program under this License may add an explicit geographical distribution limitation excluding those countries, so that distribution is permitted only in or among countries not thus excluded. In such case, this License incorporates the limitation as if written in the body of this License.

9. The Free Software Foundation may publish revised and/or new versions of the General Public License from time to time. Such new versions will be similar in spirit to the present version, but may differ in detail to address new problems or concerns.

Each version is given a distinguishing version number. If the Program specifies a version number of this License which applies to it and "any later version", you have the option of following the terms and conditions either of that version or of any later version published by the Free Software Foundation. If the Program does not specify a version number of this License, you may choose any version ever published by the Free Software Foundation.

10. If you wish to incorporate parts of the Program into other free programs whose distribution conditions are different, write to the author to ask for permission. For software which is copyrighted by the Free Software Foundation, write to the Free Software Foundation; we sometimes make exceptions for this. Our decision will be guided by the two goals of preserving the free status of all derivatives of our free software and of promoting the sharing and reuse of software generally.

The above paragraph mentions the possibility of the Free Software Foundation or other bodies using the GPL making exceptions to its licensing terms in certain circumstances. If you perceive a conflict with another package, it is well worth contacting the copyright holder to see whether the conflict is easily resolvable – one way is by dual (or multiple) licensing, where a product is released under more than one license at the same time.

NO WARRANTY

11. BECAUSE THE PROGRAM IS LICENSED FREE OF CHARGE, THERE IS NO WARRANTY FOR THE PROGRAM, TO THE EXTENT PERMITTED BY APPLICABLE LAW. EXCEPT WHEN OTHERWISE STATED IN WRITING THE COPYRIGHT HOLDERS AND/OR OTHER PARTIES PROVIDE THE PROGRAM "AS IS" WITHOUT WARRANTY OF ANY KIND, EITHER EXPRESSED OR IMPLIED, INCLUDING, BUT NOT LIMITED TO, THE IMPLIED WARRANTIES OF MERCHANTABILITY AND FITNESS FOR A PARTICULAR PURPOSE. THE ENTIRE RISK AS TO THE QUALITY AND PERFORMANCE OF THE PROGRAM IS WITH YOU. SHOULD THE PROGRAM PROVE DEFECTIVE, YOU ASSUME THE COST OF ALL NECESSARY SERVICING, REPAIR OR CORRECTION.

12. IN NO EVENT UNLESS REQUIRED BY APPLICABLE LAW OR AGREED TO IN WRITING WILL ANY COPYRIGHT HOLDER, OR ANY OTHER PARTY WHO MAY MODIFY AND/OR REDISTRIBUTE THE PROGRAM AS PERMITTED ABOVE, BE LIABLE TO YOU FOR DAMAGES, INCLUDING ANY GENERAL, SPECIAL, INCIDENTAL OR CONSEQUENTIAL DAMAGES ARISING OUT OF

Overview of Open Source 261

```
THE USE OR INABILITY TO USE THE PROGRAM (INCLUDING
BUT NOT LIMITED TO LOSS OF DATA OR DATA BEING REN-
DERED INACCURATE OR LOSSES SUSTAINED BY YOU OR THIRD
PARTIES OR A FAILURE OF THE PROGRAM TO OPERATE WITH
ANY OTHER PROGRAMS), EVEN IF SUCH HOLDER OR OTHER
PARTY HAS BEEN ADVISED OF THE POSSIBILITY OF SUCH
DAMAGES.
```

The main body of the GPL ends with the relatively standard disclaimer of liability, which is an essential part of all licenses. It is followed by instructions for applying the GPL to your own works – something that does not necessarily apply to applications created with a GPL-licensed framework. The option always exists, of course, and many applications are indeed licensed in this way according to this procedure.

```
                END OF TERMS AND CONDITIONS

         How to Apply These Terms to Your New Programs

  If you develop a new program, and you want it to be of
the greatest possible use to the public, the best way to
achieve this is to make it free software which everyone
can redistribute and change under these terms.
  To do so, attach the following notices to the pro-
gram. It is safest to attach them to the start of each
source file to most effectively convey the exclusion of
warranty; and each file should have at least the "copy-
right" line and a pointer to where the full notice is
found.
<one line to give the program's name and a brief idea of
what it does.>
Copyright (C) <year> <name of author>
This program is free software; you can redistribute
it and/or modify it under the terms of the GNU General
Public License as published by the Free Software Foun-
dation; either version 2 of the License, or (at your
option) any later version.
This program is distributed in the hope that it will
be useful, but WITHOUT ANY WARRANTY; without even the
implied warranty of MERCHANTABILITY or FITNESS FOR A
```

PARTICULAR PURPOSE. See the GNU General Public License for more details.

You should have received a copy of the GNU General Public License along with this program; if not, write to the Free Software Foundation, Inc., 59 Temple Place, Suite 330, Boston, MA 02111-1307 USA.

Also add information on how to contact you by electronic and paper mail.

If the program is interactive, make it output a short notice like this when it starts in an interactive mode:

Gnomovision version 69, Copyright (C) year name of author Gnomovision comes with ABSOLUTELY NO WARRANTY; for details type 'show w'. This is free software, and you are welcome to redistribute it under certain conditions; type 'show c' for details.

The hypothetical commands 'show w' and 'show c' should show the appropriate parts of the General Public License. Of course, the commands you use may be called something other than 'show w' and 'show c'; they could even be mouse-clicks or menu items--whatever suits your program.

You should also get your employer (if you work as a programmer) or your school, if any, to sign a "copyright disclaimer" for the program, if necessary. Here is a sample; alter the names:

Yoyodyne, Inc., hereby disclaims all copyright interest in the program 'Gnomovision' (which makes passes at compilers) written by James Hacker.

<signature of Ty Coon>, 1 April 1989

Ty Coon, President of Vice

This General Public License does not permit incorporating your program into proprietary programs. If your program is a subroutine library, you may consider it more useful to permit linking proprietary applications with the library. If this is what you want to do, use the GNU Library General Public License instead of this License.

The GNU General Public license is a fairly long document, at least as compared to some other OSS licenses. It begins with a preamble that clearly explains the intent of the license, including its intent to guarantee the freedom to share and change free software. It does not limit the ability to charge money for the *distribution* of the software, but it does impose a number of other limitations. It requires the user of the software to pass on the same rights to the software that they have to any subsequent users – thus, guaranteeing the same free access to the software that the first user enjoyed. It also specifically places restrictions on the patenting of software derived from the licensed software.

The GPL clearly explains the terms and conditions – this is one thing that adds to its length. It also includes a specimen copyright notice, and a detailed explanation of how to apply its terms to new packages that are created.

As with the Apache license, the GPL requires that the copyright and license information be duplicated in any new copies or derivatives of the software.

Most importantly for some purposes, the GPL requires that products that contain the licensed software must be "licensed as a whole at no charge to all third parties under the terms of this License." There is some debate about the precise meaning, but the general consensus is that this makes software licensed under the GPL unsuitable for use in commercial applications where the software is being resold. Some consider this a misinterpretation of the purpose of the GPL, but the possibility alone is sometimes enough to discourage commercial application of products that are based on the GPL. In the case of frameworks, it may be reasonably argued that any application built using the framework might fall under the GPL if the framework itself was licensed that way, and this is unacceptable to many organizations. This is sometimes referred to as a "viral" license, in the sense that it "infects" the applications built with it or on top of it with its own specific licensing constraints.

The second GNU license is called the GNU Library Public License, often abbreviated LGPL. This is a variation of the GPL that is often applied to libraries, or software that is specifically intended to be incorporated into other works. The LGPL still guarantees the right of the users of the application to access the source code of the package. The LGPL, however, has special modifications that permit the library so licensed to be incorporated into "nonfree" programs. The key definition in this license is the difference between a "work based on the library" and a "work that uses the library."

There is an active debate between proponents of the Apache license, and similar "Apache-style" licenses, and proponents of the GNU licenses. Those who favor the GNU license maintain that it enforces essential rights of the user, and that its application to derived works of the original product is an essential part of this enforcement. Advocates of the Apache license maintain that the very act of enforcing these rights is an infringement on the freedom that open source (and free software) hopes to maintain. Some developers say that even the Apache license contains too many restrictions, and prefer the BSD license, which is essentially little more than a disclaimer of liability. Less is more, these developers believe, when it comes to licensing.

In some framework projects, in fact efforts are made so as not to "mix" types of licenses. For example, most Apache projects cannot make use of any components that are licensed under the GPL (because the GPL states that works derived from it must themselves be licensed under the GPL). The LGPL was created specifically to address this requirement, and is often used for this purpose.

7.1.4.4 Mozilla License

The popular Web browser application's introduction to the open-source community spawned a new type of open-source license. Many other open-source projects have emulated this license, and although they are not exact replicas, they can fairly be called "Mozilla-type" licenses.

The Mozilla license defines its terms very carefully, and specifies exactly what is meant by "modifications," an important term in this license. It grants permission for worldwide and royalty-free licensing from both the original developers of the application, and from all subsequent contributors explicitly. (Many other licenses do not explicitly grant this permission for subsequent contributors.) It also mentions that all modifications created or contributed are covered by the same license, effectively extending the license to all extensions of the product. It includes the usual admonitions about including a copy of the license in any distributions or derived works as well, as most licenses do.

The Mozilla license states that the modifications you might perform must be documented in a file included with the modifications. It also specifies that "Larger Works" may be created that are *not* necessarily released under the same license, but that Covered Code (code originally licensed under the Mozilla license) is still covered by the Mozilla license.

The Mozilla Public License is still a fairly extensive license, and has many definitions that are important to be clarified before using software released this way. Let us have a look at the license itself:

```
Mozilla Public License Version 1.0

1. Definitions.
   1.1. "Contributor" means each entity that creates or
        contributes to the creation of Modifications.
   1.2. "Contributor Version" means the combination of
```

Overview of Open Source

>   the Original Code, prior Modifications used by a
>   Contributor, and the Modifications made by that
>   particular Contributor.
> 1.3. "Covered Code" means the Original Code or Mod-
>   ifications or the combination of the Original
>   Code and Modifications, in each case including
>   portions thereof.
> 1.4. "Electronic Distribution Mechanism" means a
>   mechanism generally accepted in the software
>   development community for the electronic
>   transfer of data.
> 1.5. "Executable" means Covered Code in any form
>   other than Source Code.
> 1.6. "Initial Developer" means the individual or
>   entity identified as the Initial Developer in
>   the Source Code notice required by Exhibit A.
> 1.7. "Larger Work" means a work which combines
>   Covered Code or portions thereof with code not
>   governed by the terms of this License.

Generally, an application created using a Mozilla-licensed framework would be considered a "larger work."

> 1.8. "License" means this document.
> 1.9. "Modifications" means any addition to or dele-
>   tion from the substance or structure of either the
>   Original Code or any previous Modifications. When
>   Covered Code is released as a series of files, a
>   Modification is:
>
> A. Any addition to or deletion from the contents of a
>   file containing Original Code or previous Modifica-
>   tions.
> B. Any new file that contains any part of the Original
>   Code or previous Modifications.
>
> 1.10. "Original Code" means Source Code of computer
>   software code which is described in the Source
>   Code notice required by Exhibit A as Original

Code, and which, at the time of its release under this License is not already Covered Code governed by this License.

1.11. "Source Code" means the preferred form of the Covered Code for making modifications to it, including all modules it contains, plus any associated interface definition files, scripts used to control compilation and installation of an Executable, or a list of source code differential comparisons against either the Original Code or another well known, available Covered Code of the Contributor's choice. The Source Code can be in a compressed or archival form, provided the appropriate decompression or de-archiving software is widely available for no charge.

1.12. "You" means an individual or a legal entity exercising rights under, and complying with all of the terms of, this License or a future version of this License issued under Section 6.1. For legal entities, "You" includes any entity which controls, is controlled by, or is under common control with You. For purposes of this definition, "control" means (a) the power, direct or indirect, to cause the direction or management of such entity, whether by contract or otherwise, or (b) ownership of fifty percent (50%) or more of the outstanding shares or beneficial ownership of such entity.

2. Source Code License.
   2.1. The Initial Developer Grant.
   The Initial Developer hereby grants You a worldwide, royalty-free, non-exclusive license, subject to third party intellectual property claims:
   (a) to use, reproduce, modify, display, perform, sublicense and distribute the Original Code (or portions thereof) with or without Modifications, or as part of a Larger Work; and

```
    (b) under patents now or hereafter owned or con-
        trolled by Initial Developer, to make, have made,
        use and sell ("Utilize") the Original Code (or
        portions thereof), but solely to the extent that
        any such patent is reasonably necessary to enable
        You to Utilize the Original Code (or portions
        thereof) and not to any greater extent that may
        be necessary to Utilize further Modifications or
        combinations.
    2.2. Contributor Grant.
    Each Contributor hereby grants You a world-wide,
    royalty-free, non-exclusive license, subject to third
    party intellectual property claims:
    (a) to use, reproduce, modify, display, perform, sub-
        license and distribute the Modifications created
        by such Contributor (or portions thereof) either
        on an unmodified basis, with other Modifications,
        as Covered Code or as part of a Larger Work; and
    (b) under patents now or hereafter owned or con-
        trolled by Contributor, to Utilize the Contrib-
        utor Version (or portions thereof), but solely
        to the extent that any such patent is reasonably
        necessary to enable You to Utilize the Contribu-
        tor Version (or portions thereof), and not to any
        greater extent that may be necessary to Utilize
        further Modifications or combinations.
```

The above terms expressly address the licensing of code donated by contributors to the project – most projects licensed under other licenses also take at least some steps to ensure that "donated" code becomes legally the copyright of the primary copyright holder. Some organizations even have a specific "contributor agreement" that ensures this copyright transfer is handled correctly. There are no universally accepted standards on how this is handled, and in practice it has not often been a serious concern.

```
    3. Distribution Obligations.
        3.1. Application of License.
        The Modifications which You create or to which You
        contribute are governed by the terms of this License,
```

including without limitation Section 2.2. The Source Code version of Covered Code may be distributed only under the terms of this License or a future version of this License released under Section 6.1, and You must include a copy of this License with every copy of the Source Code You distribute. You may not offer or impose any terms on any Source Code version that alters or restricts the applicable version of this License or the recipients' rights hereunder. However, You may include an additional document offering the additional rights described in Section 3.5.

3.2. Availability of Source Code.

Any Modification which You create or to which You contribute must be made available in Source Code form under the terms of this License either on the same media as an Executable version or via an accepted Electronic Distribution Mechanism to anyone to whom you made an Executable version available; and if made available via Electronic Distribution Mechanism, must remain available for at least twelve (12) months after the date it initially became available, or at least six (6) months after a subsequent version of that particular Modification has been made available to such recipients. You are responsible for ensuring that the Source Code version remains available even if the Electronic Distribution Mechanism is maintained by a third party.

The above term implies that the framework you construct your application with would need to be available in source code form to anyone you license your application – an important responsibility that is also required by the GNU public license and several others.

3.3. Description of Modifications.

You must cause all Covered Code to which you contribute to contain a file documenting the changes You made to create that Covered Code and the date of any change. You must include a prominent statement that the Modification

is derived, directly or indirectly, from Original Code
provided by the Initial Developer and including the name
of the Initial Developer in (a) the Source Code, and (b)
in any notice in an Executable version or related documentation in which You describe the origin or ownership
of the Covered Code.

3.4. Intellectual Property Matters

(a) Third Party Claims.

If You have knowledge that a party claims an intellectual property right in particular functionality or
code (or its utilization under this License), you must
include a text file with the source code distribution
titled "LEGAL" which describes the claim and the party
making the claim in sufficient detail that a recipient
will know whom to contact. If you obtain such knowledge
after You make Your Modification available as described
in Section 3.2, You shall promptly modify the LEGAL file
in all copies You make available thereafter and shall
take other steps (such as notifying appropriate mailing
lists or newsgroups) reasonably calculated to inform
those who received the Covered Code that new knowledge
has been obtained.

(b) Contributor APIs.

If Your Modification is an application programming interface and You own or control patents which are reasonably necessary to implement that API, you must also
include this information in the LEGAL file.

3.5. Required Notices.

You must duplicate the notice in Exhibit A in each file
of the Source Code, and this License in any documentation for the Source Code, where You describe recipients'
rights relating to Covered Code. If You created one or

more Modification(s), You may add your name as a Contributor to the notice described in Exhibit A. If it is not possible to put such notice in a particular Source Code file due to its structure, then you must include such notice in a location (such as a relevant directory file) where a user would be likely to look for such a notice. You may choose to offer, and to charge a fee for, warranty, support, indemnity or liability obligations to one or more recipients of Covered Code. However, You may do so only on Your own behalf, and not on behalf of the Initial Developer or any Contributor. You must make it absolutely clear than any such warranty, support, indemnity or liability obligation is offered by You alone, and You hereby agree to indemnify the Initial Developer and every Contributor for any liability incurred by the Initial Developer or such Contributor as a result of warranty, support, indemnity or liability terms You offer.

3.6. Distribution of Executable Versions.

You may distribute Covered Code in Executable form only if the requirements of Section 3.1-3.5 have been met for that Covered Code, and if You include a notice stating that the Source Code version of the Covered Code is available under the terms of this License, including a description of how and where You have fulfilled the obligations of Section 3.2. The notice must be conspicuously included in any notice in an Executable version, related documentation or collateral in which You describe recipients' rights relating to the Covered Code. You may distribute the Executable version of Covered Code under a license of Your choice, which may contain terms different from this License, provided that You are in compliance with the terms of this License and that the license for the Executable version does not attempt to limit or alter the recipient's rights in the Source Code version from the rights set forth in this License. If You distribute the Executable version under a different license You must make it absolutely clear

Overview of Open Source

```
that any terms which differ from this License are of-
fered by You alone, not by the Initial Developer or any
Contributor. You hereby agree to indemnify the Initial
Developer and every Contributor for any liability in-
curred by the Initial Developer or such Contributor as a
result of any such terms You offer.

3.7. Larger Works.

You may create a Larger Work by combining Covered Code
with other code not governed by the terms of this Li-
cense and distribute the Larger Work as a single prod-
uct. In such a case, You must make sure the requirements
of this License are fulfilled for the Covered Code.
```

Because applications built with a framework licensed under these terms are likely to be considered "larger works," this term is important in that it ensures that when you redistribute the framework with your application, it must remain licensed under the original Mozilla license, even though your application may use a different license.

```
4. Inability to Comply Due to Statute or Regulation.

If it is impossible for You to comply with any of the
terms of this License with respect to some or all of the
Covered Code due to statute or regulation then You must:
(a) comply with the terms of this License to the maximum
extent possible; and (b) describe the limitations and
the code they affect. Such description must be included
in the LEGAL file described in Section 3.4 and must be
included with all distributions of the Source Code. Ex-
cept to the extent prohibited by statute or regulation,
such description must be sufficiently detailed for a
recipient of ordinary skill to be able to understand it.

5. Application of this License.
   This License applies to code to which the Initial De-
   veloper has attached the notice in Exhibit A, and to
   related Covered Code.
```

6. Versions of the License.

6.1. New Versions.

Netscape Communications Corporation ("Netscape") may publish revised and/or new versions of the License from time to time. Each version will be given a distinguishing version number.

6.2. Effect of New Versions.

Once Covered Code has been published under a particular version of the License, You may always continue to use it under the terms of that version. You may also choose to use such Covered Code under the terms of any subsequent version of the License published by Netscape. No one other than Netscape has the right to modify the terms applicable to Covered Code created under this License.

6.3. Derivative Works.

If you create or use a modified version of this License (which you may only do in order to apply it to code which is not already Covered Code governed by this License), you must (a) rename Your license so that the phrases "Mozilla", "MOZILLAPL", "MOZPL", "Netscape", "NPL" or any confusingly similar phrase do not appear anywhere in your license and (b) otherwise make it clear that your version of the license contains terms which differ from the Mozilla Public License and Netscape Public License. (Filling in the name of the Initial Developer, Original Code or Contributor in the notice described in Exhibit A shall not of themselves be deemed to be modifications of this License.)

Taking an approach similar to the one the Apache license takes into account for its projects, the Mozilla license requires that if you copy it, you may not use a similar name for your copy or modification of the license itself.

7. DISCLAIMER OF WARRANTY.

COVERED CODE IS PROVIDED UNDER THIS LICENSE ON AN "AS IS" BASIS, WITHOUT WARRANTY OF ANY KIND, EITHER EXPRESSED OR IMPLIED, INCLUDING, WITHOUT LIMITATION, WARRANTIES THAT THE COVERED CODE IS FREE OF DEFECTS, MERCHANTABLE, FIT FOR A PARTICULAR PURPOSE OR NON-INFRINGING. THE ENTIRE RISK AS TO THE QUALITY AND PERFORMANCE OF THE COVERED CODE IS WITH YOU. SHOULD ANY COVERED CODE PROVE DEFECTIVE IN ANY RESPECT, YOU (NOT THE INITIAL DEVELOPER OR ANY OTHER CONTRIBUTOR) ASSUME THE COST OF ANY NECESSARY SERVICING, REPAIR OR CORRECTION. THIS DISCLAIMER OF WARRANTY CONSTITUTES AN ESSENTIAL PART OF THIS LICENSE. NO USE OF ANY COVERED CODE IS AUTHORIZED HEREUNDER EXCEPT UNDER THIS DISCLAIMER.

8. TERMINATION.

This License and the rights granted hereunder will terminate automatically if You fail to comply with terms herein and fail to cure such breach within 30 days of becoming aware of the breach. All sublicenses to the Covered Code which are properly granted shall survive any termination of this License. Provisions which, by their nature, must remain in effect beyond the ternination of this License shall survive.

9. LIMITATION OF LIABILITY.

UNDER NO CIRCUMSTANCES AND UNDER NO LEGAL THEORY, WHETHER TORT (INCLUDING NEGLIGENCE), CONTRACT, OR OTHERWISE, SHALL THE INITIAL DEVELOPER, ANY OTHER CONTRIBUTOR, OR ANY DISTRIBUTOR OF COVERED CODE, OR ANY SUPPLIER OF ANY OF SUCH PARTIES, BE LIABLE TO YOU OR ANY OTHER PERSON FOR ANY INDIRECT, SPECIAL, INCIDENTAL, OR CONSEQUENTIAL DAMAGES OF ANY CHARACTER INCLUDING, WITHOUT LIMITATION, DAMAGES FOR LOSS OF GOODWILL, WORK STOPPAGE, COMPUTER FAILURE OR MALFUNCTION, OR ANY AND ALL OTHER COMMERCIAL DAMAGES OR LOSSES, EVEN IF SUCH PARTY

SHALL HAVE BEEN INFORMED OF THE POSSIBILITY OF SUCH DAM-
AGES. THIS LIMITATION OF LIABILITY SHALL NOT APPLY TO
LIABILITY FOR DEATH OR PERSONAL INJURY RESULTING FROM
SUCH PARTY'S NEGLIGENCE TO THE EXTENT APPLICABLE LAW
PROHIBITS SUCH LIMITATION. SOME JURISDICTIONS DO NOT
ALLOW THE EXCLUSION OR LIMITATION OF INCIDENTAL OR CON-
SEQUENTIAL DAMAGES, SO THAT EXCLUSION AND LIMITATION MAY
NOT APPLY TO YOU.

10. U.S. GOVERNMENT END USERS.

The Covered Code is a "commercial item," as that term
is defined in 48 C.F.R. 2.101 (Oct. 1995), consisting of
"commercial computer software" and "commercial computer
software documentation," as such terms are used in 48
C.F.R. 12.212 (Sept. 1995). Consistent with 48 C.F.R.
12.212 and 48 C.F.R. 227.7202-1 through 227.7202-4 (June
1995), all
U.S. Government End Users acquire Covered Code with only
those rights set forth herein.

Some licenses, including the Mozilla license, have special terms explaining the impact of the license as it relates to U.S. government use. Many licenses, such as the BSD license, need no such terms due to their simplicity.

11. MISCELLANEOUS.

This License represents the complete agreement concern-
ing subject matter hereof.
If any provision of this License is held to be unenforceable, such provision shall be reformed only to the
extent necessary to make it enforceable. This License
shall be governed by California law provisions (except
to the extent applicable law, if any, provides otherwise), excluding its conflict-of-law provisions. With
respect to disputes in which at least one party is a
citizen of, or an entity chartered or registered to do
business in, the United States of America: (a) unless
otherwise agreed in writing, all disputes relating to

this License (excepting any dispute relating to intellectual property rights) shall be subject to final and binding arbitration, with the losing party paying all costs of arbitration; (b) any arbitration relating to this Agreement shall be held in Santa Clara County, California, under the auspices of JAMS/EndDispute; and (c) any litigation relating to this Agreement shall be subject to the jurisdiction of the Federal Courts of the Northern District of California, with venue lying in Santa Clara County, California, with the losing party responsible for costs, including without limitation, court costs and reasonable attorneys fees and expenses. The application of the United Nations Convention on Contracts for the International Sale of Goods is expressly excluded. Any law or regulation which provides that the language of a contract shall be construed against the drafter shall not apply to this License.

12. RESPONSIBILITY FOR CLAIMS.

Except in cases where another Contributor has failed to comply with Section 3.4, You are responsible for damages arising, directly or indirectly, out of Your utilization of rights under this License, based on the number of copies of Covered Code you made available, the revenues you received from utilizing such rights, and other relevant factors. You agree to work with affected parties to distribute responsibility on an equitable basis.

Like the GPL, the Mozilla license now provides an example "notice" to include in your own code if you are licensing it under these terms.

EXHIBIT A.
"The contents of this file are subject to the Mozilla Public License Version 1.0 (the "License"); you may not use this file except in compliance with the License. You may obtain a copy of the License at http://www.mozilla.org/MPL/

```
Software distributed under the License is distributed on
an "AS IS" basis, WITHOUT WARRANTY OF ANY KIND, either
express or implied. See the License for the specific
language governing rights and limitations under the
License.
The Original Code is _____.
The Initial Developer of the Original Code is
_____. Portions created by _____are
Copyright (C) _____. All Rights Reserved.
Contributor(s): _____."
```

The Mozilla license, like the GPL and others, expressly concerns itself with an end user's access to source code. When creating your application, the requirements of these licenses must be taken into account. When planning the distribution of your finished application, specific steps are recommended by some licenses to ensure you are in compliance with their terms about source access. It is essential to know what is required to avoid future problems, not to mention the simple courtesy of respecting the wishes of the copyright holder. You use their code for free, after all, so compliance is a small price to pay, literally and figuratively.

7.1.4.5 Dual/Multiple Licensing

Some projects take an unusual approach to the constraints of having to choose a particular license – they release the code under more than one license. Although there is a concern that mutually exclusive licenses might conflict, this approach has apparently some merits – the copyright holders of the project, after all, have the ability to release their code under any license they wish.

If a framework you are interested is not available under a license that you find acceptable, you may wish to request the copyright holders if this is a possibility.

Dual licensing means that some projects that were otherwise unavailable to projects that use the GPL or LGPL can, in fact, be used, and this method is gaining in popularity because it is used more extensively.

7.1.5 The Advantages of Open Source

Much has been written about the advantages of open-source software, but often the information presented is anecdotal, and not based on hard business realities. Many comparisons also concentrate on the technical advantages of open source, which, although quite real in the right situations, are not the whole story. A purely technical perspective seems to be inapplicable to the actual development needs of organizations. It is important to realize that although there are indeed some advantages that are unique to open-source products, many of the features touted as unique to open source are just as applicable to many commercial, proprietary products, and sometimes even more so. Do not believe that just because it is open source, it somehow magically confers advantages that make it superior to proprietary competitors.

Although the arguments in favor of open source as a philosophy and its merits from an ethical point of view may be very compelling, they are seldom a sufficient incentive for organizations to adopt open source.

Market acceptance and the size of a user base cannot be the only criteria by which software is judged. This is not to say that it is not important – in fact, it is particularly so with application frameworks – but it is often overemphasized. Frameworks that have larger user bases do get more applications developed with them, and by the very nature of a framework this can be a positive thing; however, just because the herd is stampeding in a certain direction does not make it the direction you want to go. Often relatively poorly designed frameworks are promoted to the point where the user base is caught up in a snowball effect: so many people are using this, therefore, it must be good, right?

7.2 FRAMEWORKS AND OPEN SOURCE

In this section we explore how frameworks fit into the open-source picture by first looking at the development process that frameworks undergo, and how this process benefits from the open-source approach. We then explain the benefits to the user of the frameworks developed with this approach.

7.2.1 The Development of Frameworks

Frameworks, like many things, are often born out of necessity. In the process of creating multiple applications, developers discover that there are some areas of functionality that are common. These areas are then abstracted and generalized to form the features of the framework. Often, the process of abstracting generalized classes from concrete examples produces a better framework than if the generalized classes were designed independently of concrete examples.

This generalization is iterative: the framework becomes more and more widely applicable as it becomes more generalized. This happens because more applications are built with the framework – it is an evolutionary process.

Obtaining many different points of view helps this generalization process, and speeds the development of the framework. More eyes on the project mean that the existing design must be explained (and in some cases, defended) many times, and this is a learning experience for everyone involved.

Theoretically, the ideal procedure for creating a framework would be to analyze the entire problem domain (e.g., all Web applications), extract all relevant abstractions, and then create many different examples of applications. You would want to extract abstractions that can be easily extended and specialized to implement the examples, and derive further abstractions from these specializations. In other words, derive one way of doing each task, and reuse that way for each subsequent example.

In reality, this is easier said than done. What tends to happen, instead, is that some portions of an existing application or an application under development get abstracted: this forms the core of the new framework. As other applications are built, further abstractions are derived, and more generic components are built into the framework. The framework develops along with the example applications.

Ideally, there should be two or more application-development projects going on independently, in parallel with the development of the framework.

As development goes on, some application functions will not be met by the framework. This either defines the boundaries of the framework (specifying something that it is not intended to provide), or results in further growth as it expands to meet the new need. It is important at this stage to avoid having many different ways to do one job – this can lead to fragmentation of the framework and defeats reuse.

Many of these techniques are common to all object-oriented design, for example, the process of generalization and abstraction. They are taken a bit further in framework design, but the principals are the same.

With an ordinary object-oriented application, testing is done via example datasets, or use scenarios of the application. With a framework, its testing implies *building* other applications using the framework itself.

The category of applications used to test a framework determines the applicability of that framework: if your examples are from a specific application domain (such as accounting, manufacturing, etc.), then the framework will likely develop specific functionality in that area. A wider scope of applications will develop a more widely applicable framework.

An application framework is difficult to create. It is difficult, not so much because the code is difficult to write, or that there is a large amount of code. Indeed, many enterprise applications have several times more code than the frameworks that helped create them. The code of a framework is often complex; however, proper design helps to make it understandable. This complexity, though, is not the reason for frameworks being so difficult to create. The difficulty lies in obtaining the experience that is distilled into them. Frameworks evolve from the effort to reuse both design and code, and from repeated refactoring that results in widely applicable services and components. This is what is difficult about their creation.

Convincing an organization's management that in this kind of infrastructure-building, long-term effort is a good investment is often difficult. Given the amount of time that goes into frameworks, many organizations simply do not have the resources to create them, irrespective of how convinced they may be of their advantages.

Because frameworks tend to be large and fairly complex pieces of software, they are often not a cost-effective project for a single organization. It is also a good thing when a particular framework is used in many projects – it grows, it becomes a de facto standard to a degree, and the organizations using it get the benefits. All of these factors mean that frameworks are good candidates for open-source projects, and indeed many of the best frameworks are open source.

The secret of open source is knowing what to use and when. Many criteria help in choosing an OSS project: license, support availability, user base size, community, and suitability to the task.

Why would a developer or company release a framework as open source anyway? What could be the motivation for such an action? An application framework is a major development effort for any individual or group. Why write it and then give it away? Actually, there are some very good reasons, all of which are quite practical.

When you refactor, repair, or improve core elements of a framework, the entire user base benefits. This then amortizes the costs of the effort to make such a refactor or improvement across all the beneficiaries.

If you consider commercial applications, the benefits to a software developer, or to a company contracting software development services, become clear. If such a developer can begin with the advantages of a sophisticated framework without having to finance the entire cost of developing such a framework, bidding on some jobs is now viable in terms of cost, where it would not have been before. This means more business for the developer, and more deployments for the framework, which is a true win–win scenario.

7.2.2 The Advantages of Open Source for Frameworks

The nature of a framework, with its wide applicability, benefits from many eyes and many users, which open source provides. A framework also benefits from widespread use, and from many developers in many different situations putting it through its paces. From this kind of exposure, a framework benefits by receiving what amounts to a very thorough quality assurance.

Of course, the reverse is also true; a company producing a commercial product on a well-established open-source framework can benefit from the popularity of the framework itself.

Certain categories of software appear to respond well to the open-source process. One of the most well-known examples of open-source development, the Linux operating system shares many attributes with Web-application frameworks. It is large, complex, and highly horizontal – that is, it is applicable to many different problem domains. It is highly used by developers, and the people who work "where the rubber meets the road" in the development of real-world business systems. Linux is also focused primarily on the server.

Much can be learned about open-source techniques because they can be applied to frameworks by examining other similar projects. Experience with other projects indicates that a certain development style works best in open source. Projects released early in their development cycles increase their exposure and this exposure widens the user and developer base, which benefits the project's development.

The different agendas and goals of all of the different parties involved in a popular open-source project would seem at first glance to be a detriment. In fact, the opposite is true – these different agendas can actually be a benefit in the right kind of project. Frameworks are one such kind of a project – the convergence of many different agendas keeps the framework flexible. No one direction of development overwhelms the others – they all must converge on a common goal.

The nature of a framework means that its users are also developers. This makes an ideal situation for open-source development, because open-source projects benefit and grow mostly by acquiring new developers and contributors, and not just users.

Traditionally, large and complex projects were released infrequently, say every six months at a maximum. The goal was to minimize problems and bugs, so after each release a new development/enhancement cycle would begin, followed by an extensive quality assurance period, and then the next release.

Open-source projects follow a different cycle. They are released early in their development phase, sometimes when they are little more than a prototype. Frequent incremental releases follow – sometimes as often as once every few days during intense periods of development. This allows the results of the group's efforts into everyone's hands quickly and often. There is no period of behind-closed-doors development followed by the fanfare of a release. Instead, development becomes a continuous process, an evolution, punctuated by many smaller milestone releases. Given the fundamentally evolutionary nature of the development of frameworks, where patterns and generalizations are derived from repeated reuse, this makes them well suited to this development model.

The modern open-source development environment – the Internet – promotes the kind of widescale exposure of open-source framework projects that cannot be achieved by proprietary efforts.

A kind of unexpected synergy develops in projects with such a wide developer base, making the project both more flexible and yet more robust at the same time. Problems are quickly identified when the framework is in use in many different environments, and as most developers already know, *finding* a bug is usually more difficult than fixing it.

Large frameworks are very complex systems, and as the example of Linux has shown, large and complex systems can be created and made reliable by a diverse group of geographically distributed developers.

In high-performance computing, an algorithm is often broken into many portions, each of which runs in parallel and often on a separate system. Indeed, this is one of the basic precepts of distributed systems, and where much of the scalability of J2EE comes from. Some problems lend themselves well to decomposition into parallel parts, and these problems work well on such parallel processing systems. It turns out that, by analogy, framework development is one such problem. It "parallelizes" well.

Communication is as much a central part of open-source framework development as the code itself. For the project to truly benefit from the many different perspectives of its developer/user base, there must be an understanding, at least at a high level, of the approach each contributor adopts. Understanding the *why* behind code is at least as important as understanding the exact process it uses to achieve its result. This requires good communication in the project, both in written form via documentation and in the direct communication between development team members. Collaborative online forums and mailing lists provide ideal tools for this form of development. They are asynchronous in that geographic differences can be minimized – people in Japan can post their contributions during their day and similarly the people in New York can contribute when most convenient to them. They are self-archiving – a written record exists that can later be searched, and builds an ongoing record and a knowledge base for the project automatically. They are also inherently one-to-many, allowing each developer's input to be shared immediately with the entire distributed team – sometimes this is difficult, expensive, and time consuming with other models of communication. Finally, they are also "filterable," that is, each developer can focus on the part of the project discussion that he cares about, while at the same time remaining informed on other areas of the project work.

One of the more powerful advantages of frameworks is the design patterns they bring to a project. In much of the framework, these patterns emerge iteratively from practical applications. A framework developed open source has the opportunity to encompass design patterns from a larger set of samples, and grows as a result. It is important that the core developer group realizes the good input from even casual users of the framework. Their feedback and responses can be valuable sources of new design patterns and antipatterns (structures and practices recognized as best avoided). Sometimes this input can even highlight the fact that the design patterns and structures of the framework are incorrect – if a feedback indicates that the framework is seldom used correctly, the fault may be with the framework (or possibly the documentation), and not with the users. This kind of feedback may be a good indicator of a need to refactor.

7.2.3 Using Open-Source Frameworks

Now that we have defined open source itself looked at some of its more popular licensing schemes, and examined how open source and frameworks make a good fit, let us examine how open-source frameworks are put to work in commercial software development.

7.2.3.1 Open Source in the Corporate World

A common and highly successful technique that has been adopted by companies in recent years is to use open-source projects as the basis of commercial products. Supplying the "polish" to an OSS project, supplementing it with support, documentation, training, and perhaps even new features has become an industry of its own. "People are giving away bricks for free, but you must still assemble your own house."

Open source can be a "hard sell" in the corporate environment. The "suits" (I can say that, I have been one) believe that you cannot get something for nothing. They are right. Open source *is* an exchange, just a different type of exchange than the corporate world is used to. In OSS, the exchange is more like a barter than a cash deal. It is a trade of time: one developer's time is exchanged for the results of a group of others. It is true that this exchange takes place only between the contributors to a project – at least it seems this way. As it turns out, even the people who just "use" an open-source project contribute back, in a different way. They might send in bug reports, hoping that the project community will fix them for "free." Actually, they have been paid in advance – by the time spent finding and reporting the bug. Even users who never send in a bug still play their part: by using the project, they increase the size of the user base. The larger the user base, the more interest generated in the project – the more interest in a project, the better the chance of attracting more users and developers who *do* contribute in more concrete ways. So, by describing the open-source project in these decidedly capitalistic terms, you may find that acceptance becomes slightly easier.

Of course, an understanding of the economics involved is not the only impediment to management's acceptance to open source. In some cases, commercial software companies spread – some would say intentionally – information about the disadvantages of open-source software seeding "FUD," or Fear, Uncertainty, and Doubt. For managers who do not fully understand the risks and benefits of open source, it does not require much "FUD" to undermine their confidence. The best defense against this, of course, is fact and education.

7.2.3.2 Evaluating Open-Source Frameworks

In previous chapters, we discussed how to compare and choose frameworks. There are a few elements that are unique to open-source frameworks in this process, which we explore here.

7.2.3.2.1 Suitability to the Task

The most important of all of the criteria has to be the suitability of a framework to the task at hand, for both open-source and proprietary frameworks. The framework may have the right license, good support availability, and a healthy user base and still be the wrong tool for the job. We discuss, in other areas of the book, how to choose the right tool – none of the other criteria are as important as this. Just *because* a framework is open source is no reason to think that it fits your particular project's needs any better than a commercial offering.

It may be a really great hammer, but if what you need is a screwdriver, then this is not very helpful.

7.2.3.2.2 User Base Size
The number of people currently using the framework can be an important factor – it gives, at least, a gauge of how useful others find the tool. As a statistic for choosing a framework, however, it can be misleading in a number of ways. The framework may be new, and although it is perfect for the job, well supported, distributed under an appropriate license, and otherwise ideal for your project, there may not *yet* be a large user community. It is also important to examine the kinds of projects in which it is used – just because there are many people doing one kind of project with this framework does not make it the right choice for *your* project.

It is also possible that the framework has been used in a large number of highly successful projects, but that this information is poorly presented or absent in the framework's website. Look into the archive of the framework's mailing list for other information about this kind of history.

Of course, just determining what the user base size is can be a difficult process. Counting downloads is only, at best, an indicator, because it does not separate the "tire-kickers" from the actual users.

The contributor base is a little easier to count, but is not necessarily related to the number of users. Some frameworks developed by one or two individuals are extremely popular, lending some truth to the supposition about too many cooks spoiling the broth.

7.2.3.2.3 Community
Not only the size, but also the *quality* of the community of users, developers, and contributors to a framework must be taken into account. Take a look at the archives of the email list or forums that are always found for such a tool: is the interaction productive and courteous? Are newcomers welcomed and directed to the appropriate resources to get started? Are input and criticism well received and handled? If all you see are flame wars and personality conflicts, it may be a bad sign for the overall health of the community. This does not necessarily mean that it is the wrong tool for you, but it means there is one more factor to be considered.

The culture of a community is also very important; for instance, some open-source groups are opposed on principal to commercial implementations of their works (although these are fewer more recently). This would be an adverse culture for some projects. Other projects have a highly expert group of developers involved, and might not be a good first project for beginners. Culture does count.

7.2.3.3 Releases and Scheduling in the Open-Source World

The process of releasing new packages and the schedule under which such releases are made is a bit more transparent in the open-source world. This is the benefit: it becomes fairly evident by following the discussions on the development lists and watching the releases of beta versions when a release will be made. Typically, open-source projects follow the philosophy promoted by many in the Apache group: release early, release often.

The downside is that most open-source projects do not have any full-time paid staff working on them. Their development is done by what amounts to time contributions, and therefore the user base has no particular right to expect a given release schedule to be adhered to. New packages are released when they are ready, as opposed to when the calendar says that they should be released. Often, this leads to higher quality software, but it can be frustrating to an organization used to the more rigid schedules of commercial development. Not to say that commercial companies always (or often!) meet their release deadlines, but they at least *have* deadlines. Most open-source projects do not – the speed with which new features are implemented and released is directly proportional to the amount of time the various contributors put into their development. Often, what this amounts to is that the features that the core group of developers requires in its own projects gets the maximum time and attention, which is perfectly logical. Frequently, contributors also pay attention to the frequency of requests from the user community; however, if a feature is requested a great deal, contributors focus more time on it – but such features typically come second in priority to the features that the contributor requires.

So what is the best method of encouraging the development of new features in an open-source project? The first way is to volunteer: suggest that you lead or participate in the development of the feature you want. This may encourage others who also want the feature to come forward and join you in its development. The next way is to request it, along with a justification of why it is useful to the project as a whole. This again provides a motivation for other contributors to want to develop the feature, even if you cannot assist directly in the development. Above all, do not demand: there is no room, in an open-source project, for demanding that a particular feature be incorporated just because someone wants it – remember, open source is largely a volunteer effort, hence you must motivate, not dictate.

7.2.3.3.1 CVS

CVS, or the "concurrent versioning system," is a highly essential resource for many frameworks, particularly for open-source frameworks, and deserves a quick introduction here. CVS is an open-source project itself, one that has been around a long time, and is in extremely widespread use.

CVS serves two essential purposes in software project development. The first is collaboration: enabling multiple – sometimes geographically scattered – developers to work together efficiently on projects. It takes a somewhat unfamiliar approach to management of this collaboration, as we will see.

A second essential, but sometimes overlooked, capability of CVS is tracking. CVS serves as a shared log of all changes made to the software, along with details of developers who made them, when, and why (if the developers were considerate enough to annotate their changes correctly). More than this, CVS can produce a copy of the software at any point in time, allowing a copy of the system at any stable point to be produced on demand. It is even possible to have multiple versions of the project being maintained at once, in a single repository. The ability to restore or recover a previous version is particularly powerful, especially in the situation where a new feature has broken an existing functionality – the precise changes that caused the problem can be easily examined and reviewed.

Other version control systems take an exclusive approach to versioning. When one developer wants to work on a particular piece of code, a "lock" is put on that code, so that no other developer can modify it until the lock is released. This is reasonable only in the situation where there is close coordination between the developers. If there is a conflict, close coordination in real-time communication can solve the problem. In many projects today, however, developers are not even in the same time zone, and much less in the same office. A different approach is needed in these situations.

CVS's approach fits better with the distributed development environment. The developer requests, or "checks out" a working copy of the source code repository and then works on the source independently, with no locking taking place. This sounds unreliable and contradictory, but it works. Each developer has an independent copy of the source code. Many edits may be made at once, even to the same files.

When developers are finished with a set of code changes, they "commit" them. Committing is the write operation, updating the central repository with the changes. During the commit process, the CVS requests a description of the changes and notes the date, time, and the identity of the developer who made the changes. While changes are happening, any of the developers in the community can request updated versions of the entire or part of the archive at any time. This is in fact the primary use of CVS by nondevelopers – to get updates of the latest and best code without having to wait for a bundled release to be created. In this way, a user can get access to patches and fixes literally as soon as the developers do.

Now, of course, the process opens the opportunity for more than one developer to work on the same file at the same time. CVS makes no particular effort to avoid such conflicts, or collisions, but it does provide powerful mechanisms for helping the developer resolve them.

If developers update their own local copy from the repository frequently, the opportunity for such a conflict is reduced. If one developer commits changes to the same file while the original developer is still working on it, however, conflict resolution must be applied. The developer who commits first has no problem – his changes are immediately applied to the master copy. When the second developer commits, however, his changes are rejected. Instead, he must *merge* the changes made by the first developer to commit into his local copy. If the changes were actually made to different areas of the file, then the merge is successful; the second developer can then commit the merged result, and the master copy will contain the sum total of both sets of changes. If the changes were made to the same lines, however, the second developer's copy will contain both sets of changes, and the conflicting lines are marked. The developer must then resolve the conflict, either choosing one of the changes, or combining them as appropriate, and then commits to the repository again. At all times, the repository contains a consistent version, because the file cannot be checked-in until the conflicts are resolved.

CVS stores a complete record of each of the changes in detail – it does not actually store separate copies of each version. This allows any given version of the file to be reproduced. It is a normal practice for developers to check in only when their changes are at least compiling, and some teams prefer that the change is verified and tested first.

When a specific set of revisions is ready for release, CVS provides the means to "tag" the files and revisions of these files with a specific string, which is usually the release number or some derivation of it. This allows developers and users to retrieve all files in the tagged version, enabling a stable release to be created while development continues unabated. Setting up CVS for a project is not particularly simple, but using it is.

The release process for many open-source projects follows a common pattern. The very first source for a project is normally only found somewhere in a CVS repository. When it reaches a level where at least its most basic features can be tested, it is often released with a 0.01 or 0.1 version number, to indicate that it is "prerelease" and is not yet expected to be of production quality. After this, there will likely be a number of incremental "point" releases, such as perhaps

0.02, 0.03, and so forth. Many projects also produce a "beta" or a "release candidate" version when they approach a release. This gives the community of both users and developers a chance to finalize the features in the upcoming release, while putting a temporary "freeze" on new features until the existing ones are debugged. Most projects persist with the notation of the number preceding the decimal indicating a "major" release. Typically, this means new functionality, not just bug fixes or improvements to existing features. A major release is also indicated when there is an issue of backward-compatibility with older releases: if the new release, for example, requires files created with an older version to be converted, this would be a good point for a "major" release, such as from 1.05 to 2.0. Subsequent minor enhancements and bug-fixes use the digits following the decimal, such as 2.01, 2.1, 2.2, and so forth. The details of the scheme vary slightly from one project to another, but this method is common enough in both open-source and commercial software projects to be considered a de facto standard.

7.2.3.4 Support

Particularly in a corporate environment, the availability of support for a framework can be a great advantage. Many OSS projects depend on the community of users and developers for support. Depending on the use you have in mind for the project, how critical it is, and how complex the OSS project itself is, this may or may not be enough.

Like OSS itself, community support can be a hard sell in the corporate world.

The other option, of course, is commercial, paid support. This is often provided by a third party – for example, someone other than the developers or hosts of the OSS project. The quality of support can range from feeble to top-notch, and it is helpful to have some existing customer comments to judge by.

Often, the mere availability of commercial support, even if it is never purchased or used, is enough to make use of an OSS project more palatable to the corporate types.

7.2.3.5 Learning and Open Source

An open-source framework can often have an advantage when considering the learning curve. When first adopting a given framework, open source or not, much time must be put into getting developers up to speed. The real benefits of framework and component development start to emerge once the tool is relatively well understood.

During the learning process, the source code to the framework itself is the final word on how things work. Particularly, if the code is well commented, it is often better and easier to examine its function directly in the source code rather than examining it in documentation. By checking functionality directly in the code, we can also avoid the problem of the code and the documentation being out-of-sync with each other. If you are looking at the actual code you are running, there is no ambiguity.

Having the code on hand is also invaluable during the all-important process of selecting a framework in the first place. You can learn much about the quality and care taken to develop a framework by examining the code. Is the code well commented? Is it written conforming to a consistent coding standard? Are there many deprecated methods? Can you understand the package structure?

Having access to the source of an example application is as important as having a source to the framework. The framework itself is an excellent reference, but a good example can truly jump-start your development, particularly if it is allowable to copy and modify the example. It is important that the example be an instance of an application built with the framework in such a way that the facilities of the framework can be properly used. There is such a thing as a bad example, and poor usage practices can result from emulating such an example.

Often complete application frameworks require more than one example, because one example cannot reasonably use all of the pertinent features at once. So, often you will find a whole set of examples, from the obligatory "Hello World" on up in complexity. In the ideal case, an example will also be a full-blown, usable application, which shows the use of the framework in a more realistic setting than a contrived example. If the example is open source as well, and similar in functionality to your required application, so much the better – you have a ready-made template to customize from, as well as learn from.

7.2.3.6 How to Get Help

It is important to take the right approach when looking for help in an open-source project. Almost all such projects are supported and maintained by volunteers. You cannot expect to demand support in the same way you might for a commercial product, or you may find yourself offered a full refund of your purchase price instead.

Always make sure to check the FAQ, the mailing list archives (or forum archives), and the documentation before asking. No one likes to answer the same question twice and much less to answer it dozens of times.

If you are reasonably sure that you have hit a question whose answer cannot be easily found, then by all means ask. A forum or listserv is the best place to post your question, unless the project FAQ allows you to ask new questions.

If the project has an automated bug tracker or help-desk system, this is also a possibility if you have encountered what appears to be an actual problem with the framework.

When you ask your question, provide enough relevant detail so that the people whom you are asking do not have to ask for more information. For example, what environment (operating system, JDK, Web server) are you using, and what is the context of the problem (e.g., what were you trying to accomplish when the question or problem arose). Do not write a novel, however – be succinct. Code snippets, if appropriate, are often appreciated, but do not use attachments to a mailing list, which, unless specifically asked, is generally considered bad etiquette.

Do not email your questions to users from the list directly (e.g., off-list) unless invited.

7.2.3.7 How to Get Involved

Getting involved in an open-source project is very simple: by just being a user of the project, you are to some degree "involved." If you submit clear, well-defined bug reports, all the better. If you submit bug reports *with* the solution to the bug, better still! In many projects, most of the community are involved at a fairly low level of commitment, so it is not necessary to dedicate a great deal of time. A core developer community tends to form, and in better projects it is not an exclusive circle – anyone willing to spend time and effort into understanding the framework well enough to contribute significantly becomes a new core developer.

The key to all successful attempts to get involved in a project is communication. This usually starts by getting in touch with the maintainer or the core developer group of a project, or joining an appropriate mailing list. The mailing list has the advantage that you can listen for a while, reading other postings and getting a feel for the current discussions, before chipping in. The direct contact approach has the advantage of putting you directly in touch with the core person/group of the project, although in very popular projects that person or group might be very busy, and it may take some time before your email is answered.

In short, there are many levels of involvement. Roughly in order of increasing time commitment required, they often fall into one of the following categories:

- **User:** Even just using a project is contributing – you contribute to the user base, the popularity of the project, and to the overall knowledge base available about the project.

- **Feedback:** At the next level of involvement, you begin the process of contributing back by providing feedback to the development/project team. Even nothing more than saying "great product, thanks!" goes a long way. Consider that almost all open-source projects are staffed by volunteers. The feedback from users actually getting value from their creation is part of their "pay," and in fact, is one of the most enjoyable aspects. Sometimes users of an open-source project hesitate to provide a feedback, thinking they are "bothering" the development team, or because they somehow feel uncomfortable actually making use of a free product. Nothing could be further from the truth – an open-source project *needs* this kind of feedback to survive and prosper. It tells the development team that is doing something right – and as any dog owner knows, most creatures including programmers respond better to positive than negative reinforcement.

    Also, offering to have the URL of your completed application listed (if possible) as a reference of something that was created using the framework is always greatly appreciated.

- **Bug Reports:** The time spent to submit bug reports is probably one of the most valuable things a relatively casual user of the project can do. Any project group worth its salt will appreciate the bug report – particularly if it is sufficiently detailed to help in tracking down a problem. At a minimum it should include the basics, such as details about your system and configuration, the version of the project you were using, any supporting software (e.g., whether the JDK or Database was used), and the steps taken to reproduce the problem. At this level, still no actual *development* takes place, but you still contribute very much!

- **Website Contributions:** Simply chipping in some materials for the website of the project is usually much appreciated. The website of a project sometimes gets the same level of attention as the documentation; in other words, not enough attention. Better presentation can provide the whole project with a more professional and competent feel, which in turn attracts new users and helps the project as a whole. It can also simplify the work of the project team in coordinating development.

- **Graphical/Artistic Contributions:** Closely related to website contributions are graphical or artistic contributions. The user who has the ability to create logos, diagrams, artwork, and related materials is often greatly appreciated and prized by a development team. It often seems to be the case that those who are expert at software development lack the skills to also be competent visual artists. There are, of course, exceptions, but most open-source teams would very much welcome a graphical design from someone with that skill, for use both on the website and in other related project materials, such as logos and documentation.

- **Documentation Contributions:** Documentation is often the last place that many developers would choose to spend their time. Unfortunately, it is a key element of any software, and is particularly important to open-source software. Often the documentation is the most important guide to a product, because commercial support may be unavailable. It is important that the documentation is complete and up-to-date. Even an initial effort to produce first-rate documentation is not enough, because most open-source projects are in a constant state of enhancement and change – the documentation must keep up. In light of this, one of the most valuable contributions a project can receive is in the area of documentation. This can range from simple corrections to minor enhancements to entire documentation projects. Often, the less-experienced users of a project are in a position to actually document some things *better* than the core development team. The core team is experienced with the product, and sometimes cannot imagine the steps that a novice user goes through, whereas a more casual user, who started as just a novice, can provide valuable insight. A beginners' guide to the project is often created through such an insight. Because all new users to the project need such a guide, at least at first, it often becomes one of the most important parts of a project's documentation – and makes an excellent candidate for contributions. Frequently, the documentation for an open-source project is also stored in the CVS repository for the project, allowing it to be versioned and maintained just like the source code – so at least a working knowledge of CVS is useful when contributing documentation.

  Related to but distinct from documentation is the contribution of written work *about* the project, for publication either online or in the trade press publications. For people with an ability to communicate clearly, this is an excellent avenue to not only learn about the project, but to spread knowledge of it to other interested parties. This kind of "press" can be very valuable to a project, and can again result in other kinds of contributions that it otherwise would not have had access to.

- **Support Services:** You might not think of providing paid support services for the project or product as a contribution, but it is, and an important one at that.

The availability of commercial, paid support often proves to be a turning point for an open-source project. It legitimizes the project and often takes it past the last hurdle for acceptance in many organizations, which otherwise would not use it. This can not only increase the level of interest in the project, swelling its user base, but also increase its user base in a very desirable direction: business and professional users, who may well have much more to contribute to a project once their company adopts it for internal use. Of course, providing commercial support for the project requires substantial knowledge of the project itself – but once the project is used in your development, your team must acquire that knowledge in any case to make best use of the project. Reselling it is then another way of capitalizing on that experience and sharing it with others.

- **Packaging/Redistribution**: Increasing the distribution base of the project is also very important: Most projects start out by only being available as a download from the project's home page, but this can prove inadequate over time. Demand for a popular project can outstrip the capability of a single server, and offering a "mirror," or alternate download site, can be one type of contribution. Making the project available in different build formats or installation settings is another way to contribute to its packaging and redistribution. Many popular projects even lend themselves to a commercial distribution, perhaps with additional supporting documentation, or on a CD format for easy installation. All of these methods contribute to the overall popularity of the project and attract other contributions.

- **Design Contributions**: Another area of contribution that is sometimes not considered is design: often design is "extracted" from user requests over time, so it is important to ask if you see a project that does not have a feature you need. Ask whether the feature is present, but not yet documented (as is often the case), and if the answer is no, ask whether it is or could be planned for a future release. The more detailed the design input, the more likely it will become a concrete part of the product. It is important to consider whether the type of project is appropriate to the feature – for example, there is no point in asking for database support in a framework that is oriented to presentation. If it is a logical extension, however, detail how you see it working, and most importantly, what the advantages would be. Requesting new features and contributing design to an open-source project is partly a sales job: you must convince the other contributors, particularly the hard-core coders, that this new feature or attribute is a good idea, and that it brings real benefit to the project as a whole.

- **Code Contributions:** Code contributions can also have one of several levels. At the basic level, just enhancing the online program documentation and comments can be very useful – and also can be a highly effective way of learning the code itself for the contributor. Beyond this are the coding of unit tests, additional logging and debugging, and various other fairly minor coding tasks. There is also the job of code formatting, which is an excellent place to begin for a novice code contributor. More advanced, of course, are actual contributions of new functionality, bug fixes, and enhancements to the project itself. This level of contribution implies an understanding of the overall project at a fairly good level – although the more modular projects facilitate this kind of contribution, because you can be involved in the development on a single module and need not be an expert in the other modules. Usually, at this level of contribution a developer will be given access to the primary CVS (or other version control) repository for the project – sometimes called being a "committer" to the project, which refers to the "commit" command used to actually post changes into the code repository. This is usually one of the highest levels of involvement with the project, although, of course, some committers contribute more than others.

- **Financial Contributions:** One final means of contributing back to an open-source project is financial. Many open-source projects (such as all the Apache projects) are hosted and copyrighted by nonprofit organizations. These organizations are often set up to accept contributions, both major and minor, and are then able to put these to use in furthering the goals of the project. Web hosting, for example, must be paid for, as must server space for development (unless contributors use their own servers for everything except the common CVS archive, which often happens). Some organizations (such as the JBoss group) sell commercial versions of the project documentation as a means for users to financially support the project. Just because a project is open source does not mean it is allergic to money!

This sums up some of the more common ways of getting involved in an open-source project. This is by no means a complete list. As we said earlier, it is important to communicate with the project group. Ask them what they need, what would be of most use to the project at this point. Describe your own capabilities and desires, what you can do, and what you would like to do – the team can then match this with the needs of the project and advise you as to how to get involved.

7.2.3.8 Contributing Back: Component Reuse on a Grander Scale

Component reuse within a project is a good thing. Component reuse within an organization, that is, using the same components on more than one project, is even better. The savings increase exponentially, assuming that the components that are reused were engineered well in the first place. At an even higher level of reuse, open-source (or collaborative source) projects reuse components *between* organizations. This has a number of advantages that are not obvious at first glance. By enabling reuse between projects and organizations, code has additional quality constraints imposed on it: different people have to understand and work with the components, so the documentation and interfaces must be clearer. Portability issues that might not crop up within one organization (using, say, only one type of hardware or one particular database system) may well be found through reuse.

7.3 SUMMARY

Open source does not necessarily mean what you think it does: although it usually means free, the definition of free must be clearly understood, and seldom means "do whatever you want." Even open-source projects have constraints and responsibilities associated with them, and it is important to understand what they are.

Open source and frameworks, however, are an excellent fit, and many of the best frameworks are open source. If you know exactly what license you are dealing with, and understand how to put the advantages of open source to use, you can reap many benefits for your own development projects.

CHAPTER 8

Development Methodologies and Design Patterns

8.1 Frameworks and Methodologies

A software methodology is a set of guidelines, rules and, practices used in development projects. Some methodologies have more rules than others, and have a greater impact on the development process. As software development evolves, and comes closer to being recognized as an engineering discipline than an art, practices that work well are discovered through experience, and these practices are formalized over time into methodologies. Simply adding more rules and procedures, however, does not necessarily result in better methodology, in the same way that adding new functionality to a framework does not necessarily result in a better framework. Methodologies that are "lightweight," but highly effective, are often the easiest to apply and the best in practice, as they impose relatively few burdens on the development process – and are therefore more likely to be actually used!

There are many parallels between development methodologies and frameworks, and we explore here how the two interrelate, and how your development methodology has an impact on your choice of framework, and vice versa.

Use of a framework does not necessarily imply that you have to work with a particular development methodology. Some frameworks have, however, been created with such methodologies in mind – a good example is the JUnit unit test framework. It was developed with the Extreme Programming methodology in mind, and is in fact ideally suited for use with this technique. Other frameworks were designed with Aspect Oriented Programming, or another similar methodology. Unfortunately or fortunately, depending on your perspective, there is an overabundance of methodologies, particularly in the object-oriented development area.

It is important to understand whether a particular framework leans toward a specific methodology, and how firmly it embraces it. For example, although JUnit grew from the need for a testing framework when applying the Extreme Programming methodology, it is not necessary to use Extreme Programming to use JUnit – it works perfectly well when applied to a project created with different methodologies.

Just as with frameworks, there is no hard and fast rule to select the "best" software development methodology for a particular project. Beware of the framework that insists it can only be used within a specific methodology, and that the methodology is the One True Methodology. While almost all Java Web frameworks will lean somewhat toward Object-Oriented Design and Object-Oriented Analysis, it is not always the perfect approach either. Flexibility is essential.

A complete software development methodology is far more than a notation standard, a procedure or process, and its supporting tools. Many books include development methodology in detail, and we will not attempt to do so here.

Often a methodology attempts to provide a complete life-cycle plan for software, from inception to obsolescence. They might include everything from project management to cost estimating, measuring and metric methods, quality assurance, developer role definitions, detailed examples and training recommendations, and even methods for extending and enhancing the method! Others take a more simplistic approach, outlining a few basic methods and guidelines and leaving the rest to the particular project implementor.

Having made that disclaimer, let us examine some of the aspects of a development methodology and how they are affected, or have an impact on, your choice of framework.

- **Concepts and Terminology**: Different methodologies sometimes choose specific terminology. For instance, it is important to understand the meaning of "object," "class," and "operation" within the specific methodology. Methods also have different root concepts – for example, some are very much oriented around a database, and others are very specific to a particular programming language or notation methodology. It is important to know whether your development methodology fits well with your choice of framework from a terminology point of view. If something in the methodology is called a "procedure" and in the framework that maps to a "controller" or "action," you must be aware of these mappings to use them together effectively.

- **Notation:** Most methods involve a specific notation, often a graphical model, of the system being analyzed or designed. It is important to understand how this notation will relate to the services of the chosen framework. Ideally, there should be a diagram or model of the framework itself, and possibly a couple of example applications built with the framework, using the selected notation. It is then simple to apply the same approach to the new application being built. If there is no such diagram, an attempt to create it might reveal any potential areas of "impedance mismatch" between the design methodology and the framework.

    The notation of a method should be a complete and self-consistent description of the application being built. Once the mapping from the notation and terminology of the method to the framework is made, application design will be greatly simplified. A notation often provides a set of means for breaking the project into manageable components – the way this translates to the framework's notion of application components is also important, and the scalability of the methodology is integral to this. Both the framework and the notation should allow multiple parts of the overall application to be under design/development at the same time if the project is large and involves more than one developer.

- **Procedures and practical use:** The practical use of the methodology and how it interfaces with the development techniques of the framework are also important. Some frameworks and methodologies are better suited to new software development than the reengineering or extension of existing legacy systems. Some methodologies advocate prototyping as one of their primary design methods – frameworks tend to support this well, as a rule, and also the extension of the prototype into the finished system. Of course, methodologies that have specific procedures that support reuse are also usually good fits for frameworks.

Example Methodologies 299

The portion of the life cycle of a project that the methodology addresses (e.g., entire life cycle, design/development only, or development/implementation only) is usually less critical in relation to its fit with a framework. Most frameworks are applicable at a late design stage and throughout the development stage of an application's life cycle. Many are also involved in the deployment stage, at least to some degree. Whether the methodology supports each of these stages is not critical.

- **Software engineering approach:** The software engineering approach taken by a methodology is also important for its use with a framework. As discussed before, an emphasis on reuse is helpful in the methodology, because in most frameworks it is assumed that reuse of components is a design priority to a certain degree. The method should be widely applicable to different problem domains (for general-purpose application frameworks), or at least to the specific problem domain being considered (for application-specific frameworks). A framework that supports multiple levels of testability and unit tests is best suited to a method that includes this principal, for example, Extreme Programming when coupled with a framework that incorporates unit test capability.

These are some of the factors that can help determine if your chosen methodology is a good fit with the framework you wish to use (or the reverse). It is an important question, particularly if a number of large projects are to be undertaken with the combination, and the work up front to get a good match will be worthwhile.

8.2 EXAMPLE METHODOLOGIES

Let us examine a few traditional and current software methodologies and see how they fit with component-based and framework development:

8.2.1 Waterfall Method

One of the simplest and oldest methodologies is the so-called waterfall method. Development in this method proceeds in a linear fashion from one step to the next, with limited feedback and few or no iterations over a step.

Waterfall development does not place any emphasis on a prototype stage, reuse, or componentization. The big picture of the project must be defined at the start in this simple sequence-oriented method.

Framework and component development tends to be more iterative, with repetitions over steps as the functionality is built up in blocks, and allows a greater degree of parallelism than is possible with the older waterfall method.

The traditional waterfall method performs rather poorly when specifications change frequently and rapidly, and is not a good fit for many of today's Web-application development projects.

The amount of risk in the waterfall method remains essentially the same throughout the project until well into the testing stage when problems (which might have begun at the design stage) are identified.

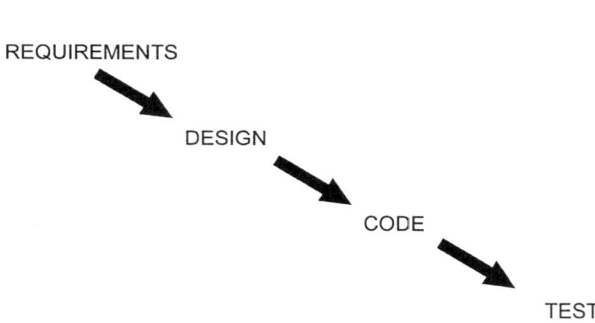

8.2.2 Incremental/Iterative Method

More sophisticated than the waterfall method, the iterative method is still simplistic, and only describes an overall approach to the development process. Many methodologies in real use today are far more complex, but still have aspects of the incremental approach within them.

Iterative methods imply a cycle of adding functionality, testing, perhaps documenting, and then adding more functionality, growing the project in cycles that add incremental functionality at each stage.

Although this fits somewhat better with the use of frameworks and components, it does not take into account the "assembly" of completed parts

Example Methodologies

(components) with functionality that is already operational. In this sense, it is also at best a sloppy fit with framework and component-based Web-application development.

The amount of risk in the incremental method is reduced at each iteration – when a particular iteration is tested, problems in that iteration can be identified and resolved before the next iteration begins.

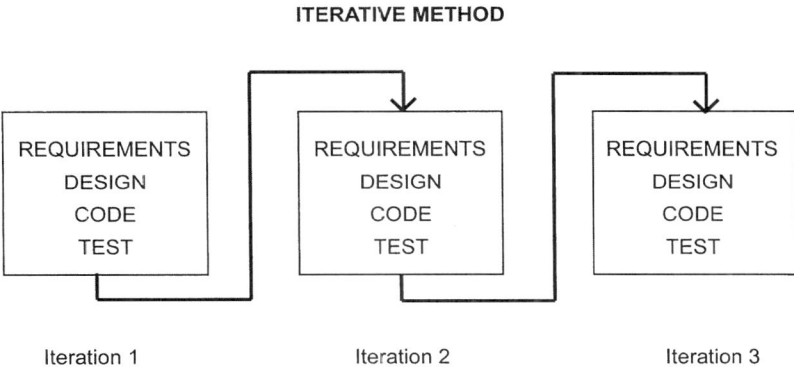

8.2.3 Open-Source Method

For lack of a better term, a kind of methodology has evolved that we term the "open-source" methodology. In this instance, we are not discussing a licensing scheme, as in Chapter 7, we are talking about the development life cycle and technique that is common to open-source projects. It can also be applied to commercial "closed-source" packages, although in some ways it tends to work better with larger developer communities. Although not a formalized and documented methodology, this technique is probably used by one of the largest developer communities, and is well worth our examination.

This methodology concentrates on many small incremental enhancements made in parallel. The overall "vision" of the package is kept somewhat flexible quite intentionally: its goals can change significantly between creation and completion, which is a good fit with today's Web applications. The open-source method emphasizes frequent minor point releases and as much feedback on these releases as possible with a generally large developer community. The central point of organization of this method is often the code itself, often somewhere in a CVS repository.

An open-source method project *evolves* more than it develops – it responds much more rapidly to changing needs of its various contributors/developers. Structure and organization evolve from the project itself, rather than from other methods that tend to impose a structure from the outside.

The open-source method works reasonably well with frameworks, although the component-based assembly of a framework-based project often requires more design discipline than is seen in open-source projects. The various competing interests in an open-source-method project tend to help develop the project quickly, but with a fair bit of "not invented here" syndrome in the mix: the urge to create a particular piece of functionality quickly often overrides the more structured approach of working out how to integrate another project that already has the needed functionality. This sometimes leads to excess duplication *between* projects, which is in conflict with the reuse philosophy of frameworks to some degree.

The separation of the roles implied in component-based development (e.g., separation into the supplier of components, manager/administrator of components, and consumer/assembler of components) is often emphasized in the open-source method: because of the nature of the larger community of users and contributors, some of the community members concentrate on just one of these roles.

Risk in the open-source method is reduced in the same way as in the iterative method: with each incremental release, the iteration and all the enhancements made in this iteration are tested, and problems are identified in this cycle. This method brings even more eyes to bear on the problems, however, and usually tests the entire project (not a subset) in many different environments, thereby enhancing final quality.

An important point to understand is that the open-source method does not address the *management* of a project. Although decision making is often distributed and democratic in many open-source projects, the overall vision, the monitoring, and the championing of a project still must take place. Often these functions are the responsibilities of one or very few people, even in projects that have hundreds of developers involved. The management of a project is no less essential in an open-source project than in any other; in fact, sometimes quite the opposite is true: an open-source project with no core person or group is likely to drift for a while and then peter out, much like a commercial project that loses its management advocate, exhausts its budget, and withers away. There is no magic in the open-source method that can avoid this, and it happens all too often.

Example Methodologies

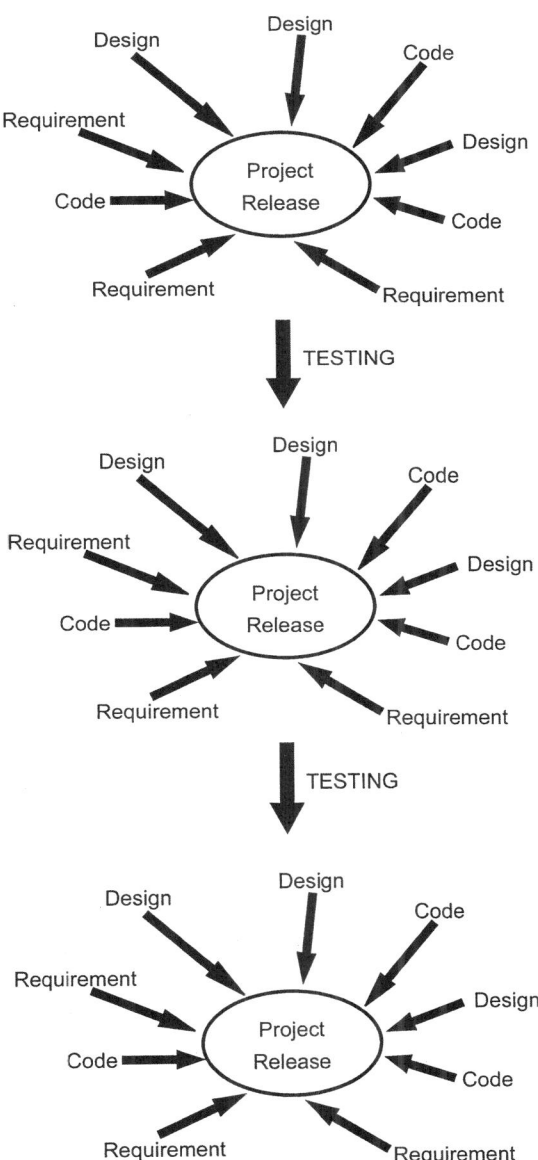

8.2.4 Rapid Application Development

More of a technique than a formalized methodology, Rapid Application Development (RAD) is a process whereby the speed of creation of a product is used as part of the methodology in its creation.

RAD can actually be an aspect of many other methodologies, and relies on highly skilled developers, powerful software development tools, application of best techniques, management of deliverables, and often the use of CASE or other software engineering support tools. All of this is managed within a structure designed to produce rapid results in short increments. Prototyping is a tool often used in an RAD project to solicit early feedback on design, and often the prototype is then expanded into the finished application by the application of high-level software tools.

RAD is a technique well supported by frameworks and components, because its requirements for high-level tools are met by the component framework itself. Prototyping is easy when an assembly of components results in an operational application early in the development cycle.

We will see elements of RAD in many different formal methodologies, especially in Extreme Programming, which we explore below.

8.2.5 Rational Unified Process

The Rational Unified Process is a commercial development of Rational Software. It provides a structured and well-controlled methodology for managing a software creation process, with special attention to the production of quality finished applications. It aims to provide a predictable budget of both time and resources for project creation.

The Rational methodology focuses on the creation and maintenance of models of the system being built, and relies on the use of Unified Modeling Language (UML) to communicate its design. UML was originally created at Rational, and they provide some of the most well-known tools for creating and using UML models. The easiest application of the Rational Unified Model is through the use of tools supplied by Rational.

The Rational approach codifies best practices gleaned from many projects into a methodology that encourages iterative development, carefully managed and monitored requirement analysis, and a component-based development process. As a result, it is well suited to development with frameworks and components. It encourages use of visual models of the design and software process, and tightly controlled change management.

This methodology can be a good fit with frameworks, particularly with frameworks that have existing visual models that can be used as a starting point for new projects. It is important, however, that the design of the architecture for the application being built be created with the structure of the chosen framework in mind. If an entirely different architecture is planned, shoehorning it into a particular framework can be very difficult after the fact. Introduce the framework early in the process to avoid this problem.

8.3 Select Perspective

The Select Perspective methodology from Aonix is another development methodology we examine briefly. Like Extreme Programming, which we examine later, it supports a relatively low-overhead methodology approach, and does not burden the development process with excessive formal procedures.

The Select Perspective emphasizes a collaborative approach between all parties involved in the development process including the user. It advocates (like the open-source method) frequent delivery of product with incremented functionality, and judges the progress of a project based on the fitness of each of the deliverables for the given business purpose.

Select Perspective is flexible and customizable, and is being adapted to fit the unique requirements of each project. It allows ongoing risk management throughout the life cycle of the project, and incorporates actual project data into the decision-making process during the development process. This methodology relies more heavily on modeling techniques, such as UML, than do other lightweight methodologies (such as Extreme Programming). A number of commercial products have been developed to facilitate the application of Select Perspective to projects.

In the next section, we explore in detail a more recently evolved methodology that has some elements of the incremental method, some elements of (and compatibility with) the open-source method, and a few unique aspects of its own. Some consider it to be the best fit with framework and component development, and a powerful methodology for any project, framework-based or otherwise.

8.4 Testing and Extreme Programming

Testing is an essential part of any development methodology; indeed, some methodologies make it a core part of their philosophy. One such methodology that has gained many adherents is Extreme Programming whose surging popularity, and the general opinion that it works well, along with its applicability to frameworks and framework projects, make it worthy of our closer examination here.

Extreme Programming is a methodology that has been shown to be highly effective in real-world use, and is in fact used in the development of a number of application frameworks. It carefully imposes a limited number of rules on the development process – rules that are unusual, even somewhat radical, when compared to other development methodologies.

Several excellent books have been written about this methodology, so we will just include the highlights here.

8.4.1 Extreme Programming Overview

In this section, we take a look at the Extreme Programming technique with a high-level overview and make some observations about how this technique applies to framework and component-based development. We spend a bit more time on Extreme Programming than other techniques particularly because it is frequently applied to frameworks and framework-dependent projects.

8.4.1.1 Project Organization

Instead of a monolithic design document, Extreme Programming advocates the use of "User Stories." These are descriptions, created by project users using their own terminology, of processes in the finished system. These reports are then used to create a release plan, designating the states of the development process, and the acceptance, or sign-off tests that will be applied to each report. These short "chunks" of development (less than 3 weeks for each report) become the milestones and measurable deliverables of the project. Completion of each of these user reports indicates progress in the project, and how rapidly they are completed is a measure of how much is getting done on the project. As most developers know, the number of people churning away on a project is no indicator of actual accomplishment, and generally it is a known fact that adding more developers to a project going over schedule is a good way to make it go even further over schedule. Better to take bite-sized pieces in the first place, so that problems are seen early and often and can be corrected with minimal impact.

The release plan of the project should allow for frequent incremental releases, with relatively small increments between releases. This "release early, release often" approach has proved its advantages in many open-source projects, and can be applied equally well to commercial or in-house development.

Extreme Programming also advocates cross-training, and getting more than one developer involved in each part of the project to avoid bottlenecks and disasters if staff are lost or reassigned. This also fosters good communication, which is essential between developers, and easier to facilitate with small groups. This kind of communication and cross-training is also fostered by one of Extreme Programming's more unusual approaches: it advocates using "pair programming," that is, two developers working at a single workstation for all code creation that goes into the finished product. Experience with the method has shown that when properly applied, productivity equals or betters the productivity when both individuals work separately, but that the quality of the created code is higher. This is one aspect of Extreme Programming that is difficult for many developers to accept, although the statistics and results bear out its effectiveness.

8.4.1.2 Design

Extreme Programming advocates simplicity in design as a guiding principle. Always find the simplest way to do something, and consider that a design is finished when there is nothing left to take away, and not when there is nothing left to add. This tends to keep focus on the original design goals, and avoids unnecessary or undesired features from creeping into the process. Small experimental programs are often written to explore the proposed solution, to see if it is as simple as it seems, and then these are refined until they encompass the requirements. It is important for developers to agree on an overall system metaphor for the design, and to stick with this through the development process. Often this mirrors the problem domain itself, although sometimes an even simpler metaphor can be found.

Refactoring is another approach used aggressively in Extreme Programming. It is gaining popularity as a "buzzword" in software development circles, but is still sometimes difficult for developers to adopt. Refactoring refers to the approach of reviewing a solution that already exists and works, but is not ideal or easily extensible, and redesigning and reimplementing it in a better way. It involves discarding code, work, and often design as well, which is never an altogether easy thing to do. However, the benefits of refactoring and applying it whenever possible to improve a solution pay dividends. It is important for developers to see code that ends up being discarded when refactoring as valuable guideposts along the way to the final design, not mistakes that are simply rejected and waste time.

8.4.1.3 Testing

Testing is a central concept to Extreme Programming, and in fact is probably one of its better known aspects. All code created with the methodology must possess a unit test, and the test is created *before* the code is created. In other words, you first create a test that would be satisfied by code that fulfills the user report being worked on, then you create code that satisfies the test. This is often facilitated by a unit test framework, such as JUnit. Many Web-application frameworks include JUnit, or easily allow it to be integrated, bringing consistency to their tests, and allowing an entire sequence of tests to be run to verify entire systems. Whenever a problem is found that was not detected by a test, a new test is coded to identify that problem, and then the code is corrected; in this way, the same kind of problem cannot slip through again, and the code (and the tests) increase steadily in quality. A final type of test applied in Extreme Programming is an acceptance test – that is, a test that ensures that a particular user record has been satisfied. Completion of these tests is made known to the entire group, because it is an essential statistic of progress on the project.

8.4.1.4 Development

The development phase of an Extreme Programming project is not characterized by developers going away and sitting over their terminals in seclusion, and then coming back with the answer. The end user is involved in the entire process as much as possible, and must be constantly available for communication by the project team.

Code must be created according to specific coding standards; ideally, it should be impossible to easily tell which member of a project team created which particular section of code, where in many projects it is simple to pick out a particular coding style. Pair programming is used to create all of the actual code going into the project, with only one pair doing actual integration of the code into the core project at a time. In this way, integration conflicts are found early and resolved on the spot, and integration with obsolete versions is avoided.

The code developed is seen in an Extreme Programming project as a community resource – the concept of "code ownership" by individual teams or developers is discouraged. Shifting development teams onto different areas of the code is one way to avoid this kind of an issue. Performance and optimization issues are deferred until the end of the project, because it is much more essential to have functionality in place and working properly than to have the wrong application running quickly. Lastly, the development phase of an Extreme Programming project plans for no overtime on the part of developers. The tale of development going on into the wee hours of the morning to meet deadlines is repeated so often that it is often assumed that the developer is a nocturnal species. Overtime is counterproductive, and is indicative of a problem in the planning or in the application of the methodology. Instead of throwing more time, resources, or, worst of all, more people on a problem, it is better to change the scope or the schedule of the project.

Extreme Programming is a methodology that works well in situations where requirements and specifications undergo rapid and constant change. In the ideal development world, a set of concise and well-formed specifications are submitted to the development team, and they then create the software that fulfills these specifications. Unfortunately, in the real world, the specification often does not even get time to cool off from the laser printer before the changes begin, and projects frequently evolve substantially while they are still in the early stages of development. Worse, sometimes the specification never really freezes at all – either because customers of the project do not have a 100 percent firm idea of what they want, or because the requirements really change quickly. Extreme Programming applies well in these situations, helping contain project risk caused by either shifting specifications or hard deadlines.

In today's environment of shrinking software development resources, Extreme Programming's applicability to small development groups is particularly valuable. In fact, it does not necessarily scale well to large groups of developers (more than twelve, e.g., on the same project). Some would say that software development itself does not scale to such large groups in any case, and that most highly successful software has been created by "groups" of one or two developers, and sometimes as many as three. However small your team may be, reports of enhanced productivity by the use of Extreme Programming are encouraging. Extreme Programming actually brings more resources to bear on the problem, in a sense, as it actively involves the customer, manager, designer, and other interested parties early and often in the development process. By achieving "buy-in" and involving all concerned parties, not just the developers, Extreme Programming increases the chance of the project's success, because more people are motivated to do what needs to be done to make it all come together. Extreme Programming's philosophy of "test first" increases the quality of software in ways that are not immediately apparent: by designing a system to be easier to test, and to facilitate automated testing, you often build the kind of robustness required in a highly reliable system as a by-product. This, of course, is an essential attribute for frameworks themselves, as their multiple applications in multiple environments require this level of robustness.

8.5 UML

The UML standard, created by the Object Management Group (OMG) organization, has been widely adopted as a cross-language notation for system design and description. Many developers in today's environment begin their development process with diagrams as an essential part of the design process, and with UML as the standard for diagramming and describing software projects.

UML is independent of any one software methodology, but can be successfully applied to many different methodologies. As a result, it has been adopted as the standard diagramming technique for many different development projects. This has resulted in UML being widely understood in the development community, making it especially useful for diagramming the design of frameworks. A framework, by its nature, needs to be understood and used repeatedly by a diverse group of developers of all skill levels. A single well-known diagramming standard to describe its design is a valuable tool in educating developers and potential users about the framework.

UML defines twelve standard diagram types. Not all UML tools utilize all of these types, just a few can still be used quite effectively, depending on the project. These are the diagrams describing structure, the class, object, component, and deployment diagrams, the diagrams describing behavior or operations, which include the use-case, sequence, activity, collaboration and state-chart diagrams, and finally the diagrams describing the model and its overall organization, which are the package, subsystem and model diagrams. Many UML tools can examine existing systems and produce representative diagrams directly from the code, which can then be refined as required for a finished product – for large existing systems this can be a valuable time saver.

Often frameworks make some use of use-case diagrams, particularly when describing overall capabilities or giving examples, and more extensive use of the package, class, object, and component diagrams. Other than in specific cases and examples, behavior diagrams are less frequently used.

Let us examine some of the more commonly used UML diagrams and how their usage is affected by using a framework and components in your development process.

8.5.1 Use-Case Diagrams

A use-case diagram is used to identify application requirements at a high level. It is not concerned with implementation details or specific classes or components but instead provides a functional description of a part of the finished application. In this sense, use-case diagrams are similar to the "user stories" used in the Extreme Programming method – they capture a part of the interaction of the user with the system (or sometimes with one part of a system with another, or even between two systems).

The major elements in a use-case diagram are the "actors," most often representing hypothetical users of the system, but sometimes include another kind of "client," such as a device or other application, and the use-cases themselves, representing a service provided by the application being designed. These elements are connected by lines that indicate interactions – a kind of communication between the actor and the use-case. Each use-case diagram is accompanied by a narrative description of the use-case being described, which includes a step-by-step sequence of the interactions being modeled.

For example, a simplistic use-case diagram of a user logging in to authenticate with an application might look like

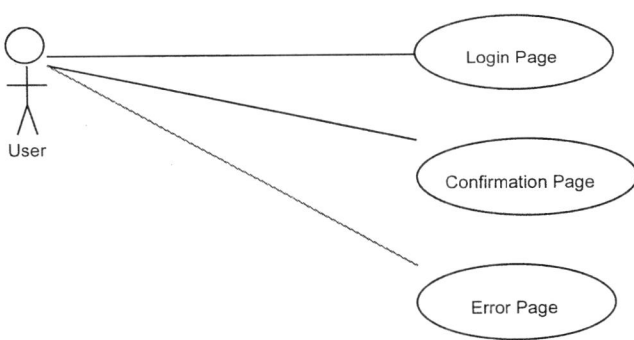

The narrative that goes with it might be :

- Users direct their Web browser to the application.
- The system provides the login screen.
- The user keys in his or her login name and password and then clicks a button.
- The system then validates the entered information and determines whether the login is correct, thereby authenticating the user.
- The system responds with a message indicating a successful login and presents the application's main menu.

- ALTERNATIVE: if the login name or password is not acceptable, the system presents a generic rejection message (without indicating the specific problem) and waits for three seconds and presents the login page again.

Most use-cases, of course, are slightly more complex, but the general principle is the same.

In framework and component design, the use-cases themselves are often services provided by the framework or existing components. For our example, our framework almost certainly includes a kind of existing login service and a default page to interact with it. So our use-cases tend, with frameworks, to begin with existing services, or aggregations of existing services. As more application-specific features are designed, custom services are created, but always keeping in mind the framework's capabilities to support specific sequences – for example, if we design with Struts, we know that it is easy to create logic to accept a form, validate that form, and present the same form again if any invalid data is found. If we work *with* the capabilities of our framework, use-cases are easier to create, and tend to be more consistent than when starting from scratch.

It is also important to keep in mind that use-cases may model the interaction of one system (or part of the system) with another – in other words, the "user" may be another application or module. This method can therefore be used to model noninteractive tasks as well as user interactions at a high level.

8.5.2 Class and Object Diagrams

Class diagrams show classes and the relationships between classes, interfaces, and their implementations, and sometimes they show even actual instances of the classes and their interactions. They also indicate the attributes (variables) of instances of the class, and the methods available in each class (or interface). Frequently, they encompass only a section of the class hierarchy of an application – perhaps one package, or an even smaller subset.

When designing with frameworks, the high-level classes usually belong to the framework, so the top-level class diagrams are those of the framework itself. The specific classes created for an application are usually subclasses of abstract classes provided by the framework, or implementations of interfaces defined in the framework. They typically also utilize services of the framework by calling methods on those classes. Therefore, your own class diagrams will need to interact frequently with those of the framework. It is helpful if the framework has its own class diagrams, and even better if they are in a format that is compatible with your own UML design tool. In this way you can start with a copy of the framework's own class diagrams and extend as required for your application.

Sometimes the framework provides "stereotypes" from which to build additional diagrams, allowing you to represent the assembly of existing services within the framework more easily.

8.5.3 Sequence and Collaboration Diagrams

Although use-cases describe sequences, they diagram only a static point in the application's life cycle. Class diagrams also show a single moment in time. Sequence diagrams and collaboration diagrams show how an application's state is intended to change over time – they show the dynamic operation of the application being designed. They are also a key tool to understanding the flow and processing of a framework, enabling it to be used correctly.

Sequence diagrams are probably the most frequently used UML diagram after class diagrams – they show the interactions between classes as the application is executed, thereby showing the classes involved across the page from left to right, and also showing the sequences as lines between the columns containing the classes. These lines indicate messages are being passed from one class to another, and the diagram indicates time by the first interaction being at the top of the page, and each subsequent interaction lower down with time increasing toward the bottom of the diagram. We saw an example of a sequence diagram in Chapter 3:

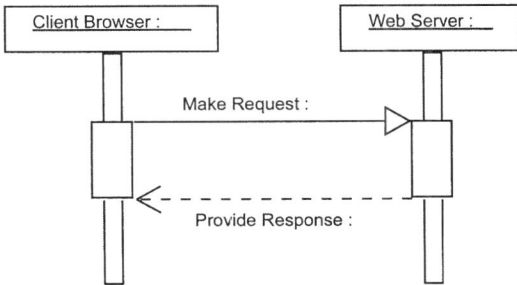

When designing with frameworks, the interactions available are usually constrained to the available interactions between components in the framework.

The framework provides a pattern that structures the flow of sequences – for example, some frameworks use the command pattern and others rely on events. These sequence mechanisms influence the interactions that are available in your sequence diagrams. Ideally, your system should rely on the sequence mechanisms supported by the framework – if you have to create your own, at least for relatively high-level objects, you are not getting maximum benefit out of the component and flow services provided by your framework. At a lower level, of course, your own custom objects will sometimes need to interact, but the more this happens the less flexible the finished application, as you introduce more component dependencies (or object dependencies, at the more detailed level).

8.5.4 Package, Component, and Deployment Diagrams

Some of the other UML diagrams in common use are package, component, and deployment diagrams. Each of these is influenced somewhat by the use of a framework in your development process.

Package diagrams are used for showing the structure of the packages that make up the application. Frequently, the framework you use has a certain set of guidelines for separating your classes into packages, so this diagram is influenced by the recommended practices in a particular framework. Avalon, for example, encourages the separation of the package for the interfaces for a component or service and the implementation. Expresso encourages the packaging together of an application's data persistence objects into a single subpackage. As you follow these guidelines, your package diagrams will reflect these decisions.

A component diagram is sometimes ignored in traditional application development as being similar to a package diagram. When designing with frameworks and components, however, a component diagram provides an essential high-level view of how the classes in your application are collected into specific components and services. Use of a framework frequently encourages heavier use of this structure, and hence this diagram. If you follow the recommended decomposition method for your framework, you will see the appropriate level of design that components occupy: for example, if you decompose your application into services, components, and classes that implement these components, the component diagram is an essential view.

The final diagram we examine briefly is the deployment diagram. This is a diagram showing each of the "nodes" or processing elements of the finished application as they would appear in the proposed configuration for production. Sometimes this is high level, with each node being a server in a clustered server application, and sometimes it is lower level, in which case each node can represent a "service" of the finished application, irrespective of the server on which this service is deployed. The options available in a deployment diagram depend much on the possible configurations of the component model that your framework provides. For frameworks that support the full J2EE/EJB component mechanism, multiple servers might indeed play a part in your deployment diagram. For most frameworks, the specific separation of services across servers is a configuration decision, and not a design decision, and the deployment diagram can be used to indicate this layout.

8.6 MVC Architecture

The majority of frameworks follow, in one way or another, the model–view–controller (MVC) architecture for separating user interface from logic. Although not a development "methodology" per se, MVC has been with us since the days of SmallTalk, and variants on it are very popular in Web-application development. In general, the principle of separating the view from the model and the controller has been a topic of great importance, particularly when the view changes with the speed of the changing presentation technologies of the Web.

MVC aims to separate business logic and processing (model) from the UI, or presentation (view) from navigation and input (controller). The reason for this is to achieve independence between these areas: it is much more difficult to change the visual presentation if it is dependent on and built into the business logic. The reverse is also true: it is harder to make changes to the processing if the presentation is hard-coded into it. Separation of these areas results in a vastly more flexible system.

8.6.1 Model 1

Model 1 of MVC results when the request to and the response from the Web browser are handled by a single component: either a JSP page or a Servlet, for example. Business logic may be separated, but both the request and the response are dealt with together.

8.6.2 Model 2

Model 2 refers to the case when the request from the browser is handled by one component (typically a Servlet), and the response is handled by another

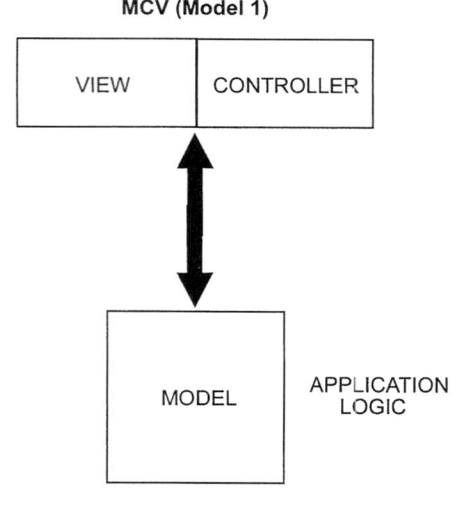

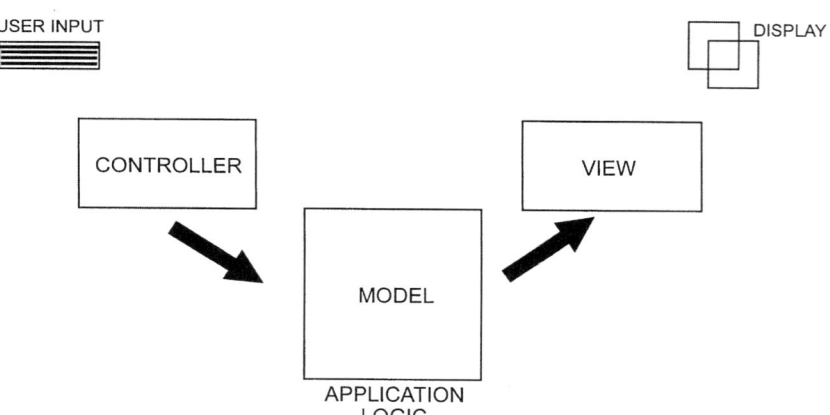

(often a JSP page but just as easily another Servlet). This provides for a better isolation among the MVC areas of responsibility. A particular request can be redirected to a different view, for example, and the view logic is isolated from the request-handling logic. Typically, a third component handles the actual business logic.

In a nutshell, Model 1 separates the model from the view and controller, whereas Model 2 separates all three.

8.6.3 HMVC

Another term, related to MVC and its two "models," that is sometimes used in connection with framework design patterns is HMVC, or hierarchical model–view–controller. This is very similar to another pattern called "presentation–abstraction–control," which is a pattern whereby the MVC structure is further decomposed into a series of "layers," in a hierarchical arrangement. This structure is more commonly used in Swing or AWT-based client applications. It is not entirely applicable to "thin-client" Web applications.

8.7 DESIGN PATTERNS

Frameworks provide much more than a powerful tool box to your application development process. They provide *design patterns* that greatly streamline not only the development process, but the design process as well.

Design patterns are not an exact science. They are more generalized, and constantly evolving as they are used. The same general pattern can be used in many different concrete implementations. Frequently, UML diagrams are used to describe a design pattern and its implementation.

Patterns can exist at all levels of detail, aiding design at every stage, from initial design, prototype, extended development and deployment phases.

A pattern consists of a recurring set of relationships between services, components, and objects. Repeated use of a certain set of relationships uncovers certain advantages, and these become regularized into design patterns. Like reusable components, design patterns develop in an iterative and evolving process through repeated reuse.

Patterns can actually be applied at a number of different levels. Coding standards are one type of pattern – the use of a particular style of indentation, for example, is a basic pattern.

Any pattern should be applied consistently, and should have the ability to be easily reused in many different situations. It should be possible to describe the pattern, and to verify that it has been applied correctly when it is used.

Any set of patterns to be used on a single project should have the ability to be combined – that is, they should not be mutually exclusive or prevent each other from being used.

Also, generally patterns are not dependent on a specific programming language – they are often applied in many different languages.

Applying a pattern in any given situation does not necessarily result in the easiest or fastest solution. Applying the correct patterns appropriately through the entire project, however, will often reduce the overall effort of both development and long-term maintenance. Just like frameworks, patterns are most effective when consistently applied to a project.

Some patterns, such as interfaces, inheritance from a single class, and method call-backs, follow naturally from the structure of the Java language. Other common patterns, such as pooling and the creation of implementations via factory classes, are seen repeatedly in the standard Java APIs.

Let us examine a few common patterns and explore how frameworks support their use.

8.7.1 Composition and Extension

The two patterns that are best known to most Java programmers are also common in Web-application frameworks: composition and extension. You use composition every time you use a Vector or ArrayList in Java: it is the pattern of combining objects into a grouped object so that they can be manipulated as a set. Some frameworks extend Java's inherent composition capabilities with their own strongly-typed version for special purposes. Java collection objects are effectively weakly-typed, because they can hold objects of any type, and even different types of objects in the same collections.

Extension is also common in Java: you use it every time you extend a class to create a subclass. Frameworks often make heavy use of extension, by providing a rich set of extensible classes for use in your own applications. However, there are some disadvantages to extension in some situations, and many frameworks provide other means as well. In Java, for example, classes can only inherit from one other class – interfaces can be used to avoid this restriction to some degree.

The design patterns known to most programmers stop with extension. This is sometimes a reason for delays in the adoption of frameworks – the more advanced design patterns are unfamiliar to some.

8.7.2 Delegates and Proxies

Delegation is the next more complex pattern seen often in frameworks and is a kind of "container" pattern. It is a type of advanced composition in that it passes on behavior to other classes, and is very flexible and dynamic.

The object containing the referred-to object is called the delegator, and the contained or referred-to object is called the delegate. The delegate is often an instance of a particular interface. In our example, we might have a delegator that expects a class that implements "UserInfo." Multiple classes can be created, all with slightly different behaviors, all of which implement "UserInfo." The delegator then uses some conditions, say a configuration setting, to determine which delegate to use. This provides a framework with "pluggable" capability, where the exact implementation for a particular functionality can be replaced as easily as flipping a switch. Many frameworks take advantage of this pattern for that very reason.

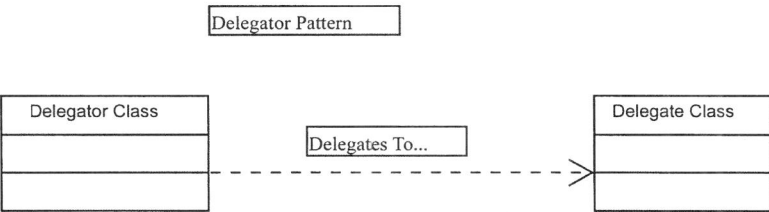

If the delegate is not "private" to the delegator class, but is used directly by other parts of the system, it is known as the "proxy" pattern because the delegator, in fact, acts as proxy for the delegate.

8.7.3 Interface

The delegate and the proxy patterns both require use of an even simpler pattern: the interface. An interface is a contract – the class implementing the interface agreed to implement a certain functionality, and to have a certain design signature. This allows other classes to treat implementations as though they were an instantiation of a particular class.

Other than their uses as an enabler of delegation, interfaces can be used to do something very similar to multiple inheritance. When *combined* with delegates (or proxies), we find a combination pattern that has many of the advantages of multiple inheritance but without the complexities and potential pitfalls. Frameworks can use this combination to good effect, allowing an application to do its own inheritance rather than forcing it into the framework inheritance hierarchy, while at the same time, allowing access to the framework's functionality.

Another valuable use of interfaces used by some frameworks is the "marker" interface. This allows an interface with no methods to be used to "mark" a

EXAMPLE OF THE DELEGATION DESIGN PATTERN

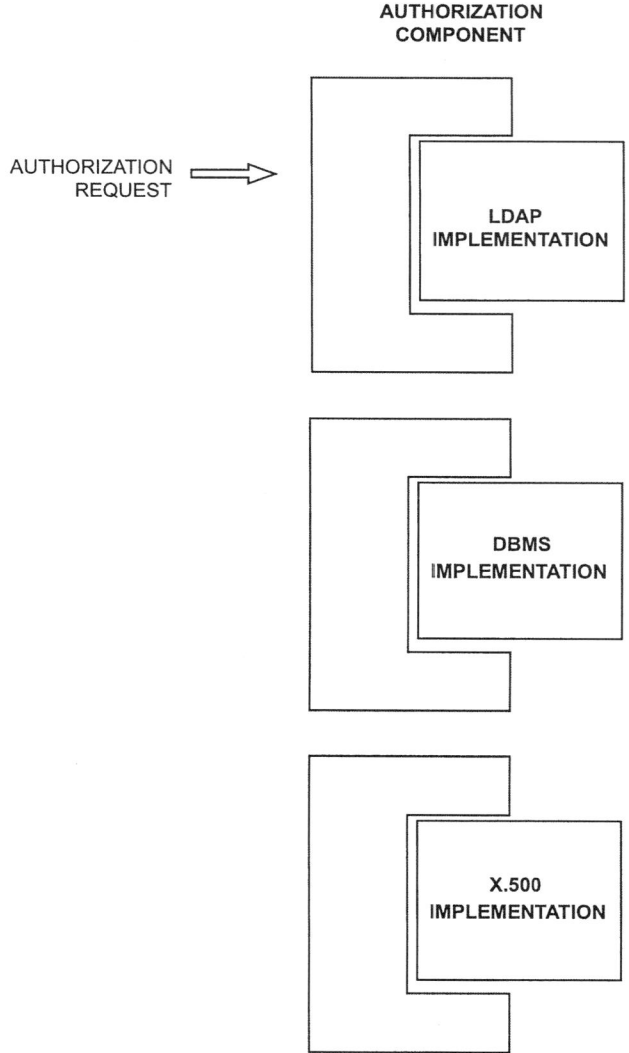

class, for example, to note whether it belongs to a particular group or category. Avalon, for example, uses this pattern to mark classes that can be managed by a ComponentManager. (Actually, this has changed in later versions of Avalon, but it does provide a good example.)

Often, the marker interface is used to denote instances of another pattern that we discuss later – the utility class.

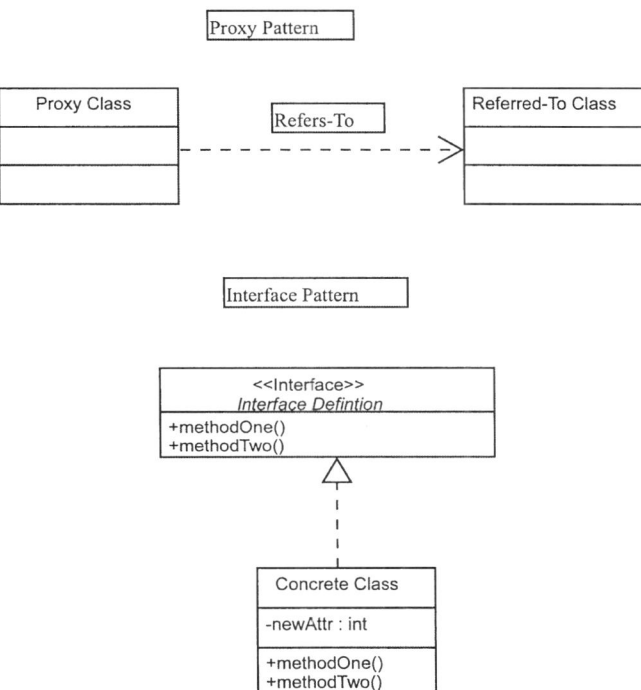

8.7.4 Factories

Many Java standard APIs make use of the next design pattern: the factory pattern. Normal, direct instantiation, either with the "new" operator, or via the newInstance method of the class (often used for dynamic class loading). The factory pattern involves accessing a Factory class for new instances, such as:

```
SomeClass object = Factory.newInstance
```

This example shows a static factory method, but sometimes nonstatic factories may be used:

```
1. SomeFactory myFactory = newFactory();
2. SomeClass object = myFactory.instantiate();
```

This can be very valuable where the factory itself is a pluggable implementation, using perhaps a delegate or proxy pattern.

This is an example of the kit pattern, or the toolkit pattern: a static factory is used with the delegate pattern to create instances of another factory. Different factories can be created as required from the same static factory.

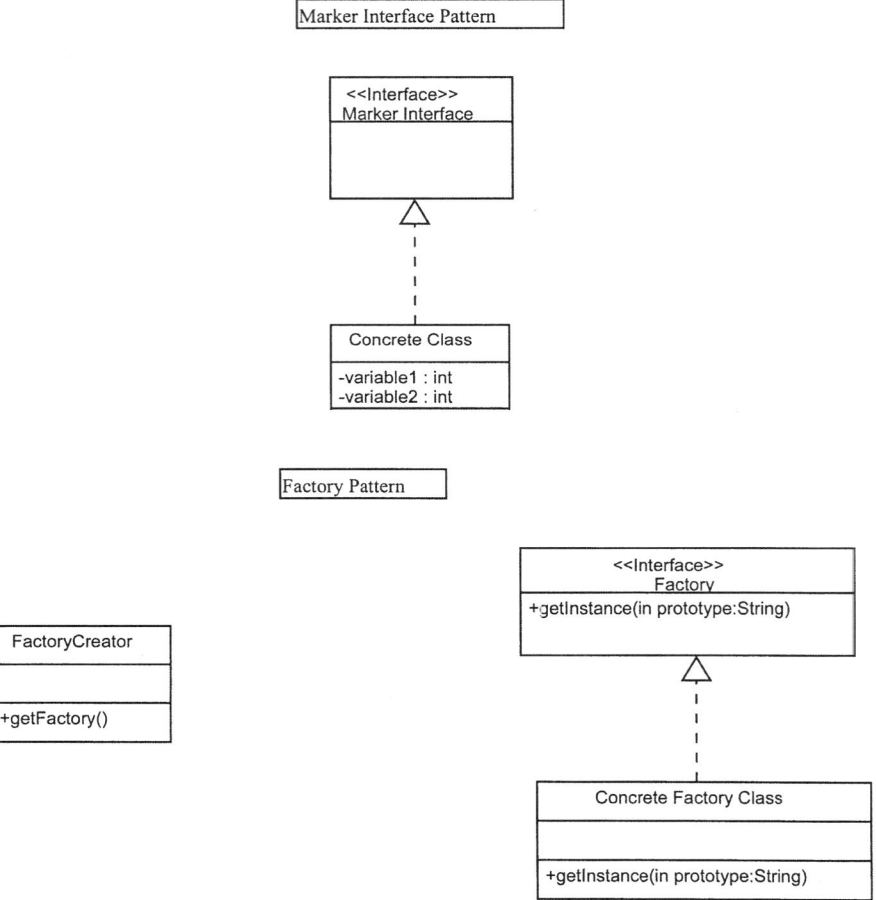

A further refinement of the factory pattern can incorporate an existing instance as a parameter. This is called the prototype pattern. A factory is used to create an instance from another instance. The resulting prototypes are instances that operate like classes, and they are copied from the prototype class – sometimes with specific modifications.

8.7.5 Pooling

Another pattern that is common in frameworks is the pooling pattern. Although the most popular example of pooling is for database connections, it can be applied in many other ways whenever there is a situation where instantiating new instances is expensive or inefficient. It can also be applied in situations where locking is required for concurrent access.

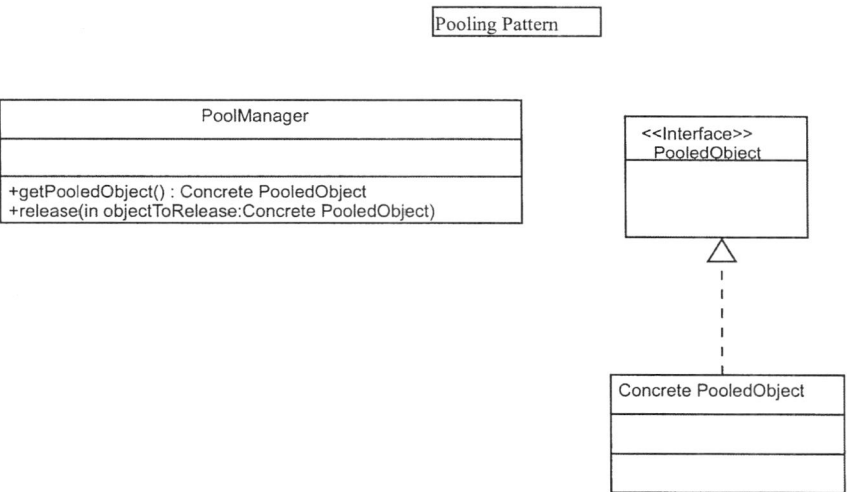

Often, the class implementing the pool has only one instance – it is an example of our final design pattern, the Singleton. A Singleton is a very simple pattern – it is a class that can only have one instance. Singletons are often created as factories. They frequently have a getInstance() method that returns the one and only instance of the class.

8.7.6 Singleton

A Singleton is a common pattern found in frameworks. A Singleton is simply a class that is only instantiated once – there is a single instance of the class. All attempts to instantiate another instance simply return the one shared instance.

This pattern is frequently used for classes where only a single instance is possible, such as a Cache Manager or global configuration class. In the factory pattern, for example, we see where individual factories could be created by a single "factory maker" class – a kind of a factory of factories. This "factory maker" is frequently a Singleton class.

Usually the Singleton is implemented by defining a private constructor, such as:

```
public class TheSingleton {
   private TheSingleton() {
   }
}
```

As you can see, the constructor does nothing. Of course, of this was all we had in the Singleton, there would be no way to access it at all. The Singleton class is distinct from a class with only static methods – a utility class. Unlike a utility class, which is never instantiated at all, a Singleton *is* instantiated – but only once. The single instance is normally stored as a class static variable, and the objects that need access to the instance call a "getInstance()" method to retrieve it. A Singleton class may use class or instance variables as required, also unlike a utility class.

```
public class TheSingleton {
   private static TheSingleton myInstance = null;
   private TheSingleton() {
   }
   final public synchronized static TheSingleton
     getInstance() {
     if (myInstance == null) {
        myInstance = new TheSingleton();
     }
     return myInstance;
   }
   final public Object clone() throws CloneNotSupported
     Exception {
     throw new CloneNotSupportedException();
   }
}
```

As you can see from above, the getInstance method immediately creates a new instance (which it alone is allowed to do) if the single instance (myInstance) is not already initialized. Once the single instance is initialized, it is simply handed back to the caller. The addition of an empty "clone" method prevents the caller from obtaining the single instance then calling the "clone" method (defined in java.lang.Object) to create a second instance – not that any user of the singleton should do so, but it is a good practice to prevent it in any case. As you can see, the two methods are declared "final," preventing even an extension of the singleton from being instantiated more than once.

The methods of a singleton should be thread-safe – either synchronized in their entirety (as we have done here), or using synchronized sections (critical sections) for access to common data. The methods of the singleton need not be static, however.

```
          Singleton Pattern

          Singleton Class
-onlyInstance : Singleton Class
+getInstance()
```

8.7.7 Utility

A utility class is a pattern found in almost every framework. Simple methods, such as copying a file, encoding a string, formatting a date, and so forth, are collected into classes. These classes usually provide a related set of methods, such as file-handling (which is a common example). The utility class is never instantiated. Instead, all of its methods are static, and are called directly as required from other objects. There are usually no instances or class variables in a utility class, so in this sense a utility class is akin to the "subroutines" of older languages: it is just a collection of methods made available for reuse.

Utility classes are often declared "final," and are not intended to be extended by subclassing. They are often the easiest parts of a framework to use, because they require no special preparation: just call the method you need, with the appropriate parameter, receive the return value, and carry on.

The methods collected into utility classes should be very generic: too many parameters is a good indication that the method might be better off in a separate object, where data and methods are combined. A framework with too many utility classes, or too much of its functionality embodied in utility classes, may make insufficient use of other more powerful design patterns.

8.7.8 Thread-Safe

Thread-safety is more of a technique than a pattern per se. It involves ensuring that a particular method, or an entire class, can be executed at the same time by more than one thread, and that these executions do not interfere with each other in any way. It is related to multithreaded programming, which is something that any capable framework should provide assistance with by providing prebuilt classes and hierarchies of classes that take this kind of scalability into account.

One way of making a method thread-safe is simply to synchronize it. This prevents multiple executions from interfering with each other, but may have a detrimental effect on the whole application as a result. Synchronization is a "blocking" mechanism, whereas thread-safety is not. Making a method thread-safe involves ensuring that the method does not use any variables outside its own scope during its execution. For example:

```
public class SomeClass {
  private Integer x = 0;
  public Integer someMethod() {
    ... use x in some calculation ...
      return result;
  }
}
```

This class leaves open the opportunity for the int "x" to be accessed by two simultaneous invocations of "someMethod," resulting in an unexpected result. To solve this with synchronization, we might say

```
public synchronized Integer someMethod()
...
```

Or even:

```
public synchronized Integer someMethod() {
  .....
  synchronized(x) {
  .... use x for calculation ...
  }
  return result;
}
```

But both of them can impose blocking constraints on the operating application. The severity of the problem will vary widely, of course, depending on exactly what happens in someMethod that utilizes "x." A thread-safe approach might be as follows:

```
public Integer someMethod(Integer x) {
   .... use x for calculation ...
   return result;
}
```

As you can see, we are not synchronizing x any longer, because it is passed as a parameter — its scope is now limited to the single thread of the method, and synchronization is not required.

Thread-safety is not a pattern that can be used in all situations, nor is this the only (or even the best, in all circumstances) way to go about it. It is, however, an important but subtle pattern that is used frequently in frameworks, particularly in the logic container or application component support areas.

8.7.9 Separation of Concerns

Separation of concerns, like the service pattern we examine next, is a higher level design pattern, usually used in an entire development project. It is found frequently throughout the structure of a framework. Separation of concerns involves breaking a problem into different points of view, or "concerns." It is sometimes difficult to point to a piece of code and show the pattern in use, but any well-designed framework will incorporate it extensively.

The interface pattern is almost always an example of separation of concerns at work: the definition of the contract of a class is being separated from the implementation. A common indicator of separation of concerns is the existence of classes that implement a number of different interfaces. Each interface deals with a single concern, even though the class may be involved in a number of different concern areas when taken as a whole.

When applied correctly, the separation of concerns pattern results in appropriate modularization of a system, breaking it into digestible and maintainable pieces. Object-oriented development, and in particular Java, lends itself well to this very process.

As a very simple example, take an object that represents a customer, with a method for calculating the customer's total debt:

```
public class Customer implements PersistentObject {
   Integer customerID;
   String customerName;
   .....

   public Double calculateReceivable() {
   ....
   }
}
```

You see that our example object implements an interface "PersistentObject." In our hypothetical framework, this indicates that the object can be read from and written to some kind of persistent storage: a database, for example. The customer class, however, is not concerned with this directly. Its job is to deal with the customer and to calculate the customer's receivable amount. The "concern" of persistence is isolated by the interface.

Often, separation of concerns is much more pervasive and subtle than in our simple example, but you should see indications of how the individual elements of a framework deal with one area of priority at a time, at the same time allowing your application to make use of all of these elements at once.

8.7.10 Service Pattern

The service pattern is another high-level pattern that is common in frameworks. It lends itself well to the reusability of frameworks, and this fit has contributed to its popularity.

The service pattern involves decomposing the application problem into a number of services, where a "service" is a component, or possibly a collection of components, providing a specific function to the overall solution. For example, a service might be an authorization component or a job scheduler. These are examples of "system services," or services that are not specific to a particular application's business functionality. A service that produces customer bills, for example, would be a business service.

Generally speaking, a framework provides system services that are then used by your application-specific services. For example, the customer billing service might use the persistence service to access customer data and the scheduling service to send reminder notices or dunning letters.

When decomposing a particular application problem into services, the services named explicitly in the specification are often business or application services: billing the customer, shipping the part, and producing the financial statement. The ones that are left unsaid are often the implied system services: providing login processing and authentication, storing the data, and so forth.

8.7.11 Command

In frameworks, the command pattern is used less frequently than some other patterns. It is similar to delegation in that it may involve a request for a particular operation being "passed along" to another object, which does the actual processing. The command pattern is, however, more than this and refers to the general arrangement where a single class handles multiple "commands," or requests for processing. It may handle some of the requests itself, or may use the delegation pattern (or the proxy pattern) to refer requests to other objects.

A scheduling class might be an example of a command pattern. Many classes can call the scheduling class, requesting that functions be scheduled for later execution. The scheduling class, in turn, may refer some (or all) requests to other classes at the appropriate time.

Frequently, the command pattern uses another simple pattern: the so-called functor pattern. This pattern brings the equivalent of pointers to functions to Java, allowing a form of "call-backs" to be used to select the appropriate functionality. In our example of a scheduling class, for instance, the method call to schedule an operation might look like

```
schedule(Date dateToRun, Runnable objectToRun);
```

The dateToRun provides a date object, specifying when the process is to be started, and the objectToRun specifies the actual object that is to be executed at the proper time. The Runnable interface (from java.lang.Runnable) is used to indicate that the objectToRun possesses the "run()" method, which is called when the at the appropriate time.

In this example, the scheduling object is the command processor, and the objectToRun is the *functor* – the object that is "called back" when the scheduled time becomes current.

8.8 DEVELOPMENT PHASES

Design patterns are applied at all levels of a project's development life cycle, and certain patterns are particularly applicable to certain phases. Let us examine the common phases and see how they relate to some of our patterns.

8.8.1 Prototyping

In response to the pressure to produce tangible results as early as possible, prototyping has emerged as a high-level design pattern that leads smoothly to development. This pattern also has the advantage of permitting user feedback and involvement very early in the design/development process. Creating applications, even with powerful framework assistance, is still a difficult, expensive, and time-consuming process. The earlier the design can be introduced to the people who will actually use it, the earlier services design changes can be made, minimizing their impact on the process.

Some important considerations should be applied to this pattern: because it is a prototype, it is important to get something running in a short time, not to overgeneralize, or to try to make enabling reuse a high priority. Frameworks, with their abilities to free the developer from having to worry about the infrastructure "plumbing," facilitate rapid prototyping. Often, the prototype can be extended into the finished application – but this should *not* be the goal. A prototype should be considered a throw-away, a first pass.

In the prototyping phase, the design pattern where decomposing the specification into nouns, which relate to objects, and verbs, which relate to actions, can be applied. Emphasis should be placed on basic functionality, with the refinement deferred until the next phase.

8.8.2 Development

The development phase consists, to oversimplify, of taking the lessons learned in the prototype and scaling them up to a complete and working application. Although the prototype concentrates on demonstrating functionality quickly and easily, the goal in development is to create a more enduring design for the production application.

Frequently, a pattern of decomposition is applied, as shown in the following diagram. The overall application is decomposed into the required services. An example of this process is seen in the design of our case study in the Appendix.

The required services are then mapped to the available services of the chosen framework. Services that the framework provides are then used to implement the components for each required service. Services that are not provided must be coded directly.

This, as discussed previously, is a good place to evaluate the fit of a particular framework. If many or all of the required services are provided by the chosen

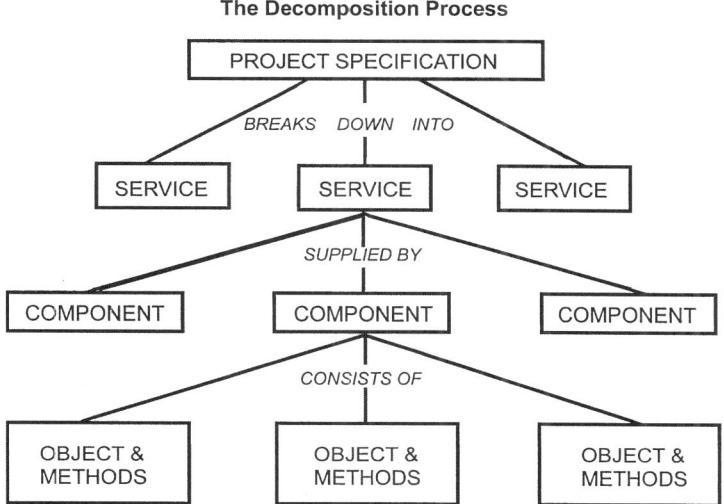

framework, it is a good fit. If many services have to be custom-developed, then perhaps another framework would be a better choice.

In the development phase, frameworks support the subclass pattern very well, by providing a rich set of classes for applications to extend with their custom requirements. This is where the more extensive full-application frameworks provide their best value – they provide superclasses for many different uses, from data access to work flow to messaging. This is in contrast to APIs, whose services are usually accessed by calling methods of other objects, and not so much by subclassing.

In the development phase it is still important to avoid building in reusability too early – the first priority must be the application specification. Refinement and generalization for reuse can be deferred until the next phase.

8.8.3 Evolution and Reuse

Once the basic development of the application is completed, the overall life of the project begins. Refinement and extension to existing applications are often more cost effective than new development, and applications built with frameworks provide significant advantages in this phase.

If much of the application is developed as subclasses and refinements of generic services, further refinements are simplified, because the base service is already designed for use in many different situations, not just the specific needs of the initial specification.

Refactoring to enhance reusability is another pattern often used at this stage. Objects, components, and services are consolidated and generalized. Built-in functionality and hard-wired logic are parameterized and made configurable, allowing reuse. That such generalization is deferred until this stage should not be considered a defect – it is normal and desirable for generalization to wait until basic functionality is well established.

8.9 Designing with Frameworks

The process of design is aided by the use of the design patterns inherent in your chosen framework. These design patterns may not be formally stated, but they are present nonetheless.

The design patterns help you decompose the specification of your project into the services, components, and objects that are required to build the application.

In the case studies discussed in the Appendix, you will see how a simple application requirement is decomposed using several popular frameworks. When reading the examples, it is not so much the differences between the frameworks that become clear as the similarities in their design process. Every framework's design process begins with the determination of the services required by the application. These services are then matched to the services provided by the framework.

Some of the most flexible frameworks available use a design pattern known as the "delegate" pattern to provide "pluggable" implementations of some services.

As an example of this pattern, consider the authorization component of a typical framework. The component is used for authorization throughout the framework, and must be flexible when deployed in different environments. In some cases, it reads its user and group information from an LDAP server, such as OpenLDAP. In other deployments, the component reads its information from tables in a relational database.

In the example in section 8.7.3, you can see the general structure of delegation: the authorization component presents a common API to all requests. It then refers or "delegates" these requests to the appropriate deployment-specific implementation, deciding on the correct version often by means of configuration settings. The different implementations usually implement a specific interface, mapping the generalized methods of the interface to the specific calls needed by the custom implementation. However, delegation can be applied in a situation where the underlying implementation does not implement a compatible interface. In this situation, the delegator (the authorization component) might have to do a bit more work to "map" the functionality required to the implementation provided. In both cases, the result is to "hide" the details of the implementation behind the delegator.

8.10 SUMMARY

In this chapter, we have explored some of the more common design patterns that are seen in frameworks. The design patterns used in a framework often provide one of the more powerful features in your development process, and are often one of the least understood. Take time to explore the framework's design, and understand its structure – it will pay off rapidly in the use of the framework, even though it may take some effort up front.

We have also seen how various design methodologies fit with framework and component-based development, and explored how frameworks benefit each methodology. Component-based development is a central aspect of using frameworks for your Web application, and any methodology you use must allow this technique to be a good fit.

CHAPTER 9

Integrated Development Environments

9.1 GENERAL PRINCIPLES OF IDEs IN FRAMEWORK/COMPONENT DEVELOPMENT

Integrated Development Environments (IDEs) are often a software developer's most intensively used tool, and this is often true of Web-application development. Until recently, IDEs had few special features for Web-application development, but this has changed. IDEs have become more flexible and easily configured, and their increased capabilities make them a better fit with frameworks. In this chapter we examine IDEs and how they relate to frameworks, with a few specific examples as well as some general observations and best practices.

IDEs and frameworks actually have much in common. They are tools that allow you to build your applications. The difference is that whereas an IDE provides tools for manipulating code, editing, searching, compiling, and so forth, a framework also provides services to be used by your code. A framework does not generally help you manipulate code (although some do generate code), it instead provides you with structure and services to build your application faster and easier.

Sometimes the line blurs a little between a framework and an IDE. Some IDEs provide libraries or APIs that are intended to be used in combination with your finished application at run time – this means they have at least some of the elements of a framework. Some frameworks provide graphical or command-line frontends to help you generate code, where the generated code is commonly a subclass of one of the abstract classes provided by the framework – in this sense, the framework provides some of the capabilities of an IDE.

Particularly in the area of UIs, we are seeing more and more overlap of frameworks and IDEs. The HyperQbs presentation framework, for example, can be used in conjunction with the Dragon visual assembly tool to create sophisticated user interfaces. HyperQbs itself is a framework, whereas Dragon has some of the attributes of an IDE. It is not a completely integrated development environment, it concentrates entirely on the building of UIs, but Dragon itself is not linked with your code at run time, whereas HyperQbs is linked.

9.1.1 Included Tools

So what does an IDE integrate? What tools does it provide to the development process? Let us look at what we are likely to find in a typical IDE:

- **Project Manager:** Most IDEs work with the concept of a "project," where a project consists of a particular set of files related to a single application. Many of the files are Java source code, but there may be a number of other files associated with the project as well, such as HTML, JSP, XML configurations, even text files, and documentation. Ideally, your IDE allows you to associate any arbitrary file type with the project, making it easier to organize the work. Some frameworks use specific template files; for example, the Velocity presentation framework uses Velocity Macro (.vm) files – an IDE should allow you to include such files in a project, and also allow at least a default text editor to manipulate them.

    The concept of a project relates to the idea of an "application" in most frameworks. Although a Web application is generally thought of as the contents of a Web application archive (WAR) file, with Java classes, configuration files, library jar files, and so forth, some frameworks have the notion of a "subapplication," or a separate unit of functionality within a single Web application. An IDE that works well with such a framework allows you to set the top-level directory of your "projects" at any level of the Web application, allowing separation of such "subapplications" and also allowing work to be broken down into more logical units.

The project manager in most IDEs allows the classpath to be customized, including .jar files that are outside the actual project being developed. This is where the access to framework services is normally made: a framework typically provides a number of jar files that define its classes and services that your application can access. These jars are then included in the IDEs classpath, so that your application refers to a class from the framework from which the compiler can resolve the reference. Normally these jar files are deployed with your finished application.

- **Editor:** Probably, the element of any IDE with which a developer spends the most time is the editor. Typically, IDEs feature a highly configurable editor that has features such as syntax highlighting, bookmarking, auto-completion, and other powerful facilities to let you move around your code quickly and easily.

  Normally, the regular Java editor provided with any IDE is quite adequate, although some developers have very strong affinities to specific editors, such as VI or Emacs – many IDEs address this issue through "emulations," where the keystrokes for Emacs, for example, are recognized by the IDE's own editor. The difficulty with frameworks sometimes lies in the file types used. Most frameworks have configuration files, which are often either property files or XML files – both of which are common formats with which most IDEs have no problems. More unusual file types, however, such as velocity macro files, template files, and other special configuration and option files are sometimes not as easy. In some cases the IDE might not recognize their file formats as part of the project. If they can be included in the project, the default editor might not be capable of opening them. Ideally, an IDE should have some kind of "fall back," where an unrecognized file format can be opened and edited as a text file, with no special editor features. Framework files seldom need anything more, but if it is possible to customize the editor to recognize special syntax (such as template tags), then the integration of the framework and the IDE is all the smoother.

- **Class Browser:** Class browsing is a powerful capability that allows quick and easy access to large hierarchies of classes. Often a class browser is modeled around the class browsers found in SmallTalk systems: a hierarchy of packages are shown, allowing you to choose a package. Once a package is selected, the "member" classes of that package are displayed, possibly with a description or other statistics. Selecting a particular class then displays the variables (attributes) and methods of that class, often using various icons to indicate private and public attributes and methods. Selecting a method often brings up the code for that method. This allows a very focused development, where individual files are less important than the actual structure of the class hierarchy of the application.

General Principles of IDEs in Framework/Component Development   337

Class browsing, as mentioned previously, is an ideal way to explore the structure of the classes in a framework, and can often be easier than browsing source files directly. It is important, however, to understand the difference between the class hierarchy of a framework and that of your own application. Often, using a framework involves subclassing abstract classes that are provided by the framework, or implementing certain interfaces. A class browser that shows the associated hierarchies might not make a clear-enough division between your own code and the framework's code; one way to avoid this is to use separate packages – always a good practice in any case. Take care not to browse "up" and unintentionally edit methods in the framework itself – you stand the risk of creating your own "custom" version unintentionally, and making it difficult to upgrade in the future.

- **Project Browser:** We have already discussed how an IDE usually provides some kind of project management. Typically, when a particular project is selected, a project browser or file browser is used to navigate within the application. This is distinct from the class browser, in that it is structured on the basis of the file and directory structure of the project, and not the Java class hierarchy. This means it can access files other than the Java classes, such as templates, macro files, scripting, and configuration files that might be part of your application. Often a framework uses such files, particularly templating presentation frameworks, and this is how you usually access them from within your IDE.

  A technique that is helpful in some IDEs is to configure the framework itself (including source code, if available) as one project, and then your own application as a separate project. You then include the .jar files of the framework in your own application's project (with no source). This allows you to keep the isolation complete between the two, and still have the convenience of going to the project containing the framework when browsing and looking up for things in the framework's source code.

- **Compiler:** IDEs always provide some access to a compiler. Typically, this is a connection to the usual external "javac" tool provided with your JDK, but some IDEs offer "internal" compilation (such as IBM's VisualAge). This can present an issue to the use of frameworks for a couple of reasons: sometimes these internal compilers have problems with external jar files. The jar must be loaded "into" the IDE before it can be accessed, and the large structures of some frameworks exceed the reasonable size of a class structure that can be handled by the IDE, making all other operations very slow. Sometimes the internal compiler includes specific versions of the JDK, for example, JDK 1.2.2. This makes using this IDE with a framework that requires JDK 1.3 a problem. The same is true of referenced libraries – if the internal compilation uses a particular version of the Servlet API, for instance, the version required by your framework must match.

All of these potential problem areas have resulted in most IDEs providing the ability to use an external compiler, at least as an option. Although external compilation might be slower, it is almost always the safest bet in terms of compatibility.

- **Build Manager**: The process of compiling all of the files that are required to create a finished application involves the use of a build manager. Rather than compiling all files, build managers figure out for you those files that require compilation, and do no more work than is necessary. Often they are also involved in creating jar archives, generating documentation, and other functions necessary for the preparation of a releasable package.

   IDEs sometimes include a build manager within their features, although they may allow the integration with an external stand-alone build manager, such as the Apache Ant tool. It is essential that whatever build system is available be compatible with the recommended method of deploying applications for your chosen framework. Most IDEs that support Web applications can generate either jar files or possibly the entire "war" (Web application archive) or "ear" (enterprise application archive) files – but they may not generate them in the exact structure that your framework works with best. For example, a server-side application created for use with the Apache Avalon framework (or, more specifically, the Phoenix server) must be generated in a "sar" archive (a .jar archive with a different name, containing the files necessary for a single service). Ant can easily be configured to handle this, but some internal build systems in IDEs cannot.

- **Version Control**: Almost all IDEs provide some means of access to external version control systems. Versioning is an essential part of the management of your own application development, and for open-source projects this almost always means use of the CVS version control system. Although many IDEs provide access to CVS, not all of them allow CVS to be easily accessed from behind a firewall, which is often required in corporate development projects.

   It is also important, when working with frameworks, that your IDE allows more than one CVS repository to be used – one for the framework itself, probably read-only, and one for your application. Often, however, an external CVS application can be used to access the framework, because you probably would not want to upgrade the version of the framework you are using during the actual development of your application.

- **GUI Builder**: Many IDEs contain special features for creating the user interface of your application. Some allow the UI to be "painted" using a graphical

General Principles of IDEs in Framework/Component Development   339

tool – often these tools are specific to the Swing UI library, and are not particularly useful for Web applications that intend to use Servlets or JSPs as their frontend. More Web-oriented IDEs allow you to create and edit JSP pages or other template pages, however. If the generated template code is compatible with your framework, then this can be a valuable facility. This is one reason for the popularity of JSP – because it is a well-established standard, a number of visual tools exist for creating them, including tools integrated with popular IDEs.

Often, however, the GUI-building capabilities of an IDE rely on a specific library – either Swing or a custom graphics library included with the IDE – which are either not used at all, or are not applicable to Web-application development. As templating standards become better established, this is likely to change, but at the moment most UI creations for Web applications still happen within a regular text editor, whether an IDE is used or not.

Of particular interest here is an emerging standard related to UI development: XSL. Extensible style sheets are gaining wider acceptance as a means of separating presentation from logic, and also a means of layering even the presentation so that the look and feel of a site can be changed with a simple alteration to a style sheet. IDEs that support the creation of XSL in visual UI builders are particularly useful for creating this kind of flexible UI. Very few exist so far, but this is changing as well.

- **Debugger**: Many IDEs also contain a debugging capability – again, sometimes linked to an external debugger application. It can be particularly difficult to configure these debugging capabilities with a framework, but once properly configured they can be very valuable tools. It is important to understand when debugging and tracing runs display the code belonging to the framework, and when they display code that is in your application – usually the package name is shown, and this is a good differentiator.
- **Internationalization**: Facilities that make it easier to internationalize your application often include a utility to locate and "extract" text strings from your application, replacing them, instead, with a reference to a key that refers to an external text file. Java provides some built-in capabilities for managing such external message bundle files, and most IDEs build on these capabilities.
- **Code Generation**: Code generation in an IDE is often tied to the user interface tools that are provided: once a given UI layout is "painted" using the tool, the code required to build this layout can be generated. Modern IDEs, however, take a more configurable approach, and code generation in these more recent tools is handled by plug-ins or optional modules, which allow code

to be generated for a number of different purposes – JavaBean accessors and database access code are two common examples. If this facility is sufficiently flexible, code can be generated from your IDE that extends the appropriate framework superclass.

When using frameworks within an IDE, there are some specific techniques that are helpful:

- **Do not get tangled:** It is a good idea to become familiar with the IDE and the framework separately before combining them. It is all too easy otherwise to get the facilities of one confused with the other. Know what your IDE and framework do. Keep in mind that most frameworks are portable between IDEs, whereas IDEs may have specific features that are usually only used in that environment.

  As an example, IBM's VisualAge has an advanced form designer for Swing-based GUIs. Sun's Forte has an entirely different facility, and screens created with one cannot be easily manipulated in the other. Both IDEs can be used in conjunction with, say, the Struts framework without any conflict, however, and applications created with one can easily be manipulated in the other.
- **Explore the framework:** Most IDEs have excellent facilities for browsing and navigating code – particularly large bodies of code. This makes an ideal way to learn the structure and features of a framework, because many frameworks consist of a large number of classes.

9.2 Examples of IDEs and Their Use with Frameworks

Let us look at a couple of popular IDEs and how they are used in conjunction with frameworks.

9.2.1 Eclipse

www.eclipse.org

The Eclipse project is a collaborative effort, led by companies such as Borland, IBM, Merant, QNX Software Systems, Rational Software, RedHat, SuSE, TogetherSoft, and WebGain, to create an interoperable platform for development tools.

The Eclipse project is separated into the Eclipse project itself, which aims to provide a platform for integrated tool development, and the Eclipse Tools project, intended to be a development center for tools meant to work with and on the Eclipse platform. The main Eclipse project is further subdivided into several portions:

- *Platform*, which provides a framework and set of common services to serve as the backbone for tool integration, including the user interface and project management capabilities, and version control.
- *The JDT*, or Java Development Tools, which provides the connection for plug-ins to be integrated into the platform, and a number of code-handling and creation tools.
- *The PDE*, or plug-in development subproject, which provides tools and editors facilitating development of plug-ins for Eclipse, much the same way that the Forte tool (or Netbeans) is designed to be extended via plug-ins.

Eclipse is seen by some as IBM's answer (among other companies) to the Sun Forte IDE, which is based on the open-source Netbeans project. Certainly, the design goals are similar, and notably absent among the tool vendors committing to the eclipse standard is Sun Microsystems themselves. However, competition in this area has resulted in many highly valuable new features being created for both IDEs, so a little competition is, as is often the case, a good thing.

Eclipse is actually, in and of itself, an application-specific framework: it is designed for the creation and integration of IDEs and their related tools. The Eclipse IDE, technically, is just one of the number of possible projects that can be created with this framework.

Beyond this, its extensible plug-in-oriented nature is ideally suited for use with Web-application-building frameworks. It allows the IDE to be customized and connected to the capabilities of a framework – for example, it is possible to create a template-editing plug-in to allow Velocity templates to be easily generated and edited, making it easier to take advantage of frameworks that use Velocity as one of the choices for building the UI.

As in the case of Netbeans, the extensible nature of the platform can also be used to create custom-code-generating plug-ins that create appropriate code using the capabilities of an underlying framework, but allow you to work within the tightly integrated UI of the Eclipse-based IDE, rather than at the command line, which so many frameworks now require you to do.

Eclipse also incorporates an integration with the Apache Ant toolkit (as a provided plug-in), allowing Ant's powerful build and dependency management features to be used directly in your Eclipse projects.

A powerful debugger that is included rounds out the Eclipse IDE. Source files can be "attached" to bytecode-only jar files to allow the debugger to track the source for even dependent libraries, a very valuable addition particularly for open-source projects, where the source is likely to be available.

9.2.2 NetBeans

www.netbeans.org

Netbeans is another example of an IDE that is also a framework – actually, two frameworks. The first is the Netbeans *platform*, which provides a backbone for desktop applications, including UI management, storage and configuration management, and editing. The second is the *IDE*, which provides the version control integration, syntax highlighting, pluggable compiler supports, and much more. The separation promotes better reusability of the underlying components.

Sun Microsystem's Forte product line is based on NetBeans. It offers enhanced and commercially supported products that include extra plug-ins and J2EE support.

Netbeans, like Eclipse, supports a powerful API for integration of pluggable modules. This includes a very useful "AutoUpdate" module, which can query an update server to locate new versions of modules and the platform itself, and then offers to assist the user in downloading and installing them, helping users to keep themselves updated with the latest Netbeans version.

Pluggable modules provide an ideal way to integrate with features of many frameworks. For example, the Torque database and code-generating facility from Turbine could be added as a module, making it easily accessible from the regular Netbeans menus and user interface.

In addition, Netbeans supports templates for creating new classes. This makes it easy to create templates that create classes for use in your particular framework: a good example would be a template for creating new Struts Action classes. This simplifies the code-creation process and makes it more straightforward to access the features of your chosen framework. A number of projects are underway to provide such integration features for a number of more popular frameworks.

9.2.3 JDEE

jdee.sunsite.dk

Another interesting option as an IDE is the Java Development Environment (JDEE for Emacs). It takes the approach of building the IDE effectively into the editor – the editor in this case is the powerful and venerable Emacs tool, a classic that, for many developers, needs no introduction.

Emacs is more than just an editor – it is a toolset designed specifically to be extensible, and a great many "modes" or plug-ins are available to customize its behavior. JDEE is one such "mode," and brings many Java-development-specific features to Emacs, including commands to compile, run, debug, build, browse, and manage projects.

It provides syntax coloring for Java programs, auto-indentation for code formatting, and linking between compile-time errors and the original source code, making it quick and easy to find errors.

One reason we highlight this particular IDE, from amongst all of the excellent choices available, is because of its incredible configurability. Even more than many IDEs, JDEE can be extended and customized to be a perfect fit with your choice of application framework. Largely because of the power of the underlying Emacs platform and editor, it is possible to use JDEE with other modes that provide specific features for use with frameworks, such as the vtl-mode for syntax-highlighting Velocity templates, and JSP modes for frameworks such as Struts. Emacs also has capable plug-ins for editing XML, which is heavily used by a number of frameworks.

The ability to tailor the environment to work with your precise choice of framework is a powerful benefit for this particular IDE – although many other IDEs are indeed heading in this direction, becoming more configurable and customizable.

9.2.4 No IDE at All: One Option

Even with so many powerful IDE choices available in the development market today, some developers do not use any IDE at all. They, instead, use a number of tools in combination that produce what we might call a "nonintegrated" development environment. Why would someone make this choice? What could the advantages possibly be?

One factor that might cause a developer to consider this choice is the features he wants to use: if the particular development tools a developer uses are not supported in combination by any one IDE, it may be easier and faster to simply use these tools independently. For example, the Ant build-management product, an open-source Apache offering, was not supported until recently by any IDE explicitly. If you wanted to use Ant in your project, you either jumped outside your development environment, or did not use one at all. Even if a particular tool is supported, its support may not be configurable in the way a particular developer wants it to be. For example, say certain features of the CVS version control system are available from Netbeans. It calls CVS from a graphical menu within the IDE, and is very convenient. If, however, you need to prefix your access to CVS with another command – say, for example, to route the CVS commands via a firewall – you may need options that are not supported by the IDE, even though they are supported by CVS itself. The lack of ability to configure CVS the way developers want leads some developers to simply use CVS from the command line, instead of the graphical menu. Once you do this, it is a small step to do all of your development from the command line, and the IDE is abandoned.

The reasons we have given above for choosing not to use an IDE, however, are being addressed as better and more flexible IDEs become available. Netbeans, for example, has added considerably to the number of configuration options you can use with its CVS access. Eclipse, Netbeans, Elixir, and other IDEs now support "plug-in" modules to add custom capabilities. Most modern IDEs let you configure menus, change options, and adjust their behavior significantly, overcoming most of the objections that developers might have based on a lack of flexibility.

Apart from lack of some specialized features that some developers cite as the reason for choosing to avoid IDEs, some developers simply regard the so-called command-line development as more efficient. Ideally, both your development environment and your framework should give you the choice of both graphical and command-line user interfaces to all of their tools and services. In reality, this is seldom the case: tools tend to present one or the other option, not both.

The perception of greater flexibility in command-line development is sometimes driven by the features of the underlying platform. Unix, for example, was created to support development with a huge array of command-line utilities, and having access to these is often very valuable to the experienced developer. Often the native tools of the operating system are combined with one or more higher level tools, such as Apache's Ant.

Although a few years ago this was perhaps a more valid choice, given the low quality of many IDEs, their slow performance, and their high-priced commercial alternatives, this argument is less valid today. With the advent of several top-notch, reliable, and even open-source IDEs, the advantages in productivity gained by their use is more difficult to argue with than it was once.

9.3 Selecting Tools and IDEs

It is important to understand the relationship between your IDE and your chosen framework, and if you have an opportunity to select an IDE, there are some factors that must be taken into consideration. Not every developer has this opportunity, but with more IDEs becoming available at either low cost or no cost at all, changing to another IDE is no longer the multi-thousand-dollar stumbling block it was at one time.

IDEs are becoming more modular and configurable, and this sometimes leads to a situation where it is difficult to say where the IDE ends and the framework begins. Keeping a clear distinction in mind allows you to take your pick of tools, and to move up when something better comes along, as well as makes it easy to continue to use non-IDE tools, many of which have such a valuable place in application development with frameworks.

CHAPTER 10

Strategies for Using Frameworks: Best Practices

Over a number of years of working with frameworks, and being involved in their development and use, I have found that a few recurrent themes have come up. A number of issues arise again and again, and various solutions are tried. Sometimes the solutions work out, and apply to the same kind of problem when it comes up again in the future. Just like the design patterns and structure that evolve in a framework, these kinds of "best practices" that have evolved over time can save you considerable effort when applying frameworks to your own development projects.

In this chapter, we explore some of these practices and discuss how they came about, and how they can be applied to your own situation.

10.1 INITIAL ADOPTION

The first group of best practices that we discuss relates to the initial adoption stage of the use of frameworks: when you are just getting started there are some points to consider. This is the stage where a good number of mistakes are made, sometimes resulting in an otherwise promising framework being abandoned.

10.1.1 Take the Plunge

The first most important strategy for using frameworks and components in your development process is to make the decision to do so in the first place. We have explained in great detail, in the preceding chapters, how frameworks bring benefits to the development process, discussed what these benefits are, and examined concrete examples of frameworks. We have even discussed how to make your choice of framework from among the many possibilities. None of these help, however, if you do not actually take the plunge. The days of writing applications on top of nothing but the operating system are long gone, and applications are getting too complex to be created entirely from scratch anymore. So, the first step is to pick a framework, go through the learning curve, and get started.

Although getting started might sound like a strange item to include in best practices, it is perhaps the one that most developers have the biggest problem with. They might evaluate frameworks, might even do a sample project with one, but many factors conspire to convince them not to adopt the framework, at least not right away.

10.1.2 Frameworks: Not Just for Breakfast Any More

It is important to consider a framework as a tool for your entire project development, not just something to jump-start it. Earlier, when Java Web-application frameworks were in their infancy, some frameworks were fine for getting started, but they ran out of steam when it came to the "hard" parts of application development. Some, for example, provided good functionality in the area of creating the user interface, but the application logic, configuration, database access, and so forth were still very much a do-it-yourself proposition. This has led some developers to consider frameworks well and good for beginners, but something that a professional developer should avoid.

Although there may have been some truth to this at one time, it is certainly not true anymore. Frameworks today provide a rich set of services to all areas of the application. Those frameworks that focus on one area, such as presentation or database, do so intentionally, and it is straightforward to use such frameworks in combination with other frameworks that provide what they do not. Frameworks today are very much not just for beginners – in fact, almost the opposite is true. The more sophisticated and complex your application development project is, the more you need to take a component and framework-based approach, to deal with that complexity.

Do not underestimate what frameworks today are capable of. Particularly, given the open source availability of many of the most powerful frameworks, it simply does not make business sense to reinvent the wheel.

10.1.3 Patterns, Patterns, Patterns

After getting started, without underestimating your framework, probably the most important practice that has emerged over years of using frameworks has been the habit of working from patterns. The first step in this is to understand the patterns used in your framework, both the low-level design patterns such as proxies, delegators, factories, and so forth, and the high-level structures. Understand how your framework of choice is *meant* to be used, and what kind of structure best fits the way it provides services. We discuss this in more detail below.

As explained in Chapter 1, a framework is not merely code – it is structure *and* code. In fact, the structure is the more important of the two, and understanding and following the high-level design patterns of a framework are essential to get the most out of your tool.

10.2 THE FIRST PROJECT

Let us assume now that you are really going to undertake a project using a framework, and that you have made your choice with regard to which framework to use. We can now discuss strategies and practices applicable to the first few projects created with the framework.

10.2.1 Development Process

When you start using a framework to develop your application, a few general techniques apply. You should spend much of your development time on creating new subclasses of existing framework classes, configuring objects together, and modifying existing examples to work for your particular application, for example. If you find you have written much of your code from scratch, something is wrong: you have likely not taken advantage of the framework properly. Keep in mind that the time spent getting to know the framework – even if it involves creating a few simple "throwaway" projects – is not wasted, it is time spent well that is more than repaid later. This is where the quality of the documentation for your chosen framework makes a significant difference. It is not possible to overemphasize the old adage "seek first to understand...."

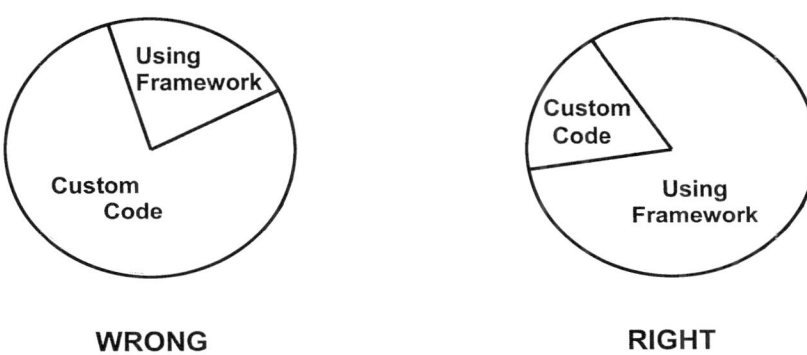

You will see some of the general techniques of framework development applied in our case studies in the Appendix.

Development of an application with a framework generally involves the following sequence:

- **Design – problem decomposition**: We have discussed previously how the requirement of sequence of decomposing an individual application into the appropriate components and services is somewhat specific to a given framework. In general, however, an application requirement is "mapped" to the services available in your framework. The more experienced you are with the framework, the more you find that the requirements can be mapped to things that already exist in the framework, and the less you find yourself saying "that needs custom code." We discussed the stages of component-based development Chapter 1 -- these apply here and throughout the development process.
- **Create an empty application**: Most Web-application frameworks provide a means to create an "empty" application – that is, to generate all of the required objects for an application with no logic and no customizations. Into this shell, we add our own specific logic and presentation design to create the finished application. Some frameworks, such as Turbine, include a mechanism to generate a bit more than an empty shell: they allow you to specify your required database schema, and create some classes via code generation

automatically. Other frameworks have a separate tool to do this, such as WebAppWriter for the Expresso framework, and allow much of the logic of the application to be created, at least the outline, as well as database access.
- **Build components/services**: The next step is where the rubber really meets the road: creating the actual components and services for your application. This is where you first concentrate on assembly: using existing components and services to, as far as possible, create the application by putting these components together and configuring them correctly. Once this is done, you are left with the custom work – specific services or components that must be created, or, preferably, made as extensions and subclasses to existing templates or abstract classes. Often this takes place in parallel with the next stage: creating the presentation layer.
- **Create presentation**: Most frameworks allow the presentation portion, or the user interface, of your new application to be built in parallel with the components and services. The UI can often be created by a nonprogrammer, or preferably by someone with the specialized skill set of a Web designer. If possible, "designer" tools are used at this stage, and the user interface is mostly "painted," and then wired up to the application logic created in the previous step.
- **Testing**: Proponents of Extreme Programming say that this is an ongoing process, in fact, a process that begins before the first line of code is written. Wherever it happens, testing and verification are an essential part of the development process, and most frameworks provide you with a layer and mechanism to build in tests early in the game.
- **Packaging and deployment**: Some frameworks provide additional tools or scripts to assist with the process of taking your development copy and preparing it for a production environment. Others simply assume you create a Web application archive (war) file. Often, the creation of the first war file is only the first iteration – the application can then be tested in a testing environment or an application server, an essential step for verifying the integrity of the build process, and development then continues on the development server.

These steps may, of course, vary depending on your particular development methodology, and the particular structure of your framework.

10.2.2 Do Not Fight the Framework

Whenever I begin working with a new framework, it seems strange and unusual compared to the last framework I was using. Every framework takes a different approach, has different strengths, and probably takes a different view of problem solving than the development you were doing previously. When I first work with a new framework, issues that I think should be simple seem difficult – then I start to understand the viewpoint of the new framework, and start to work with it instead of working against it, and things become easier. For a while, it still seems almost like it requires more effort to use the framework than to simply code directly, but a bit of persistence shows this is seldom the case.

It is important to understand the general high-level design and structure of an application framework, so that structure can be taken advantage of. Even more important is to avoid "fighting the framework," that is, using the facilities of the framework in a way they were not intended and designed. Just like using a screwdriver to hammer in a nail, it can be done, but not very well and not very effectively. However, if all you know is hammers, everything starts to look very much like a nail.

It is essential to understand the *assumptions* that developers of a framework have made – for example, many Web-application development frameworks assume a specific kind of UI, whether it is JSP, straight HTML, a templating language, or Applets. Although it may not be obvious when reading about the framework itself, this can often be discovered by examining the kinds of applications that are built with the framework – are they all Applet based? Do they all rely on a relational database? Do they use XSL style sheets to define their user interface? Understanding these assumptions tells you a lot about the kinds of applications that the framework is best suited toward and about the kinds of applications it is not suited for.

The assumptions of the developers of a framework might also include expectations of the deployment environment: clearly a framework that depends on EJBs, for example, assumes that the deployment environment is capable of supporting them. These are the kinds of system requirements that should be stated fairly clearly in the framework's documentation – but sometimes are not.

A framework is, in part, a description of how to decompose an application design, and how to apply specific solutions to each part of the application. If you understand how a particular framework does its particular decomposition, it becomes much easier to apply it correctly.

A good indicator of whether you are struggling with the framework is when you are creating a large amount of custom code to solve part of a problem. Perhaps the framework does not have a service that addresses what you are trying to do – but often it does, and you simply do not see it yet. Or you believe you see it, but you are using the hammer to drive in a screw. This can be very subtle, and the documentation of the framework is not the only guide to use to avoid it. You must examine examples of applications built using the framework and not just any applications: these should be applications that are considered to be proper examples of how to *best* apply the services that the framework provides. There is nothing more frustrating than following an example, only to discover the example was poorly constructed in the first place, and you have just spent a lot of time learning bad habits.

10.2.3 Use the Web

For today's Web-application developer, this advice may sound redundant, but it is very relevant. Use the Web – not just to obtain and research the framework you work with, but to see examples of the kinds of applications built with frameworks, and to interact with the developer community.

The resources available to you start with the website of the framework. Frequently, this site provides you with one or more mailing list addresses. These mailing lists often form the backbone of the community support for the product, and must be used like the valuable resources that they are. Be sure to find out what the proper etiquette is for each of the supplied lists – otherwise your questions may remain unanswered.

Some of the key resources for researching frameworks on the Web are as follows:

- **The Apache Software Foundation**
  www.apache.org

    A key resource for many different open-source projects, including several of the frameworks we review, the Apache Foundation is an essential place to research some of the most active and useful framework projects. In addition, the many other key open-source projects that are hosted here are essential to many frameworks. These include the XML parser Xerces, the XSL transform tool Xalan, the Jakarta Commons project, with its many tools and utilities, and of course, the frameworks Turbine, Avalon, Cocoon, Slide, and Jetspeed. New projects are always starting and the news is frequently updated and current.

- **The open-source development network**
  www.osdn.com
  www.sourceforge.net
  www.slashdot.org
  www.freshmeat.net

    The open-source development network (OSDN) group of sites also provides essential resources for framework research and selection. The Source

Forge project acts as a repository and home to literally thousands of open-source projects, many of which are either frameworks or framework-related components or tools. Slashdot, of course, needs no introduction as a source of timely, relevant, and often irreverent news and discussion on all developments that are software related – with a particular emphasis on open source. The freshmeat.net site lists and provides a point of announcement for hundreds of new software releases each month, including many frameworks and framework tools, and is an excellent place to begin a search for a framework for a specific project, and to research its release history.

- **The Java page of the Free Software Foundation**
  www.fsf.org/software/java/java-software.html

  Although not rich in full frameworks, the list of Java software maintained by the Free Software Foundation is a valuable resource, and often provides tools and utilities that can be used in conjunction with frameworks, or as Servlet containers (such as the GNU/Paperclips project).

- **The Giant Java Tree**
  www.gjt.org

  The Giant Java Tree is a project consisting of a large "tree" of free Java software, licensed under the General Public License. It provides another valuable resource for components and extensions to frameworks, and serves as an experiment in distributed software development for large projects.

There are many others; these are just a few to get you started. Sun Microsystems' site is also an excellent place to find links to resources. News sites and industry magazine sites are also excellent sources of information.

Also, it is important not to assume that the project's "official" page is the only source of information about it. Often there are a number of related sites, and the general newsgroups (nntp groups) are often good sources of information above and beyond the original site of the framework. Get out your favorite search engine and start digging!

Another valuable Web resource is the online FAQ for the product, particularly if it is a FAQ that allows new questions to be dynamically added. This can be the most valuable place for a beginner to start. It is always appropriate to check the FAQ and the mailing list archives before asking questions of the listserv community.

Be sure to put your favorite search engine to use – the Web changes on a daily basis, and just because a site is not well known (yet) does not mean that it might not have valuable information for your project.

10.3 PROBLEMS AND PITFALLS

Once you have gotten over the trials of the initial adoption of a framework and component model, you have done your first project, and as you start other projects, certain issues start to arise. In this section, we examine some of these issues and point out ways to avoid or minimize them.

10.3.1 What *Not* to Do

Some of the lessons gleaned from experience with frameworks are better expressed as things *not* to do – kinds of practical antipatterns for using frameworks. We discuss some of the things to avoid here.

10.3.1.1 Orphans

On my island home at Grand Bahama, almost all of the houses are built out of concrete block. There are a number of reasons for this, not the least of which is the hurricane-prone climate. Some of the other reasons, though, teach us something about another kind of construction: there is a concrete-block production facility, and local construction companies are familiar with the method of block construction. In software development, this is like having a certain development environment available, and being familiar with a specific method. Introducing a new framework to many companies is like introducing poured-concrete construction. The people engaged in the constructions know the materials in general, but they are used in a different way. The results may be faster, may be more efficient, may even produce better results – but there is still some resistance to new ways. Sometimes this resistance is founded on good reasons, but it is always worthwhile finding out.

Although there is nothing to stop you "branching out" from what a framework offers with your own custom tools and extensions, it is important to be aware of the potential pitfalls when deciding to do this, however, and how to avoid these pitfalls by extending the framework in a future-compatible manner.

If you go about your customizations the wrong way, you can end up with an "orphan" version of the framework – one that differs sufficiently from the "standard" version that you can no longer easily take advantage of new releases of the framework. When working on applications, because the bulk of the time is spent on *maintenance*, not initial development, it does not often make sense to sacrifice compatibility for short-term advantage.

So what can you do if the framework does not offer a service that you need for your application? You do not want to create an orphan, and you are convinced that you are not overlooking a way to do what you want within the bounds of the framework. In such a situation, the choices sometimes depend on the licensing of the framework, the goals of the project, and the nature of the enhancement. If the new service is generic enough that you believe it could be reusable, and the framework is open source, you may want to consider contributing your enhancement to the framework. This is not as altruistic as it sounds – although it is true that others will benefit from your work, you also get a lot of feedback, testing, and probably debugging of your new service as part of the bargain. Your enhancement benefits by being kept up-to-date with future releases. You get many developers' opinions on your enhancement, and probably end up with a better enhancement than you otherwise would have had.

Sometimes this approach is not possible due to the politics of the project. Almost every framework has a mechanism for dealing with custom enhancements correctly. With Avalon, by way of example, you can create a custom implementation of any component, registering it with the same "role" as an existing component. It is then simply a matter of configuration to tell the application to use your custom enhancement instead of the "normal" service or component. This allows you to keep your work separate from the framework, and does not prevent you from upgrading to the latest version later. The only thing you must watch for is that if the API of the service you have extended is changed, you may need to update your customizations. In practice, this does not happen often enough to be a major maintenance burden, and is much better than the alternative of creating an "orphan" version.

10.3.1.2 Do not Open that Box

Two terms that are sometimes used in discussing components are "white box" and "black box." A "white box" framework allows you to "see inside" the services and component capabilities it provides. "White box" implies that it is easier or more efficient to use the service when you understand *how* it provides its results – in other words, when you can see the implementation details. This is not just the difference between open source and proprietary – being *able* to see the details is not the same as *needing* to see them. White box implies a blurring of the line between interface and implementation. One sign of a white-box-type approach is where the implementation is accessed directly – no intermediary interface is used to isolate the implementation from its API.

A much more modular approach is sometimes called "black box." Just as in engineering, a black box is understood entirely in terms of its inputs and outputs. You do not know, or need to know, *how* it does what it does, you simply need to know how to use it. A good indicator of a black-box approach is separation of interface and implementation (an important component design pattern). Some frameworks even package the interface for a service and its implementation in separate Java packages – this helps enforce the separation, and makes sure the box remains closed. As users of the black box, we need to understand *only* its interface – where to connect up the wires, so to speak, and we need not care about what goes on inside.

10.3.1.3 Do not Give up

In 1940, Sir Winston Churchill said, "We shall never surrender!" This must be your attitude when trying to master a development framework as well, though hopefully the battle is somewhat easier than Dunkirk. The learning curve for mastering a framework, particularly a powerful one, is steep – whereas this is a good thing in that you will do a lot of learning in a short period of time, it is also a bad thing for the same reason. Fortunately, most good programmers actually like learning, and the biggest challenge is getting them to allocate the amount of time required to do a proper job of it. Several times during the process you feel constrained by the new limitations the framework no doubt imposes on you – this is normal; work through it. There are reasons for the limitations, and you will soon see them. Do not let the "not invented here" syndrome, or lack of appropriate persistence, deprive you of a powerful ally in your application development process. Sir Winston also once said, "Never in the field of human conflict was so much owed by so many to so few." Hopefully, you will end up feeling this way about the designers of your framework of choice, once you are over the top of the learning curve!

You should allow longer than you might think for the learning process, and it is essential that it remains just that: a learning process. Although at a certain point you can tackle a prototype application, initial learning with a framework should be done on a "throwaway" example project, there is nothing you want to keep. Make sure your manager or supervisor has bought in to the time required – you cannot learn a framework "in between" things, at least not properly. Keep at it – there is light at the end of the tunnel, and the benefits are worth it.

10.3.2 Deployment Environments

Although the final deployment environment for an application might be a cluster of J2EE application servers, this is probably not the ideal environment in

Problems and Pitfalls 357

which to develop. Although realistic testing in the deployment environment is, of course, necessary at some point, it is usually better to start off with the simplest possible deployment environment. Frameworks are often complex beasts and taming one is best done in the cage of a single, straightforward server setup, and not out in the wilds of a full-blown app server cluster. A simple environment lets you deal with one issue at a time, and as your familiarity with the framework grows, you find that adding complexity to the deployment environment is less of a problem.

10.3.3 Team Development with Frameworks and Components

By providing a backbone for a development project and establishing development guidelines, a framework can actually assist in team development. If everyone uses the same framework, they can more easily read each other's code, and assembling sections written by different developers is much easier.

At the same time, coordination of a team development effort is no less important in a framework environment than in any other kind of development. Just because you use a framework does not mean that any less attention can be paid on coordination, it is just that that coordination should be a bit easier to accomplish.

Team development becomes easier when the team operates with a common set of design patterns, so the design patterns inherent in the structure of the chosen framework are again beneficial here.

I have been involved in both the development of frameworks themselves, and in the creation of applications using frameworks. Over time, a few repetitive themes have emerged, and I will attempt to share the results of producing the flat spot on my forehead with you and try to spare you having to pound your head on the same walls.

10.3.4 Start Small

Do not bite off more than you can chew at first.

Although it is very tempting to dive right into the project at hand, this is seldom the best approach. It is usually far better to tackle something small using the chosen framework – even if it is a prototype of the complete project, or an unrelated project. This gives you a chance to learn about the capabilities of a framework in actual use, rather than concentrating on the functionality of your own application. Just make sure that you consider these initial attempts as disposable.

Often, the framework has one or more example applications – dissecting them is an excellent way to begin.

Your greatest productivity boost with a framework is *after* you have climbed the learning curve – so it makes sense to spend time working on a minor project intended specifically as a learning experience. Then, when you start on your "real" project, you have a better chance of applying the framework correctly and getting the most out of it.

10.3.5 Read More Than You Write

Just as I said above, it is never wise to "fight the framework." The best way to avoid this is to read more code than you write, especially at first. In rich frameworks, many of the things you want to get done in your application already have a way of getting done by using the framework. It is important to know what is and what is not provided for, because nothing is more frustrating than spending time coding a piece of functionality only to find out that the framework provides it automatically, or with a single method call. This goes back to the discussion of the learning curve: it really is downhill on the other side. To paraphrase an old saying, "seek first to understand, then write your code."

A framework, by its nature, should impose a collaborative model on your development that you should adapt to. The type of model is an indicator of the "personality" of the framework. It shows how the framework tackles certain design problems. You must work with it, or writing your application with the framework is more difficult than not using it at all.

A framework's goals are to let you write more application with less code: if you find you are not building your application mostly from preexisting components, either you have chosen the wrong framework or you are not using it correctly. You should use a limited number of components repeatedly, thereby not having to reinvent any wheels.

10.3.6 Throw Some Code Away (Refactor)

Many developers, having built a piece of code that does the job, hold onto it like grim death. Even when their expanded knowledge of the framework makes

Problems and Pitfalls   359

it clear that they are doing a task the "hard way," they are loathe to go back and change existing code. Although I am definitely a proponent of the "ain't broke, don't fix it" school of thought myself, there are times when going back and changing existing code is still the right thing to do.

Here are some of the signs that indicate it is time to refactor when using a framework:

- **Having to adapt new code:** When you find yourself having to adapt new code to fit with the way you have done something in earlier code, it may be time to reexamine the older code. Either you are doing it wrong now, or (more likely) you did it wrong before, and having become more familiar with the framework, you have now started working with it more effectively. Never hesitate to go back and refactor – the instinct to leave code that is working alone is strong, but the grief when you eventually have to go back and work on that code makes it well worth fixing as soon as possible. Remember, the lifetime of a good application mostly depends on its maintenance, not its initial development, so that old code *will* come back to haunt you eventually.
- **New code is significantly shorter/easier:** You may not have any problems interfacing with older code, but still find that you are now doing the same kinds of tasks in a shorter and easier way. Again, you have probably learned the framework more thoroughly by now, and are simply using it more effectively. This is again the right time to go back and have a look at the older code you have written and see if it is time to up date. Books such as *Refactoring: Improving the Design of Existing Code* written by Martin Fowler, and its related website http://www.refactoring.com, deal in detail of how to make the decision about when refactoring is required.
- **Noncomponent code:** When you find that a fair amount of code has crept into your application that is *not* separated into components, it may be time to refactor. When you create new functionality, sometimes it is not clear as to how it should be packaged into components, but as the remainder of the application is fleshed out, it becomes more apparent. Never hesitate to go back and "clean up"– it pays dividends in future reuse and flexibility.

There are, of course, many other factors that indicate that it is time to consider refactoring in general, and these factors apply equally well to code written when using a framework as they do at any other time.

10.4 FUTURE-PROOFING

Once you have successfully adopted a framework, and are happily cranking out projects with it, avoiding the pitfalls along the way, there are still some points to consider. How do you ensure that you will continue to receive maximum benefit from your development tool over time? Here we discuss how to future-proof your use of components and frameworks by adopting practices that help protect your investment.

10.4.1 Learning Never Stops

As mentioned earlier, if all you know is hammers, everything looks like a nail. Once you know your framework of choice well – perhaps *very* well, it is important not to get stuck in a rut, and start thinking of everything in terms of that framework. When you work with, for example, the Struts framework, there is a specific method of decomposing an application that fits with that framework. You think of things in terms of separate views for presentation, and you consider application logic as it fits the "Action" object, which is the Struts way of performing such logic. That is great – for Struts. There is nothing wrong with this method of decomposing a problem and considering a solution, but it is not the only one. Keep an open mind to other techniques, and your own development benefits. You are also better prepared if you find that a new technique offers special advantages for a particular project, and better suited to take advantage of it.

When working with a particular framework, it is easy to lose sight of other developments and projects going on. Many frameworks are large beasts, after all, and just keeping up with their development can take up a great deal of time. It is worth browsing information about other frameworks from time to time, however. Sometimes you will come across a discussion on a mailing list for another framework that leaves you saying "wow, I'm glad I'm using my framework, not that one." At the same time, every now and then you come across a discussion that leaves you thinking "hmm, I wonder if I could apply that to my project." This can lead to a new way of thinking about your own application, even using your existing framework.

With the present trend in frameworks toward greater modularization and a more "plug-in"-based approach, it becomes easier to use more than one framework. It is possible to choose from the best parts of several frameworks and put them together, making it even more important to keep an open mind and keep updated with alternative approaches.

In Chapter 11, we will consider a new approach to frameworks that is specifically designed to allow quick and easy interoperability *between* frameworks, and to allow a developer to apply several different frameworks to a single project.

10.4.2 Community Directions, New Versions

Even though you have chosen one (or several) framework(s) to work with, the framework itself is usually a moving target. Open-source frameworks in particular tend to evolve and change fairly rapidly. As new facilities are created and bugs are found and fixed, you naturally want to upgrade to the latest and best version. If you have followed my advice about not creating an orphan, this is usually fairly straightforward. Any upgrade, particularly one to a framework, brings with it the risk of breaking something, however. It is usually wise to attempt the upgrade with a demo or prototype application, before diving in with your most important package. Of course, it goes without saying that proper version control and backups are an essential part of this process, as in any major upgrade. You must understand what has changed since the previous version, and what it does to your application. This is the key aspect of "backwards compatibility," and as frameworks evolve sometimes the development team makes the decision that backward compatibility is less important than new features. The best designs, however, allow both: they are structured so that new features can be used while at the same time supporting code created to work with older versions of the framework – this is, after all, one of the benefits of the component model.

As a framework evolves and grows over time, it is important to keep up with not only the changes that are being made, but also the expected future direction. Where is the framework going? How is it adapting to new technologies and new changes in industry requirements and standards. A good example is seen in EJB. When Enterprise JavaBeans and the J2EE platform were first introduced, many frameworks were already mature and in use. Most adapted to the new technology, allowing EJBs to coexist with the component model already in use by the framework. Some took longer to adapt than others, and some never did – choosing instead to support their own component model. Another example that is current to many frameworks is their direction for providing Web services. How is the framework going to deal with potential demand for its applications to be accessed as Web services? By following discussions in the framework's mailing list, and by keeping current on the road map and future plans, you can be prepared for future trends and how your chosen framework will adapt to them. This helps avoid a sudden discontinuity when you upgrade at some time in the future.

10.4.3 Reusability

If your framework begins with the right kind of component design, reusability of your components developed with that design is enabled, it is not guaranteed, just enabled. You have the *opportunity* to create a component or custom service that can be reused in your own (or other) future applications. It still takes careful design of the component or service to make the promise of reusability a reality. Sometimes time constraints move reusability concerns to the back burner – it is more important to get the component to work than to worry about its potential reuse. This is not necessarily a barrier to future reuse. Indeed, most reusable components start off being more fixed-purpose, then they are extended and generalized over time as they are used in different projects. A certain amount of thought toward reuse early on, however, can make this process much easier. Not only do components built with reuse in mind provide a ready toolbox for future development, they are also usually much easier to maintain. Think ahead – a bit of additional design work now can pay off handsomely later.

10.4.4 New Technology

The Web-application development world is often a place of rapid development of new technologies. Unlike previous application environments, the evolution of these new technologies is vastly accelerated in the Web, and often their adoption is likewise a rush to keep up. Wireless devices are a fine example of this: applications created for the desktop browser were not necessarily well suited to the wireless device. Frameworks, by their nature, should help with this issue. By application of configurable components at all levels, they help avoid lock-in to a specific technology or implementation. Again, the high-level component design is an essential part of future-proofing your applications.

It has been said that the more things change, the more they stay the same. There is some truth to this, as is seen in Web applications. The Web is indeed a new environment, and as more devices are connected to the Internet, the entire spectrum of applications that is possible expands. However, many constants remain. Data is still data. It must be stored, accessed, and presented. Users still expect certain levels of responsiveness, even as they demand more services from their Internet-enabled services. These common elements, if abstracted correctly, allow an application built using a framework to remain insulated from the low-level details of technology. Indeed, many Web applications provide capabilities to allow legacy applications, which were written years before the popularity of the Net exploded, to be "Web-enabled," as we have seen. No application lasts forever, but many have lasted decades beyond their original designers' wildest dreams. Maintaining the right level of isolation from the underlying services and technologies with your application can make it as "future-proof" as possible.

10.5 SUMMARY

We have seen, in this chapter, some of the practices and techniques that have proven useful over a number of years when using and working with frameworks. Applying these techniques can help ease your transition into using frameworks and components in your projects, and help you avoid some of the well-known potholes on the road.

You will no doubt find your own techniques to add to these techniques as your experience and the tools themselves continue to evolve.

CHAPTER 11

Conclusions: The Future of Frameworks and Components

In this chapter we summarize the discussions in the previous chapters to highlight the most significant points and discuss the future of frameworks and components. We look briefly at the trends that are leading the way to the future of application development, and how frameworks and components fit in.

11.1 Emerging Framework/Component Technologies

Frameworks are gradually expanding their reach into other areas of Web-application development. Combined with Java's advances with new and extended standard libraries, it means future Web applications will use some exciting new technologies.

The fastest growing segment of the Web-application community is the area of mobile and wireless application. Although some frameworks already focus on this market segment (Roaming Media Framework and Java Micro Framework), others also provide services to both desktop and mobile clients, such as Cocoon with its advanced WML support.

11.1.1 New Interface Paradigms and Frameworks

We have already discussed in previous chapters the importance of Web applications having highly flexible user interfaces. With the wealth of new devices being connected to the Internet today, your application will be called on to interact with everything from devices with effectively no visual interface at all (such as appliances, and even the fridge) to mobile devices with a functional but limited interface (such as Web-enabled televisions, cell phones, pagers, and other wireless clients), all the way to devices with extremely rich interface capabilities, such as full-blown desktop browsers with scripting support.

In addition to these kinds of interfaces, however, applications that run on the Internet will be called on to support even more varied styles of user interaction. Speech interfaces, for example, are becoming a popular way for companies to extend their Web applications and make them available via a telephone. Ideally, the same application logic and data available over the Web should be available through such an interface.

Some of what have been considered the more "exotic" user interface styles will be seen more frequent as Web applications become more substantial, and begin handling more of an organization's day-to-day business operations. The data repository collected by such applications will be a key resource for the financial management of the organization, and will need to be accessed in many different ways to support analysis. For example, it should be possible to extract sales data into popular spreadsheet formats – a simple interface that is already supported by many traditional applications. Data will also need to be accessible for multidimensional analysis, which may involve an external OLAP (online analytical processing) application. New standards now being finalized that provide for Java access to such multidimensional data sources will facilitate this type of access.

Often Web accessibility to a company's information and applications results in much wider use of these resources than was possible before. This in turn leads to very large datasets being created, as more and more detailed information is collected about a company's operation by its applications. These large datasets often contain more information than is obvious, and sometimes specialized tools such as intelligent data mining are used to extract this "hidden" data. The nature of the Web application itself then facilitates dissemination of this newly "discovered" information, which means that Web applications must be able to interact with such external tools in a "two-way" manner. They do not just spit out data, and let the external data mining or OLAP tool crunch it – the resulting analysis represents essential decision-support knowledge, and the

Web itself (where the raw data may have been gathered in the first place) is the ideal medium to publish it (always with due consideration to security).

Organizations that rely on the interactivity of the Internet are not satisfied with infrequent batch updates for analysis – they will be moving at Internet speed, and will require online near-real-time views of their information. Emerging standards in the area of virtual reality will likely be used to allow users to view collected data via a VRML (virtual reality modeling language) plug-in on their Web browsers, and Web applications must be ready for this kind of unorthodox interaction. Again, applications created for client-server, mini, and mainframe environments often provide the ability to access data in these ways – Web applications must do no less, and in fact, must provide even greater transparency, and at the same time deal with the complex security constraints inherent in the Web environment.

The component-based development encouraged by frameworks is an ideal environment to support these new interface paradigms. Web applications, because of the nature of the environment in which they operate, tend to be more interface independent. APIs such as JDBC provide a layer of independence from data sources, flexible UI layers provide independence from a particular markup, and frameworks such as Avalon even provide independence from actual implementation of services. This means that application logic remains available and usable even with these new interface requirements, and that the framework itself can be extended to provide these as options, future-proofing your applications nicely in the process.

11.1.2 Web Services

Web services have actually been around ever since the Internet first came into existence: but the "client," so far, has been people, and not programs! Regular HTML over HTTP is an example of a simple kind of Web service: you type a URL and get a page. Web services as a method for applications to interact with other applications, though, are a different story.

Web services have recently acquired a new definition in the Web-application scene, and this new combination of existing technologies has already had a large impact on many organizations' development plans.

Web services refer to a new way of "packaging" Web-application functionality. Web services are self-contained and self-describing applications that can be located and invoked via standard Web services and protocols. Frameworks are an important part of the development and an important reason behind the popularity of Web services, because they allow existing applications to quickly (in some cases, immediately) take advantage of this new technology.

There are a number of reasons why Web services have suddenly become an important buzzword in our industry, not the least of which is the amount of marketing effort put into it by various companies. It is not all hype, however; a number of key technologies that Web services depend on have achieved certain levels of standardization just when the need for interoperability is very large. Many applications are Web enabled, and more of a company's business transactions happen over the Web. This drives a need for applications to interoperate – to exchange more than just data. They need to be able to automatically invoke each other's functionality when appropriate, even when the interacting applications are on different servers and belong to different companies. Web services provide this capability in such a way that existing applications can participate without undergoing major renovations. This makes Web services a very interesting topic for companies investing in Web applications, and for the developers responsible for creating them.

Fundamentally, a Web service is a mechanism for accessing a software service via a standard protocol. Most often this protocol is HTTP but alternatives, such as SMTP, are quite possible.

Web services should not only be available via standard Web protocols such as HTTP or SMTP, but also be self-describing and "discoverable," so that other applications can find that the service exists and what it does programmatically. XML is also frequently seen as the ideal data format for this process, because it is self-describing and language-neutral. A number of methods are beginning to emerge as promising standards to act as the discovery and access method for Web services.

Let us examine some of the fundamental technologies involved in Web services, and how frameworks help you leverage them.

11.1.2.1 XML

The emergence of XML and various standards for its use has provided powerful tools for data sharing. Particularly, with the use of transformation technology such as XSL/XSLT, XML has quickly become the lingua franca for data exchange, particularly on the Web. XML, when used in conjunction with data type definitions (DTDs), provides a self-describing and structured data transport.

What was needed to put XML to work in Web services was a means to use it to access *methods*, or business logic, as well as data.

11.1.2.2 SOAP

SOAP, or Simple Object Access Protocol, is an XML-based lightweight protocol designed for exchanging information in a distributed environment, either locally or via a WAN such as the Internet. It is commonly used for accessing Web services. The protocol normally uses HTTP as its transport mechanism, but can also utilize SMTP, JMS, or other communication mechanisms.

SOAP was developed in response to the need to combine information and requests for processing. SOAP defines an XML standard for passing *messages*, where a message can contain both data and requests for methods to act on that data. It is an XML-based client/server protocol, independent of the transport used to communicate the message. The client sends a message and the server receives it, acts on it, and (usually) sends a message back in response.

A SOAP server "publishes" a Web service, providing the ability to respond to appropriate XML messages, much like a website is "published" with a Web server, providing the ability to respond to URL requests. Specific port numbers are used to separate HTTP requests for Web services from requests for traditional HTML pages. SOAP messages are not dependent on the server's programming language – in this way, SOAP provides an ideal mechanism for integrating between, for example, J2EE applications and applications built with Microsoft's .NET architecture.

SOAP provides a mechanism for an application to make any of its services available to other application clients. The publishing application and the client can interact with objects without being concerned with SOAP and Web services. This is a perfect entry point for frameworks – they are able to provide SOAP-based Web services to all their applications and logic components, without any modification.

The SOAP specification defines three parts to the protocol: an "envelope," which defines a means of describing what is in a particular message and what should be done with it, a data-type handling mechanism and set of definitions, and a way to specify remote procedure calls and their responses.

SOAP messages can be quite simple: as a trivial example, let us look at a particular SOAP message that requests the square of a number. We ignore for the moment the process of locating the Web service (which is the job of UDDI and WSDL), and concentrate on the actual message passing.

The call to the remote procedure, or *service*, consists of an XML fragment such as

```
<GetSquare>
  <OriginalValue>10</OriginalValue>
</GetSquare>
```

As you can see, the fragment is relatively human-readable: we pass a value of 10, and apparently ask for a square in return. In actual practice, this fragment is enclosed in a SOAP "envelope," which specifies the name space of the method call we asked for, as well as the URN of the actual service we use:

```
<SOAP:Envelope xmlns:SOAP="urn:schemas-xml soap-
  org:soap.v1">
  <SOAP:Header></SOAP:Header>
   <SOAP:Body>
     <m:GetSquare xmlns:m="urn:localserver/soap:
        SquareValue">
       <OriginalValue>10</OriginalValue>
     </m:GetSquare>
   </SOAP:Body>
</SOAP:Envelope>
```

The appropriate SOAP server receives this message, changes it back from an XML stream to an actual procedure call, and forms a response. The response follows a similar format:

```
<SOAP:Envelope xmlns:SOAP="urn:schemas-xmlsoap-
  org:soap.v1">
  <SOAP:Header></SOAP:Header>
   <SOAP:Body>
     <m:GetSquareResponse xmlns:m="urn:localserver/soap:
        SquareValue">
       <SquareValue>100</SquareValue>
     </m:GetSquareResponse>
   </SOAP:Body>
</SOAP:Envelope>
```

This corresponds quite closely to the normal call and response of any method, and indeed mapping from regular method calls to SOAP request/response calls is not difficult. Many tools provide the means to do this easily, and frameworks are rapidly taking advantage of them. The one important fact to note is that the request and response did not imply anything about the particular language providing the service (or requesting it, for that matter). This provides an important interconnection point between Java and other languages, particularly Microsoft's .NET platform, which also has many tools for easy creation of Web services.

11.1.2.3 Web Services Definition Language (WSDL)

The SOAP specification has had a long and somewhat turbulent history. In development since 1998, SOAP predates the XML Schema language on which it now depends.

Politics and FUD (Fear, Uncertainty, and Doubt) among vendors and standards organizations prevented SOAP from being widely adopted for a long time. This was largely because vendors did not perceive an advantage in interoperability – in fact, quite the opposite is true. Vendors would like to have organizations dependent on a capability available from that vendor alone. Fortunately, the market demands otherwise, and vendors have – in some cases reluctantly – complied. The XML-RPC specification (a standard for remote procedure calls via XML) was released before SOAP and provides useful functionality in many applications even now.

By the fourth quarter of 1999, the SOAP specification was publicly available, and the W3C XML Schema language had progressed to the point where the need for the two standards to interact was evident.

SOAP extends the type-representing system of XML Schemas to provide reference and array types, and adds the concept of behavioral types and methods. This enables SOAP to not only transport data, but also specify the methods to be applied to the data.

Now that the XML Schema specification has stabilized, providing a defined means for applying types to XML, and that SOAP itself is now the focus of a W3C working group, the standard is sufficiently mature for vendors to know what they are dealing with.

The essential addition of Web services definition language (WSDL) makes SOAP a truly viable contender as a standard for sending transient XML to trigger responses from Web applications.

In Java terms, WSDL is like the interface specification for the Web service: it gives information to the caller about what the Web service is capable of, and how to invoke it.

We list the WSDL definition for our simple "square the number" service used in our examples:

```xml
<?xml version="1.0" encoding="UTF-8"?>
<definitions name="SquareService"
    targetNamespace="http://localhost/wsdl/SquareService.
      wsdl"
    xmlns="http://schemas.xmlsoap.org/wsdl/"
    xmlns:soap="http://schemas.xmlsoap.org/wsdl/soap/"
    xmlns:tns="http://localhost/wsdl/SquareService.wsdl"
    xmlns:xsd="http://www.w3.org/2001/XMLSchema">

<message name="GetSquare">
    <part name="OriginalValue" type="xsd:integer"/>
</message>
<message name="GetSquareResponse">
    <part name="SquareValue" type="xsd:integer"/>
</message>

<portType name="SquarePort">
    <operation name="GetSquare">
        <input message="tns:GetSquare"/>
        <output message="tns:GetSquareResponse"/>
    </operation>
</portType>

<binding name="SquareBinding" type="tns:SquarePort">
    <soap:binding style="rpc"
      transport="http://schemas.xmlsoap.org/soap/http"/>
<operation name="GetSquare">
    <soap:operation soapAction="GetSquare"/>
    <input>
      <soap:body
         encodingStyle="http://schemas.xmlsoap.org/soap/
           encoding/"
         namespace="urn:examples:squareservice"
         use="encoded"/>
    </input>
```

```
      <output>
        <soap:body
          encodingStyle="http://schemas.xmlsoap.org/soap/
          encoding/"
          namespace="urn:examples:squareservice"
          use="encoded"/>
      </output>
    </operation>
  </binding>

  <service name="SquareService">
    <documentation>Return the Square of an
      Integer</documentation>
    <port binding="tns:SquareBinding" name="SquarePort">
      <soap:address
        location="http://localhost:8080/soap/servlet/
        rpcrouter"/>
    </port>
  </service>
</definitions>
```

This WSDL file is simply stored where it can be accessed like any other document, via HTTP. When the client wishes to access a particular Web service, it can read the WSDL to find out what it needs to know to prepare its request appropriately.

11.1.2.4 UDDI

Universal description, discovery, and integration service, or UDDI, provides the "discovery" and "description" part for Web services. It is a standard XML format that provides a way for an application running as a Web service to describe itself to potential clients. A client queries the application, and it responds with a specially formatted XML message that describes the services it offers. IBM and Microsoft are very active in the promotion and standardization of UDDI.

The information provided in a UDDI registry allows Web applications to locate available Web services. The registry is commonly separated into the following components:

- **White Pages:** Just like the section of a phone book by the same name, the white pages portion of a UDDI registry lists basic identification information, such as address and contact.
- **Yellow Pages:** Also like their paper namesake, the UDDI yellow pages provide categorized listings, which are based on standardized categories. This allows an organization that provides Web services to list themselves by their business function, and for potential clients to search by these functions and categories.
- **Green Pages:** With no direct parallel in print, the green pages in a UDDI registry include technical information about Web services made available by the listed organization. The closest parallel might be the familiar domain name service (DNS) for looking up IP addresses given a domain name. A human-readable name is mapped to the various URL and file references required to actually invoke the Web services that are listed.

UDDI registries provide the first link in the chain of services that enable the whole Web services infrastructure. As Web services become more common, UDDI registries will become an essential service, just as DNS is today, in enabling Web applications to interoperate. Frameworks and component models that are developed now include access to such services.

11.1.3 Jini

As the Internet develops it grows into new areas. The traditional PC or desktop workstation will soon be supplanted as the most common Internet device: more portable devices such as cell phones, PDAs, and other consumer electronic devices will interact over the Net. The dynamic nature of the Net and the wireless revolution mean that the devices participating in a particular network are no longer static. As devices and their services are ever changing, applications that use these services must adapt, and this is where the Jini technology comes into play.

Jini provides a mechanism for services to "advertise" themselves as they become available, and for other elements of the network to find and communicate with these services. Instead of configuring a specific set of services ahead of time, a network that uses Jini can expand and adapt dynamically – new services become available and unavailable all the time, and applications and devices find the services they need dynamically. Jini is independent of any specific wire protocol, such as CORBA or RMI.

As application frameworks extend to support this kind of dynamic service infrastructure, the ability to create Web applications that are able to adapt to changing environments and different service availabilities will emerge. Because the application requires access to mobile devices or services, it will be able to discover these via Jini, download the appropriate interface, and interact with the service.

11.1.4 JavaSpaces

One Jini-based service that is sure to have an impact on applications developed in the future is JavaSpaces. JavaSpaces is a means for creating collaborative and distributed applications. It provides a high-level *coordination* mechanism for distributed components. Like a good component system, it strives to provide a simple and readily adopted component mechanism.

JavaSpaces takes a different approach to application development: an "application" in JavaSpaces is defined as a collection of distributed processes. These processes cooperate and interact with each other through objects that are placed into and removed from one or more "spaces."

A "space" is an object repository, a place where persistent objects reside on the network and can be accessed. Each application process communicates only through these objects – never directly. A process can write a new object into a space, make a copy of an object in a space (to manipulate it, because objects within the space are read-only), and remove objects from a space. Processes locate objects in a space by means of an object template. A prototype object – the template – is created, and the known values are specified. This object is then used as the search criteria in the space. If it is found that there is no object that matches the required value , a process can block, or wait, until one "arrives" – for example, until a suitable object is placed there by another process. Unlike persistent objects in many other application models, the objects in a space are handled as data-only. Once they are removed (or copied) from the space, however, their methods can be invoked just like any other object.

More than almost any other application development technique, JavaSpaces requires a unique way of approaching applications. Few frameworks exist that support its capabilities, but this will likely change over time, particularly for more process-intensive applications that are distributed over server clusters.

11.1.5 Agents and Machine Intelligence

As we saw in Chapter 6, frameworks for creating Web-based applications using agents already exist. The nature of the Web and the portability of Java combine to make agents a natural progression, and frameworks to allow application logic to be distributed in this way make agents accessible. Often, as agents undertake their tasks and relocate themselves as necessary, they need to make decisions that are more complex than a nonagent application. This brings agents into the realm of machine intelligence, allowing them to solve problems through the application fuzzy logic and learned knowledge bases. Advanced applications that take advantage of these kinds of capabilities are emerging in a few specialized areas, but framework support for such capabilities is currently very thin.

11.2 FRAMEWORK INTEROPERABILITY

In Chapter 6 we discussed the advantages and disadvantages of combining frameworks – of using more than one application framework to provide services to your custom application. Most application-specific frameworks combine well with others. Many complete application frameworks do not – they provide a fairly constrained structure to the finished application that makes it difficult to incorporate services from any other framework.

One direction that is sure to be seen in the development of frameworks is increased interoperability. As standards emerge for technologies such as SOAP and JMS, frameworks will provide access to their services via these standards, and a certain amount of interoperability will be achieved as a result. The ability to connect application logic written for different component models will take a bit more – and again frameworks are adapted to provide the high degree of configurability that makes this possible.

11.3 META-FRAMEWORKS

Another new approach to frameworks and related technology is the concept of a "meta-framework." That is, a framework that specifically bridges and integrates the best capabilities of many different frameworks, allowing them to be used together on a single application. By defining sufficiently high-level design patterns and structures, this approach can bring the best of many different frameworks to bear on an application, making it a powerful tool. As frameworks and components are improved, this meta-framework approach allows new components with improved capabilities to be used without changing the application itself.

At least one project (Keel, at *www.keelframework.org*) is underway to provide a backbone designed to connect multiple frameworks, and to allow developers to choose the implementation of the various framework services best suited to their needs. Some complete application frameworks make a start in this direction: most notably Turbine and Avalon, with their highly "pluggable" architectures, but a meta-framework takes this one step further. It provides almost no services directly; instead, it defines a layer of generic services by means of interfaces. These interfaces then have their concrete implementations in the services provided by other frameworks.

Meta-frameworks are aided in their efforts by the development of more pluggable services in frameworks – making it easier for a meta-framework to connect to the services of the various underlying frameworks themselves. As with interoperability, the goal here is to allow the application developer to choose services that are not available from a single framework and combine them to solve application problems. Components that are written using different component architectures can be combined – such as EJBs interacting with Struts Action objects, or Avalon components collaborating with JavaSpaces processes.

11.4 Summary

We have explored what we mean by components and frameworks, examined what they provide, and discussed how to compare and select frameworks. We have seen how the benefits and disadvantages of using a framework can be compared and how to tell when the trade-offs make it worthwhile.

The bottom line is that usually considerable effort has to be put into adopting and learning a framework, and that the selection has to be made very carefully, taking a large number of factors into account.

The advantage is nearly always worth it, however, and the resultant boost in productivity and quality of the finished application almost always more than makes up for the initial steep learning curve.

Our final examination of frameworks is given in the Appendix, where we implement the same application using four different frameworks. We include extensive comments in between the code to explain how each of the services are accessed and what benefits are achieved. This allows you to see how the design patterns and framework principles are applied in a real, albeit simple, application, and how the services of the different frameworks are put to use to dramatically reduce the development time and effort.

Appendix

Case Studies

A.1 Introduction

The best way to get a "feel" for different frameworks when choosing between them is to use them – to put them to work thereby creating an actual application. In actual practice, this is seldom done. No one has enough time to spend creating throw-away applications in several different frameworks. Once a developer begins to use a particular framework, and dedicates time to learn it well enough to do the example, it is easy to continue, and to take advantage of what has been learned so far. To switch tracks and use another framework is difficult, and things that have been learned about the first framework must often be unlearned to properly use another.

The comparison is still very helpful; however, seldom it is done. Creating a similar application in multiple frameworks, even a very simple one such as the one used here, allows a point-for-point comparison between frameworks. If one of the frameworks you are giving serious consideration to is not one of the ones we have chosen for a case study, you might find it helpful to implement the same sample application as a starting point.

In this Appendix, we use several detailed code examples, so that you can see what developing the same application with different frameworks is like. We do not, for lack of space, list every source code line here. You can download a zip file of the complete source code from http://www.cup.org/titles/catalogue.asp?isbn=0521520592. Place this file in any convenient directory and unzip it – the filenames we give in the following text are all relative to that directory.

A.2 Design

To perform a realistic analysis and comparison of different frameworks, we provide here the source code of a simple application as implemented with the aid of several different frameworks. It is not our intention here to try to teach the use of a framework, or even produce an ideal example of that framework's use. Indeed, our case study applications could be improved considerably. What we are trying to do is show a realistic sample of how the same problem would be tackled by four very different frameworks. We explore in some detail the differences in the design, development, and deployment process for each of the applications to contrast the approaches taken by the frameworks – not just the differences, but also the similarities. You will see how the design patterns we have discussed come into play, and how the frameworks provide structure and services to our simple application.

We include detailed excerpts from the source code to each of the applications, along with observations on both the code and the development process that created it.

The application to be created will be the same, functionally, for each of the frameworks, allowing us to see how each framework aids the process. In a very broad sense, the following are the design goals of our case study application:

- A basic asset inventory management application, which is designed to keep track of the various pieces of equipment and assets of a company. It will allow entry and lookup of asset information and related transactions stored in a relational database, and will support login authentication and basic internationalization.
- The application, in keeping with our focus on Web-application frameworks, will be Web based: that is, it should be fully accessible via a standard Web browser, with no special client requirements.
- Provide the ability to enter and record Assets in a relational database. Assets can be listed and searched for by using at least a number and description. Assets can also be retrieved and edited.
- Allow only authorized users to enter and update all data – implying an authentication and authorization scheme for users to log in to the application.
- Allow for the entry of transactions that affect the status and the value of each asset: for example, initial purchase, depreciation, sale, and write-off.
- Prepare current values of assets on demand.
- Provide a basic means to navigate the application and access its features.

Design

The following diagram shows what those features might look like as a simple UML Use-Case:

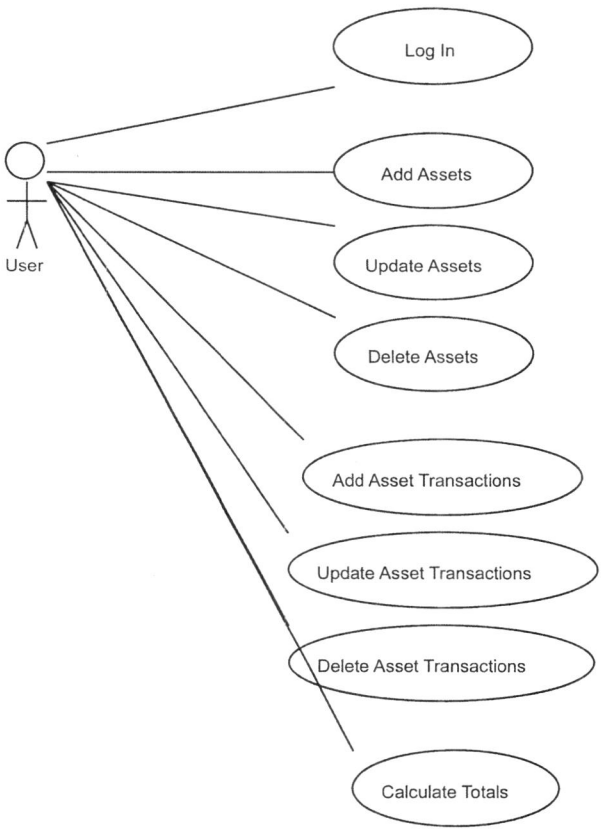

Although it is quite possible to provide a minimal implementation of these features, we have specifically attempted to satisfy the requirements in a way that is extensible: for example, something that could be developed into a full-featured asset management application. Most of us are not trying to develop "demo" Web applications, but the real thing, and an example that ignores the requirements of real-world deployment and use skips the very part of development that frameworks can help us most with. By necessity of space, the examples are shorter and less complete than a fully developed application – but we have nonetheless not cut any corners. Although we describe the installation process of the frameworks in brief, as well as an outline of the development process, refer to the documentation of the framework of your choice – these kinds of procedures change rapidly sometimes, and again we have no desire to reproduce the usually excellent documentation that frameworks themselves provide.

For an operating environment, we assume that we are operating on a Linux-based system (RedHat 6.2, specifically), with JDK 1.3.1 and the Tomcat 4.0 Servlet engine. For a database we use MySQL 3.23.33, which runs on the same system as everything else. Due to the nature of Java and Web applications, your results will probably be very similar even if these specifics are different.

A.3 Initial Design

In Chapter 8, we described a design process of decomposing a specification into services, components, and then specific subclassed objects. Let us apply this process to our sample specification, first independently of any framework, to see the overall picture, and then by mapping to the services and components provided by a specific framework.

The specification discusses asset items – a noun, indicating an object or a data, and the entry or lookup of these items – a verb (two, actually), indicating an action or a process. So we immediately see one service we need: a service providing entry or lookup of the asset information. We could view this as either a single service with two capabilities (entry and lookup), or two separate services. Applying the design pattern of deferring aggregation or generalization until later, we choose to consider them separately.

The specification then describes asset transactions, and an entry and lookup capability for them as well. These are then our second two services; again we can immediately see the similarity to the first two – we are discussing entry and lookup, just of a different data set, but we avoid bundling them together and parameterizing at this phase of design.

The specification next discusses the details of tracking the entry and update of assets and their transactions, and implies the existence of an authorization and authentication service. We need users to be able to identify themselves via logins, and be granted/denied permission to the various functions of our system.

So far we have the following services:

- authenticate (log in)
- enter assets

Initial Design 381

- lookup assets
- edit assets
- enter asset transactions
- lookup asset transactions
- edit asset transactions

The specification discusses another explicit service – the ability to calculate current values of assets on demand. This is our next service.

Finally, the specification calls for a way to navigate the application and access all of our services. Often this is an implied requirement and is the last of our services.

So the list of services in total includes the following:

- authenticate
- enter assets
- lookup assets
- edit assets
- enter asset transactions
- lookup asset transactions
- edit asset transactions
- calculate current values
- navigate the application

This high-level decomposition must now be further decomposed into components that are used to provide these services. For our example, we do this both at a high level and in the context of each of our frameworks.

A.3.1 Authenticate

This service implies a persistent store of user information, to authenticate users. So we have the following:

- User Component (Persistent)

and the action of logging is implied:

- Login Component (action)

A.3.2 Enter Assets

This service again implies an asset component, as a persistent object, and the action of entering and asset:

- Asset (Persistent)
- Enter Asset (action)

A.3.3 Lookup Asset

This service again needs access to the persistent asset object, and a component to perform the lookup:

- Lookup Asset (action)

A.3.4 Edit Asset

Similarly, edit adds just a single additional action. Implied here, though, is a relationship with the lookup function: we need to be able to specify or select an asset to edit.

A.3.5 Enter Asset Transaction

This service requires the persistent asset transaction object, and the action of entering such a transaction:

- Asset Transaction (Persistent)
- Enter Asset Transaction (action)

A.3.6 Lookup Asset Transaction

We again just add a new action component, which refers to the persistent asset transaction:

- Lookup Asset Transaction (action)

A.3.7 Edit Asset Transaction

We again just add a new action component, to allow editing of an existing persistent asset transaction:

- Edit Asset Transaction (action)

A.3.8 Calculate Current Values

Assuming the totals for an asset's value are stored in the same persistent components as the asset itself, this service implies that there are no additional elements:

- Calculate Current Values (action)

A.3.9 Navigate

The same is true of navigation, although the flow of the application might be stored in a persistent object in some implementation.

- Navigate (action)

Now we apply our design to each of our chosen frameworks and see how the services and components map to the capabilities that are provided.

A.3.10 Database Design

Our specifications can be used to derive a general database design. Some frameworks (such as Struts and Cocoon) require the database tables to be created by means of SQL statements, whereas others (such as Turbine and Expresso) can do this for you – by generating the appropriate SQL from a separate definition of the fields. We end up with the following database design, using the MySQL database as a basis:

A.3.10.1 Asset Table

Field	Type	Null	Key	Default	Extra
AssetId	int(11)		PRI	NULL	auto-increment
Descrip	varchar(80)	YES		NULL	
TotalValue	float	YES		NULL	

A.3.10.2 Asset Transaction Table

Field	Type	Null	Key	Default	Extra
AssetId	int(11)		PRI	NULL	
TrxDate	datetime		PRI	NULL	
TrxType	char(1)			NULL	
TrxValue	float			NULL	

If our database modeling mechanism for our framework uses classes to map to tables, we might have a UML class diagram something like this:

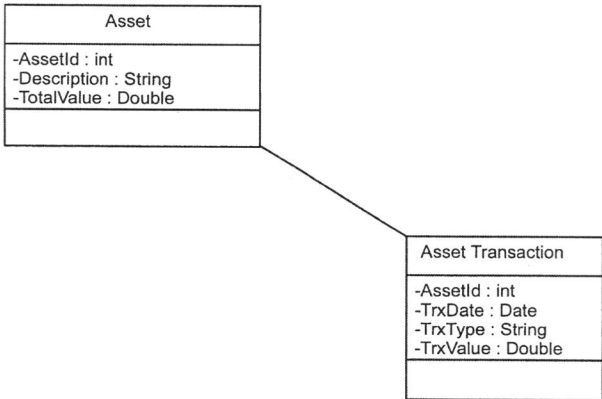

A.4 Case Study: Struts

Although Struts brings a lot of power to the presentation side of an application's construction, through its extensive tag library, it can easily be used to develop entire applications. Our first case-study application is created with Struts, version 1.0.

A.4.1 Installation

Struts does not include a Servlet engine bundled with its download, so our installation began by downloading a copy of Tomcat 4.0 and installing it independently, according to its normal installation process.

Case Study: Struts

Struts is downloaded as a single .tar.gz or .zip file, and is unzipped into a suitable directory. In the "webapps" directory of this new directory, a number of .war files will be found, each of which is a specific Struts Web application. These must then be installed into a separate Tomcat Servlet engine to enable them. For our purposes, we create a separate "inventory" directory within our Tomcat web-apps subdirectory to contain our new application.

In this web-apps directory we installed (using the "struts-blank.war" Struts application as a model) the required WEB-INF directory and a number of .jar files containing the required Struts classes. A number of "starter" applications, including a "blank" application, are included with Struts and can be used as the starting point for your own applications.

Because we require authentication via a login, according to our specification, we again take the route of least resistance, and use the basic authentication provided by the container application, Tomcat.

To set this up, we must make a couple of configuration changes to Tomcat. In the Tomcat installation directory, there is a subdirectory "conf" within which we find tomcat-users.xml, which lists the defined user names, passwords, and associated roles. The default looks like:

tomcat-users.xml

```
 1: <!--
 2:   NOTE: By default, no user is included in the "manager"
 3: role required
 4:   to operate the "/manager" web application. If you wish
 5: to use this app,
 6:   you must define such a user - the username and password
 7: are arbitrary.
 8: -->
 9: <tomcat-users>
10:   <user name="tomcat" password="tomcat" roles="tomcat"
11: />
12:   <user name="role1" password="tomcat" roles="role1"
13: />
14:   <user name="both" password="tomcat"
15: roles="tomcat,role1" />
16:   <user name="manager" password="manager"
17. roles="manager" />
18. </tomcat-users>
```

For the purposes of our simple example, we just stick with the default, and use the login name "tomcat" with its default password. For an actual deployment, of course, this is exactly what we must *not* do: default passwords should be changed immediately, and we would probably want a more substantial authentication mechanism in any case.

To enable protection for our application, we also include an additional section in our web.xml file:

web.xml

```
 1: <security-constraint>
 2:    <web-resource-collection>
 3:       <web-resource-name>
 4:          struts
 5:       </web-resource-name>
 6:       <url-pattern>
 7:          /*
 8:       </url-pattern>
 9:       <http-method>
10:          GET
11:       </http-method>
12:       <http-method>
13:          POST
14:       </http-method>
15:    </web-resource-collection>
16:    <auth-constraint>
17:       <role-name>
18:          tomcat
19:       </role-name>
20:    </auth-constraint>
21: </security-constraint>
22: <login-config>
23:    <auth-method>
24:       BASIC
25:    </auth-method>
26:
27:    <realm-name>
28:
29:       Default
30:    </realm-name>
```

Case Study: Struts

```
31:
32: </login-config>
33: <security-role>
34:    <role-name>
35:       tomcat
36:    </role-name>
37: </security-role>
```

IMPORTANT: this kind of security configuration, although very similar in other containers, is specific to Tomcat. Your own container will have a slightly different way of setting up basic authentication.

In the struts-config.xml file, it is possible to specify data sources to connect to databases via JDBC. These data sources provide automatic connection pooling, making it easy to use them in our application without a lot of extra code. The struts-config.xml section for data sources is edited to look like this:

struts-config.xml

```
<!-- ========== Data Source Configuration ========== -->
<data-sources>
  <data-source
     autoCommit="true"
    description="Asset Data Source"
    driverClass="org.gjt.mm.mysql.Driver"
     maxCount="4"
     minCount="2"
     password=""
        url="jdbc:mysql://localhost/inventory"
        user="root"
   />
</data-sources>
```

We examine the remainder of the struts-config.xml file later.

A.4.2 Design Process

The basic unit of business logic in Struts is the "Action"; therefore, to contain the business logic for our sample, a number of Action objects will be required.

- Add Assets
- List Assets
- Update Asset
- Delete Asset
- Add Asset Transactions
- List Asset Transactions
- Update Asset Transaction
- Delete Asset Transaction
- Calculate Asset Values

For the user interface, the preferred method in Struts is JSP pages; therefore, a page for each of the primary functions allowed by our Action objects is needed. These pages are associated with the appropriate action object as part of the "mapping" process, the definition of which is contained in the struts-config.xml file.

A.4.3 Development Process

The Struts application begins with a series of JSP pages, which later evolve into the "views" for our "actions". We began with the data entry page for Assets, and then for Asset Transactions. An essentially identical page is used for updating (in fact it would be quite possible to use the same page, with conditional code). Asset and Transaction listings are also straightforward. In our application, we also created the "confirmation" page used to acknowledge completion of various functions.

Once we created all of the required JSP pages, the Actions had to be coded, and associations had to be made between Action and view. There is essentially one Action for each of the basic operations listed above for our application, and these call SQL directly where database access is required, utilizing Struts' own built-in connection pool.

A final "menu" page was created to link all the other pages together, and our simple application was up and running. Let us look at the finished code.

A.4.4 Finished Application

The bulk of our finished application for Struts consists of Action objects and JSP pages that are all linked together by the struts-config.xml file,

Case Study: Struts

(See the full text of the file in the struts/struts-config.xml file from the website.)
The two form beans that we will use are defined below, with a short "name" and the associated full class names.

```
48:      <form-beans>
49:
50:      <form-bean    name="AssetForm"
51:                    type="com.yourcompany.forms. AssetForm"/>
52:
53:      <form-bean    name="AssetTrxForm"
54:
55: type="com.yourcompany.forms.AssetTrxForm"/>
56:
57:      </form-beans>
```

The two "global" forwards that we will refer to from within our Action objects are given below. We can use the generic names "error" and "success," and then associate these names with specific jsp pages here in the configuration. In this way, the application need not change if we want to use a different error or confirmation page some time in the future.

```
68:      <forward name="error"
69: path="/error.jsp"/>
70:      <forward name="success"
71: path="/confirm.jsp"/>
72:
73:   </global-forwards>
74:
75:
76:   <!-- ========= Action Mapping Definitions
77: ============================ -->
78:   <action-mappings>
79:
80:      <!-- Example logoff action
81:      <action path="/logoff"
82:
83: type="org.apache.struts.example.LogoffAction">
84:       <forward name="success"
85: path="/index.jsp"/>
```

```
86:        </action>
87:        -->
88:
```

We define below all of the Action objects, associating them with a URL path and (if required) with a form bean object. When issuing the URLs, our web.xml defines the ".do" suffix as the identifier for the Struts Controller Servlet – so "ListAssets.do" is used to invoke the "ListAssets" action, and so forth.

```
 89:    <action    path="/ListAssets"
 90:               type="com.yourcompany.actions.ListAssets"
 91:               scope="request">
 92:      <forward name="success" path="/listAssets.jsp"/>
 93:    </action>
 94:
 95:    <action    path="/ListAssetTrx"
 96:               type="com.yourcompany.actions.ListAssetTrx"
 97:               scope="request">
 98:      <forward name="success" path="/listAssetTrx. jsp"/>
 99:    </action>
100:
101:    <action    path="/AddAsset"
102:               type="com.yourcompany.actions.AddAsset"
103:               name="AssetForm"
104:               scope="request">
105:    </action>
106:
107:    <action    path="/AddAssetTrx"
108:               type="com.yourcompany.actions.AddAssetTrx"
109:               name="AssetTrxForm"
110:               scope="request">
111:    </action>
112:
113:    <action    path="/PromptUpdateAsset"
114:
115: type="com.yourcompany.actions.PromptUpdateAsset"
116:               name="AssetForm"
117:               scope="request">
```

Case Study: Struts

```
118:       <forward name="update" path="/updateAsset.jsp"/>
119:     </action>
120:
121:     <action   path="/UpdateAsset"
122:              type="com.yourcompany.actions.UpdateAsset"
123:              name="AssetForm"
124:              scope="request">
125:     </action>
126:
127:     <action   path="/DeleteAsset"
128:              type="com.yourcompany.actions.DeleteAsset">
129:     </action>
130:
131:     <action   path="/UpdateAssetTrx"
132:              type="com.yourcompany.actions.UpdateAssetTrx"
133:              name="AssetTrxForm"
134:              scope="request">
135:       <forward name="update"
136: path="/updateAssetTrx.jsp"/>
137:     </action>
138:
139:     <action   path="/PromptUpdateAssetTrx"
140:
141: type="com.yourcompany.actions.PromptUpdateAssetTrx"
142:              name="AssetTrxForm"
143:              scope="request">
144:       <forward name="update"
145: path="/updateAssetTrx.jsp"/>
146:     </action>
147:
148:     <action   path="/DeleteAssetTrx"
149:
150: type="com.yourcompany.actions.DeleteAssetTrx">
151:     </action>
152:
153:     <action   path="/Calculate"
154:              type="com.yourcompany.actions.Calculate">
155:     </action>
```

The initial file in our application is a simple "menu" – just a list of links to the other functions:

(See the file struts/index.jsp for this listing.)

```
 1: <%@ page language="java" %>
 2: <%@ taglib uri="/WEB-INF/struts-bean.tld" prefix="bean" %>
 3: <%@ taglib uri="/WEB-INF/struts-html.tld" prefix="html" %>
 4: <%@ taglib uri="/WEB-INF/struts-logic.tld" prefix="logic" %>
 5:
 6: <html:html locale="true">
 7: <head>
```

The use of the "bean:message" tag is as shown below, accessing a localized message from an external message bundle file. For our application to be fully internationalized, all messages should be accessed in this manner.

```
 8: <title><bean:message key="index.title"/></title>
 9: <html:base/>
10: </head>
11: <body bgcolor="white">
12:
13: <logic:notPresent name="org.apache.struts.action.MESSAGE"
14: scope="application">
15:   <font color="red">
16:     ERROR: Application resources not loaded -- check
17: servlet container
18:     logs for error messages.
19:   </font>
20: </logic:notPresent>
21:
22: <h3 align="center">Asset Inventory</h3>
23:
24: <p align="center">
25: <a href="ListAssets.do">List Assets</a>
26: </p>
27: <p align="center">
28: <a href="promptAsset.jsp">Add Assets</a>
29: </p>
30: <p align="center">
```

Case Study: Struts

```
31: <a href="ListAssetTrx.do">List Asset Transactions</a>
32: </p>
33: <p align="center">
34: <a href="promptAssetTrx.jsp">Add Asset Transactions</a>
35: </p>
36: <p align="center">
37: <a href="Calculate.do">Calculate Asset Values</a>
38: </p>
```
...

As you can see, we refer to the following action objects in the strutsconfig:

- AddAsset
- UpdateAsset
- DeleteAsset
- ListAssets
- AddAssetTrx
- UpdateAssetTrx
- DeleteAssetTrx
- ListAssetTrx
- Calculate

Let us examine how each of these things are implemented, beginning with adding new assets:

Add assets begins with a simple JSP form, associated with a particular "form bean," from which the action objects obtain the form values:

(See the file struts/promptAsset.jsp.)

```
 1: <%@ page language="java" %>
 2: <%@ taglib uri="/WEB-INF/struts-bean.tld" prefix="bean" %>
 3: <%@ taglib uri="/WEB-INF/struts-html.tld" prefix="html" %>
 4: <%@ taglib uri="/WEB-INF/struts-logic.tld" prefix="logic" %>
 5:
 6: <html:html locale="true">
 7: <head>
 8: <title>Add Asset</title>
 9: <html:base/>
10: </head>
11: <body bgcolor="white">
```

```
12:
13: <h3>Add Assets</h3>
14:
```

We see below the reference to the AddAsset action object. The ".do" suffix is not required in this case, and the form bean object is automatically looked up by association from the struts-config.xml file.

```
15: <html:form action="AddAsset">
16: <table border="0">
17: <tr>
18: <td>Asset Description:</td>
19: <td><html:text property="descrip"/></td>
20: </tr>
21: </table>
22: <p><input type="submit" value="Add"/></p>
23: </html:form>
24:
25: </body>
26: </html:html>
```

This page is associated with the form bean AssetForm. Given below are the key methods in this class:

(See the file struts/AssetForm.java a full listing.)

```
...
  13: public final class AssetForm extends ActionForm {
...
  23:     public int getId() {
...
  26:     public String getDescrip() {
...
  29:     public void setDescrip(String newDescrip) {
...
  32:     public void setId(int newId) {
...
  35:     public void setTotalValue(double newValue) {
...
  38:     public double getTotalValue() {
...
```

Case Study: Struts

When this form is submitted, it calls an action AddAsset, which is mapped to our first "action" object, the key method of which is shown below:
(See the file struts/AddAsset.java for a full listing.)

...
```
30: public final class AddAsset extends Action {
31:   public ActionForward perform(ActionMapping mapping,
32:     ActionForm form, HttpServletRequest request,
33:     HttpServletResponse response)
34:   throws IOException, ServletException {
35:     Connection myConnection = null;
36:     try {
```

We establish below our connection to the data source as defined in the struts-config.xml file, and then build our SQL statement from the values in the form bean. The form bean has been automatically populated with the values from our HTML form by the framework.

```
37:       DataSource dataSource =
38: servlet.findDataSource(null);
39:       myConnection = dataSource.getConnection();
40:       AssetForm myForm = (AssetForm) form;
41:       Statement s = myConnection.createStatement();
42:       s.execute("INSERT INTO ASSET " +
43:         "(Descrip) VALUES ('" + myForm.getDescrip() +
44: "')");
45:   } catch (SQLException sqle) {
```
...

To return the connection back to the pool in the event of success or failure, we use the "finally" block.

```
48:   } finally {
49:     try {
50:       if (myConnection != null) {
51:         myConnection.close();
52:       }
53:     } catch (SQLException e) {
```
...

```
56:        }
57:    }
```

The final step is to return a "forward" to the appropriate symbolic name – in this case, the global "success" page that was also defined in struts-config.xml earlier.

```
58:        return (mapping.findForward("success"));
59:    }
60: }
```

The above action receives information from the form bean, and uses a pooled connection to the database to execute a simple SQL for inserting the data into the proper table. The "view" for this action simply confirms that the action is complete:

(For a complete listing, see struts/confirm.jsp.)

...
```
 6: <head>
 7: <title>Operation Complete</title>
 8: <html:base/>
 9: </head>
10: <body bgcolor="white">
11: <h3 align="center">Asset Inventory</h3>
12: <p align="center">
13: Operation Complete
14: </p>
15: <p><a href="index.jsp">Back</a></p>
```
...

unless there was some kind of an error, in which case we direct to a different view:

(For a complete listing, see struts/error.jsp.)

...
```
13: <h3 align="center">Asset Inventory: Error</h3>
14: <p align="center">
15: An error occurred
16: </p>
```

Case Study: Struts

In the following example, we simply use the exception stored in the page context by our Action object to display the stack trace.

```
17: <blockquote>
18: <% ByteArrayOutputStream bos = new ByteArrayOutputStream();
19:    Exception e = (Exception) request.getAttribute ("error");
20:    e.printStackTrace(new PrintStream(bos));
21:    out.println(bos.toString());
22: %>
23: </blockquote>
24: <p><a href="index.jsp">Back</a></p>
...
```

Addition of asset transactions is essentially identical.
(See struts/promptAssetTrx.jsp for the full listing.)

```
...
 7: <title>Add Asset Transaction</title>
...
12: <html:form action="AddAssetTrx">
13: <table border="0">
14: <tr>
15: <td>Asset Id:</td>
```

The property names used here correspond to the properties in the appropriate form bean, and are populated automatically by the framework.

```
16: <td><html:text property="id"/></td>
17: </tr>
18: <tr>
19: <td>Trx Date:</td>
20: <td><html:text property="dte"/></td>
21: </tr>
...
```

A form passes the data along to a form bean.
(See struts/promptAssetTrxForm.java for a full listing.)

```
...
13: public final class AssetTrxForm extends ActionForm {
```

```
 14:       private int id = 0;
 15:       private String type = null;
 16:       private String dte = null;
 17:       private double val = 0;
...
 21:       public int getId() {
...
 24:       public void setId(int newId) {
...
 77:       public ActionErrors validate(ActionMapping mapping,
 78:                        HttpServletRequest
 79: request) {
```

In our example, we have no validation. It would normally be performed at this point.

```
 80:       ActionErrors errors = new ActionErrors();
 81:       return errors;
 82:    }
 83: }
```

... which collects the data, which is then accessed by the AddAssetTrx action to add it to the database:
(See the file struts/AddAssetTrx.java for a full listing.)

```
...
 30: public final class AddAssetTrx extends Action {
 31:    public ActionForward perform(ActionMapping mapping,
 32:       ActionForm form, HttpServletRequest request,
 33:       HttpServletResponse response)
 34:    throws IOException, ServletException {
 35:       Connection myConnection = null;
 36:       try {
 37:          DataSource dataSource =
 38: servlet.findDataSource(null);
 39:          myConnection = dataSource.getConnection();
 40:          AssetTrxForm myForm = (AssetTrxForm) form;
 41:          Statement s = myConnection.createStatement();
 42:
```

Case Study: Struts

```
43:          String insertStatement = "INSERT INTO ASSET TRX " +
44:            "(AssetId, TrxType, TrxDate, TrxValue) VALUES ("
45:            + myForm.getId() + ", '"
46:            + myForm.getType() + "','"
47:            + myForm.getDte() + "',"
48:            + myForm.getVal() + ")";
49:            s.executeUpdate(insertStatement);
50:        } catch (SQLException sqle) {
...
```

This action uses our "confirm" page to acknowledge the action, and goes back to the data entry form if there is an error, allowing the user to try again.

We use Action objects to prepare the prompt forms as well. It is a good practice in Struts to always make transitions between pages the result of an action – for example, not to call a JSP directly from another JSP. This allows the application to be controlled by the application logic, and makes reconfiguring which pages are used a simple matter of editing the struts-config.xml file.

Listing assets and asset transactions is even easier. We use a ListAssets action to prepare our asset listing...

(See struts/ListAssets.java for a full listing.)

```
...
32: public final class ListAssets extends Action {
33:   public ActionForward perform(ActionMapping mapping,
34:       ActionForm form, HttpServletRequest request,
35:       HttpServletResponse response)
36:   throws IOException, ServletException {
37:   Connection myConnection = null;
38:   try {
39:     DataSource dataSource = servlet.findDataSource (null);
40:     myConnection = dataSource.getConnection();
41:     Statement s = myConnection.createStatement();
```

An ArrayList is defined below, which will be stored in the current page context and made available to our JSP page...

```
42:          ArrayList myList = new ArrayList();
43:          ResultSet rs = s.executeQuery("SELECT AssetId,
44: Descrip, TotalValue FROM ASSET");
```

```
45:      while (rs.next()) {
46:          System.err.println("One row");
47:          AssetForm af = new AssetForm();
48:          af.setId(rs.getInt(1));
49:          af.setDescrip(rs.getString(2));
50:          af.setTotalValue(rs.getDouble(3));
51:          myList.add(af);
52:      }
53:          request.setAttribute("List", myList);
```
...

The forward "success" in the case of this action is defined as the page that displays the listing of assets

```
67: return (mapping.findForward("success"));
```
...

and an associated JSP is defined as the view to display the results.
(See the file struts/listAssets.jsp for a complete listing.)

...
```
  11: <h3 align="center">List Assets</h3>
  12: <table align="center" border="1">
  13: <tr>
  14: <td><strong>Asset Id</strong></td>
...other headings
  19: </tr>
  20: <logic:present name="List">
  21: <logic:iterate id="oneAsset" name="List">
```

In the lines below, we use the "List" that we stored in the Action object and iterate through its member objects to display each asset.

```
  22: <tr>
  23: <td><bean:write name="oneAsset" property="id"/></td>
  24: <td><bean:write name="oneAsset" property= "descrip"/></td>
  25: <td><bean:write name="oneAsset"
  26: property="totalValue"/></td>
```

Case Study: Struts

```
27: <td><html:link href="/struts/PromptUpdateAsset.do"
28: paramId="id"
29:    paramName="oneAsset"
30: paramProperty="id">Update</html:link></td>
31: <td><html:link href="/struts/DeleteAsset.do" paramId="id"
32:    paramName="oneAsset"
33: paramProperty="id">Delete</html:link></td>
34: </tr>
```
...

The same technique is used for listing Asset Transactions.
(For a full listing, see the file struts/ListAssetTrx.java.)

```
...
33: public final class ListAssetTrx extends Action {
34:    public ActionForward perform(ActionMapping mapping,
35:      ActionForm form, HttpServletRequest request,
36:      HttpServletResponse response)
37:    throws IOException, ServletException {
...
44:      ResultSet rs = s.executeQuery("SELECT AssetId,
45: TrxType, TrxDate, TrxValue FROM ASSETTRX");
46:      while (rs.next()) {
47:        AssetTrxForm af = new AssetTrxForm();
48:        af.setId(rs.getInt(1));
49:        af.setType(rs.getString(2));
50:        af.setDte(rs.getString(3));
51:        af.setVal(rs.getDouble(4));
52:        myList.add(af);
53:      }
54:      request.setAttribute("List", myList);
...
```

When updating assets, we access the update Action from a link on the List Assets page. In this case, we first call a "prompt" action to retrieve the current asset record and populate a form bean with the proper values for editing.

(For a full listing, see struts/PromptUpdateAsset.java.)

```
...
  32: public final class PromptUpdateAsset extends Action {
...
  38:    String id = request.getParameter("id");
...
  44:      ResultSet rs = s.executeQuery("SELECT AssetId,
  45: Descrip, TotalValue FROM ASSET WHERE AssetId = " + id);
  46:      AssetForm af = new AssetForm();
  47:      if (rs.next()) {
  48:      af.setId(rs.getInt(1));
  49:      af.setDescrip(rs.getString(2));
  50:      af.setTotalValue(rs.getDouble(3));
  51:      }
  52:      request.setAttribute("asset", af);
  53:      return (mapping.findForward("update"));
...
```

The PromptUpdateAsset action retrieves the current values of the given asset, and calls the update view to present our form.

(For a complete listing, see struts/updateAsset.jsp.)

```
...
  12: <html:form action="UpdateAsset">
  13: <table border="0">
  14: <tr>
  15: <td>Asset Id:</td>
  16: <td><bean:write name="asset" property="id"/>
  17: <html:hidden name="asset" property="id"/>
  18: </td>
  19: </tr>
...
```

Our update form's action is UpdateAsset, which calls the simple Action to write the results to the database.

(See struts/UpdateAsset.java for a full listing.)

```
...
  30: public final class UpdateAsset extends Action {
```

Case Study: Struts

We use the AssetForm bean to determine the id of the asset we will be updating:

```
35:     AssetForm af = (AssetForm) form;
36:     int id = af.getId();
37:     String descrip = af.getDescrip();
38:     Connection myConnection = null;
39:     try {
40:        DataSource dataSource =
41: servlet.findDataSource(null);
42:        myConnection = dataSource.getConnection();
43:        Statement s = myConnection.createStatement();
44:        s.executeUpdate("UPDATE ASSET SET Descrip = '" +
45: descrip
46:                + "' WHERE AssetId = " + id);
...
```

The same techniques are used with Asset Transactions. First, we have our "prompt" action to populate the form:

(See struts/PromptUpdateAssetTrx.java for a full listing.)

```
...
31: public final class PromptUpdateAssetTrx extends Action {
```

Here we access the URL parameters passed to this action, which tell us which Asset Transaction we are going to present for update:

```
37:     String id = request.getParameter("id");
38:     String dte = request.getParameter("dte");
...
44:       ResultSet rs = s.executeQuery("SELECT AssetId,
45: TrxDate, "
46:         + "TrxType, TrxValue FROM ASSETTRX WHERE AssetId
47: = " + id
48:         + " AND TrxDate = '" + dte + "'");
49:     AssetTrxForm af = new AssetTrxForm();
50:     if (rs.next()) {
51:       af.setId(rs.getInt(1));
52:       af.setDte(rs.getString(2));
```

```
   53:      af.setType(rs.getString(3));
   54:      af.setVal(rs.getDouble(4));
   55:    }
   56:    request.setAttribute("trx", af);
   57:    return (mapping.findForward("update"));
...
```

Our prompt action then uses the "update" form to collect the data.
(See struts/updateAssetTrx.jsp for a complete listing.)

```
...
   12: <html:form action="UpdateAssetTrx">
   13: <table border="0">
   14: <tr>
   15: <td>Asset Id:</td>
   16: <td><bean:write name="trx" property="id"/>
   17: <html:hidden name="trx" property="id"/></td>
   18: </tr>
...repeat for other fields
   33: <p><input type="submit" value="Update"/></p>
...
```

This then calls the appropriate update action to store the data to the database as before.
(See struts/UpdateAssetTrx.java for a full listing.)

```
...
   30: public final class UpdateAssetTrx extends Action {
...
   35:   AssetTrxForm af = (AssetTrxForm) form;
   36:   int id = af.getId();
   37:   String dte = af.getDte();
   38:   String type = af.getType();
   39:   double val = af.getVal();
...
   46:     s.executeUpdate("UPDATE ASSETTRX SET TrxType = '"
   47:       + type + "', TrxValue = " + val
   48:       + " WHERE AssetId = " + id
   49:       + " AND TrxDate = '"
   50:       + dte + "'");
...
```

Case Study: Struts

Delete is very similar to update, except that no intermediary form is required – the user can delete an asset directly from the listing page. Delete calls the following action object:

(See struts/DeleteAsset.java for a complete listing.)

```
...
  29: public final class DeleteAsset extends Action {
...
  34:    String id = request.getParameter("id");
...
  42:      s.executeUpdate("DELETE FROM ASSET WHERE AssetId
  43: = " + id);
...
```

Deleting an asset transaction is essentially identical to deleting an asset, except that the form must pass a two-part primary key to indicate the appropriate transaction to be deleted.

(See struts/DeleteAssetTrx.java for a complete listing.)

```
...
  29: public final class DeleteAssetTrx extends Action {
...
```

Two parameters from the URL are passed to us below – the "id" and the "trxdate" of the Asset Transaction to be deleted.

```
  34:    String id = request.getParameter("id");
  42:      s.executeUpdate("DELETE FROM ASSET WHERE id = " +
  43: id + " and trxdate = '" + trxdate + "'");
...
```

Our final Action object contains the application logic to sum up all of the asset transactions for a particular asset and write the totals to the Asset table itself. Like the Delete operations, it simply confirms its results or calls the error view to display the problem, if any.

(See struts/Calculate.java for a full listing.)

```
...
  33: public final class Calculate extends Action {
...
```

```
47:      ResultSet rs = s.executeQuery("SELECT AssetId FROM
48: ASSET");
49:      while (rs.next()) {
50:        oneId = rs.getInt(1);
51:        myList.add(new Integer(oneId));
52:      }
```

In the above example, we have built a list of all of the assets available, storing their identifiers. This list is used to repeatedly call the SQL "sum" function to produce our totals, storing the totals back in the original asset record:

```
53:      for (Iterator i = myList.iterator(); i.hasNext();)
54: {
55:        oneInt = (Integer) i.next();
56:        oneId = oneInt.intValue();
57:        s = myConnection.createStatement();
58:        rs = s.executeQuery("SELECT SUM(TrxValue) FROM
59: ASSETTRX "
60:          + "WHERE AssetId = " + oneId);
61:        if (rs.next()) {
62:          String oneTot = rs.getString(1);
63:          Connection myUpdateConnection =
64: dataSource.getConnection();
65:          Statement updateStatement =
66: myUpdateConnection.createStatement();
67:          s.executeUpdate("UPDATE ASSET SET TotalValue = "
68:            + oneTot + " WHERE AssetId = " + oneId);
69:         myUpdateConnection.close();
70:        }
71:      }
...
```

A.4.5 Struts Summary

Struts allows the application problem to be easily decomposed into individual elements, and the Action object maps well to each of these simple elements. The application development process is fast and flexible, and it is easy to understand the mechanisms that should be used at each stage of the process. This is one of Strut's greatest strengths: it is simple enough to understand and apply very quickly, and this shows especially well in this simple application.

Of course, our Struts case study is not ideal – many improvements are immediately obvious. Some of them that would probably be a high priority are:

- **Refactor database actions**: It would not be difficult to combine the operations that delete records, update records, add records, and so forth, resulting in the creation of a more generic and reusable database maintenance service. Parameters can then be used to indicate the table we want to add, update, and so forth. This would reduce the amount of code we have and make it more useful in future projects.

- **Improve Error Handling**: The error handling in our sample is primitive, and is not applied 100 percent consistently. More advanced error handling, including more user-friendly error messages, would probably be a requirement for production use.

- **Functionality Improvements**: A number of functional improvements are obvious, such as taking into account the meaning of the transaction-type field, some controls on the dates and values of the transactions, and so forth.

A.5 CASE STUDY: COCOON

As discussed in Chapter 5, Cocoon is a powerful and flexible Web-application framework. It concentrates on providing XML-based services to its websites and applications: through its generation, transformation, and formatting capabilities, Cocoon serves content from almost any source, including application logic, in almost any desired format.

Cocoon especially shines in situations where the same data needs to be presented in different formats, because the data source can remain constant, cleanly separated from the templates that transform it into appropriate presentation. We do not show this capability well in our simple example, but you do nonetheless see some of the expressive powers of one of Cocoon's capabilities: XSP (eXtensible Server Page).

A.5.1 Installation

The standard installation of the Cocoon framework is normally quite straightforward: it is bundled as a .war file, and can be installed directly into many servlet containers. Our specific installation, with Cocoon 2.0.2 and Tomcat 4.0.3, was slightly more difficult due to some conflicting versions of XML parsers. This is a common problem in frameworks – a framework requires, for example, a specific version of the Xerces XML parser, and the servlet container includes a different one. This causes some strange "class not found"-type messages to appear on startup, and is usually resolved by changing the version used by the servlet container. Theoretically, in the case of the Servlet API 2.3 this problem is solved – the class loader used by the servlet container should be completely independent of that used by the actual Web application, allowing both to run two different versions of the same package. In practice, it is often not quite that cut-and-dried.

Once Cocoon was built according to special instructions for the particular configuration we were using, however, it was installed as a .war file and was immediately made operational. A number of samples are included that allow the installation to be verified as operational.

As part of our specification calls for a secured application, we have used the easiest route to this again: basic authentication via the Tomcat container/server application. It is quite possible to configure Cocoon to perform database-based authentication as well (in fact, it includes an example of just this), but because we use this technique in two of the other Web-application case studies, we stick with the basic authentication for Cocoon. The configuration is identical to that shown for our Struts example, with the exception that the application path is secured.

A.5.2 Design Process

The design process for Cocoon depends to a large degree on which of Cocoon's different techniques you adopt for creating an application. We chose to create the application as a set of XSP pages, so the design concentrated mostly on determining what pages we needed, and the underlying SQL to make the pages interact with the database.

There are at least a couple of other options with Cocoon: possibly better options, as they increase the reusability of our components over the XSP choice.

One option is to use Action objects to perform our database manipulations. Action objects allow the pipeline of a request to be modified dynamically. Run time parameters allow the action to determine the appropriate action to take, and its results are then available to transformers and serializers further down the pipe. Another possibility is to use a custom Generator. Generators are the originators of pipelines, and can create XML from whatever is appropriate – including application logic. More complex applications might prefer to take this approach – we examine this alternative in more detail later in this case study.

A.5.3 Development Process

The development process for the Cocoon example began by configuring Cocoon to access our database. The version of Cocoon we used (2.0.2) contained the option to work with a nontransactional database (by leaving the auto-commit function set to true), but this option was not operating correctly, so we did this one case study with PostgresSQL, another open-source database engine, which does support transactions.

This requires the postgres JDBC driver, downloaded from the Postgres website, to be installed in the WEB-INF/lib directory of the Cocoon Web application. It is also necessary to tell Cocoon to load this class by adding an initial parameter to the Cocoon2 Servlet in the web.xml file (in the WEB-INF directory). In the section specifying the load-class parameter, we added the postgresql.Driver class

web.xml

```
1:    <init-param>
2:      <param-name> load-class</param-name>
3:      <param-value>
4:        <!-- For IBM WebSphere:
5:        com.ibm.servlet.classloader.Handler -->
6:        <!-- For Database Driver: -->
7:        <!-- org.gjt.mm.mysql.Driver -->
8:        postgresql.Driver
9:        <!-- For parent ComponentManager sample:
```

```
10:          org.apache.cocoon.samples.parentcm.Configurator
11:          -->
12:       </param-value>
13:    </init-param>
```

The key line above is line 8 – the remaining lines were already present.

The next stage is to configure a data source to provide the connection to the database itself. This is configured as part of the main Cocoon configuration file: cocoon.xconf. An existing sample data-sources entry can be copied and modified:

cocoon.xconf

```
 1:   <datasources>
 2:     <jdbc logger="core.datasources.personnel"
 3: name="assets">
 4:       <!--
 5:         If you have an Oracle database, and are using the
 6: the
 7:       pool-controller below, you should add the attribute
 8:       "oradb" and set it to true.
 9:       <pool-controller min="5" max="10" oradb="true"/>
10:       That way the test to see if the server has
11: disconnected
12:       the JdbcConnection will function properly.
13:       -->
14:       <pool-controller max="10" min="5"/>
15:       <!--
16:         If you need to ensure an auto-commit is set to
17: true or
18:       false, then create the "auto-commit" element below.
19:       <auto-commit>true</auto-commit>
20:       The default is true.
21:       -->
22:
23: <dburl>jdbc:postgresql://jglobal:5432/assets</dburl
24: >
25:       <user>someuser</user>
```

```
26:         <password>somepassword</password>
27:     </jdbc>
28: </datasources>
```

A.5.4 Finished Application

Every URL handled by Cocoon is "matched" to an appropriate pipeline via the *Sitemap*. We discussed the Sitemap in Chapter 5, and it is the essential starting point for any Cocoon application. In our case, we use XSP, and .xsp files are already "matched" in the Cocoon default site map. Sitemaps can "reference" other sitemaps, creating a hierarchy where a sitemap for a particular "subapplication" can be maintained independently of the top-level sitemap. The primary Cocoon sitemap is in a file called webapps/cocoon/sitemap.xmap, within our Tomcat installation directory. It contains the following reference to the "samples" sub-sitemap:

```
    <map:match pattern="samples/**">
        <map:mount check-reload="yes" src="samples/"
 uri-prefix="samples"/>
    </map:match>
```

These lines indicate that the sub-sitemap is to be checked for changes, and also indicate the URL prefix for our sample applications ("samples"). For simplicity, we have only mapped our application in the primary sitemap – if you were intending to distribute your new application independently, a sub-sitemap would be more appropriate.

The sections relevant to XSP files are in the top-level Cocoon sitemap. First, the generator for XSP files is defined:

```
      <map:generator label="content,data"
 logger="sitemap.generator.serverpages" name="serverpages"
 pool-grow="2" pool-max="32" pool-min="4"
 src="org.apache.cocoon.generation. ServerPagesGenerator'/>
```

This defines the XSP generator with the name "serverpages." The Java object that actually performs the generation is in the class org.apache.cocoon. generation.ServerPagesGenerator. We then see the default pipeline for XSP pages defined further down in the sitemap:

```
<map:match pattern="assets/*">
   <map:generate src="docs/samples/assets/{1}.xsp"
type="serverpages"/>
   <map:transform
```

The line below defines the standard style sheet for transforming the output of an XSP page into HTML.

```
src="stylesheets/dynamic-page2html.xsl">
        <map:parameter name="view-source"
value="docs/samples/assets/{1}.xsp"/>
    </map:transform>
    <map:serialize/>
 </map:match>
```

This defines URLs matching our pattern (assets/*) to have their source in the subdirectory "docs/samples/assets." They use the serverpages generated as defined above, and their output is transformed via the default transformed XSLT and using the style-sheet dynamic-page2html.xsl, which provides basic HTML transformations. The result of this transformation is then serialized – in this case, via the default serializer, which simply writes the HTML to the user's browser.

The finished application for Cocoon consists of the required configuration, which we have shown above, and the XSP files for each of the pages in our application.

An important point to note about our simple Cocoon application is that it is not obvious from the source code that we have adhered to the MVC paradigm of separating logic and presentation. In fact, the XSP pages you see listed here are just logic. What appears to be HTML embedded between the SQL and other logic statements is actually XML markup, which is transformed via a style sheet to create the actual HTML that the browser sees. In our case, the default mapping of XSP output to HTML was used – it is a style sheet built into Cocoon and is called dynamic-page2html.xsl. We could just as easily have mapped our particular XSP pages to another style sheet, to "dress up" the HTML output. This would have allowed us to use "custom" tags in our XSP, for example, to represent common markups for a "look and feel" specific to our site. Even more sophisticated techniques can be used in Cocoon to more explicitly separate the visual presentation from the logic, but this gives you an idea of the basics.

Case Study: Cocoon 413

The primary page in our finished application is navigate.xsp, which provides links to all of the other forms and actions we need:

(See cocoon/navigate.xsp for a complete listing.)

```
...standard pre-amble
    9:    <page>
   10:      <title>Asset Inventory</title>
   11: <content>
   12:      <para>Please Select...</para>
   13:      <para><a href="add-asset">Add Assets</a></para>
   14:      <para><a href="list-assets">List Assets</a></para>
   15:      <br/>
   16:      <para><a href="add-assettrx">Add Asset
   17: Transactions</a>
   18:      <para><a href="list-assettrx">List Asset
   19: Transactions</a></para>
   20:      <br/>
   21:      <para><a href="calculate">Calculate Asset
   22: Values</a></para>
   23:    </content>
   24:    </page>
...
```

We access this page with the following URL:

```
http://localhost:8080/cocoon/assets/navigate
```

This page simply provides a set of links to our other functions – it performs no logic on its own. The logic pages include one for each of the actions, beginning with addition of new assets. The XSP below prompts for the one field we need to enter to define a new asset – the description – and passes this on to another page that interacts with the database:

(See cocoon/add-asset.xsp for a complete listing.)

```
...
    7:    <title>Add New Asset</title>
    8:    <content>
    9:    <form action="process-add-asset" method="POST">
   10:      <input name="process" type="hidden" value="Add"/>
```

```
11:     <para>Asset Description:
12:       <input name="descrip" type="text"/>
13:     </para>
14:     <input type="submit" value="Add"/>
15:   </form>
16: </content>
17: <para>
18:   <a href="navigate">Back to the main page</a>
19: </para>
```
...

Our process-add-asset.xsp page actually calls the database to add the new record, and confirms the result:

(See cocoon/process-add-asset.xsp for a full listing.)

...
```
 9: <xsp:logic>
10:   String descrip = null;
11:   int currId = -1;
12: </xsp:logic>
13: <page>
14:   <xsp:logic>
15:     descrip = <xsp-request:get-parameter name="descrip"/>;
16:   </xsp:logic>
17:   <title>Add Asset Processed</title>
18:   <content>
```

We establish a connection to the data source called "assets," as defined in our configuration:

```
19: <esql:connection>
20:   <esql:pool>assets</esql:pool>
21:   <esql:execute-query>
22:     <esql:query>
```

First, we establish the current maximum asset id. It is possible to rely on the database to assign this serial number, but doing so might not be portable across all databases.

Case Study: Cocoon

```
23:      select max(id) as maxid from asset
24:    </esql:query>
25:      <esql:results>
26:     <esql:row-results>
27:      <xsp:logic>
28:        currId = <esql:get-int column="maxid"/>;
29:      </xsp:logic>
30:       <esql:execute-query>
31:         <esql:query>
32:          insert into asset (id, descrip) values (
33:
34: (<esql:parameter><xsp:expr>currId</xsp:expr></esql:
    parameter
35: > + 1),
36:
37: <esql:parameter><xsp:expr>descrip</xsp:expr></esql:
    parameter
38: >
39:         )
40:         </esql:query>
41:        </esql:execute-query>
42:     </esql:row-results>
43:       </esql:results>
44:     </esql:execute-query>
45:   </esql:connection>
...
```

The same technique is used for adding asset transactions, with add-assettrx.xsp having the form:

(See the file cocoon/add-assettrx.xsp for a full listing.)

```
...
  9:    <form action="process-assettrx" method="POST">
 10:      <input name="process" type="hidden" value="Add"/>
 11:      <para>Asset ID: <input name="id" type="text"/></para>
 12:      <para>Transaction Type:
 13:        <input name="trxtype" type="text"/>
 14:      </para>
...repeat for remaining fields.
```

```
21:        <input type="submit" value="Add"/>
22:    </form>
```
...

This form passes on its request to process-add-assettrx.xsp in turn:
(See the file process-add-assettrx.xsp for a full listing.)

...
```
11:    String id = null;
12:    String trxdate = null;
13:    String trxtype = null;
14:    String trxvalue = null;
```
...

In the lines below, we access the parameters passed with the POST request from the previous form:

```
17:    <xsp:logic>
18:
19:      id = <xsp-request:get-parameter name="id"/>;
20:      trxdate = <xsp-request:get-parameter name="trxdate"/>;
21:      trxtype = <xsp-request:get-parameter name="trxtype"/>;
22:      trxvalue = <xsp-request:get-parameter
23: name="trxvalue"/>;
24:    </xsp:logic>
25:    <title><xsp:expr>process</xsp:expr> Asset Transaction
26: Processed</title>
27:    <content>
28:      <esql:connection>
29:        <esql:pool>assets</esql:pool>
30:      <esql:execute-query>
31:        <esql:query>
32:          .insert into assettrx (id, trxdate, trxtype,
33: trxvalue) values (
34:
35: <esql:parameter><xsp:expr>id</xsp:expr></esql: parameter>,
36:
37: <esql:parameter><xsp:expr>trxdate</xsp:expr></esql:
    parameter
```

Case Study: Cocoon   417

```
38: >,
39:
40: <esql:parameter><xsp:expr>trxtype</xsp:expr></esql:
    parameter
41: >,
42:
43: <esql:parameter><xsp:expr>trxvalue</xsp:expr></esql:
    paramete
44: r>)
45:     </esql:query>
46:    </esql:execute-query>
47:   </esql:connection>
```
...

These pages give us the "add" capability we need. Now we need similar pages for listing and editing assets and their transactions:
(See the file cocoon/list-assets.xsp for a full listing.)

```
...
 9:    String prefix = "asset?id=";
10:    String assetID = null;
...
14:      <esql:connection>
15:       <esql:pool>assets</esql:pool>
16:        <esql:execute-query>
17:         <esql:query>select id, descrip, totalvalue
18: from asset order by id</esql:query>
19:          <esql:results>
20:           <table border="1">
21:            <tr>
22:             <th>Asset Id</th>
```
...other headings
```
27:            </tr>
```

We use the "row-results" tag to specify that a row is added to our table for each record retrieved from the database:

```
28:           <esql:row-results>
29:            <xsp:logic>
```

```
30:            assetID = <esql:get-string
31: column="id"/>;
32:        </xsp:logic>
33:        <tr>
34:        <td><esql:get-string column="id"/></td>
35:
36:        <td><esql:get-string
37: column="descrip"/></td>
38:        <td><esql:get-string
39: column="totalvalue"/></td>
40:        <td>
41:          <A>
42:           <xsp:attribute name="href">
43:           asset?id=
44:           <xsp:expr>assetID</xsp:expr>
45:           </xsp:attribute>
46:           Edit Asset
47:          </A>
48:        </td>
49:        <td>
50:          <A>
51:           <xsp:attribute name="href">
52:           process-delete-asset?id=
53:           <xsp:expr>assetID</xsp:expr>
54:           </xsp:attribute>
55:           Delete Asset
56:          </A>
57:        </td>
58:        </tr>
59:        </esql:row-results>
60:        </table>
...
```

The list-assets page displays a link alongside each of the asset records that allows us to call an update or delete function. Updates are very simple, because there is only one asset field that can be directly updated: the description. We do require, however, a form to key in the new description, or edit the old one; so, the first XSP simply presents the following form:

Case Study: Cocoon

(See the file cocoon/asset.xsp for a full listing.)

...
```
 9:     String assetID = request.getParameter("id");
10:     String descrip = null;
11:     String totalvalue = null;
```
...

First, we access the existing asset record so that we can display its current information,

...
```
16:    <esql:query>select id, descrip, totalvalue
17:         from asset
18:         where id =
19: <xsp:expr>assetID</xsp:expr></esql:query>
20:      <esql:results>
21:       <esql:row-results>
22:         <xsp:logic>
23:           descrip = <esql:get-string column="descrip"/>;
24:         </xsp:logic>
25:         <xsp:logic>
26:           totalvalue = <esql:get-string
27: column="totalvalue"/>;
28:         </xsp:logic>
29:    </esql:row-results>
```
...

and then, we display the update form for the user to make changes.

```
33:    <title>Update Asset</title>
34:    <content>
35:     <form action="process-update-asset" method="POST"
36: name="AssetEntry">
37:       <input type="hidden" name="id">
38:       <xsp:attribute name="value">
39:         <xsp:expr>assetID</xsp:expr>
40:       </xsp:attribute>
```

```
41:        </input>
42:        <para>Asset Id:
43:        <xsp:expr>assetID</xsp:expr>
44:        </para>
45:        <para>Asset Description:
46:          <input name="descrip" type="text">
47:            <xsp:attribute name="value">
48:              <xsp:expr>descrip</xsp:expr>
49:            </xsp:attribute>
50:          </input>
51:        </para>
52:        <para>Asset Value:
53:          <xsp:expr>totalvalue</xsp:expr>
54:        </para>
55:        <input type="submit" name="cocoon-action- Update"
56: value="Update"/>
...
```

The update form calls our XSP that actually performs the database update, just like add:
(See cocoon/process-update-asset.xsp for a full listing.)

```
...
  15:    descrip = request.getParameter("descrip");
  16:    id = request.getParameter("id");
...
  23:        <esql:query>
  24:          update asset set descrip =
  25: <esql:parameter><xsp:expr>descrip</xsp:expr></esql:
      parameter
  26: >
  27:          where id =
  28: <esql:parameter><xsp:expr>id</xsp:expr></esql: parameter>
  29:        </esql:query>
...
```

Deletion is equally simple – the asset identifier is passed to an XSP that calls the database to remove the record and any related transaction records.

Case Study: Cocoon

(See cocoon/process-delete-asset.xsp for a full listing.)

```
...
  22:      <esql:query>
  23:      delete from assettrx
  24:      where id =
  25: <esql:parameter><xsp:expr>id</xsp:expr></esql: parameter>
  26:      </esql:query>
  27:      </esql:execute-query>
  28:    </esql:connection>
  29:    <esql:connection>
  30:      <esql:pool>assets</esql:pool>
  31:      <esql:execute-query>
  32:        <esql:query>
  33:          delete from asset
  34:          where id =
  35: <esql:parameter><xsp:expr>id</xsp:expr></esql: parameter>
  36:          </esql:query>
...
```

The sequence for editing asset transactions is identical to that for assets, except that there are more fields to deal with. We start with our listing form, which has the "edit" and "delete" links just like our asset listing form:

(See cocoon/list-assettrx.xsp for a complete listing.)

```
...
  16:      <esql:execute-query>
  17:        <esql:query>select id, trxdate, trxtype,
  18: trxvalue from assettrx order by trxdate</esql:query>
  19:        <esql:results>
  20:          <table border="1">
  21:          <tr>
  22:          <th>Asset Id</th>
...headers for other fields
  28:          </tr>
  29:          <esql:row-results>
  30:          <tr>
  31:          <td><esql:get-string column="id"/></td>
```

```
 32:
 33:        <xsp:logic>
 34:         id = <esql:get-string column="id"/>;
 35:        </xsp:logic>
 36:        <td><esql:get-string
 37: column="trxdate"/></td>
 38:        <td><esql:get-string
 39: column="trxtype"/></td>
 40:        <td><esql:get-string
 41: column="trxvalue"/></td>
 42:        <xsp:logic>
 43:          tdate = <esql:get-string
 44: column="trxdate"/>;
 45:        </xsp:logic>
 46:        <td>
 47:          <A>
 48:            <xsp:attribute name="href">
 49:             assettrx?id=
 50:             <xsp:expr>id</xsp:expr>
 51:
 52: & trxdate=<xsp:expr>tdate</xsp:expr>
 53:            </xsp:attribute>
 54:            Edit
 55:          </A>
 56:        </td>
 57:        <td>
...repeat for "delete" action
 71:    </esql:results>
...
```

These two pages have links for each asset or asset transaction to allow us to proceed to the pages for editing and deleting assets or transactions. On selecting "edit," we are led to our asset transaction edit form:

(See cocoon/assettrx.xsp for a full listing.)

```
...
 17:    <esql:query>select id, trxdate, trxtype, trxvalue
 18:       from assettrx
 19:       where id =
```

Case Study: Cocoon

```
20:    <xsp:expr>assetID</xsp:expr></esql:query>
21:         and trxdate = <xsp:expr>trxdate</xsp:expr>
22:    <esql:results>
23:      <esql:row-results>
24:        <xsp:logic>trxvalue = <esql:get-string
25: column="trxvalue"/>;</xsp:logic>
26:        <xsp:logic>trxtype = <esql:get-string
27: column="trxtype"/>;</xsp:logic>
28:      </esql:row-results>
29:    </esql:results>
...
32:    <title>Edit Asset Transaction</title>
33:    <content>
34:      <form action="process-update-assettrx" method="POST">
35:      <para>Asset Id:
36:        <xsp:expr>assetID</xsp:expr>
37:        <input type="hidden" name="id">
38:         <xsp:attribute name="value">
39:           <xsp:expr>assetID</xsp:expr>
40:         </xsp:attribute>
41:        </input>
42: </para>
43:
...repeat for remaining fields
65:        <xsp:logic>
66:         <input type="submit" name="cocoon-action-Update"
67: value="Update"/>
68:        </xsp:logic>
...
```

and then to our asset update page itself:
(See cocoon/process-update-assettrx.xsp for a full listing.)

```
...
17:    id = request.getParameter("id");
18:    trxdate = request.getParameter("trxdate");
19:    trxtype = request.getParameter("trxtype");
20:    trxvalue = request.getParameter("trxvalue");
...
```

```
27:      <esql:query>
28:        update assettrx set trxtype =
29: <esql:parameter><xsp:expr>trxtype</xsp:expr></esql:
    parameter
30: >,
31:          trxvalue =
32: <esql:parameter><xsp:expr>trxvalue</xsp:expr></esql:
    paramete
33: r>
34:        where id =
35: <esql:parameter><xsp:expr>id</xsp:expr></esql: parameter>
36:        and trxdate =
37: <esql:parameter><xsp:expr>trxdate</xsp:expr></esql:
    parameter
38: >
39:      </esql:query>
...
```

"Delete" is again equally straightforward. Note that we must pass all of the parts of the combination key to delete only the one transaction – just as in the update.

(See cocoon/process-delete-assettrx.xsp for a complete listing.)

```
...
21: <esql:execute-query>
22:    <esql:query>
23:      delete from asset
24:      where id =
25: <esql:parameter><xsp:expr>id</xsp:expr></esql: parameter>
26:    </esql:query>
27: </esql:execute-query>
...
```

The pages we have seen so far provide – albeit in a very simple and rather repetitive way – all of the database maintenance we need for our application. Now we consider the calculate operation, which sums up the asset transactions and updates the asset master records with the results. This takes the form of a single page that calls the database directly to create the required totals:

Case Study: Cocoon

(See cocoon/calculate.xsp for a complete listing.)

...
```
  25: <esql:query>
  26:    select id from asset
  27: </esql:query>
```
...
```
  30:    <!-- for each asset -->
```
...
```
  32:         currId = <esql:get-string column="id"/>;
```
...
```
  37:          <esql:query>
  38:             select sum(trxvalue) as tot from
  39: assettrx
  40:             where id =
  41: <esql:parameter><xsp:expr>currId</xsp:expr></esql:
      parameter>
  42:          </esql:query>
  43:          <esql:results>
  44:          <esql:row-results>
  45:             <xsp:logic>
  46:                currentTotal = <esql:get-float
  47: column="tot"/>;
  48:             </xsp:logic>
  49:          </esql:row-results>
  50:          </esql:results>
  51:        </esql:execute-query>
  52:        </esql:connection>

  53:        <para>Asset <xsp:expr>currId</xsp:expr>,
  54: Total <xsp:expr>currentTotal</xsp:expr></para>

  55:                 <!-- now update the asset -->
```
...
```
  59:                    <esql:query>
  60:                       update asset set totalvalue =
  61: <esql:parameter><xsp:expr>currentTotal</xsp:expr></esql:
      para
  62: meter>
  63:                       where id =
```

```
64: <esql:parameter><xsp:expr>currId</xsp:expr>
    </esql:parameter>
65:                                 </esql:query>
...
```

A.5.5 Cocoon Summary

Our Cocoon application so far is actually a comparatively poor example of the benefits that can be derived from this powerful framework. It is, however, what a new Cocoon user might actually write in an attempt to fulfill the specifications, and it in fact does the job.

What is poor about it is that there is not enough separation of application logic from at least the core elements of the presentation – they both are in the same XSP page. Indeed, a skilled JSP developer with a bit of familiarity in SQL could produce the same application with JSP just as easily. In fact, if you compare our Cocoon solution using XSP with the Struts case study, you can find a great similarity. Other than the use of the Action objects in Struts, which provides better separation of logic and presentation, the two are quite similar. In the case of Cocoon, an XSP page is used for each of the "actions." Of course, the Cocoon application has the advantage of being somewhat separated from its actual presentation – it would not be difficult to define a separate style sheet that would allow this entire application to be accessed via WML, rather than via HTML, or to change the "look" of all of the generated pages by altering a few lines in a style sheet. These kinds of changes would not be as easy with JSP.

We can, however, do better – by digging into Cocoon a little deeper, we find that application logic can, in fact, be introduced at several different points in the framework. XSP is just one of them, and although it may be the most convenient, it is not necessarily the most powerful. One step towards improvement would be to use the equivalent of tag libraries in JSP – logicsheets. Logicsheets allow us to put the application logic into separate XSP files, and then reuse these logicsheets as required in our application. Another option for a refactored version of our example could be the use of Cocoon's Action objects, providing for a complete separation of the database access logic and the presentation.

Of course, the functional and other improvements that we discussed for the previous case study could also be applied to our Cocoon version. Cocoon's latest version includes, for example, an advanced form-handling capability,

XMLForm, which would permit basic validation to be introduced by creating simple configuration entries.

A.6 CASE STUDY: EXPRESSO

Now we examine our case study created in yet a different complete-application framework: Expresso.

A.6.1 Installation

The path of least resistance for Expresso's installation involved downloading the "Expresso Complete" download bundle. Packaged as a .jar file, this file is un-jar-ed into a suitable directory, and includes Expresso, its administrative interface, a copy of Tomcat 4.0 preconfigured for Expresso, and a Hypersonic database engine, which is also preconfigured.

To meet our case study parameters of using MySQL, we had to do the following:

- Install the mysql driver: involved only copying the mysql_comp.jar file to the webapps/expresso/WEB-INF/lib directory.
- Configure the connection for Expresso: this is accomplished by editing the expresso-config.xml file in webapps/expresso/WEB-INF/config, and adding a section such as:

expresso-config.xml

```
<context name="inventory">
  <description>Case Study<description>
  <jdbc
    driver="org.gjt.mm.mysql.Driver"
    url="jdbc:mysql://localhost/inventory"
    connectFormat="4"
    login="root"
    password=""
    cache="y" />
  <type-mapping>
    <java-type>>LONGVARCHAR<java-type>
    <db-type>text<db-type>
```

```
    <type-mapping>
    <images>%context%/%expresso-dir%/images<images>
    <startJobHandler>y<startJobHandler>
    <showStackTrace>y<showStackTrace>
</context>
```

This section is a duplicate of an example context provided in the file, with a new name (inventory) and the configuration for MySQL instead of the included Hypersonic. Documentation for a number of database engines is provided on the Expresso website.

After this configuration, Expresso is started along with Tomcat by running the "startup.sh" script in the "bin" subdirectory. A number of additional messages are seen in the regular Tomcat startup sequence, confirming that both Expresso and Struts have initialized properly.

A.6.2 Design Process

The design process for the Expresso version of the case study begins with a Schema object, which "defines" the new application being created. A portion of the Schema object, called AssetSchema, is shown below in the Finished Application section.

The other two major objects we use in designing our Expresso asset program are *DBObjects* and *Controller* objects. DBObjects are used to define our persistent objects, namely assets and asset transactions, and Controller objects are used to define the logic of our application.

A.6.3 Development Process

To create the Expresso application, we started by generating default code from a related project: WebAppWriter, which can be found at www.webappwriter.com. The downloaded code included a Schema object, two DBMaint objects, and a Controller object. We then customized these objects to meet the specification exactly, and to incorporate the calculation logic, which is not generated for us.

A.6.4 Finished Application

The finished application for Expresso consists of a relatively small number of source files, and a few customized JSP files as the user interface/navigation

Case Study: Expresso

capability. The default for user interface in Expresso is to use Struts-enabled JSP pages, so this is what we have used in this instance. We assume we are using Expresso's own built-in authorization (Login) and authentication (Security) modules. Let us examine the results:

The first file is the Schema for our new application. This is the hub that defines the other objects we will use, and it also defines a few essential settings for our new application.

(See expresso/AssetSchema.java for a complete listing.)

```
...
  29: public class AssetSchema extends Schema {
...
```

We define the two DBObjects and the one Controller object we will use in our application:

```
  36: add(new Asset());
  37: add(new AssetTrx());
  38: add(new CalculateTotals());
...standard code for setting up security, etc.
```

Now let us examine the two Database Object definitions created for this application: one defines the asset master object and the other defines the asset transactions:

(See expresso/Asset.java for a full listing.)

```
...
   23: public class Asset extends SecuredDBObject {
...
   25:     public static final String FLD_AssetId = "AssetId";
   26:     public static final String FLD_DESCRIP= "Descrip";
   27:     public static final String FLD_TotalValue =
   28: "TotalValue";
...
   50:     /**
   51:      * Method called when the record is added - allows us to
   52: specify default values
   53:      *
   54:      * @throws DBException
```

```
 55:        */
 56:       public void add() throws DBException {
 57:           setField("TotalValue", "0");
 58:           setField("AddedOn", DateTime.getDateTimeForDB());
 59:           setField("UpdatedOn", DateTime.getDateTimeForDB());
 60:           super.add();
 61:       }/* add() */
...
 77:       public void setupFields() throws DBException {
 78:           setTargetTable("Asset");
 79:           setDescription("Asset");
 80:           setCharset("ISO-8859-1");
...
 82:           addField(FLD_AssetId, "auto-inc", 0, false, "Asset
 83: Identifier");
 84:           addField(FLD_DESCRIP, "varchar", 80, true,
 85: "Description");
 86:           addField(FLD_TotalValue, "double", 0, false, "Total
 87: Value");
 88:           addField("AddedOn", "datetime", 0, true, "Added
 89: On");
 90:           addField("UpdatedOn", "datetime", 0, true, "Updated
 91: On");
 92:           setReadOnly(FLD_TotalValue);
 93:           setReadOnly("AddedOn");
 94:           setReadOnly("UpdatedOn");
 95:
 96:           addKey("AssetId");
...
104:       public void update() throws DBException {
105:           setField("UpdatedOn", DateTime.getDateTimeForDB());
106:           super.update();
107:       }/* update() */
...
```

The "meat" in the above DBObject is in the setupFields() method. This is where the fields that the DBObject maintains are specified, and special conditions are placed on some fields such as the "auto-inc" for the Asset ID field, indicating that it will be an automatic incrementing sequential number. The

Case Study: Expresso

other interesting parts are the add() and update() methods, where the normal add method is extended to set the last update date and time fields. The rest of the DBObject is "standard," generally, although further customization is always possible if required.

Now let us look at the detail object, the Asset Transactions themselves:
(See expresso/AssetTrx.java for a complete listing.)

```
...
  23: public class AssetTrx extends SecuredDBObject {
  24:    public static final String FLD_AssetId= "AssetId";
  25:    public static final String FLD_TRXDATE= "TrxDate";
  26:    public static final String FLD_TRXTYPE= "TrxType";
  27:    public static final String FLD_TrxValue = "TrxValue";
...
  54:    public void add() throws DBException {
  55:        setField("AddedOn", DateTime.getDateTimeForDB());
  56:        setField("UpdatedOn", DateTime.getDateTimeForDB());
...
  69:    public Vector getValidValues(String fieldName) throws
  70: DBException {
  71:        Vector myValues = new Vector(4);
  72:        if (fieldName.equals("TrxType")) {
  73:            myValues.addElement(new ValidValue("Acquire",
  74: "Acquire"));
  75:            myValues.addElement(new ValidValue(" Dispose",
  76: " Dispose"));
  77:            myValues.addElement(new ValidValue("
  78: Depreciate", " Depreciate"));
  79:        return myValues;
  80:        }
  81:        return super.getValidValues(fieldName);
...
  88:    public void setupFields() throws DBException {
  89:       setTargetTable("AssetTrx");
  90:       setDescription("AssetTrx");
  91:       setCharset("ISO-8859-1");
  92:
  93:       addField(FLD_AssetId, "int", 0, false, "Asset');
  94:       addField(FLD_TRXDATE, "datetime", 0, false,
```

```
 95: "Transaction Date");
 96:        addField(FLD_TRXTYPE, "char", 1, false,
 97: "Transaction Type");
 98:        addField(FLD_TrxValue, "double", 0, false,
 99: "Transaction Value");
100:
101:        addField("AddedOn", "datetime", 0, true, "Added
102: On");
103:        addField("UpdatedOn", "datetime", 0, true, "Updated
104: On");
105:        setReadOnly("AddedOn");
106:        setReadOnly("UpdatedOn");
107:
108:        addKey("AssetId");
109:        addKey("TrxDate");
110:        setMultiValued("TrxType");
111: }
...
118:    public void update() throws DBException {
119:
120:        setField("UpdatedOn", DateTime.getDateTimeForDB());
121:        super.update();
...
```

The final class created was to implement the logic (the calculation of values) of our application, and was an extension of Expresso's DBController class. The controller is invoked via a special URL that we will see used on our JSP pages. This particular controller only has a single state, because it does only one thing. The state, or the method that performs the logic, is "internal," that is, it is part of the Controller class itself – often these States are contained in external State objects in a more complex application.

(See expresso/CalculateTotals.java for a full listing.)

```
...
 25: public class CalculateTotals extends DBController {
...
 30:    public CalculateTotals() {
 31:
```

Case Study: Expresso

```
32:        setSchema("com.yourcompany.assets.AssetSchema');
33:
34:        State calc = new State("calc", "Calculate Totals");
35:        addState(calc);
36:        setInitialState("calc");
...
52:     public void runCalcState(ControllerRequest req,
53: ControllerResponse res) throws ControllerException {
54:        try {
...prepare and access a list of transactions
65:            for (Iterator eachAsset
66:                =
67: assetList.searchAndRetrieveList().iterator();
68:                eachAsset.hasNext(); ) {
69:
70:                oneAsset = (Asset) eachAsset.next();
71:
72:                trx.clear();
73:                trx.setField(AssetTrx.FLD_AssetId,
74:                    oneAsset.getField(Asset. FLD_AssetId));
75:
76:                /* Now get the asset transactions total */
77:                oneTotal = trx.sum("TrxValue");
78:
79:                oneAsset.setField(Asset. FLD_TotalValue, new
80: Double(oneTotal).toString());
81:                oneAsset.update();
82:                updatedCount++;
83:            }
84:
85:            res.addOutput(new Output("Updated " +
86: updatedCount + " assets."));
...
```

Having created and compiled all of these objects, we then proceeded to the installation/configuration process. This consisted of "registering" our Schema object on the "Applications" page of Expresso. We then ran the "Create/Verify

Database Structure and Perform Initial Setup" link from Expresso's "Setup" page – this generated the appropriate tables in the MySQL database. One observation was that a lot more of the configuration and setup for Expresso was done within the Web browser than outside the browser with the command line, which was more common with the other frameworks.

Once the database was generated and the Schema object was registered, we turned our attention to creating a simple navigation scheme, because this was part of our specification. By copying some simple JSP pages from Expresso's eForum example application, we created a basic frame-set and a single page to access all of the applications' functionality.

Taking the path of least resistance, setting up a user interface for our new application involved editing a JSP file to customize the "menu" copied from another Expresso application:

(See toc.jsp for a complete listing.)

```
...standard pre-amble
  11:    Vector tocContents = new Vector();
  12:    tocContents.addElement("Asset Data|Maintain Asset
  13: Tables|" + contextPath
  14:        + "/assets.jsp");
  15:    tocContents.addElement("Calculate Totals|Calculate Asset
  16: Total Values|"
  17:        + "/expresso/assets/CalculateTotals.do");
  18: %>
...
```

We then customized one more page, using some special-purpose JSP tags to provide navigation links to the database editing capabilities for our two database tables:

(See the file expresso/assets.jsp for a full listing.)

```
...
  24: <p class="jc-pageheader">Asset Inventory Data <a
  25: href="help/assets.html" target="new"><img src="<%= images
  26: %>/help.png" alt="General Help about Asset Inventory"
  27: border="0"></A></p>
  28:
  29: <table align="center" border="1" cellpadding="2"
  30: cellspacing="0" bordercolordark="#008080"
```

Case Study: Expresso

```
31: bordercolorlight="#FFCC33">
32:     <expresso:TableHead
33: value="Item|List|Add|Search|Help"/>
34:
35:     <expresso:DBMaint
36: dbobj="com.yourcompany.assets.dbobj.Asset" label="Assets"
37: help="help/assets.html"/>
38:     <expresso:DBMaint
39: dbobj="com.yourcompany.assets.dbobj.AssetTrx" label="Asset
40: Transactions" help="help/assettrx.html"/>
...
```

We must also "register" our new Controller object with Struts, so that it can be accessed via a particular URL pattern from our new user interface. This involves creating a new assets-config.xml file and placing it in the WEB-INF/config directory. Expresso's configuration system loads all XML files that match the appropriate DTD on startup, so just having the file in the right directory is enough – it need not be listed anywhere else.

To create our mapping file, we edited a copy of the example application configuration file, substituting our own mapping:

(*See assets-config.xml.*)

```
 1: <?xml version="1.0" encoding="ISO-8859-1"?>
 2: <!DOCTYPE struts-config PUBLIC "-//Apache Software
 3: Foundation//DTD Struts Configuration 1.0//EN"
 4:
 5: "http://jakarta.apache.org/struts/dtds/struts-config_1_0.
    dtd
 6: ">
 7: <struts-config>
 8:   <action-mappings>
 9:     <!-- Calculate Totals -->
10:     <action path="/assets/CalculateTotals"
11: type="com.yourcompany.assets.controller.Calculate Totals"
12: scope="request" name="default" validate="false">
13:     </action>
14:   </action-mappings>
15: </struts-config>
```

As we have only one mapping in our application, the file is very simple. We make use of the default mapping in Expresso for the remainder of the actions our applications need to take – such as database maintenance.

If we install our finished application in a default Expresso installation, it can be invoked by going to the URL

```
http://localhost:8080/expresso/components/assets/frame.jsp.
```

This takes us to a frame-set that shows our menu on the left-hand side. Our first menu choice (Asset Data) brings up a page that gives us access to add, update, search for and delete both Asset and Asset Transaction data. Our second choice (Calculate Totals) immediately invokes the Controller we wrote above, and produces a simple confirmation page that tells us that processing is complete. We can then view the totals by listing the Asset master records and viewing the newly calculated fields.

A.6.5 Expresso Summary

Our Expresso application is a good example of the kind of application to which Expresso lends itself very well. The framework is highly database oriented, and provides robust services in this area. Because a lot of our functionality in this example comprises database maintenance, the ability to use Expresso's built-in database maintenance logic eliminates the need to do much coding. Another, more logic-oriented application might require more Controller objects to be created. We might also wish to customize the user interface more extensively than we have, and would create custom JSP pages as "views" for database maintenance than simply using the defaults provided by the framework.

Some of the other possible improvements to our simple application might include better validation and error handling, in addition to any other core features that an expanded design might demand.

A.7 CASE STUDY: TURBINE

Now we create our case study application again, this time using the powerful Turbine-application framework. As seen in Chapter 5, Turbine provides not only flexible user interface support, but also a highly capable object/relational mapping layer. We see the advantages this brings to our example.

A.7.1 Installation

Installation of Turbine entails downloading the Turbine Development Kit (TDK), which is a bundle of Turbine and Tomcat setup and preconfigured to allow for easy installation of the development environment. This file is supplied as a .tar.gz or a .zip archive, and is un-tar-ed into an appropriate directory. The TDK 2.1 was used for our example.

A.7.2 Design Process

In Turbine, application logic is contained by *Screen* and *Action* objects – for our application, we need a number of screens: to add, edit, and list Assets, and to Add, edit and List Asset Transactions. In addition, we need logic to calculate the current asset value.

The default user interface choice in Turbine (although several are available) consists of Velocity templates. We create a template to list, edit, and add each of our persistent objects, at a minimum. The path of least resistance, when learning Velocity, is to modify existing templates, using them as a starting point, and expanding until we have the "view" we require.

A.7.3 Development Process

Using the instructions on the default page in the TDK, the development process begins by generating the application skeleton.

- In the TDK's root directory, we first edit the *newapp.props* file, changing the turbine.app.name to "inventory" and the turbine.app.type to "peer" (because we use a database to store our persistent objects).
- The target.package was set to com.jglobal.turbine.inventory and the target.directory was set to com/jglobal/turbine/inventory.
- Then we execute ./newapp.sh inventory, which creates the skeleton of the new application automatically. When this process completes, it refers you to a GETTING_STARTED.txt file in the newly generated web-app's directory for instructions on how to proceed.
- As directed by this file, we then edited the ./project/inventory.properties file. The only change required in our case (because we were using the default MySQL database) was to set the password and user name for access to the database.

- In addition to the inventory.properties file, there is an inventory-schema.xml file present in the project subdirectory. This file can be edited to specify the database tables and fields required by our new application. The Turbine subproject Torque is then able to automatically generate the appropriate object/relational mapping classes for our new application. We populated this file appropriately, using the example RDF table to work, and created two database tables: an Asset table and an AssetTrx (Asset Transaction) table.
- We had to remove a couple of DOCTYPE lines from XML files, because the system on which we were building the application did not have Internet access – this is a problem that sometimes crops up using DTD that refers to a URL, because the XML parser tries to access the site referred to in order to read the DTD.
- At this point it was necessary to restart the servlet engine. (The instructions do not mention this, but unless class reloading is enabled it is always a good policy after application changes.)
- Then we browse the

    ```
    http://localhost:8080/inventory/servlet/inventory
    ```

    URL. This brings up the Turbine Data Manager page for the newly generated sample application.

Now that we have a sample to work on, the customization of this sample into our finished Turbine application can begin:

- First, we added new Velocity templates to the templates/screens subdirectory for our Asset and Asset Transaction tables. They began as a copy of the default generated templates and were modified to suit, retaining the same basic look and feel.
- We then added macro code to the DefaultBottom.vm template in the templates/navigation directory to provide links to our new tables. These links are used as navigation in all pages in our new application.

For each of the new tables, we need to extend VelocityScreen to create a screen class. In the /WEB-INF/src/java/com/jglobal/turbine/inventory/modules/screens directory, we add AssetForm.java and AssetTrxForm.java, again starting from the example code as a basis.

A.7.4 Finished Application

The completed application consists of a number of objects, most of which were generated more or less automatically by the Torque subproject of Turbine: in the "modules/actions" package within our application, there are two "Action" objects that handle the actual interaction with the database, one for each of our persistent objects. These actions are then called by the Velocity templates when specific commands are issued by the user on clicking a button.

(See turbine/AssetSQL.java for a full listing.)

```
...
  100: public class AssetSQL extends VelocityAction
  101: {
...
  112:    public void doInsert(RunData data, Context context)
  113:       throws Exception
  114:    {
  115:      Asset entry = new Asset();
  116:      data.getParameters().setProperties(entry);
  117:      entry.save();
  118:    }
...
  128:    public void doUpdate(RunData data, Context context)
  129:       throws Exception
  130:    {
  131:      Asset entry = new Asset();
  132:      data.getParameters().setProperties(entry);
  133:      entry.setModified(true);
  134:      entry.setNew(false);
  135:      entry.save();
  136:    }
...
  141:    public void doDelete(RunData data, Context context)
  142:       throws Exception
  143:    {
  144:      Criteria criteria = new Criteria();
  145:      criteria.add(AssetPeer.ASSETID,
  146: data.getParameters().getInt("assetid"));
  147:      AssetPeer.doDelete(criteria);
```

```
148:   }
...
153:   public void doPerform(RunData data, Context context)
154:     throws Exception
155:   {
156:     data.setMessage("Can't find the button!");
157:   }
...
```

Please note that in source file listings we omit the license preamble at the top of the file for brevity – however, each actual source file should contain the license in full.

In the AssettrxSQL.java source below, you can see the minor changes that specify the appropriate Peer object to be used for database access for asset transactions instead of assets.

(See turbine/AssettrxSQL.java for the complete listing.)

```
...
  15: public class AssettrxSQL extends VelocityAction
...
  27:      public void doInsert(RunData data, Context context)
...
  43:      public void doUpdate(RunData data, Context context)
...
  56:      public void doDelete(RunData data, Context context)
...
  70:      public void doPerform(RunData data, Context context)
...
```

The "modules/actions" package also contains some default actions created by the code generation phase, including LoginUser, LogoutUser, SQL, and SecureAction classes. These default files were not altered, and were not used by our example application.

The "actions/screens" package contains the "Screen" classes, one for each of our Velocity templates. Templates are located (by default) in the "templates" subdirectory of the Web-application root directory. The first template is the Asset form, which is used for both initial input and updates to the Asset records themselves.

Case Study: Turbine

(See turbine/AssetForm.java for the complete listing.)

```
...
 19: public class AssetForm extends VelocityScreen
...
 26:     public void doBuildTemplate( RunData data, Context
 27: context )
...
 31:         int entry_id =
 32: data.getParameters().getInt("ASSETID");
 33:         Criteria criteria = new Criteria();
 34:         criteria.add(AssetPeer.ASSETID, entry_id);
 35:         Asset asset = (Asset)
 36: AssetPeer.doSelect(criteria).elementAt(0);
 37:         System.err.println("Here");
 38:         context.put("new", new Boolean(false));
 39:         context.put("entry", asset);
...
```

This action is associated (by its name) with the AssetForm.vm template, shown below:

(See turbine/AssetForm.vm for a complete listing.)

```
  1: $page.setTitle("Add Asset")
... standard HTML pre-amble
  7: <form method="post"
  8: action="$link.setPage("ListAssets.vm").setAction("AssetSQL")
  9: ">
 10:   <div align="left">
 11:     <table bgcolor="#ffffff" cellpadding="5">
 12:       #if ($new)
 13:         #formRow ("Descrip" "Descrip" $!entry.Descrip)
 14:       #else
 15:         #headerCell ("Asset Id")
 16:         #entryCell ($entry.Assetid)
 17:         #formRow ("Descrip" "Descrip" $!entry.Descrip)
 18:         #headerCell ("Total Value")
 19:         #entryCell ($entry.Totalvalue)
```

```
20:        #end
21:      </table>
22:
23:      <input type="hidden" name="AssetId"
24: value="$entry.Assetid"/>
25:      #if ($new)
26:      <input type="submit" name="eventSubmit_doInsert"
27: value="Insert"/>
28:      #else
29:      <input type="submit" name="eventSubmit_doUpdate"
30: value="Update"/>
31:      <input type="submit" name="eventSubmit_doDelete"
32: value="Delete"/>
33:      #end
34:    </div>
...
```

As you can see, Velocity templates are very straightforward, and even simpler than many JSP pages. Embedded HTML is simply included at the point it occurs. The next screen is the Asset Transaction form, which is used for entry and update of the transaction records

(See turbine/AssettrxForm.java for complete listing.)

```
...
  19: public class AssettrxForm extends VelocityScreen
...
  26:    public void doBuildTemplate( RunData data, Context
  27: context )
...
  31:        int entry_id =
  32: data.getParameters().getInt("ASSETTRX");
  33:        Criteria criteria = new Criteria();
  34:        criteria.add(AssettrxPeer.ASSETID, entry_id);
  35:        Assettrx assetTrx = (Assettrx)
  36: AssettrxPeer.doSelect(criteria).elementAt(0);
  37:        context.put("entry", assetTrx);
  38:        context.put("new", new Boolean(false));
...
```

Case Study: Turbine

and their associated Velocity templates.
(See turbine/AssettrxForm.vm for a full listing.)

```
 1: $page.setTitle("Add Transaction")
...standard HTML
 7: <form method="post"
 8: action="$link.setPage("ListAssettrx.vm").
       setAction("Assettrx
 9: SQL")">
10:    <div align="left">
11:      <table bgcolor="#ffffff" cellpadding="5">
12:        #if ($new)
13:          #formRow ("Asset Id" "AssetId" $!entry.Assetid)
14:          #formRow ("Trx Date" "Trxdate" $!entry.Trxdate)
15:        #else
16:          #headerCell ("Asset Id")
17:          #entryCell ($!entry.Assetid)
18:          </tr>
19:          #headerCell ("Trx Date")
20:          #entryCell ($!entry.Trxdate)
21:        #end
22:        #formRow ("Trx Type" "Trxtype" $!entry.Trxtype)
23:        #formRow ("Trx Value" "Trxvalue" $!entry.Trxvalue)
24:      </table>
...command buttons as in previous form
```

Custom screen objects were also created to "list" the two types of records, first the Assets:

(See turbine/ListAssets.java for a full listing.)

```
...
19: public class ListAssets extends VelocityScreen
...
25:    public void doBuildTemplate( RunData data, Context
26: context )
27:    {
28:        context.put("entries", getEntries());
29:    }
...
```

```
 36:     private Vector getEntries()
```
...specify an empty criteria (e.g. get all records)
```
 40:             Criteria criteria = new Criteria();
 41:             return AssetPeer.doSelect(criteria);
```
...

which correspond to the ListAssets Velocity template:
(See turbine/ListAssets.vm for a full listing.)

```
  1: $page.setTitle("List Assets")
```
...headings
```
 15:     #foreach ($entry in $entries)
 16:     <tr>
 17:        #entryCell ($entry.Assetid)
 18:        #entryCell ($entry.Descrip)
 19:        #entryCell ($entry.Totalvalue)
 20:        <td><a
 21: href="$link.setPage("AssetForm.vm").addPathInfo ("assetid",
 22: $entry.Assetid)">Edit</td>
 23:     </tr>
 24:     #end
```
...

and then the Asset transactions:
(See turbine/ListAssettrx.java for a complete listing.)

```
  1: package com.jglobal.turbine.inventory.modules. screens;
  2: /*
  3:  * License omitted for brevity
  4:  */
  5: import java.util.Vector;
  6: import org.apache.turbine.modules.screens.Velocity Screen;
  7: import org.apache.turbine.util.RunData;
  8: import org.apache.turbine.util.db.Criteria;
  9: import com.jglobal.turbine.inventory.om.peer.AssettrxPeer;
 10: import org.apache.velocity.context.Context;
 11: /**
 12:  * Grab all the records in a table using a Peer, and
```

```
13:    * place the Vector of data objects in the context
14:    * where they can be displayed by a #foreach loop.
15:    *
16:    *
17:
18:    */
19: public class ListAssettrx extends VelocityScreen
20: {
21:     /**
22:      * Place all the data object in the context
23:      * for use in the template.
24:      */
25:     public void doBuildTemplate( RunData data, Context
26: context )
27:     {
28:         context.put("entries", getEntries());
29:     }
30:     /**
31:      * This will return all the asset transactions records
32: in
33:      * the database but they have been mapped to
34:      * Assettrx objects so they can be directly used
35:      * in the Velocity template.
36:      */
37:     private Vector getEntries()
38:     {
39:         try
40:         {
41:           Criteria criteria = new Criteria();
42:           return AssettrxPeer.doSelect(criteria);
43:         }
44:         catch (Exception e)
45:         {
46:           e.printStackTrace(System.err);
47:           return null;
48:         }
49:     }
50: }
```

This class in turn goes with the ListAssettrx template:
(See turbine/ListAssettrx.vm for a complete listing.)

```
...headings
  15:        #foreach ($entry in $entries)
  16:        <tr>
  17:            #entryCell ($entry.Assetid)
...repeat for each field
  21:            <td><a
  22: href="$link.setPage("AssettrxForm.vm").addPathInfo
       ("assetid"
  23: , $entry.Assetid).addPathInfo("trxdate",
  24: $entry.encode()")>Edit</td>
  25:        </tr>
...
```

Each of our "list" templates has an "Edit" link for each record. These edit links call the appropriate update form, which is populated with the existing values for the record. Each update form also provides "delete" functionality.

Each of our database tables and associated objects also have a MapBuilder object created for them automatically. We do not have to alter these classes either – the following is an example for the Asset table:
(See turbine/AssetMapBuilder.java for full listing.)

```
...
  57:       public void doBuild ( ) throws Exception
  58:       {
  59:          dbMap = TurbineDB.getDatabaseMap("default");
  60:          dbMap.addTable(getTable());
  61:          TableMap tMap = dbMap.getTable(getTable());
  62:          tMap.setPrimaryKeyMethod(TableMap.IDBROKERTABLE);
  63:           tMap.addPrimaryKey ( getAsset_Assetid(),
  64: new Integer(0) );
  65:
  66:          tMap.addColumn ( getAsset_Descrip(), new
  67: String() );
  68:
```

Case Study: Turbine

```
  69:             tMap.addColumn ( getAsset_Totalvalue(),
  70: new Double(0) );
...
```

The MapBuilder object is used to specify the fields and their types when accessing each Peer object. Each table also has one of these "Peer" objects generated for it – actually, a *Base* peer and a regular *Peer* – which allows us to customize the behavior of the object by altering the peer object, while still allowing the flexibility to change the database scheme and regenerate the associated BasePeer. This permits much easier changes to the structure of the underlying database, and avoids the danger of generated code overwriting customized logic.

The BaseAssetPeer class, for example, is the generated class for our asset table. It is rather long, so we just present the method signatures here, but the details are worth studying, and the comments in the code do a good job of explaining the various methods. We do not have to edit this code at all.

(See turbine/BaseAssetPeer.java for the full listing.)

```
...
  19: abstract class BaseAssetPeer extends BasePeer
...
  40:    public static Object doInsert(Criteria criteria)
...
  55:    public static Object doInsert( Criteria criteria,
  56: DBConnection dbCon ) throws Exception
...
  64:    public static void addSelectColumns ( Criteria criteria)
  65: throws Exception
...
  80:    public static Asset row2Object (Record row, int offset,
  81: Class cls ) throws Exception
...
  96:    public static Vector doSelect( Criteria criteria )
  97: throws Exception
...
 111:    public static Vector doSelect( Criteria criteria,
 112: DBConnection dbCon ) throws Exception
...
 123:    public static Vector doSelect( Criteria criteria,
```

```
124: String className, DBConnection dbCon ) throws Exception
...
157:    public static void doUpdate(Criteria criteria) throws
158: Exception
...
178:    public static void doUpdate(Criteria criteria,
179: DBConnection dbCon) throws Exception
180: {
...
196:    public static void doDelete(Criteria criteria) throws
197: Exception
...
214:    public static void doDelete(Criteria criteria,
215: DBConnection dbCon) throws Exception
...
223:    public static void doInsert( Asset obj ) throws
224: Exception
...
233:    public static void doUpdate(Asset obj) throws Exception
...
240:    public static void doDelete(Asset obj) throws Exception
...
254:    public static void doInsert( Asset obj, DBConnection
255: dbCon) throws Exception
...
270:    public static void doUpdate(Asset obj, DBConnection
271: dbCon) throws Exception
...
284:    public static void doDelete(Asset obj, DBConnection
285: dbCon) throws Exception
...
291:    public static Criteria buildCriteria( Asset obj )
...
310:    public static Asset retrieveById(Object pkid)
311:          throws Exception
...
332:    public static Asset retrieveByPK(
333:                    int assetid
...
```

Case Study: Turbine

Then the much simpler peer class:
(See turbine/AssetPeer.java for a complete listing.)

```
...
  26: public class AssetPeer extends BaseAssetPeer
  27: {
  28: }
```

The same is true for the Asset transaction table, which also has a BasePeer:
(See turbine/BaseAssettrxPeer.java for details.)

```
...
  19: abstract class BaseAssettrxPeer extends BasePeer
...
  44:    public static Object doInsert( Criteria criteria )
...
  58:    public static Object doInsert( Criteria criteria,
  59: DBConnection dbCon ) throws Exception
...
  66:    public static void addSelectColumns (Criteria criteria)
...
  83:    public static Assettrx row2Object (Record row, int
  84: offset, Class cls )
...
 100:    public static Vector doSelect( Criteria criteria)
...
 116:    public static Vector doSelect( Criteria criteria,
 117: DBConnection dbCon ) throws Exception
...
 129:    public static Vector doSelect( Criteria criteria,
 130: String className, DBConnection dbCon) throws Exception
...
 164:    public static void doUpdate(Criteria criteria) throws
...
 186:    public static void doUpdate(Criteria criteria,
 187: DBConnection dbCon) throws Exception
...
 204:    public static void doDelete(Criteria criteria) throws
...
```

```
 222:     public static void doDelete(Criteria criteria,
 223: DBConnection dbCon) throws Exception
...
 231:     public static void doInsert(Assettrx obj) throws
...
 240:     public static void doUpdate(Assettrx obj) throws
...
 248:     public static void doDelete(Assettrx obj) throws
...
 263:     public static void doInsert(Assettrx obj, DBConnection
 264: dbCon) throws Exception
...
 279:     public static void doUpdate(Assettrx obj, DBConnection
 280: dbCon) throws Exception
...
 293:     public static void doDelete(Assettrx obj, DBConnection
 294: dbCon) throws Exception
...
 300:     public static Criteria buildCriteria (Assettrx obj)
...
 321:     public static Assettrx retrieveById(Object pkid)
...
 343:     public static Assettrx retrieveByPK(
 344:             int assetid)
...
```

and another simple peer object associated with it.
(See turbine/AssettrxPeer.java for the full listing.)

```
...
 26: public class AssettrxPeer extends BaseAssettrxPeer
 27: {
 28: }
```

A number of other standard classes are generated for our example application, but these are the primary objects that our application logic needs to deal with. A production application would likely customize the Action and Peer objects further, and would incorporate application-level authentication and authorization.

A.7.5 Turbine Summary

Although the specifics of the code for the Turbine application are quite different from our other case studies, there are a number of significant similarities. Like Struts, Turbine associates a particular "view" with an "action," but keeps the two isolated. Velocity, the default user interface tool, permits only very basic conditionals and other basic logic, thereby ensuring that application logic does not creep into the templates. Strut's tag library provides the same function, although it is possible to sidestep this and write code into JSPs – a practice that is not recommended.

Like Expresso, Turbine is well suited to database-oriented applications, and its object/relational mapping layer makes it easy to produce the kind of database maintenance functionality we need, albeit with little more actual code than Expresso.

As with all of our examples, the Turbine sample has much room for improvement. We could, at the begining, use Turbine's own authentication mechanism instead of the shortcut of using Tomcat for this function. Turbine's authentication and authorization mechanism is highly capable, and able to communicate with many different storage systems for user information (such as LDAP). We could also effect improvement in the area of validation and error handling, and of course the user interface can be enhanced considerably from the default.

A.8 Lessons Learned from the Case Studies

The specific experiences while building these case-study applications are of course influenced by the nature of the example: it was a database-oriented application, and the frameworks that focused on a specific database were a good fit. As discussed earlier, part of the reason to choose the right framework is to match the capabilities to the problem at hand. A more content-oriented application, such as a large complex website with just a few areas of logic, might be better served by a more presentation-oriented framework, or even an XML publishing framework such as Cocoon.

It is, nonetheless, interesting to simultaneously compare the same application with its counterpart from other frameworks, and we can certainly see how the "feel" of each of the selected frameworks was very different – each approached the problem from a distinct orientation and that orientation led the way for the overall development.

A.8.1 Installations

- **Struts**: Although Struts does not come bundled with an application server (such as Tomcat), its installation is straightforward and fast. Configuration did involve digging into a few XML files to connect to the database, but all frameworks require at least this level of connection to the environment.

- **Cocoon**: Cocoon's installation process is ordinarily very simple, although some specific problems were found with this particular installation. These have since been corrected in a more recent release of Cocoon. The configuration process of setting up Cocoon in a particular environment is also not complex, and the documentation is clear and complete.

- **Expresso**: Expresso's "complete" bundle allows for essentially a one-step installation, and the documentation on configuring and connecting to our database of choice is also straightforward and complete.

- **Turbine**: Turbine's TDK installation made this process extremely simple. Other than checking the port numbers that the included copy of Tomcat was set for to ensure no conflicts, the process essentially includes a single step. The installation processes for Expresso and Turbine are very similar (when using the versions bundled with Tomcat).

The installation process for the basic frameworks in all cases was fairly fast and easy. Ideally, all frameworks for web-app development should have clear documentation on the installation process, and our choices did. It is common, however, for developers to become stalled on the very first step – the installation – because they attempt to sidestep the bundled install recommended as a first stage. Often, an organization mandates use of a particular servlet engine, for example, Websphere or Orion, and not the open-source Tomcat engine. However, although it may be no easier to configure and install Tomcat than any other servlet engine, it is somewhat of a de facto standard for an initial deployment, and deploying first in the recommended environment helps considerably. It tells you whether the framework is operating correctly at least in the default environment, so that when you change your configuration to match your preferences, you start from a known point. The same is true of default database configurations: it is helpful to start with the default or preferred database for a particular framework. For example, Expresso comes bundled with the HypersonicSQL database, and it is best to get it up and running with this first, and then switch over to your own choice of DBMS. It is usually straightforward to change to another database once everything is up and running, but if you try to do all of it in one step things can get confused, and an otherwise perfectly serviceable framework might get discarded in the resulting frustration.

A.8.2 Design

With all of the frameworks, the first step before design is to understand the general design patterns and capabilities of the framework. The application problem must then be decomposed into its logic and its persistent objects, and these items are mapped to the appropriate capabilities in the framework.

- **Struts**: Views and Actions were the major items we dealt with in the Struts application. The views were JSP pages, the default view mechanism in Struts, and the Action items were determined easily from the original specification. As in the case of a couple of other cases, it is possible to improve our initial design by unifying some functions, but for our simple example the optimization is not large.

- **Cocoon**: Cocoon's design process revolved mostly around the individual pages, mapping out exactly what actions were required for each of the database maintenance steps, and then the one extra step for the calculation logic. Other than the SQL they executed, there was essentially no difference in the designs of the database maintenance pages and the calculation page. Because Cocoon does not provide an object/relational mapping layer, all of the database access required SQL statements to be built, and as a result the finished application might be slightly less portable, due to differences in the SQL syntax between different databases.

- **Expresso**: Expresso's design process revolved mostly around getting the appropriate database objects created and configured appropriately, for the database access part of our case study. The calculate logic then required some insight into Expresso's preferred method of logic handling, the Controller object. This design process was almost similar to the normal decomposition of a problem that would result from standard object-oriented design practices. It was not necessary to create individual application logic objects in Expresso's case, because its built-in DBMaint controller handled the simple maintenance tasks we required. This is a good example of a careful examination of a framework for a capability before inventing it unnecessarily.

- **Turbine:** The design process for Turbine was very database centric at first as well, like Expresso. Actions for both updating databases and calculating were handled by the same type of Action objects in Turbine, and the design process was again oriented around the data elements more than their presentation.

A.8.3 Development

The actual process of cranking out the code was quite different for each framework. The number of files that had to be dealt with varied considerably, and the automation of the process of generating an application varied significantly from frame one to another. How easy it is to get started, however, is not the complete measure of a framework: just because it is easy to create a default application does not mean that the entire development process is easy, or, more importantly, that the power to make the application flexible and maintainable is there.

- **Struts:** Development in Struts was aided by a "blank" default application provided with a framework. This provides the basis structure of a Web Application Archive, ready to be deployed, including all of the necessary jar archives, taglib definition files, and configuration files for accessing Struts itself. Starting from this "blank" also gave us a template to follow, and it was a matter of filling in our required logic and presentation.

  We dealt with three basic groups of files in developing the Struts application: first, the JSP files, which use the Struts tags. These were placed in the Web-application directory. Second, the Java source files for the Action objects, which were compiled into class files in the WEB-INF/classes directory. Lastly, the two form bean objects were created and also compiled into the WEB-INF/classes directory. The struts-config.xml file "connects" the different types of files together, specifying which action is to be called when a particular URL is invoked, and which JSP file is to be used by that action for its view, along with the form bean used.

- **Cocoon:** Of all the application frameworks, perhaps the easiest in terms of development process was Cocoon. The XSP files for our example application were in a single directory, and once edited, they were automatically compiled and ready to be executed. The only non-XSP file we had to deal with was the sitemap. As mentioned above, however, a refactoring of this application to use Action objects would result in a better finished product, and this would require Java files to be created, much in the same way as in the Struts case study.

- **Expresso:** We wrote the least amount of actual code for Expresso, even though a number of different Java classes were required (much of the code, like Turbine, was generated for us). This was largely a result of the built-in database maintenance capability, which comprised a significant portion of the code created for the other frameworks. Applications that have more custom logic would not notice as much of a difference. Most of the other frameworks involved more configuration in external files for connection to databases, whereas Expresso involved coding the fields and database mappings directly in the Java files. The code generation process for Expresso involved a tool outside the framework, so comparing it directly to, for example, Turbine meant more code to be written directly.

    For Expresso, our primary files were the new DBObject subclasses, one for each of our two tables in the sample application. A subclass of the "Schema" class, AssetSchema, holds everything together. A number of minor modifications to configuration files were also required.

- **Turbine:** Although the development process with Turbine involved more individual files, they were by and large smaller than the files generated by the Expresso development process. Each action or logic element is encapsulated individually. The file organization of the generated files was straightforward once the overall rules of organization were understood, and making customizations was quick and easy. It was necessary to create generated code, however, for basic database operations, such as Add, Update, Delete, and so forth.

    The code generation for Turbine is built into the subproject Torque, so from this point of view it required very little hand-coding to get our application up and running.

    In Turbine's case, there were a number of different files to be dealt with: first, the configuration files that control Torque's code generation, then the Velocity templates, and finally the Screen and Action classes that make up our finished application.

A.8.4 Conclusion

It is interesting to look back at our case studies and draw a few conclusions. We have seen that different application frameworks, although they take what seem to be radically different approaches, often end up requiring similar steps to create applications. This can be seen particularly clearly in the Cocoon and Struts case studies, where JSP pages and Actions compare to XSP pages. With the recommended refactoring of the Cocoon case study (separating Actions out of the XSP), the parallel would be even closer.

At the same time, we can see the unique advantages that certain framework capabilities bring to the development process. Expresso and Turbine, for example, and their advanced object-relational mapping layers, make short work of our database access needs. Indeed, because much of our example design was centered around the database, these two frameworks were particularly well suited. Of course, we could easily have combined such a tool from another framework (such as Castor) with Cocoon or Struts, and seen similar results.

In all cases, the frameworks not only provided essential services to our application, but more importantly provided a structure for us to build from. The amount of code varied a little, but was in all cases much less than we would have had to create if starting from scratch. With larger and more complex applications this difference will be much more.

No doubt, the Web applications you will create will be vastly more complex, and the framework you choose will be even more valuable to you than in this simple demonstration. Choose carefully, and maximize your Web-application-development productivity.

Glossary

4GL: Fourth-generation language. A high-level programming language intended to be more productive in development than traditional programming languages, such as C, C++, or Java. A high-level language, usually nonprocedural, to allow users inexperienced in programming to develop database applications.

Abstract Class: In object-oriented programming, a class designed only as a parent from which subclasses may be derived, but which itself is not suitable for instantiation.

ActiveX: A software development kit from Microsoft for development of Internet applications and content.

Agent: A piece of software that runs autonomously, usually helping a human being in pursuit of some knowledge-related goal.

API: Application Program Interface.

Applet: A small application, often downloaded from a remote server and run in a controlled environment.

ANSI: American National Standards Institute. This group is the U.S. member organization that belongs to the ISO, the International Organization for Standardization.

CASE: Computer Aided Software Engineering. A technique for using computers to help with the systematic analysis, design, implementation, and maintenance of software. Adoption of the CASE approach to building and maintaining systems involves software tools and training for the developers who use them.

CBD: Component-Based Development. A software development process relying primarily on the assembly of existing components into finished applications.

Client: A system or process that requests a service from another system or process.

COM: Common Object Model. An open architecture from DEC and Microsoft, allowing interoperation between ObjectBroker and OLE.

Component: An element of an application providing a specific set of services or functionality. Designed to be combined with other components to create an entire application.

COP: Component-Oriented Programming. The method of software development utilizing components as the basic unit from which applications are constructed.

Data Warehouse: A database of information intended for use as part of a decision support system. The data is typically extracted from an organization's operational databases.

DBMS: Database management system: such systems typically manage large structured sets of persistent data, offering ad hoc query facilities to many users. They are widely used in business applications: commercial examples include Ingres, Oracle, Sybase, and so forth.

DDL: Data definition language or Document Description Language.

DES: Data Encryption Standard. A NIST encryption standard.

DSS: Decision Support Systems. Software tools to help with management tasks.

DSSSL: Document Style Semantics and Specification Language. An ISO standard under preparation, addressing the semantics of high-quality composition in a manner independent of particular formatting systems or processes. DSSSL is intended as a complementary standard to SGML for the specification of semantics.

DTD: Document Type Definition. A DTD is the formal definition of elements, structures, and rules for marking up a given type of SGML document. You can store a DTD at the beginning of a document or externally in a separate file.

EJB: Enterprise JavaBeans. A component architecture intended for the development and deployment of enterprise applications. The architecture is portable between many different vendors' "container" or "server" applications, and supports distributed (i.e., multiserver) deployment of the finished application for enhanced scalability. Enterprise JavaBeans is one specification in the overall J2EE specification.

Expert system: An intelligent computer program that contains a knowledge base, specialized software, and a set of algorithms or rules that infer new facts from knowledge and from incoming data.

Garbage collection: The process of reclaiming storage that is no longer in use.

GIF: Graphics Interchange Format: a standard for digitized images compressed with the LZW algorithm.

Heuristic: A rule of thumb, simplification, or educated guess that reduces or limits the search for solutions in domains that are difficult and poorly understood. Unlike algorithms, heuristics do not guarantee solutions.

HTML: Hyper Text Mark-up Language. This is the format of files published on the Internet HTML is an application of SGML; to author in HTML using an SGML-based authoring software, you simply need the HTML DTD.

Hypertext: An approach to information management in which text is stored in a network of nodes connected by links. The nodes are meant to be viewed through an interactive browser. A link connects a piece of text to a destination piece of text; the source and destination areas are usually marked on a display by highlighting or special graphics.

IDE: Integrated Development Environment: generally, a desktop, usually a GUI-based application designed to facilitate development of software. Almost always includes the ability to edit, compile, and debug programs along with a way to manage projects made up of multiple program files.

Inheritance: In object-oriented programming, the ability to derive new classes from existing classes. A derived class inherits the instance variables and methods of the base class, and may add new instance variables and methods. A new method may be defined with the same names as one in the base class, in which case it overrides the original one.

Instantiation: A more precisely defined version of an object that was already partially defined. In object-oriented programming, a particular example of an object produced from its class template.

Interface: Interface has a specific meaning in the Java language: it is a keyword used to specify a collection of method signatures (not implementations) and constant values that are used by classes that *implement* the interface. It helps define the purpose of classes, and allows for a technique similar to multiple inheritance. Interfaces are used when the definition of an API to a component is specified completely independently from its actual implementation.

J2EE: Java 2, Enterprise Edition: differentiated from Java 2, Standard Edition (J2SE) or Java 2, Micro Edition (J2ME), J2EE is a set of standards comprising a complete environment for developing and deploying enterprise-level applications built in the Java language.

JavaBeans: A portable and flexible component model and design pattern extensively used in Java applications.

JDK: Java Development Kit: refers to the Java platform run time in conjunction with the compiler and associated development tools.

JPEG: A standardized image compression mechanism. JPEG stands for Joint Photographic Experts Group, the original name of the committee that wrote the standard. JPEG is designed for compressing either full-color or gray-scale digital images of "natural," real-world scenes. It does not work so well on nonrealistic images, such as cartoons or line drawings. JPEG does not handle black-and-white (1-bit-per-pixel) images, or motion picture compression.

JDBC: Java DataBase Connectivity. A standard used by Java for accessing practically any SQL-compatible data source. A special "driver" implementing the JDBC standard is available for almost all database engines, allowing them to be accessed from Java applications via the JDBC API.

JSP: JavaServer Pages. An extensible Java-based template technology for embedding ties to application logic into markup pages. JSP automatically generates Servlets to produce dynamic content. An XML-based set of standard "tags" can be embedded into the markup, and custom tags can easily be created to extend these capabilities.

Kerberos: An authentication system from the Athena project, adopted by OSF as the basis of security for DME.

KMS: Knowledge Management System. A distributed hypermedia system for managing knowledge in organizations. A commercial system from Knowledge Systems Inc running on workstations, based on previous research with ZOG at Carnegie Mellon University.

Knowledge Engineering: The acquisition of knowledge from a human expert or similar source and its coding in an expert system.

LDAP: Lightweight Directory Access Protocol. A subset of the X.500 protocol, which is frequently used for accessing user information and authentication information from a common network server.

Life Cycle: The software life cycle consists of the following phases: requirement analysis, design, construction, testing, and maintenance. The development process tends to run iteratively through these phases rather than linearly; several models (spiral, waterfall, etc.) have been proposed to describe this process.

Object-oriented: Applied to analysis, design, and programming. The basic concept in this approach is that of objects, which consist of data structures encapsulated with a set of routines, often called "methods" that operate on the data. Operations on the data must be performed via these methods, which are common to all instances of objects of a particular class. Thus, the interface to objects is well defined, and allows the code implementing the methods to be changed as long as the interface remains the same.

ODMG: Object Data Management Group. A vendor consortium developing standards for Object Data Definition and Manipulation Languages.

OODBMS: Object-oriented database management system.

OQL: Object Query Language from ODMG.

Pattern: A formal way to describe a solution to a commonly recurring programming problem.

RAD: Rapid Application Development.

RDBMS: Relational database management system. Differentiated from a hierarchical database or object-oriented database, although sometimes object-oriented database can also have relational capabilities. Most common relational databases use Structured Query Language (SQL) as their data query and update language.

RPC: Remote Procedure Call. A call to a routine that results in code being executed on a different system from the one where the request originated. An RPC system allows calling procedures and called procedures to execute on different systems without the programmer needing to explicitly code for this.

SOAP: Simple Object Access Protocol. SOAP uses an XML-based data structure and the HTTP protocol (among others) to provide access to data and methods via a network. It is an operating system and language portable, and is becoming widely accepted as a standard for business-to-business interaction via the Web.

Software Engineering: A systematic approach to the analysis, design, implementation, and maintenance of software. It usually involves the use of CASE tools. There are various models of the software life cycle, and many methodologies for the different phases.

Software Metrics: Measures of software quality that indicate the complexity, understandability, testability, description, and intricacy of code.

State Transition Diagram: A diagram consisting of circles to represent states and directed line segments to represent transitions between the states. One or more actions may be associated with each transition.

Superclass: The class from which another class inherits its structure.

SQL: Structured Query Language. The standardized relational database interaction language. It includes a data query and data manipulation language. Whereas individual database dialects differ slightly, SQL is a unifying standard among relational database systems, and is commonly used via the JDBC standard for database access in Web applications.

TCP/IP: A reliable connection-oriented protocol originated by DARPA for internetworking, encompassing both network and transport level protocols. Although the terms TCP and IP specify two protocols, TCP/IP is often used to refer to the entire DoD protocol suite based upon these, including Telnet, FTP, UDP, and RDP.

Transaction: A unit of interaction with a DBMS or similar system. It must be treated in a coherent and reliable way independent of other transactions.

UDP: User Datagram Protocol. The Internet standard protocol for sending datagrams between user programs. This protocol neither guarantees delivery nor requires a connection. As a result it is lightweight and efficient, but all error processing and retransmission must be taken care of by the application program. This protocol is built on top of IP and uses IP for datagram delivery (see TCP/IP).

UI: User Interface.

URI: Uniform (previously Universal) Resource Identifier. A string of characters identifying a resource. A URI is either a URL or a URN, which are both concrete instances of the abstract concept URI.

URL: Uniform (previously Universal) Resource Locator. A string identifying a resource, typically including protocol, DNS address, and detailed identifier.

URN: Uniform (previously Universal) Resource Name. A unique identifier for a resource that does not include location information, unlike a URL.

war: Acronym for Web Application Archive. A standard Java "jar" file structured to contain an entire Web application, ready to be deployed into any Servlet server/container supporting the Servlet API 2.2 or higher. The war file can contain both Java code and HTML/JSP pages, as well as other files.

Workflow: The way in which work units (information or actions) are routed through an organization. It can be formalized in terms of rules incorporating dependencies, staff roles, and so forth and hence automated.

XML: eXtensible Mark-up Language. A mark-up language where the specific "tags" or markup elements that are valid in a particular document may be adjusted via a document type definition (DTD). A fast-emerging standard for data interchange in Web applications.

Index

A "d" after a page number denotes a diagram on that page.

A

ACSJ 99, 153–55
Active Scripting 169
agent 103, 375
Aglet Workbench 103
Anakia 180
Anteater 201–2
API (Application Program Interface)
   INDI 113
   JavaMail 28, 32–33
   JMX 113
   standard 113
   vs. component 28
   vs. framework 18, 28–29, 106
   see also JDBC; JMS
application framework
   advantages of 55–58
   characteristics of 13–16
   complete (see complete application framework)
   developer need for 16–18
   difficulty in creating 279
   documentation for 14
   EJB advantage/disadvantage in 21–25
   J2EE standard and 19–21
   nonopen-source 107
   open source 106, 107, 111
   proprietary 106–7
   purpose/benefit of 12
   slow adoption of 25–27
   vs. component library 105–6
   what it is not 18–19, 28–29
   see also application framework, choosing; application-specific framework; complete application framework
application framework, choosing
   build/buy decision 129
   complexity considerations 107
   component/service 108–15
   cost-benefit analysis to aid in 126–29
   design patterns 108
   licensing considerations 106–7
   "none" as choice 125–26

specific job considerations 125
  see also
    application-specific
    framework, choosing
application logic 58d–60, 59d
  comparing among
    framework 216–18
  event driven 67–68
  scalability of 60
  tags and 117–18
application server *vs.*
    framework 18
application-specific framework
  Anteater 201–02
  Batik 209–10
  Castor 207–8
  horizontal *vs.* vertical 189
  JADE 197–98
  Jetspeed 202–4
  jRelational 208–9
  JUnit 199–201
  Object/Relational Bridge 206–7
  Openadaptor 198–99
  OpenPortal 204
  Roaming Wireless 196–97
  Simper 206
  Slide 195–96
  SOAP 29, 36, 51, 70, 101, 193, 194–95, 368–70
  UPortal 204–5
  Xalan 191–93
  Xerces 189, 190–91
  see also application framework; presentation framework
application-specific framework, choosing

database access 125
presentation 116–25
vertical market 115–16
  see also application framework, choosing
Arch4J 151–53
ASP 103–4
Aspect Oriented Programming 297
atomic transaction 63
authentication/authorization 83–85, 88
Avalon 57
  application subproject 138
  Cornerstone subproject 137
  Excalibur subproject 134–36, 139
  Framework subproject 133–34
  LogKit subproject 136
  overview of 132–33
  Phoenix subproject 136–37d, 138, 139
  Sandbox subproject 138–39
Axis 194–95

B

back up, off-system 88
Barracuda 92, 97, 169, 182–84
Batik 209–10
B2B (Business to Business) 53
B2C (Business-to-Consumer) 53
Bean API 10–11
BeanInfo object 11
BEA WebLogic 3
BeBop 99, 154
best practices
  deployment environments 356–57
  first project 348–53
  future-proofing 360–63
  initial adoption 346–48
  problems/pitfalls 354–56

Index

reading *vs.* writing code 358
refactoring 358–59
starting small 357–58
team development 357
bindings 31
Brazil 163
BSD/MIT license 247–48, 250

C

caching 62, 63, 68, 149, 225–26
Cactus project 73
case study, framework analysis/comparison
   Cocoon case study 407–27
   conclusions of study 455–56
   design comparisons among cases 453
   design of study 378–80
   development comparisons among cases 454–55
   Expresso case study 427–36
   initial design of sample specification 380–84
   installation comparisons among 452–53
   sourcecode zip file for 377
   Struts case study 384–407
   Turbine case study 436–51
Castor 207–8
CBD (component-based development)
   and B2B application 52–53
   cost of 49–50
   JavaBeans 10–12, 120, 176, 177–78
   overview of 7–9
   quality in 43–49
   server-side component 10

vs. once-off development 8d
visual component 10
closed network 75
Cocoon 97, 113, 140–44, 141d, 169
Cocoon case study
   design process 408
   development process 409–11
   finished application 411–26
   installation 408
   summary 426–27
code
   advantage/disadvantage of 56–57
   quality and 44
   reading *vs.* writing 358
   reusability of 27
code generation
   in IDE 339–40
   in Turbine 56
community support 111
complete application framework
   ACSJ 99, 153–55
   Arch4J 151–53
   Brazil 163
   choosing 114–15
   Niggle 159–61
   OpenSymphony 164–65
   realMethods Framework 162–63
   Wakesoft Architecture Server 158–59
   WASP 161–62
   see also Avalon; Cocoon; Expresso; Turbine
component
   adaptability of 50–51
   black box approach to 40
   choosing support for 114
   client-side 9–10

evolution of	40–42d
forms of	54
as integrative	51–52
reusability of	4, 13, 14–15, 44, 50, 62–63, 213, 295, 362
scalability of	51
server-side component	10
standardization of	6
time saving value of	42–43
vs. API	28
vs. framework	19
vs. object	6–7
visual component	10
see also framework/component, emerging	
component container	6, 11–12, 20
component interface	139
component library, vs. application framework	105–6
ComponentManager	133
Composable object	133
construction library	98, 116, 168–69
ControllerResponse	99–100
copyright	245, 246, 247, 248, 249, 260, 263, 267, 276
CORBA (Common Object Request Broker Architecture)	23, 31, 101
CORBA IIOP (Internet Inter-ORB Protocol)	33
COS (Common Object Services)	31
cost–benefit analysis, in choosing framework	127–29
CRM (customer relationship management)	40
CRUD (Create, Read, Update, Delete)	65
cut-and-paste development	41
CVS (concurrent versioning system)	285–88, 292, 294, 301, 338, 344

D

database	
access to	60–65, 61d, 125, 218–23, 236
generation utility for	102
Hypersonic SQL database	77
maintaining	65, 148, 223–24
managing	223–24
relational	63, 64, 65
testing	65
see also JDBC	
database event	68
data entry problem	72
data storage	86–87, 92–93
debugging	65, 66
design, reusability of	15–16
design pattern	
choosing	108
command	329
composition/extension	318
delegate/proxy	318–19d, 320d
developmental phase application of	330–32, 331d
factory	321–22d, 323–24
interface	319–21d
inversion of control	5–6
pooling	323d
quality in	46

Index **467**

separation of concerns 327–28
service pattern 328–29
singleton 323d–325d
thread-safe 326–27
utility for 325
development methodology
  Extreme Programming 297, 305–9
  incremental/iterative 300–301d
  MVC architecture and 315–17, 316d
  open-source 300–303d, 305
  RAD 304
  Rational Unified Process 304–5
  Selective Perspective 305
  UML 304, 305, 310–15, 311d, 313d, 317
distributed event handling 67
DNS (Domain Naming Service) 31
DocBookLet 109
documentation
  application framework 14
  catalog/feature list 109
  cook book 109
  design 109
  to enhance quality 48
  road-map/direction 109
  for self-support 111–12
  simplicity in 55–56
  source code 110
  status 109
domain-specific framework 115–16
DOM (Document Object Model) 169–70, 175, 182, 190
DTD (document type definition) 117

DVSL (Declarative Velocity Style Language) 180

E

e-business/commerce 52–53
Echo 98
ECS (Element Construction Set) library 98, 116, 168–69
EJB (Enterprise JavaBeans)
  advantage/disadvantage of 21–25
  code generation in 57
  execution environment for 6
  scalability and 22, 77
  Session EJB object 57
  Web-application execution and 31
email 70
encryption 80, 83, 86–87, 149
Entity beans 23, 31
EOB (Enterprise Object Broker) 139
error handling 71–73, 180, 226–27
error reporting, using template engine 121
ESC (Element Construction Set) library 98
escrow service 107
ESP (eXtensible Server Pages) 122d–125
event handling 67–68, 225
event notification 67
Expresso
  AutoDBOject in 145
  commercial support for 151
  Controllers in 146–48
  DBOject in 48, 145–46
  internationalization in 102
  Job object 148–51
  overview of 144–45

transformation in	169		open-source	
user interface in	147–48		framework;	
website	141, 144, 151		presentation	
Expresso case study			framework; *individual*	
design process	428		*framework*	
development process	428		framework, comparing	
finished application	428–36		services of	
installation	427–28		application logic	216–18
summary	436		caching	225–26
external security audit	82–83		database access	218–23
			database management	223–24
			error handling	226–27

F

file roll-over	67		event handling	225
firewall	81		JSP	234
flow of control mechanism	59		legacy application	
4GL (fourth-generation			integration	232
language)	19		logging	224–25
framework			matrix for	237–43
application-specific	115–16		monitoring/testing	227
combining services in	234–37		MVC separation	232–33
data access	125		presentation user interface	
definition of	15			228–31
designing with	332–33		push/pull presentations	233–34
(*see also* design pattern)			scheduling	231
development methodology			security	227–28
impact on	297–99		SQL insulation	219–22
development of	277–79		templating	234
domain-specific	115–16		utilities	232–33
enhancing development in	46–49		Web services	231
evolution of	39–42d		XML	234
horizontal	189		framework/component,	
meta	210–13, 237, 375–76		emerging	364
service-oriented	56		agents/machine intelligence	375
using (*see* best practices)			framework interoperability	375
vertical	189		interface paradigms	365–66
vertical market	115–16		JavaSpaces	374
what it is not	18–19		Jini	373–74
see also application			meta-framework	375–76
framework;			Web services	366–73

Index

Freemarker 121, 160, 169, 186–87
free software 245
"free" support 111

G

generalization 13, 41
generators 141d–142
getName 11
get/set pattern 12, 178
GPL (General Public License) 251–63, 275, 276
graphical menu 89–90
GUI (graphical user interface) 69, 166–67, 188

H

hardware security 78
HMVC (hierarchical model-view-controller) 176, 317
HTML (Hyper Text Markup Language) 77–78, 94, 117
HTTP 29, 77–78
HTTPS 85
HyperQbs 184–85
Hypersonic SQL database 77

I

IDE (integrated development environment)
  avoiding tanglement 340
  browsing/navigating code with 340
  build manager tool 338
  class browser tool 336–37
  code generation tool 339–40
  compiler tool 337–38
  debugger tool 339
  Eclipse 340–42
  editor tool 336
  GUI builder tool 338–39
  internationalization tool 339
  JDEE 343
  keeping separate from framework 340
  NetBeans 342
  project browser tool 337
  project manager tool 335–36
  relationship to framework 181, 334–35
  using nonintegrated IDE 343–45
  version control tool 338
  vs. framework 19
IDL (Interface Definition Language) 33
INDI 113
interface
  component 139
  configuration 4
  design pattern 319–21d
  functional 4
  GUI 69, 166–67, 188
  JNDI 20, 31–32
  UDDI 161, 372–73
  see also API; presentation/user interface; Web user interface
interface event 68
internationalization
  in Expresso 150–51
  of interface 89–93
  utility for 102
Internet 31, 75, 281
Intranet 93–94

inversion of control design
    pattern 5–6
iPlanet 3
IT (information technology)
    39, 45–46

J

JAAS standard 84–85
JabaServer 139
Jabber 139
JADE (Java Agent
    DEvelopment) 103, 197–98
JAF (JavaBeans Activation
    Framework) 33
James 139
JATLite 103
JavaBeans 10–12, 120, 176, 177–78
JavaDoc 29, 109
JavaMail 28, 32–33
Java Micro Edition 100, 104
Java Plug-In 93
JavaScript 103–4
Java security policy 80
JavaSpaces 24, 374
Java Standard Tag Library 94
Java Toolkit 101
JCE (Java Cryptography
    Extensions) 85
JCP (Java Community
    Process)
    34, 94, 112, 166
JDBC (Java DataBase
    Connectivity) 33–34, 62, 81, 101, 102, 113
JDK (Java Development Kit)
    29, 33, 80, 85
JDO (Java Data Objects) 64

J2EE (Java 2, Enterprise
    Edition) 3, 8, 20–21, 112, 113
Jesktop 139
Jetspeed 202–4
Jetty 3
Jini 24, 373–74
J2ME (Java 2 Micro Edition) 196
JMS (Java Messaging Service)
    20, 24, 32, 67, 70, 112
JMS Queue 162–63
JMX 113
JNDI (Java Naming and
    Directory Interface)
    20, 31–32
Jo! 139
jRelational 208–9
JSF (Java Server Faces) 166–70
JSP (JavaServer Pages) 3, 29
    application developer role in 167–68
    choosing 120–21
    compared with XSP 122d–125
    comparing among
        framework 234
    component developer
        role in 167
    as de facto standard 167, 168, 169
    interaction via HTTP by 29
    international templates
        using 92
    misuse of 30–31, 120–21
    overview of 166–68
    page designer in 167
    page generation and 119
    using tags in 94–95, 117, 118

Index

JSR (Java Specification
    Request)   68
JTA (Java Transaction API)   33
JTS (Java Transaction Service)   33
JUnit   150, 199–200, 297, 308

K
Keel   211–13, 376
Kerberos   83
Kettle   185

L
LDAP (Lightweight Directory
    Access Protocol)   32, 83
legacy application integration   101d, 232
LGPL (Library Public License)   263
library   13
    construction   98, 116, 168–69
    custom tag   94, 121
    ECS   98, 116, 168–69
    function   41
    Java Standard Tag Library   94
    tag   94–95, 171
license
    application framework   106–7
    see also OSS, license for
Linux   280, 281
logging   65–67, 71, 74, 133, 149–50, 224–25
log in/log out   68
Login (tag example)   95–96
Log4j   149–50

M
macro   117, 118
MacroMedia Flash   97–98
markup construction kit   168–69
markup tag   116–17, 118

Maverick   175–76
message bundle file   91, 102
messaging   32, 70–71
    see also JMS
meta-framework   210–13, 237, 375–76
meta-server   163
method signature   11
mobile wireless device   104, 115
monitoring/testing
    comparing among framework   227
    database   65
    in Expresso   150
    utility for   103
    Web-application development   73–78
Mozilla license   153, 264–76
MQ messaging system   32
MVC (Model, View, Controller)
    Architecture   30, 59, 233

N
naming service   31–32
nested exception   72–73
.NET   23, 51
.NET Studio   168
Niggle   159–61
NIS (Network Information System)   32

O
obfuscation   80
Object-Oriented Analysis   297
Object-Oriented Design   297
object-oriented development   37, 41
Object/Relational Bridge   206–7

object/relational mapping
    60–61d, 63, 102, 144
Object Transaction Service   33
Odyssey   103
OMG (Object Management
    Group)   23, 33
once-off development   8d, 44, 50
one-way encryption   86
OODBMS (object-oriented
    database management
    system)   63
Openadaptor   198–99
OpenPortal   204
open-source framework
    advantages of   280–82
    component reuse between
       organization in   295
    corporate world use of   282–83
    evaluating   283–84
    getting help for   289–90
    learning curve for   288–89
    personal involvement in
       project   290–94
    release/scheduling in   285–88
    support for   288
OpenSymphony   164–65
Oracle   77
ORDBMS (Object/Relational
    Database Systems)   63
Oreo   160
Orion   31
OSS (open-source software)   244–45
    advantages of   276–77
    free software   245
    licensing   245–47
    slow adoption of   26
OSS (open-source software),
    license for
    Apache 248–50, 256, 263–64, 272
    BSD/MIT   247–48, 250, 264
    dual/multiple   260, 276
    GNU   251–64, 268, 275, 276
    Mozilla   264–76

P

PageFactory   160
parallel development   56
parameterization   41
passive structure   5
password capture   88
PDF   96, 124
PDL (Persistence Definition
    Language)   155
Peer   156
performance, measuring   75–78
Perl   103–4
PHP   103–4
placeholder   124
point-to-point message   32
presentation framework
    Barracuda   92, 97, 169, 182–34
    combining   235–36
    commonalties among   233–34
    content generation
       approaches in   168–70
    Echo   187–88
    Freemarker   121, 160, 169, 186–87
    HyperQbs   184–85
    JSF   166–70
    Maverick   175–76
    overview of   165–66
    Scope   176
    Tapestry   180–81
    Tea   121, 169, 185–86
    Velocity   116, 117, 121, 169, 178–80

Index

WebMacro 117, 121, 160, 169, 177–78
   see also Struts
presentation/user interface 100–101, 228–31
presentation/user interface, internationalization of
   data format 91
   different display order 90
   error message 90
   menu 89–90
   message file 91
   multibyte support for presentation 90
   multibyte support for storage 90
   multiple data storage 92–93
   multiple templates 92
   numeric format/currency handling 90
   page/form 89
PrintStackTrace 73
public domain 246
publish-subscribe message 32
push *vs.* pull presentation 233–34

R
Rational Rose design tool 158
realMethods Framework 162–63
rich text format (RTF) 96
RMI (Remote Method Invokation) 33, 134–35
Roaming Media Framework 104
Roaming Wireless Framework 196–97
RTF (rich text format) 96

S
SanFrancisco 18–19
SAX (Simple API for XML) 190

scalability, system 76–77
scheduling 69–70, 231
Scope 176
scripting language support 103–4
security
   authentication/authorization 83–85, 161
   comparing among framework 227–28
   in Expresso 148–49
   of persistence object 61–62
   using inversion of control 5–6
   see also security, data; security, system
security, data
   acquisition 85
   auditing to track breach 89
   communications 86
   expiration 87
   methods of attack 87–88
   retrieval 87
   storage 86–87
security, system
   application-level 79
   browser 79
   at database connection point 81
   default password change 82, 88
   external security audit 82–83
   for files 79–81
   hardware 78
   intrusion monitoring 82
   operating system 78
   tips for 80
   unnecessary services removal 81–82
   using firewalls 81
   using secure JDBC drivers 81
security code 30
self-correction 72

self-support 111–12
serialization 11, 142–44
Servlet
   Action 172
   Freemarker 187
   Java 3
   simplicity in using 168
   Struts 30, 172
   Tea 185
   Turbine 157
   WebMacro 177
Servlet API 29, 31, 83, 94, 113
Servlet container, vs. framework 18
Session beans 31, 114
setName 11
setup file 69
Simper 206
Slide 195–96
SOAP (Simple Object Access Protocol) 29, 36, 51, 70, 101, 193, 194–95, 368–70
Software Crisis 37
software industry 35–37
software methodology 296
software project failure, reasons for 38–40
source escrow 107
Spindle 181
SQL (Structured Query Language) 62, 63, 65, 102, 219–22
SSL (secure socket layer) 78, 83, 85, 88
standards compliance 112–13
Struts 19
   actions in 170–71, 172
   component model in 57
   configuration file in 172
   controller access via 147
   controllers in 170
   Digester utility in 173
   documentation for 171
   incorporation by other framework 175
   mapping via 150
   presentation support via 158
   tag library (example) 173–72
   tags in 171
   terminology for application logic in 59
   third-party addition/extension in 173
   transformation in 169
   use of JavaServer Pages in 94
   website 170
Struts case study
   design process 387–88
   development process 388
   finished application 388–406
   installation 384–87
   summary 406–7
support service, choosing 110–12
SVG (Scalable vector Graphics) 124, 209–10
Swing 99, 182

T

tag library 94–95, 171
Tapestry 180–81
Tea 121, 169, 185–86
template
   choosing 116–19
   generation utility for 102
   in Velocity 179–80
template engine 121–22, 169

Index

templating, comparing among
    framework   234
testing. *see* monitoring/testing
Texen   180
TogetherJ   158
Tomcat   3, 29, 31
tool box. *see* Web-application development, tool box element
Torque   56
transformation, choosing   119–20
Trove subproject   186
Turbine
    actions in   157
    code generation in   56
    Fulcrum services framework in   156
    license for   249–50
    Maven project in   157
    navigation in   157–58
    overview of   155
    Stratum subproject in   156–57
    terminology for application logic in   59
    Torque persistence layer in   156
    transformation in   169
    website   155
Turbine case study
    design process   437
    development process   437–38
    finished application   439–50
    installation   437
    summary   451

U

UDDI (Universal Discovery and Directory Interface)   161, 372–73
UI/presentation-related event   67
UI (user interface)   70
    see also internationalization; presentation/user interface; Web user interface (UI) options
UML   317
    package/component/ deployment   314–15
    sequence/collaboration   313d–314
    use-case   310–12, 311d, 313
Unicode standard   91
universal client   3
Unix   101
uPortal   204–5
URL mapping   150
URL (Uniform Resource Locator)   150
utility
    bean box   11
    code generation   102
    comparing among framework   232–33
    database generation   102
    design pattern   325
    in Expresso   150
    installation bundle   103
    for internationalization   102
    for monitoring   102–3
    in Struts   173
    template generation   102
    testing   103
    Web-application development   102–3

V

Velocity   116, 117, 121, 169
    error handling in   180
    template (sample)   179

templates in	179–80
use of by other service	180
website	178
Veltag	180
vertical market framework	115–16
View Handler	147–48
VisualBasic	168
visual component	10
VM (Virtual machine)	23
Voyager	103

W

Wakesoft Architecture Server	158–59
.war (Web application aRchive)	103
WASP	161–62
waterfall	299–300d
W3C Document Object Model	182
Web application	
definition of	2–3
execution environment	29–34
security for	79
Web-application development	
application-oriented approach to	16, 17d
hierarchy of typical framework	16d
page-oriented approach to	16–17d
Web-application development, tool box element	
agent	103
application logic	58d–60, 59d
caching	62, 63, 68
configuration	69
database access	60–65, 61d
database maintenance	65
error handling	71–73
event handling	67–68
legacy application integration	101
logging	65–67
messaging	70–71
monitoring/testing	73–78
platform-specific services	104
presentation/user interface	89–101
scheduling	69–70
scripting support	103–4
security	78–89
utilities	102–3
webAppWriter project	56
WebDAV	195–96
Weblogic	29
WebMacro	117, 121, 160, 169, 177–78
Web service	
comparing	231
emerging	366–74
Websphere	3, 29
Web user interface	
applets	93–94
EML/XSL	96–97
flexible	98–100, 99d
JavaServer Pages	94–96
MacroMedia Flash	97–98
toolkit	99
Web user interface (IU). see presentation/user interface	
wireless device	100, 115
WML (wireless markup language)	124
wrapping, legacy application	57, 101d
WSDL (Web services definition language)	370–72

X

Xalan   191–93
Xerces   189, 190–91
XHTML   117
XML (Extensible Markup
    Language)   29, 31, 69,
        96–97, 117, 169,
        234, 367–68
XML Path Language (XPath)   96
XNI (Xerces Native Interface)
        190–91
XSL (eXtensible Style-sheet
    Language)   30, 96–97,
        113, 169, 191–93,
        192d
XSL-FO (XSL Formatting
    Objects)   96, 119–20,
        191–92
XSLT (XSL Transformations)
        96, 191–93
XSP (eXtensible Server Pages)
        122–25